C

Contents

Note about the F2 examination paper and practice questions in this study text

The F2 examination paper consists of 50 multiple choice questions (or 'objective testing' questions). It is therefore important that you should test your ability in answering multiple choice questions (MCQs) when you study this subject.

Some MCQs are included at the end of each chapter in this text as practice questions. If you want more practice, there are many more MCQs in the Examination Kit produced by International Financial Publishing Limited (IFP) for the F2 examination and also in IFP's distance learning materials for F2.

We take the view, however, that MCQs on their own are insufficient for practising and testing your ability. In order to understand management accounting properly, it is important to have an appreciation of the 'bigger picture' and to see 'techniques' or 'methods' of management accounting in their entirety. We have therefore included a number of longer practice questions at the end of this study text that deal with syllabus topics in a unified way. These questions deal with each topic at a suitable level for the F2 examination, even though they are too long for the examination itself.

ACCA

Paper F2

Management Accounting

Management

...eges including

International Financial Publishing in association with Emile Woolf International
Training Professionals

Second edition published by
International Financial Publishing Limited
Crowthorne Enterprise Centre, Crowthorne Business Estate, Old Wokingham Road,
Crowthorne, Berkshire RG45 6AW
Email: info@ifpbooks.com
www.ifpbooks.com

British Library Cataloguing in Publications Data
A catalogue record for this book is available from the British Library.

ISBN: 978-1-84843-004-4

Printed and bound in Great Britain.

Acknowledgements
The syllabus and study guide are reproduced by kind permission of the Association of Chartered Certified Accountants.

S

Syllabus and study guide

Aim

To develop knowledge and understanding of how to prepare and process basic cost and quantitative information to support management in planning and decision-making in a variety of business contexts.

Main capabilities

On successful completion of this paper, you should be able to:

- **A** Explain the nature and purpose of cost and management accounting
- **B** Describe costs by classification, behaviour and purpose
- **C** Apply essential business mathematics and use computer spreadsheets
- **D** Explain and apply cost accounting techniques
- **E** Prepare and coordinate budgets and standard costing for planning, feedback and control
- **F** Using management accounting techniques to make and support decision-making

Rationale

The syllabus for Paper F2, *Management Accounting*, introduces candidates to costing principles and techniques, and elements of management accounting which are used to make and support decision-making.

The syllabus starts by introducing the nature and purpose of cost accounting, distinguishing it clearly from financial accounting. The next section is cost classification and behaviour. This is followed immediately by applied business mathematics and the use of computer spreadsheets, which are essential for candidates to understand the measurement and behaviour of business costs and to be able to classify them accordingly.

The next area of the syllabus represents a central part of this paper and it introduces candidates to a variety of costing techniques used in business. It is followed by the preparation and use of budgeting and standard costing as essential tools for planning and controlling business costs. The syllabus finishes with an introduction to the use of management accounting in supporting decision-making.

Syllabus content

A The nature and purpose of cost and management accounting

1 Accounting for management
2 Cost and management accounting versus financial accounting

B Cost classification, behaviour and purpose

1 Production and non-production costs
2 Direct and indirect costs
3 Fixed and variable costs

C Business mathematics and computer spreadsheets

1 Dealing with uncertainty
2 Statistics for business
3 Use of computer spreadsheets

D Cost accounting techniques

1 Accounting for materials
2 Accounting for labour
3 Accounting for overheads
4 Marginal and absorption costing
5 Job and batch costing
6 Process costing
7 Service/operation costing

E Budgeting and standard costing

1 Nature and purpose of budgeting
2 Functional budgets
3 Flexible budgets and standard costing
4 Basic variance analysis under absorption and marginal costing
5 Reconciliation of budgeted profit to actual profit

F Short-term decision-making techniques

1 Cost-volume-profit analysis
2 Relevant costing
3 Limiting factors

Approach to examining the syllabus

The syllabus is assessed by a two hour paper-based or computer-based examination. Questions will assess all parts of the syllabus and will include both computational and non computational elements. The examination will consist of 40 two-mark questions, and 10 one-mark questions.

Study guide

This study guide provides more detailed guidance on the syllabus. You should use this as the basis of your studies.

A The nature and purpose of cost and management accounting

1 Accounting for management

(a) Distinguish between data and information.
(b) Identify and explain the attributes of good information.
(c) Outline the managerial processes of planning, decision making and control.
(d) Explain the difference between strategic, tactical and operational planning.
(e) Distinguish between cost, profit, investment and revenue centres.
(f) Describe the differing needs for information of cost, profit, investment and revenue centre managers.

2 Cost and management accounting versus financial accounting

(a) Describe the purpose and role of cost and management accounting within an organisation's management information system.
(b) Compare and contrast financial accounting with cost and management accounting.

B Cost classification, behaviour and purpose

1 Production and non-production costs

(a) Explain and illustrate production and non-production costs.
(b) Describe the different elements of production cost - materials, labour and overheads.
(c) Describe the different elements of non-production cost – administrative, selling, distribution and finance.
(d) Explain the importance of the distinction between production and non-production costs when valuing output and inventories.

2 Direct and indirect costs

(a) Distinguish between direct and indirect costs in manufacturing and non-manufacturing organisations.
(b) Identify examples of direct and indirect costs in manufacturing and non-manufacturing organisations.
(c) Explain and illustrate the concepts of cost objects, cost units and cost centres.

3 Fixed and variable costs

(a) Describe and illustrate, graphically, different types of cost behaviour.
(b) Explain and provide examples of costs that fall into the categories of fixed, stepped fixed and variable costs.
(c) Use high/low analysis to separate the fixed and variable elements of total costs including situations involving stepped fixed costs and changes in the variable cost per unit.

(d) Explain the structure of linear functions and equations.

C Business mathematics and computer spreadsheets

1 Dealing with uncertainty

(a) Explain and calculate an expected value.
(b) Demonstrate the use of expected values in simple decision making situations.
(c) Explain the limitations of the expected value technique.

Note: Decision trees and conditional profit tables are excluded.

2 Statistics for business

(a) Calculate a correlation coefficient and a coefficient of determination.
(b) Explain the concepts in (a) and interpret the coefficients calculated in (a).
(c) Establish a linear function using regression analysis and interpret the results.

3 Use of computer spreadsheets

(a) Explain the role and features of a computer spreadsheet system.
(b) Demonstrate a basic understanding of the use of computer spreadsheets.
(c) Identify applications for computer spreadsheets in cost and management accounting.

D Cost accounting techniques

1 Accounting for materials

(a) Describe the different procedures and documents necessary for the ordering, receiving and issuing of materials from inventory.
(b) Describe the control procedures used to monitor physical and 'book' inventory and to minimise discrepancies and losses.
(c) Interpret the entries and balances in the material inventory account.
(d) Identify and explain the costs of ordering and holding inventory.
(e) Calculate and interpret optimal reorder quantities.
(f) Calculate and interpret optimal reorder quantities when discounts apply.
(g) Produce calculations to minimise inventory costs when inventory is gradually replenished.
(h) Describe and apply appropriate methods for establishing reorder levels where demand in the lead time is constant.

2 Accounting for labour

(a) Calculate direct and indirect costs of labour.
(b) Explain the methods used to relate input labour costs to work done.
(c) Prepare the journal and ledger entries to record labour cost inputs and outputs.

(d) Describe different remuneration methods: time-based systems, piecework systems and individual and group incentive schemes.
(e) Calculate the level, and analyse the costs and causes of labour turnover.
(f) Explain and calculate labour efficiency, capacity and production volume ratios.
(g) Interpret the entries in the labour account.

3 Accounting for overheads

(a) Explain the different treatment of direct and indirect expenses.
(b) Describe the procedures involved in determining production overhead absorption rates.
(c) Allocate and apportion production overheads to cost centres using an appropriate basis.
(d) Reapportion service cost centre costs to production cost centres (using the reciprocal method where service cost centres work for each other).
(e) Select, apply and discuss appropriate bases for absorption rates.
(f) Prepare journal and ledger entries for manufacturing overheads incurred and absorbed.
(g) Calculate and explain the under and over absorption of overheads.
(h) Apply methods of relating non-production overheads to cost units.

4 Marginal and absorption costing

(a) Explain the importance of, and apply, the concept of contribution.
(b) Demonstrate and discuss the effect of absorption and marginal costing on inventory valuation and profit determination.
(c) Calculate profit or loss under absorption and marginal costing.
(d) Reconcile the profits or losses calculated under absorption and marginal costing.
(e) Describe the advantages and disadvantages of absorption and marginal costing.

5 Job and batch costing

(a) Describe the characteristics of job and batch costing.
(b) Describe the situations where the use of job or batch costing would be appropriate.
(c) Prepare cost records and accounts in job and batch costing situations.
(d) Establish job costs from given information.

6 Process costing

(a) Describe the characteristics of process costing.
(b) Describe the situations where the use of process costing would be appropriate.
(c) Explain the concepts of normal and abnormal losses and abnormal gains.
(d) Calculate the cost per unit of process outputs.

(e) Prepare process accounts involving normal and abnormal losses and abnormal gains.
(f) Calculate and explain the concept of equivalent units.
(g) Apportion process costs between work remaining in process and transfers out of a process using the weighted average and FIFO methods.
(h) Prepare process accounts in situations where work remains incomplete.
(i) Prepare process accounts where losses and gains are identified at different stages of the process.
(j) Distinguish between by-products and joint products.
(k) Value by-products and joint products at the point of separation.
(l) Prepare process accounts in situations where by-products and/or joint products occur.

Note: Situations involving work in process **and** losses in the same process are excluded.

7 Service/operation costing

(a) Identify situations where the use of service/operation costing is appropriate.
(b) Illustrate suitable unit cost measures that may be used in different service/operation situations.
(c) Carry out service cost analysis in simple service industry situations.

E Budgeting and standard costing

1 Nature and purpose of budgeting

(a) Explain why organisations use budgeting.
(b) Explain the administrative procedures used in the budgeting process.
(c) Describe the stages in the budgeting process.

2 Functional budgets

(a) Explain the term 'principal budget factor'.
(b) Prepare budgets for sales, production, materials (usage and purchases), labour and overheads.

3 Flexible budgets and standard costing

(a) Explain and prepare fixed, flexible and flexed budgets.
(b) Explain the purpose and principles of standard costing.
(c) Establish the standard cost per unit under absorption and marginal costing.

4 Basic variance analysis under absorption and marginal costing

(a) Calculate the following variances:
    (i) Sales price and volume
    (ii) Materials total, price and usage
    (iii) Labour total, rate and efficiency

(iv) Variable overhead total, expenditure and efficiency
(v) Fixed overhead total, expenditure and, where appropriate, volume, capacity and efficiency.

(b) Interpret all the variances in 4(a).
(c) Explain possible causes of all the variances in 4(a).
(d) Describe the interrelationships between the variances in 4(a).
(e) Calculate actual or standard figures where the variances in 4(a) are given.

5 Reconciliation of budgeted profit and actual profit

(a) Reconcile budgeted profit with actual profit under standard absorption costing.
(b) Reconcile budgeted profit or contribution with actual profit or contribution under standard marginal costing.

F Short-term decision-making techniques

1 Cost-volume-profit (CVP) analysis

(a) Calculate and interpret a break-even point and a margin of safety.
(b) Demonstrate an understanding of, and use, the concepts of a target profit or revenue and a contribution to sales ratio.
(c) Identify the elements in traditional and contribution break-even charts and profit/volume charts.
(d) Apply CVP analysis to single product situations.

Note: Multi-product break-even charts and profit/volume charts are excluded.

2 Relevant costing

(a) Explain the concept of relevant costing.
(b) Calculate the relevant costs for materials, labour and overheads.
(c) Calculate the relevant costs associated with non-current assets.
(d) Explain and apply the concept of opportunity cost.

3 Limiting factors

(a) Identify a single limiting factor.
(b) Determine the optimal production plan where an organisation is restricted by a single limiting factor.
(c) Formulate a linear programming problem involving two variables.
(d) Determine the optimal solution to a linear programming problem using a graphical approach.
(e) Use simultaneous equations, where appropriate, in the solution of a linear programming problem.

f

Formulae

Regression analysis

$$a = \frac{\sum y}{n} - \frac{b\sum x}{n}$$

$$b = \frac{n\sum xy - \sum x \sum y}{n\sum x^2 - (\sum x)^2}$$

$$r = \frac{n\sum xy - \sum x \sum y}{\sqrt{(n\sum x^2 - (\sum x)^2)\ (n\sum y^2 - (\sum y)^2)}}$$

Economic order quantity = $\sqrt{\frac{2C_0D}{C_h}}$

Economic batch quantity = $\sqrt{\frac{2C_0D}{C_h\left(1 - \frac{D}{R}\right)}}$

CHAPTER 1

The nature and purpose of cost and management accounting

Contents

Accounting for management

- Introduction to cost and management accounting
- Data and information
- Attributes of good information
- Planning, decision-making and control
- Strategic, tactical and operational planning
- Cost, revenue, profit and investment centres

1 Accounting for management

1.1 Introduction to cost and management accounting

Accounting has several purposes, but the main purposes might be stated as follows.

- To provide a record of the financial value of business transactions, and in doing so to establish financial controls and reduce the risks of fraud
- To assist with the management of the financial affairs of an entity
- To provide information - mainly information of a financial nature.

Accounting information is provided for:

- Management, so that managers have the information they need to run the company
- Other users of information, many of them outside the entity. For example, a company produces accounting information for its shareholders in the form of financial statements, and financial statements are also used by tax authorities, investors, trade union representatives and others.

Cost and management accounting is concerned with the provision of information, mainly of a financial nature, for management. A management accounting system is a management information system.

1.2 Data and information

The terms 'data' and 'information' are often used as if they have the same meaning. However, there is a difference between data and information:

- **Data** consists of unprocessed facts and statistics. Data is collected and processed to produce information. Data has no meaning until it has been processed into information.
- **Information** has a meaning and a purpose. It is produced from 'data'. It is processed data that has relevance to a particular useful purpose.

Data may be collected from many different sources, both inside and outside an organisation.

A cost accounting system records data about the costs of operations and activities within the entity. The sources of cost accounting data within an organisation include invoices, receipts, inventory records and time sheets. Many of the documents from which cost data is captured are internally-generated documents, such as time sheets and material requisition notes.

Data is analysed and processed to produce management information, often in the form of:

- routine reports, or
- specially-prepared reports, or
- answers to 'one-off' enquiries that are input to a computer system.

Information produced from cost accounting data is management accounting information. Management accounting systems also obtain information from other sources, including external sources, but the cost accounting system is a major source of management accounting information.

1.3 Attributes of good information

Information is only useful to managers if it possesses certain qualities or attributes.

- **Understandable**. Information should be understandable to the individuals who use it. For accountants, this often means having to make sure that the figures provided to managers are set out clearly and are properly explained.
- **Purpose and relevance**. Information should have a purpose and should be needed by management for a particular reason. Unless information has a purpose it has no value at all and it makes no sense to provide it. The information provided should also be relevant to this purpose.
- **Reliable**. Management information must be reliable. This means that the user of the information can rely on the information to make a decision, and should not be worried about whether the information is correct. Information does not have to be 100% accurate. In many cases, information might be provided in the form of an estimate or forecast. However, information should be as accurate or reliable as it needs to be for its purpose. It might also need to be up-to-date.
- **Sufficiently complete**. Information should be as complete as it needs to be. There should be no important omissions. However, information in management reports should not be excessive, because important information may be hidden in the unimportant information, and it will take managers too long to read and understand.
- **Timeliness**. Information must be timely. This means that it must be made available to managers in time to use it for making a decision. If information is provided too late for its purpose, it has no value. With the widespread computerisation of accounting systems, including cost accounting systems, it might be appropriate for up-to-date management accounting information to be available on line and on demand whenever it is needed.
- **Comparability**. In accounting it is often useful to make comparisons, such as comparisons of current year results with previous years, or comparisons of

actual results with planned results. To make comparisons possible, information should be prepared on the same basis, using the same methods and the same 'rules'.

- **Communicated to the right person**. Management information should be communicated to the proper person. This is the person with the authority to make a decision on the basis of the information received and who needs the information to make the decision.
- **Its value must exceed its cost**. Management information has a value. If information has no value (= no purpose) there is no point in having it. The value of information comes from improving the quality of management decisions. However providing information involves some expense. More information is worth having only if it helps to improve management decisions, and the benefits from those decisions exceed the cost of providing the additional information. This is why many small business entities do not have a formal cost accounting system – the manager is familiar with the costs and revenues of the business and the cost of operating a cost accounting system might not be worth the expense.

1.4 Planning, decision-making and control

The purpose of management information is to assist management in making decisions. Management decisions can be grouped into three broad categories:

- Planning decisions
- Control decisions
- 'One-off' decisions.

Planning

Planning involves the following:

- setting the objectives for the organisation
- making plans for achieving those objectives.

The planning process is a formal process and the end-result is a formal plan, authorised at an appropriate level in the management hierarchy. Formal plans include long-term business plans, budgets, sales plans, weekly production schedules, capital expenditure plans and so on.

Information is needed in order to make sensible plans – for example in order to prepare an annual budget, it is necessary to provide information about expected sales prices, sales quantities and costs, in the form of forecasts or estimates.

Control

Control of the performance of an organisation is an important management task. Control involves the following:

- monitoring actual performance, and comparing actual performance with the objective or plan
- taking control action where appropriate
- evaluating actual performance.

When operations appear to be getting out of control, management should be alerted so that suitable measures can be taken to deal with the problem. Control information might be provided in the form of routine performance reports or as special warnings or alerts when something unusual has occurred.

'One-off' decision making

Decisions taken by managers include planning decisions and control decisions. In addition, managers might need to make 'one-off' decisions, outside the formal planning and control systems. Management accounting information can be provided to help a manager decide what to do in any situation where a decision is needed.

1.5 Strategic, tactical and operational planning

Managers carry out their responsibilities at different levels in the hierarchy of an organisation, and decisions are made at all levels of management. These may be planning decisions, control decisions or 'one-off' decisions. Decision-making can be categorised into three levels: these different categories are probably most easily understood in relation to planning decisions.

- **Strategic planning.** Strategic planning involves setting overall objectives for the organisation and developing broad plans, mostly over a fairly long-term, about how the objectives should be achieved. An example of a strategic plan is a five-year business plan. Strategic planning is the responsibility of senior management, who plan the strategic direction that the entity should be taking. To make long-term plans, managers need information. Much of this information is not financial in nature, and much of it comes from external sources (from sources outside the organisation). However some accounting and financial information is needed for strategic planning purposes, and 'strategic management accounting' is a term for the provision of information for strategic planning purposes.
- **Tactical planning.** Tactical planning involves developing shorter-term plans to implement longer-term strategic plans. They have a shorter time frame than strategic plans, and many tactical plans cover a period of six months or one year. They might also be sub-divided into shorter control periods, such as monthly periods, for the purpose of routine control reporting. They are also more detailed than strategic plans. In a large organisation, tactical planning involves managers below the most senior level ('middle management'), although tactical plans might require senior management approval. Much of the information for tactical planning comes from sources within the organisation, such as the cost accounting system, and much of it is financial in nature. An example of a tactical plan is an annual budget.
- **Operational planning.** Operational planning is planning the operational activities of an entity in detail. Operational plans include production schedules, work schedules, machine utilisation plans, maintenance schedules, delivery schedules and so on. They are short-term plans such as daily or weekly operating schedules and most are not financial in nature. Operational planning should involve junior management and supervisors, although they might need the approval of middle management.

Management accounting information is provided mainly for strategic planning and tactical planning purposes, and for senior or middle management. However, the use of management accounting for tactical planning and control is probably more widespread than strategic management accounting.

The techniques described in later chapters of this study text relate mainly to the provision of information for planning and control at the tactical level.

1.6 Cost, revenue, profit and investment centres

Organisation structure and management responsibilities

Every business organisation has a management structure, and individual managers are given responsibility for a particular aspect of operations or activity. The operations or activity for which they are responsible can be called a **responsibility centre**. Within a large organisation, there is a hierarchy of management, with a hierarchy of delegated responsibilities.

A manager might be in charge of a department, such as a warehouse or the buying department. A part of their responsibility should be to ensure that the department operates efficiently and economically, and that costs (expenditures) are kept under control. A departmental manager is likely to be responsible for preparing the annual cost budget for the departments, subject to approval by his superiors. A manager who is made responsible for costs must have some authority over spending in his department (although a large proportion of departmental costs, such as employees' salaries, might be outside his control).

A manager might be responsible for a department or activity that earns revenue, and for the revenue earned by the department. For example a sales manager might be made responsible for the activities of a sales team and the revenue that the sales team earns. Similarly, the manager of a retail store (in a company that operates a chain of stores) might be responsible for the revenues earned by the store. A manager who is made responsible for revenues might have some authority to adjust or decide selling prices; alternatively a manager might be told what the sales prices will be and is them made responsible for the volume of sales at those prices.

When a manager is responsible for both the costs and the revenues of an operation or department, he (or she) is also responsible for the profits that it earns.

In some cases, a manager might have the responsibility to make decisions about capital investment for an operation, with authority to buy new capital equipment or sell off unwanted assets. For example in a large company or a group of companies, there might be operating divisions where the divisional manager has a large amount of autonomy, with authority over capital spending ('capital budgets') as well as revenues, costs and profits.

Definition of cost, revenue, profit and investment centres

As stated earlier, managers need management accounting information to help them make decisions. For the purpose of cost and management accounting, responsibility centres can be divided into four categories:

- **Cost centres.** A cost centre is a department or work group for which costs are established, in order to measure the cost of output produced by the centre. For example, in a factory a group of machines might be a cost centre. The costs of operating the machines would be established, and a cost could then be calculated for each unit of product manufactured by the machines.

  In a cost centre, there is no measurement of revenue or profit.

- **Profit centres.** A profit centre is a department or division within the organisation for which revenues as well as costs are established. By measuring the costs of the products or services produced by the centre, and the revenues earned from selling them, it is possible to establish the profit (or loss) that the centre makes.

Example: summarised profit centre report	$000
Revenues of the profit centre	250
Costs of the units sold by the profit centre	220
Profit (or loss) of the profit centre	30

  A profit centre might consist of several cost centres. For example, a factory might be treated as a profit centre, and within the factory, the machining department, assembly department and finishing department might be three cost centres.

- **Investment centres.** An investment centre is a division within an organisation where the management is responsible not only for the costs of the division and the revenues that it earns, but also for decisions relating to the investment in assets for the division. An investment centre manager usually has authority to purchase new assets, such as items of plant or equipment, and so should be responsible for the profit or 'return' that the division makes on the amount that it has invested.

  The performance of an investment centre might be measured by calculating the profit as a percentage of the amount invested (the return on investment or ROI).

  An investment centre might include a number of different profit centres. For example, a company manufacturing cars and trucks might have two investment centres, (1) car-making and (2) truck-making. Within the truck-making division, there might be several profit centres, each of these a separate location or factory at which trucks are manufactured and assembled.

- **Revenue centres.** A revenue centre is a department or division within the organisation for which revenues are established. In a revenue centre there is no measurement of cost or profit. Revenue centre managers will only need to have information relating to revenues and will be accountable for revenues only. For example, the income accountant in a hospital is only responsible for recording and controlling the different incomes that are received from funding bodies or other sources (for example, private patients, fundraising and so on).

Example

A media company has several divisions. One is a magazine publishing division. This division is divided into three operating units: fashion magazines, sports magazines and business magazines, which operate from different offices. The fashion magazines unit has three main functions: commissioning, editing and printing, and marketing and sales.

The media company might organise its cost and management system as follows:

- Each of the divisions in the media company, including the magazines division, might be an investment centre. The senior manager of the magazines division might have the authority to incur capital expenditure to acquire new assets for the division. The performance of the magazines division might be measured by its annual return on investment (ROI).
- Within the magazines division, the fashion magazines unit, sports magazines unit and business magazines unit might be profit centres. The manager of each unit might be responsible for the revenues and costs of the unit, and the performance of each unit would be measured by the profit that it makes.
- Within the fashions magazine unit, each of the operating functions (commissioning, editing and printing, and marketing and sales) might be a cost unit. The manager in charge of each unit is responsible for costs, and the performance of the cost unit might be measured by comparing the actual costs of the cost centre with its budgeted costs.

The differing information needs of cost, revenue, profit and investment centre management

Managers of responsibility centres are responsible for the performance of their part of the organisation and its activities. The performance of an organisation is often measured financially, in terms of:

- keeping expenditure under control
- earning a sufficient amount of revenue
- making a profit
- making a suitable return on investment.

Managers therefore need information about the costs of operations for which they are responsible. They will often also need information about revenues and profit. In some cases, they will also need information about the amount of property, plant and equipment, and other 'assets' for which they are responsible. The information they need to make decisions within their area of responsibility depends on the scope of their management authority and responsibilities.

Managers also need financial information to help them make decisions. For example, they might need information about expected costs to make a decision about how much to charge for a job for a customer. Similarly, they might need information about costs and revenues to decide whether to invest money in a new project.

Management accounting is concerned with providing information to management to help them with planning and control, and for making other decisions.

The accounting information provided to managers should help them to make decisions, and the information provided should be relevant for the decisions they have to make. Clearly, the nature and content of the accounting information required depends on the nature of the manager's responsibilities (i.e. on the type of responsibility centre).

Cost and management accounting versus financial accounting

- Purpose and role of cost and management accounting
- Comparison of financial accounting and cost and management accounting

2 Cost and management accounting versus financial accounting

2.1 Purpose and role of cost and management accounting

Cost accounting

Cost accounting is concerned with gathering data about the costs of products or services and the cost of activities. There may be a formal costing system in which data about operational activities is recorded in a 'double entry' system of cost accounts in a 'cost ledger'. The cost accounting data is captured, stored and subsequently analysed to provide management information about costs.

Information provided by cost accounting systems is financial in nature, and analysed in detail. It may be forward-looking, and used to provide information about expected costs and profits in the future. More usually, cost accounting information is historical in nature, and provides information about the actual costs of items and activities that have been incurred.

Management accounting

Management accounting is concerned with providing information to management about costs, sales revenue and profits, so that managers are able to make well-informed decisions. Management accounting information is often prepared from an analysis of cost accounting data, although cost estimates and revenue estimates may be obtained from sources other than the cost accounting system.

The purpose of management accounting is to provide detailed financial information to management, so that they can **plan and control** the activities or operations for which they are responsible. Management accounting information is also provided to help managers make other decisions. In other words, management accounting provides management information to assist with planning, control and 'one-off' decisions.

Management control systems

A management accounting system may be described as a management control system. This is an information system, largely at a **tactical information** level for middle management that helps managers to plan and control the activities of the organisation.

A management control system can be described as a system for:

- identifying the objectives of the organisation: these may be long-term objectives, or may be budget objectives for the next financial year
- setting quantified targets for achieving those objectives
- measuring actual results throughout the planning period, and comparing actual performance with the objectives and targets
- taking control action where necessary when actual results are below target, or taking control action where appropriate to sustain performance when this is better than target.

An example of a management control system is budgeting with standard costs, and measuring actual performance against the standard costs using monthly variance analysis reports. Standard costs and variance analysis are described in a later chapter.

2.2 Comparison of financial accounting and cost and management accounting

Financial accounting

A financial accounting system is used to record the financial transactions of the entity, such as transactions relating to revenue, expenses, assets and liabilities. The accounting system provides a record of the assets that the company owns, and what it owes. It also provides a record of the income that the entity has earned, and the expenditures it has incurred.

The financial accounting system provides the data that is used to prepare the financial statements of the entity at the end of each financial year (the income statement, balance sheet, cash flow statement, and so on).

The main purpose of the financial statements of companies is to inform the company's shareholders (owners) about the financial performance and financial position of the company. They are also used as a basis for preparing the 'tax accounts' and calculating the tax that the company should pay on its profits. Managers might use the information in the financial statements, but the main purpose of financial reporting is for '**external purposes**' rather than to provide management information.

Financial statements are produced at the end of the financial year. Management need information much more regularly, throughout the year. They also need much more detailed information than is provided by a company's financial statements. They often need forward-looking forecasts, rather than reports of historical performance and what has happened in the past.

There is a statutory requirement for companies to produce annual financial statements, and other business entities need to produce financial statements for the purpose of making tax returns to the tax authorities.

Managers might find financial statements useful, but the main users of the financial statements of a company should be its shareholders. Other external users, such as potential investors, employees, trade unions and banks (lenders to the business) might also use the financial statements of a company to obtain information.

Cost and management accounting

Whereas financial statements from the financial accounting system are intended mainly for external users of financial information, management accounting information (obtained from the cost accounting system) is prepared specifically for internal use by management.

An entity might have a cost accounting system as well as a financial accounting system, so that it has two separate accounting systems in operation. A cost accounting system records the costs and revenues for individual jobs, processes, activities and products or services.

- Like the financial accounting system, a cost accounting system is based on a double entry system of debits and credits.
- However, the accounts in a cost accounting system are different from the accounts in the financial accounting systems. This is because the two accounting systems have different purposes, and so record financial transactions in different ways.

There is no legal requirement for a cost accounting system. Business entities choose to have a cost accounting system, and will only do so if the perceived benefits of the system justify the cost of operating it.

(In business entities where there is no formal cost accounting system, managers still need management accounting information to run their business. Some management accounting information might be extracted from the financial accounting system, but in much less detail than a cost accounting system would provide.)

A comparison of financial and cost accounting systems of companies is summarised in the table below.

Financial accounting system	Cost accounting system
Statutory requirement	Not a statutory requirement
Used to prepare financial statements for shareholders and other external users	Used to prepare information for management (internal use only)
Might also provide some information for management	
Records revenues, expenditure, assets and liabilities	Records costs of activities and used to provide detailed information about costs, revenues and profits for specific products, operations and activities
Used mainly to provide a historical record of performance and financial position	Provides historical information, but also used extensively for forecasting (forward-looking)

Practice multiple choice questions

1 Information is processed data.

Is this statement TRUE or FALSE? ***(1 mark)***

2 Which one of the following statements is correct?

A Management accountants are responsible for planning, decision-making and control.

B The purpose of a cost accounting system is to collect information about costs.

C A management accounting system provides all the strategic and tactical information required by management.

D Management accounting information should be timely and relevant, but does not need to be 100% accurate. ***(2 marks)***

3 A company owns a factory that produces Component X. All units of Component X are transferred to the company's processing centre where a final product is assembled. Decisions about purchasing equipment for the factory are made at the company's head office. In the company's cost and management accounting system, the factory is likely to be treated as:

A A cost centre.

B A revenue centre

C A profit centre

D An investment centre. ***(2 marks)***

4 A cost centre manager needs regular information about costs incurred by the centre. In a cost and management accounting system, which of the following is the most likely frequency of regular cost reports for the centre?

A Daily

B Weekly

C Monthly

D Annual ***(2 marks)***

5 A profit centre manager needs information about which of the following?

(1) Costs incurred by the centre

(2) Revenues earned by the centre

(3) Capital investment in the centre

A (1) only

B (1) and (2) only

C (2) only

D (1), (2) and (3) ***(2 marks)***

6 A company is preparing a budget for an advertising campaign that the sales director has just ordered, subject to approval of the costs. The campaign is expected to last for just over six months. The advertising budget is an example of:

A Strategic planning

B Tactical planning

C Operational planning ***(1 mark)***

CHAPTER

2

Cost classification

Contents

Production and non-production costs

- The need to know about costs
- Materials costs, labour costs and expenses
- Manufacturing: categorising costs as 'production' or 'non-production' costs
- Elements of non-production costs
- The importance of separating production and non-production costs

1 Production and non-production costs

1.1 The need to know about costs

An organisation needs to know:

- how much it costs to make the products that it produces, or
- how much it costs to provide its services to customers.

For an organisation that is not required to make a profit (a 'not-for-profit organisation', such as a government department or state-owned agency), it is important to know how much items cost, in order to:

- plan expenditure for the future, and
- compare actual costs with planned costs, and take action to control costs when these seem too high.

For an organisation that is required to make a profit, it is also important to know how much items cost, in order to:

- make sure that the product or service will be sold at a profit
- measure the actual profit that has been made, and
- in the case of some companies, such as manufacturing companies, value inventory at the end of each accounting period.

1.2 Materials costs, labour costs and expenses

Costs can be classified as material costs, labour costs or other expenses.

- **Material costs** are the costs of any material items purchased from suppliers, with the intention of using them or consuming them in the fairly short-term future. In a manufacturing company, material costs include the cost of the raw materials that go into producing the manufactured output. In an office, costs of materials consumed include the costs of stationery and replacement printer cartridges for the office laser printers.
- Material costs do **not** include the cost of longer-term assets (non-current assets) such as plant and equipment, or new trucks for the company's fleet of delivery vehicles.
- **Labour costs** are the remuneration costs of all employees employed and paid by the entity. This includes the wages and salaries of part-time workers and the

costs of any bonuses, pension contributions and other items that are paid in addition to basic wages and salaries.

- **Other expenses** include the costs of any items that are not material costs or labour costs. They include the cost of services provided by external suppliers (the charges made by sub-contractors, charges for repairs by external contractors, rental costs, telephone costs, insurance costs, costs of energy (gas, electricity), travelling and subsistence expenses, and depreciation charges for non-current assets.

In a cost accounting system, all these items of cost must be recorded, and there needs to be an organised system for recording them. Cost items need to be grouped into categories of similar costs.

1.3 Manufacturing: categorising costs as 'production' or 'non-production' costs

In a cost accounting system for a manufacturing company, costs will be categorised as either:

- production costs (manufacturing costs) or
- non-production costs (non-manufacturing costs).

Production costs, or manufacturing costs, are the costs incurred in manufacturing finished products, up to the time that the manufacture of the goods is completed, and the goods are either transferred to the finished goods inventory or delivered immediately to the customer.

Manufacturing costs include:

- the material cost of the raw materials and components, purchased from suppliers and used in the production of the goods that are manufactured
- the labour cost of all employees working for the manufacturing function, such as machine operators, supervisors, factory supervisors and the factory manager
- other expenses of the factory, such as rental costs for the factory building, energy costs and the cost of depreciation of factory machinery.

Non-production costs are any items of cost that are not manufacturing costs.

1.4 Elements of non-production costs

Non-production costs might be divided into:

- Administration costs
- Sales and distribution costs (also called marketing costs)
- Finance costs

Administration costs

Administration costs are the costs of providing administration services for the entity. They might be called 'head office costs' and usually include the costs of the human relations department and accounting department. They should include:

- the salary costs of all the staff working in the administration departments
- the costs of the office space used by these departments, such as office rental costs
- other administration expenses, such as the costs of heating and lighting for the administration offices, the depreciation costs of equipment used by the administration departments, fees paid to the company's solicitors for legal services, costs of office stationery and so on.

Selling and distribution costs (marketing costs)

Selling and distribution costs are the costs incurred in marketing and selling goods or services to customers, and the costs of delivering the goods to customers. The costs of after-sales services, such as customer support services, are usually included in these costs. Sales and distribution costs include:

- the wages and salary costs of all employees working in the selling and distribution departments, including sales commissions for sales representatives
- advertising costs and other marketing costs
- operating costs for delivery vehicles (for delivering finished goods to customers), such as fuel costs and vehicle repair costs
- other costs, including depreciation costs for the delivery vehicles.

Finance costs

Finance costs include costs that are involved in financing the organisation, for example, loan interest or bank overdraft charges.

Finance costs might be included in general administration costs. Alternatively, finance costs might be excluded from the cost accounting system because they are relevant to financial reporting (and the financial accounting system) but are not relevant to the measurement of costs.

Other non-production costs

Non-production costs are often categorised as administration, sales and distribution or finance costs because these categories of costs are also used in financial statements produced by a financial accounting system.

In a system of cost accounting, it is not essential to use these categories of non-production costs. Sometimes, additional categories of non-production costs might be identified separately, such as costs of research and development.

Separating costs into production, administration, sales and distribution and finance costs is a division of costs according to **function**. Function refers to the nature of the activity.

Example

Functional costs might be used in an income statement to report the profit or loss of a company during a financial period, as follows:

	$000	$000
Sales revenue		600
Manufacturing cost of sales		200
Gross profit		400
Administration costs	120	
Selling and distribution costs	230	
		350
Net profit (or net loss)		50

Separating costs into the costs for each function can provide useful information for management. Functional costs show managers what they are expected to spend on each function (budgeted costs) and how much they are actually spending.

Some costs might be partly manufacturing costs, partly administration costs and partly sales and distribution costs. For example:

- The salary of the managing director, because the managing director spends time on all aspects of the company's operations.
- Building rental costs, when the same building is used by more than one function. For example administration staff and sales staff might share the same offices.

When costs are shared between two or more functions, they are divided between the functions on a fair basis. For example, the salary of the managing director might be divided equally manufacturing costs, administration costs and sales and distribution costs. Dividing shared costs on a fair basis is called **apportionment** of the cost.

Example

A company uses three categories of functional cost in its cost accounting system. These are manufacturing costs, administration costs and sales and distribution costs.

Identify the functional cost category for each of the following costs:

(1) Salary of the chief accountant
(2) Telephone charges
(3) Cost of office cleaning services
(4) Cost of warehouse staff

Answer

(1) **Chief accountant's salary**. Accounting department costs are an administration cost, and the salary of the chief accountant is treated in full as an administration costs.

(2) **Telephone charges**. These are usually treated as administration costs, unless the charges can be traced directly to telephones in the manufacturing department or the sales and distribution department. When charges can be traced directly to telephones in the manufacturing department, they should be recorded as manufacturing costs.

(3) **Office cleaning services**. These are usually treated as administration costs, unless the charges can be traced directly to offices used by the sales and distribution staff, or the production staff.

(4) **Warehouse staff**. These are manufacturing costs when the warehouse is used to store raw materials and components. They are sales and distribution costs when the warehouse is used to store finished goods. If the warehouse stores raw materials and finished goods, the wages costs should be apportioned between production costs and sales and distribution costs.

1.5 The importance of separating production and non-production costs

Inventory

In a manufacturing business, it is important to separate production costs from non-production costs. This is because at the end of any financial period, there will be some closing inventory of:

- finished goods that have been produced during the financial period but not yet sold (finished goods inventory), and
- partly-finished production, for which production is not yet compete (work-in-progress or WIP, sometimes called work-in-process).

The costs of finished goods inventory and partly-finished production (work-in-progress or WIP) consist of their production costs.

Total production costs during a period must therefore be divided or shared between:

- goods produced and sold in the period
- goods produced but not yet sold (finished goods)
- partly-produced goods in the period (work in progress).

Non-production costs must **never** be included in the cost of inventory.

Reporting profit in the income statement

An income statement reports the profit or loss earned during a financial period. Profit is the revenue for a financial period minus the costs for the period.

Manufacturing costs and non-production costs are shown separately in an income statement in both financial accounting and cost accounting because of inventory costs.

- There is a difference between the **manufacturing costs incurred** during a financial period and the **manufacturing cost of the goods sold** in the period.
- The difference between manufacturing costs incurred and the manufacturing cost of goods sold is the amount of the increase or decrease in inventory values between the beginning and end of the period.

Study the following example carefully. Illustrative numbers are included to demonstrate the calculations required.

	$	$
Opening inventory, work in progress		25,800
Manufacturing costs incurred in the period		156,000
		181,800
Less: Closing inventory, work in progress		(23,600)
Equals: Cost of goods manufactured in the period		158,200
Opening inventory, finished goods	4,000	
Closing inventory, finished goods	(8,500)	
		(4,500)
Equals: Production cost of goods sold in the period		153,700
Non-production costs		
Administration costs	62,000	
Selling and distribution costs	71,000	
		133,000
Total costs for the period in the income statement		286,700

The manufacturing costs incurred during the period were $156,000 but the manufacturing cost of goods sold was $153,700. The difference is attributable to changes in inventory levels between the beginning and the end of the period.

An income statement might be presented as follows, showing inventory changes. Although this is the format of an income statement for financial reporting (financial accounting) it might also be used in a system of cost accounting:

	$000	$000
Sales revenue		600
Opening inventory (raw materials, WIP , finished goods)	15	
Manufacturing costs in the period	210	
	225	
Closing inventory (raw materials, WIP, finished goods)	(25)	
Manufacturing cost of sales		200
Gross profit		400
Administration costs	120	
Selling and distribution costs	230	
		350
Net profit (or net loss)		50

If you have not yet studied financial accounting or financial reporting, the income statement might not yet be familiar to you. You need to learn how to calculate the cost of sales, gross profit and net profit for a financial period. Try to remember the significance of inventory in this computation, and the need to share costs of production between finished output and closing inventory.

This important topic will be explained in more detail in a later chapter.

Direct and indirect costs

- Direct costs
- Indirect costs (overheads)
- Full cost

2 Direct and indirect costs

2.1 Direct costs

In addition to classifying costs as production, administration or sales and distribution costs, costs may also be classified as:

- a direct costs, or
- indirect costs, also called **overheads**.

This means that there are direct material costs, indirect material costs, direct labour costs and indirect labour costs, and direct and indirect expenses.

A **direct cost** is a cost that can be attributed **in its entirety** to the cost of an item that is being costed.

For example, in a manufacturing company that produces television sets, the direct cost of making a television consists of direct materials and direct labour costs, and possibly some direct expenses.

- The direct materials cost is the cost of the raw materials and components that have gone into making the television.
- The direct labour cost is the cost of the labour time of the employees who have been directly involved in making the television.

Direct materials

Direct materials are materials that are used directly in the manufacture of a product or the provision of a service. For example:

- the direct materials in the manufacture of a pair of shoes might include leather and rubber heels
- the direct materials in the manufacture of an office chair include wheels, a stand, a seat (with seat cushion), back rest, arm rests and fabric.
- the direct materials in a restaurant meal are the major items of food (and drink).

Direct materials may consist of either or both:

- **raw materials**, such as glass, metals and chemicals
- **components** purchased from an external supplier: for example the direct materials of a car manufacturer include components purchased from other suppliers, such as windows, wheels and tyres.

Services might also incur some direct materials costs. For example, with catering and restaurant services the direct materials include the major items of food (and drink).

Direct labour

Direct labour is labour time that can be attributed directly to the item that is being costed. In costing a small item of manufactured output, direct labour time might be quite short, say just a few minutes per unit produced. In costing a large item such as the cost of operating a warehouse, direct labour costs include the labour cost of all employees who spend all their working time on warehouse activities.

As a general rule, labour costs are direct costs for work done by direct labour employees. Direct labour employees are employees whose time is spent directly on the item being costed. For example in a manufacturing company, direct labour employees will include:

- Machinists working in the machining department
- Assembly workers in the assembly department
- Workers in the spray painting shop

The time of these workers can be attributed directly to the production of the finished output from the manufacturing process. On the other hand some workers in a factory are not direct labour, because they do not work directly in the production of the output from the factory: Inspection staff and supervisors are examples of labour that is not direct labour when costing the output from a factory.

Non-manufacturing businesses also have direct labour employees. These are the employees directly involved in producing the output of the business or providing a service that is sold to customers. For example:

- Bricklayers are direct labour employees of a house-building firm
- Waiters and chefs are direct labour employees of a restaurant
- Miners are direct labour workers in a mining company
- Teachers are direct labour employees in a school.

Direct expenses

Direct expenses are expenses that can be attributed in full to the item being costed. In manufacturing, direct expenses are not common for manufactured units of output, and direct costs normally consist of just direct materials and direct labour costs.

However the cost of large items might include direct expenses. For example, if a construction company is building a new office building, direct expenses of constructing the building will include the rental cost of any cranes or lifting equipment hired to assist with the work. Direct expenses would also include the fees of sub-contractors who are hired to carry out some of the building work. (Work done by external sub-contractors is an expense, not a direct labour cost.).

Prime cost

The prime cost of an item is its total direct cost.

	$
Direct material cost	A
Direct labour cost	B
Direct expenses	C
Prime cost	A + B + C

2.2 Indirect costs (overheads)

An **indirect cost** or **overhead cost** is any cost that is not a direct cost, so that its entire cost cannot be attributed in full to the item that is being costed.

- Indirect labour is the cost of labour that cannot be attributed in full to the item being costed. The nature of indirect labour costs is explained in more detail later.
- Indirect expenses are expenses that cannot be attributed in full to an item that is being costed. For example, the rental costs for a factory and the costs of gas and electricity consumption for a factory cannot be attributed in full to any particular units of production. They are indirect production costs (production overheads).

In a manufacturing company, all costs of administration are usually treated as indirect costs (administration overheads) and all or most sales and distribution costs are also usually treated as sales and distribution overheads.

Indirect material costs

Indirect materials are any materials that are used or consumed that cannot be attributed in full to the item being costed. Indirect materials are treated as an overhead cost, and may be classified as production overheads, administration overheads or sales and distribution overheads.

Indirect materials in production include cleaning materials and any materials used by production departments or staff who are not engaged directly in making a product. In a restaurant, indirect materials will include the cost of salt, pepper and spices that are used by the kitchen staff for most meals, but which cannot be attributed to any specific meal.

Indirect production materials may also include some items of materials that are inexpensive and whose cost or value is immaterial. These may include nails, nuts and bolts, buttons and thread, and so on. The effort of measuring a cost for these materials is not worth the value of the cost information that would be produced; therefore these 'direct' materials are often treated as indirect materials.

Example

In which of the following types of company would fuel costs be treated as a direct material cost?

1. Manufacturing company
2. Road haulage (road transport) company

3. Construction company
4. Motorway fuel station

Solution

Manufacturing company. Fuel costs are an indirect expense. Fuel used in the company's vehicles is unlikely to be considered a material cost at all, but would be treated as an overhead expense.

Road haulage company. Since fuel is a major cost of operating a road haulage service, fuel costs are likely to be treated as a direct material cost of operations.

Construction company. Fuel costs are likely to be an indirect expense, for the same reasons that apply to a manufacturing company.

Motorway service station. This sells fuel to customers. In a retail operation, items sold to customers are direct costs of sale. The cost of the fuel sold is therefore a direct material cost (= a cost of sale).

Indirect labour costs

Indirect labour costs consist mainly of the cost of indirect labour employees. Indirect labour employees are individuals who do not work directly on the items that are produced or the services that are provided.

In a manufacturing environment, indirect labour employees include staff in the stores and materials handling department (for example, fork lift truck drivers), supervisors, and repairs and maintenance engineers.

All employees in administration departments and marketing departments (sales and distribution staff) – including management – are normally indirect employees.

2.3 Full cost

The full cost of a unit of product (or the full cost of a unit of service) is a cost that includes both direct costs and some overheads. The full cost of a unit of product might be analysed as follows:

	$	
Direct materials cost	4	
Direct labour cost	5	
Direct expenses	1	
Prime cost	10	Production cost
Manufacturing overhead (or production overhead)	8	
Full production cost	18	
Administration overhead	3	Non-production cost
Selling and distribution overhead	4	
Full cost of sale	25	

Notes:

1 Prime cost plus a share of production overheads are the **full production cost** or 'fully absorbed production cost' of the cost unit.

2 In cost accounting systems, it is common practice to include production overheads in unit costs and measure the full production cost per unit. However, administration and selling and distribution overhead costs are not usually included in the cost of each unit. Instead, they are treated in total as an expense for the period **('period costs')**.

Cost objects, cost units and cost centres

- Cost objects and cost units
- Cost centres

3 Cost objects, cost units and cost centres

3.1 Cost objects and cost units

A cost accounting system measures the costs of cost objects, and often presents the information as a cost per unit of the cost object.

- A **cost object** is an item whose cost is measured.
- A **cost unit** is a unit of the cost item.

Cost objects and cost units should be selected so as to provide management with the cost information they require.

Here are some examples of cost objects and cost units

Industry/activity	Cost object	Cost unit
Car manufacture	Cars produced	A car
Bakery	Bread produced	A batch of bread items
Steel works	Steel produced	Tonne of steel
Carpet manufacture	Carpets produced	Square metre of carpet
Retail operation	Cost of items sold	Cost per $1 sales
Passenger transport service	Cost of transporting customers	Cost per passenger/mile (i.e. average cost of transporting a passenger one mile)
Road haulage	Cost of transporting items	Cost per tonne/mile (i.e. average cost of carrying one tonne of items for one mile)
University	Cost of teaching	Cost per student

Example 1

A company manufactures tinned foods. It has two products, tinned carrots and tinned beans. In its costing system, it has two cost objects, carrots and beans. The costing system measures the costs and revenues for each cost object.

The costing system will also provide information about the cost per tin of carrots and the cost per tin of beans. These are cost units.

	Cost object	Cost unit
1	Carrots	Production cost per tin of carrots
2	Beans	Production cost per tin of beans

Example 2

Another company manufactures a single product at two factories, one in the North of the country and one in the South of the country. Its costing system might measure:

- the cost of operating the factory in the north and the factory in the south (cost objects), and also
- the total operating cost in each factory per hour of labour worked, or the total operating cost per employee at each factory (these are cost units).

Example 3

A transport company has a bus depot. The company has a cost accounting system that records and measures the cost of operating the bus depot. The costs of operating the depot are measured in three ways, as follows:

	Cost object	Cost unit
1	Buses	Operating cost per bus per month
2	Bus routes	Operating cost per month for each bus route
3	Bus drivers	Cost of operating the depot per month, per bus driver employed

3.2 Cost centres

Cost centres have been described so far in terms of management responsibilities. In a cost centre, a manager is responsible for the costs incurred, and therefore needs information about those costs.

There is a slightly different way of looking at the nature of a cost centre.

- A cost centre is a department, group of machines or activity that incurs costs.
- The cost centre produces cost units.
- Costs can therefore be traced to cost centres, and costs can be calculated for the units of output or activity of that cost centre.

Example

A group of machines produces units of Product X. During one month, the costs of operating the machines were $36,000. There are 4 machines which were each operated for 150 hours in the month. The machines produced 20,000 units of Product X.

The group of machines might be treated as a cost centre, and the costs of the cost centre in the month were $36,000.

The cost per unit of Product X produced by the cost centre was $1.80.
We can also calculate the cost per machine hour, which is $60 (= $36,000/(4 × 150)). Both units of Product X and machine hours worked can therefore be costed as cost units: one is a unit of output and the other is a unit of activity.

Cost centres: direct and indirect costs

Direct costs of a cost centre are costs that are attributable directly to the activity of the cost centre. Direct costs of a cost centre might be indirect costs of the units produced by the cost centre.

Example

The wages of a maintenance and repairs engineer might be a direct cost of the department in which he works. However, his wages are an indirect cost of each individual cost unit produced by the department. This is because the job of the engineer is to fix machines and other equipment when they break down, and he is not involved directly in producing the output of the department.

Practice multiple choice questions

1 The cost of a quality inspection checker in a factory is an indirect labour cost of items produced.

Is this statement TRUE or FALSE? ***(1 mark)***

2 Which one of the following would be classified as indirect labour?

A Paint sprayers in a car production plant

B Accountants in an audit firm

C Workers in the stores department of a brick manufacturing company

D Roofing workers in a building construction company.

(2 marks)

3 A publishing company produces books. Which of the following is a direct material cost of production?

A printing costs charged by an external printer

B a writing fee paid to the author

C the cost of copy editing

D cost of copies distributed to book reviewers. ***(2 marks)***

CHAPTER

3

Cost behaviour and cost estimation

Contents

Fixed and variable costs

- Cost behaviour: meaning
- Variable costs
- Fixed costs
- Mixed costs

1 Fixed and variable costs

1.1 Cost behaviour: meaning

Cost behaviour refers to the way in which costs change as the volume of activity changes. The volume of activity may be:

- the volume of sales
- the volume of production
- total labour hours worked, machine hours worked
- the number of production units inspected,
- the number of journeys (for buses or trains) or deliveries, and so on.

As a general rule, total costs should be expected to increase as the volume of activity rises.

Management might want information about estimated costs, or about what costs should have been. An understanding of cost behaviour is necessary in order to:

- forecast or plan what costs ought to be, and
- compare actual costs that were incurred with what the costs should have been.

The classifications of cost that were described in the previous chapter (functional costs and direct and indirect costs) are used to record and measure costs, and to report profits. However, these classifications of cost do not provide an analysis of how total costs change as more items are produced and sold, or as activity levels increase or fall.

The most important classification of costs for the purpose of cost estimation is the division of costs into fixed costs or variable costs.

1.2 Variable costs

Variable costs are costs that increase, usually by the same amount, for each additional unit of product that is made or each additional unit of service that is provided.

The variable cost of a cost unit is also called the **marginal cost** of the unit.

The variable cost per unit is often the same amount for each additional unit of output or unit of activity. This means that total variable costs increase in direct proportion to the total volume of output or activity. Here are some examples of variable cost items.

- The cost of buying a raw material item might be $5 per litre purchased, regardless of purchase quantity. If so, the variable cost is $5 per litre: the total cost of buying 1,000 litres would be $5,000 and the cost of buying 2,000 litres would be $10,000.
- The rate of pay for hourly-paid workers might be $15 per hour. If so, 400 hours of labour would cost $6,000 and 500 hours would cost $7,500.
- The time needed to produce an item of product is 4 minutes and labour is paid $15 per hour. If so, direct labour is a variable cost and the direct labour cost per unit produced is $1 (= $15 × 4/60).
- The cost of telephone calls might be $0.10 per minute. If so, the cost of telephone calls lasting 6,000 minutes in total would be $600.

1.3 Fixed costs

Fixed costs are items of cost that remain the same in total during a time period, no matter how many units are produced, and regardless of the volume or scale of activity. Fixed costs are also called **period costs,** because they are fixed for a given period of time. Total fixed costs therefore increase with time.

Here are some examples of fixed cost items.

- The rental cost of a building, which is $40,000 per month. The rental cost is fixed for a given period: $40,000 per month, or $480,000 per year.
- The salary costs of a worker who is paid $11,000 per month. The fixed cost is $11,000 per month or $132,000 per year.

Cost behaviour graphs: fixed and variable costs

Cost behaviour for items of cost (or for costs in total) can be shown in a graph. Graphs can be drawn for the total cost of an item or for the cost per unit of the item.

Cost behaviour graphs for fixed costs and variable costs are shown in the following diagram.

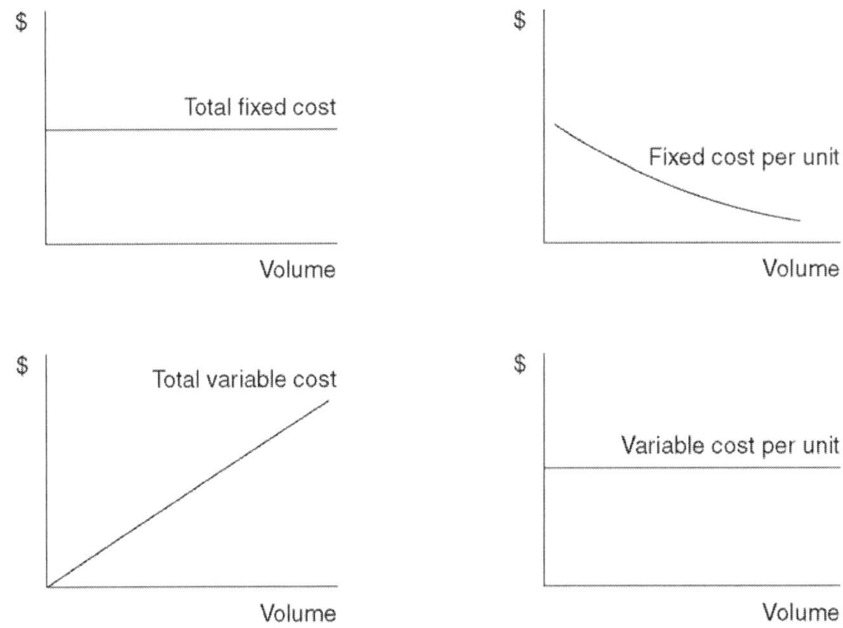

1.4 Mixed costs

A mixed cost, also called a semi-fixed cost or a semi-variable cost, is a cost that is partly fixed and partly variable. A cost behaviour graph showing the total costs for an item of mixed cost is shown below.

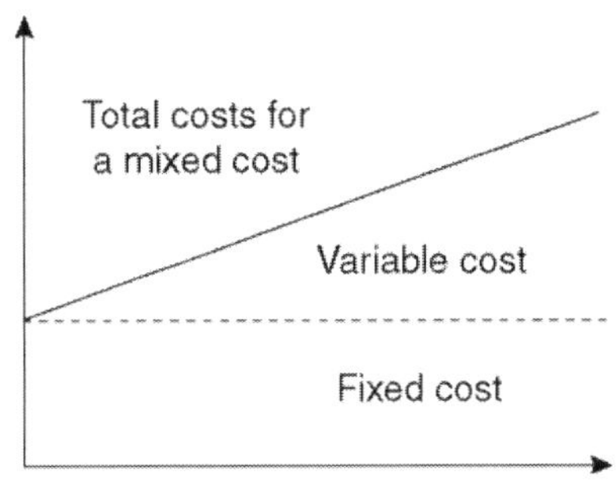

An item of cost that is a mixed cost is an item with a fixed minimum cost per period plus a variable cost for every unit of activity or output.

Example

A company uses a photocopier machine under a rental agreement. The photocopier rental cost is $400 per month plus $0.02 per copy produced.

For example, if the company makes 15,000 copies during a month, the total cost will be $400 fixed costs plus $300 variable costs (= 15,000 × $0.02), making a total cost of $700.

Mixed costs are important in cost and management accounting. It is often assumed that the total costs of an activity are mixed costs, consisting partly of fixed costs and partly of variable costs.

For example, it might be assumed that the total selling and distribution costs for a company each month are mixed costs. If this assumption is used, the total mixed costs can be divided into two separate parts, fixed costs and variable costs.

If costs can be analysed as a fixed amount of cost per period plus a variable cost per unit, estimating what future costs should be, or what actual costs should have been, becomes fairly simple.

Example

The management accountant of a manufacturing company has estimated that production costs in a factory that manufactures Product Y are fixed costs of $250,000 per month plus variable costs of $3 per unit of Product Y output.

The expected output next month is 120,000 units of Product Y. Expected total costs are therefore:

	$
Variable costs (120,000 × $3)	360,000
Fixed costs	250,000
Total costs	610,000

Other cost behaviour patterns

- Stepped fixed cost
- More unusual cost behaviour patterns

2 Other cost behaviour patterns

Some cost items are variable costs, fixed costs or mixed costs. Costs in total might have a cost behaviour pattern that is very close to being a mixed cost. However there are many cost items that have a more unusual cost behaviour pattern. Unusual cost behaviour patterns can be shown on a cost behaviour graph.

2.1 Stepped fixed cost

A **stepped fixed cost** is a cost which:

- has a fixed cost behaviour pattern within a limited range of activity, and
- goes up or down in steps when the volume of activity rises above or falls below certain levels.

On a cost behaviour graph, step fixed costs look like steps rising from left to right.

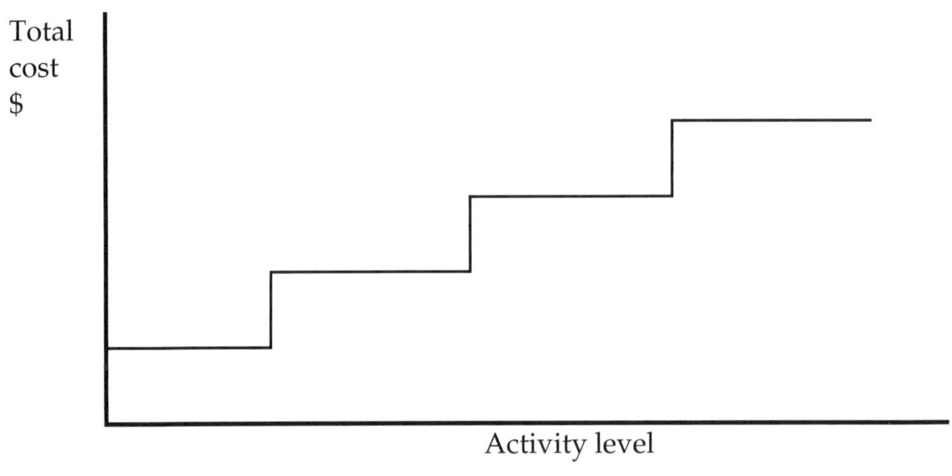

Example

A company might pay its supervisors a salary of $4,000 each month. When production is less than 3,500 hours each month, only one supervisor is needed: when production is between 3,501 and 7,000 hours each month, two supervisors are needed. When output is over 7,000 hours each month, three supervisors are needed.

These supervision costs are therefore fixed costs within a certain range of output, but go up or down in steps as the output level rises above or falls below certain levels.

A cost behaviour graph for the supervision costs can be drawn as follows.

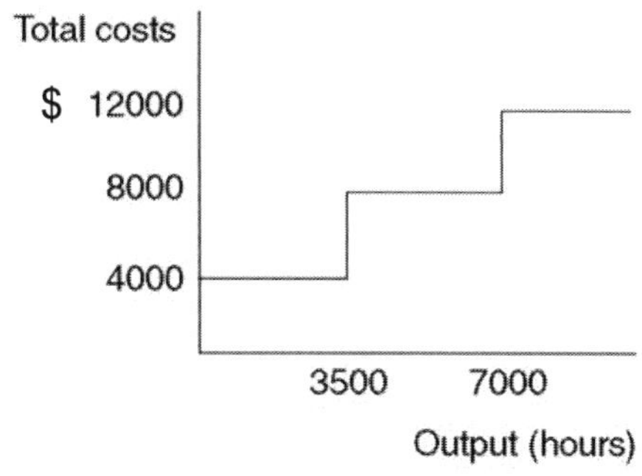

2.2 More unusual cost behaviour patterns

You may be examined on your understanding of more unusual cost behaviour patterns. Several are shown below.

Changes in total variable costs

(a)

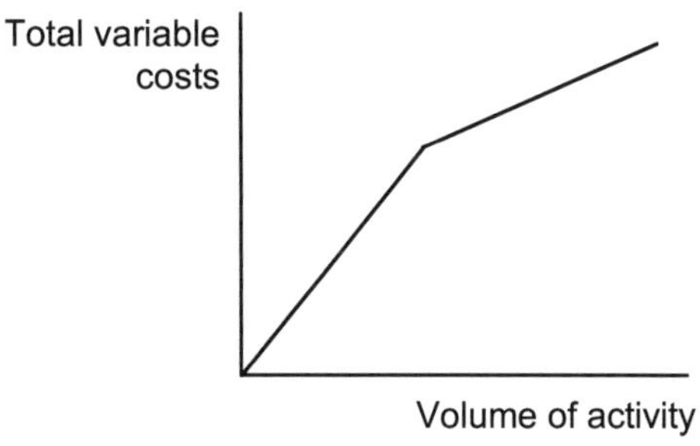

(b)

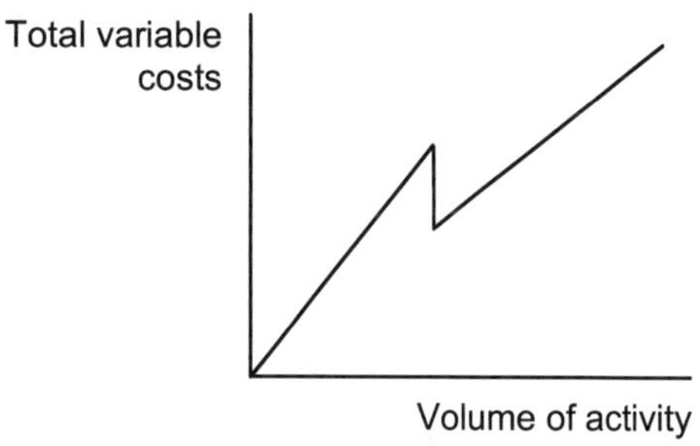

In (a), the variable cost per unit is a particular amount up to a certain level of activity or output, and is a lower amount for all units above that level of activity. For example, the cost might be $2 per unit up to 10,000 units and $1.50 per unit for each unit over 10,000 units.

In (b), the variable cost per unit is a particular amount up to a certain level of activity or output, and above that level of activity the variable cost per unit is a lower amount for all units (not just for the units above that level of activity). For example, a supplier might offer a price of $5 per unit for all units of a raw material, up to 10,000 units per order. If the size of an order is more than 10,000 units, the cost per unit will be $4.75.

Minimum and maximum charges

The cost behaviour pattern in the graph below illustrates a cost during a period when there is a charge per unit, subject to a minimum charge and a maximum charge per period.

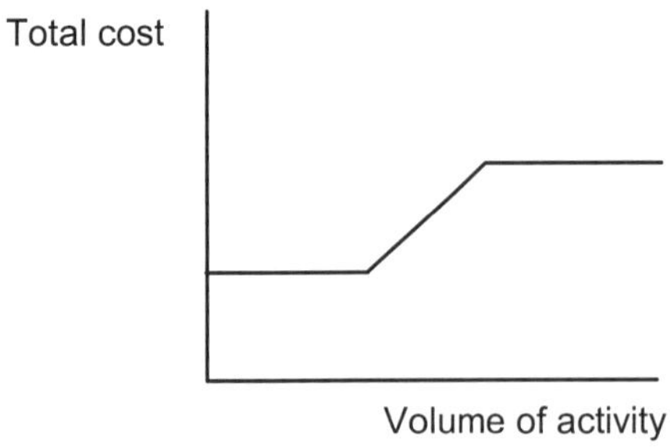

Other patterns

In your examination, you might be given another unusual cost behaviour pattern, and asked to identify the type of cost to which the cost behaviour pattern relates. You will need to study the pattern to identify its fixed and/or variable characteristics, and try to identify what type of cost fits the pattern shown. Here is just one example.

Example

Study the following cost behaviour graph and identify which of the following cost items is shown in the graph.

Total electricity charges for a factory, where the electricity supplier charges:

A a fixed annual charge plus a constant amount for each unit of electricity consumed, subject to a maximum annual charge

B a constant amount for each unit of electricity consumed up to a certain amount, and a lower charge per unit for consumption above that amount

C a constant amount for each unit of electricity consumed but if consumption exceeds a certain amount the charge is reduced to a lower amount for the total amount consumed

D a fixed charge for the year, then a constant amount for each unit of electricity consumed up to a certain amount, and a lower charge per unit for consumption above that amount

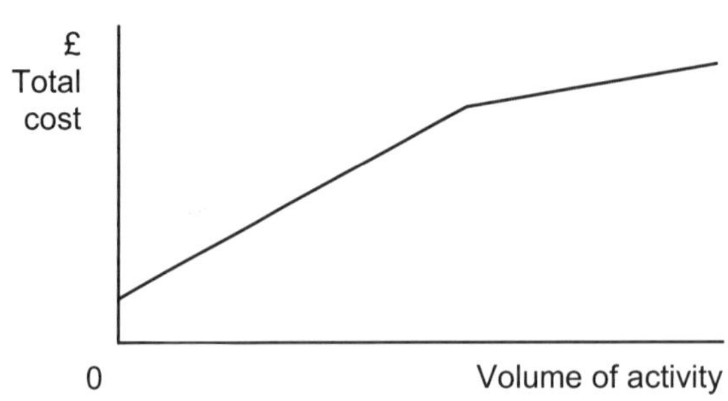

The cost behaviour graph shows that there is some charge even when consumption is zero. This means that there must be a fixed cost element in the annual charge. Total costs then rise in a straight-line fashion up to a certain level of consumption (so variable costs are a constant amount per unit) and above that level total costs continue to rise but the rate of increase is less steep (so variable costs are a new but lower constant amount per unit).

The cost item shown in the graph must therefore be D.

Cost estimation: high/low method

- Cost estimation
- A linear cost function for total costs
- High/low analysis
- High/low analysis when there is a step change in fixed costs
- High/low analysis when there is a change in the variable cost per unit

3 Cost estimation: high/low method

3.1 Cost estimation

For the purposes of planning and decision-making, it is often necessary to prepare an estimate of costs. For example, it is often necessary to estimate the total annual costs of an activity or a responsibility centre, or the total annual costs of production overheads or marketing overheads.

Unless there are reasons for a different approach, it is usual to make a cost estimate on the assumption that total costs (for a large number of different cost items together) are a mixture of fixed costs and variable costs. In order to estimate costs, it is therefore necessary to make an estimate of:

- fixed costs for the period, and
- the variable cost per unit of output or sales, or the variable cost per unit of activity (for example, the variable cost per hour worked).

In the same way, individual items of mixed cost can be divided into fixed and variable cost elements. Two cost estimation techniques are:

- high/low analysis
- linear regression analysis.

This chapter explains the high/low method. The linear regression method will be explained in a later chapter.

3.2 A linear function for total costs

If total costs can be divided into fixed costs or variable costs per unit of output or unit of activity, a formula for total costs is:

$y = a + bx$

where
y = total costs in a period
x the number of units of output or the volume of activity in the period
a = the fixed costs in the period

b = the variable cost per unit of output or unit of activity.

Graph of linear cost function

On a cost behaviour graph, total costs would be shown as a straight line, rising with the total volume of activity. (It is a cost behaviour graph for a mixed cost.) This rather simple formula is therefore a 'linear function' for total costs.

The linear cost function equation y = a + bx can be drawn as follows.

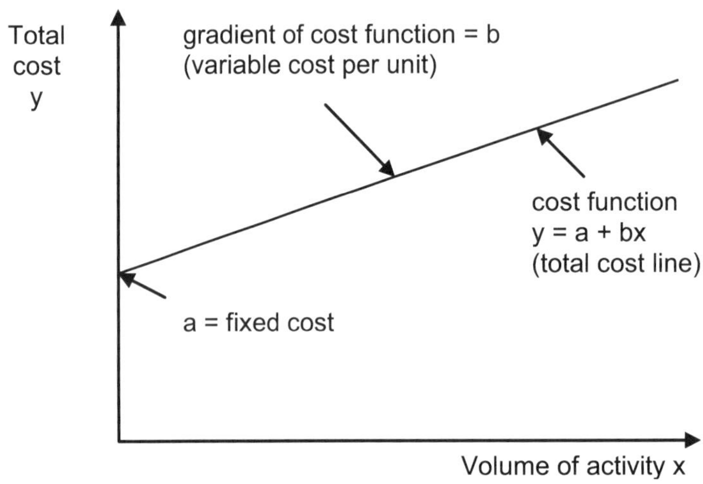

3.3 High/low analysis

High/low analysis can be used to estimate fixed costs and variable costs per unit whenever:

- there are figures available for total costs at two different levels of output or activity
- it can be assumed that fixed costs are the same in total at each level of activity, and
- the variable cost per unit is constant at both levels of activity.

High/low analysis therefore uses two historical figures for cost:

- the highest recorded output level, and its associated total cost
- the lowest recorded output level, and its associated total cost.

It is assumed that these 'high' and 'low' records of output and historical cost are representative of costs at all levels of output or activity.

The **difference** between the total cost at the high level of output and the total cost at the low level of output is **entirely variable cost**. This is because fixed costs are the same in total at both levels of output.

The method

There are just a few simple steps involved in high/low analysis.

Step 1

Take the activity level and cost for:

- the highest activity level
- the lowest activity level.

Step 2

The difference between the total cost of the highest activity level and the total cost of the lowest activity level consists entirely of variable costs. This is because the fixed costs are the same at all levels of activity.

	Activity level		$
High: Total cost of	A	=	TCa
Low: Total cost of	B	=	TCb
Difference: Variable cost of (A – B) units	(A – B)	=	TCa - TCb

From this difference, we can therefore calculate the variable cost per unit of activity.

Variable cost per unit = $(TCa – TCb)/ (A – B) units

Having calculated a variable cost per unit of activity, we can now calculate fixed costs.

Step 3

Having calculated the variable cost per unit, apply this value to the cost of either the highest or the lowest activity level. (It does not matter whether you use the high level or the low level of activity. Your calculation of fixed costs will be the same.)

Calculate the total variable costs at this activity level.

Step 4

The difference between the total cost at this activity level and the total variable cost at this activity level is the fixed cost.

Substitute in the 'low' equation	Cost
	$
Total cost of (low volume of activity)	TCb
Variable cost of (low volume of activity)	V
Therefore fixed costs per period of time	TCb - V

You now have an estimate of the variable cost per unit and the total fixed costs.

The high/low method is a simple but important technique that you need to understand. Study the following example carefully.

Example

A company has recorded the following costs in the past four months:

Month	Activity	Total cost
	Direct labour hours	$
January	5,800	40,300
February	7,700	47,100
March	8,200	48,700
April	6,100	40,650

Required

Using high/low analysis, prepare an estimate of total costs in May if output is expected to be 7,000 direct labour hours.

Answer

(1) Steps 1 and 2: Calculate the variable cost per hour

Take the highest level of activity and the lowest level of activity, and the total costs of each. Ignore the other data for levels of activity in between the highest and the lowest.

	Hours		$
High: Total cost of	8,200 hours	=	48,700
Low: Total cost of	5,800 hours	=	40,300
Difference: Variable cost of	2,400 hours	=	8,400

Therefore variable cost per direct labour hour = $8,400/2,400 hours = $3.50.

(2) Steps 3 and 4: Calculate fixed costs

Substitute in the 'high' equation	Cost
	$
Total cost of 8,200 hours	48,700
Variable cost of 8,200 hours (× $3.50 per hour)	28,700
Therefore fixed costs per month	20,000

(3) Using the cost analysis: Prepare a cost estimate

Cost estimate for May	Cost
	$
Fixed costs	20,000
Variable cost (7,000 hours × $3.50 per hour)	24,500
Estimated total costs	44,500

The technique can be used any time that you are given two figures for total costs, at different levels of activity or volumes of output, and you need to estimate fixed costs and a variable cost per unit.

3.4 High/low analysis when there is a step change in fixed costs

High/low analysis can be used even when there is a step increase in fixed costs between the 'low' and the 'high' activity levels, provided that the amount of the step increase in fixed costs is known.

The method of analysis to use depends on whether the step increase in the fixed cost is stated as a money amount of cost, or whether it is stated as a percentage increase.

The step increase in fixed costs is given as a money amount

If the step increase in fixed costs is given as a money amount, the total cost of the 'high' or the 'low' activity level should be adjusted by the amount of the increase, so that total costs for the 'high' and 'low' amounts are the same.

The high/low method can then be used in the normal way to obtain a fixed cost and a variable cost per unit. The fixed cost will be either the fixed cost at the 'high' level or at the 'low' level, depending on how you made the adjustment to fixed costs before making the high/low analysis. You can then calculate the fixed costs at the other level of activity by adding or subtracting the step change in fixed costs, as appropriate.

Example

A company has the following costs at two activity levels.

Activity	Total cost
units	$
17,000	165,000
22,000	195,000

The variable cost per unit is constant over this range of activity, but there is a step fixed cost and total fixed costs increase by $15,000 when activity level equals or exceeds 19,000 units.

Required

Using high/low analysis, calculate the total cost of 20,000 units.

Answer

There is an increase in fixed costs above 19,000 units of activity, and to use the high/low method, we need to make an adjustment for the step fixed costs. Since we are required to calculate the total cost for a volume of activity above 19,000 units, the simplest approach is to add $15,000 to the total cost of 17,000 units, so that the fixed costs of 17,000 units and 22,000 units are the same and are also the amount of fixed costs for 20,000 units.

(1) Steps 1 and 2: Calculate the variable cost per unit

	Units		$
High: Total cost	22,000 units	=	195,000
Low: Adjusted total cost: $(165,000 + 15,000)	17,000 units	=	180,000
Difference: Variable cost of	5,000 units	=	15,000

Therefore variable cost per unit = $15,000/5,000 units = $3 per unit.

(2) Steps 3 and 4: Calculate fixed costs (above 19,000 units)

Substitute in the 'high' equation	Cost
	$
Total cost of 22,000 units	195,000
Variable cost of 22,000 units (× $3 per unit)	66,000
Therefore fixed costs (above 19,000 units)	129,000

(3) Using the cost analysis: Prepare a cost estimate

Cost estimate	Cost
	$
Fixed costs (above 19,000 units)	129,000
Variable cost (20,000 units × $3)	60,000
Estimated total costs	189,000

The step increase in fixed costs is given as a percentage amount

When the step change in fixed costs between two activity levels is given as a percentage amount, the problem is a bit more complex, and to use high/low analysis we need a third figure for total cost, at another level of activity somewhere in between the 'high' and the 'low' amounts.

Total fixed costs will be the same for:

- the 'in between' activity level and
- either the 'high' or the 'low' activity level.

High/low analysis should be applied to the two costs and activity levels for which total fixed costs are the same, to obtain an estimate for the variable cost per unit and the total fixed costs at these activity levels. Total fixed costs at the third activity level (above or below the step change in fixed costs) can then be calculated making a suitable adjustment for the percentage change.

Example

A company has the following costs at three activity levels.

Activity	Total cost
units	$
5,000	180,000
8,000	240,000
11,000	276,000

The variable cost per unit is constant over this range of activity, but there is a step fixed cost and total fixed costs increase by 20% when the activity level exceeds 7,500 units.

Required
Estimate the expected total cost when the activity level is 7,000 units.

Answer

There is an increase in fixed costs above 7,500 units of activity, which means that total fixed costs and the variable cost per unit are the same for 8,000 units and 11,000 units of activity. These activity levels should be used to estimate the variable cost per unit and total fixed costs.

(1) Steps 1 and 2: Calculate the variable cost per unit

	Units		$
High: Total cost	11,000 units	=	276,000
'In-between'	8,000 units	=	240,000
Difference: Variable cost of	3,000 units	=	36,000

Therefore variable cost per unit = $36,000/3,000 units = $12 per unit.

(2) Steps 3 and 4: Calculate fixed costs (above 7,500 units)

Substitute in the 'high' equation	Cost
	$
Total cost of 11,000 units	276,000
Variable cost of 11,000 units (× $12 per unit)	132,000
Therefore fixed costs (above 7,500 units)	144,000

(3) Calculate fixed costs at activity levels below 7,500 units

Fixed costs increase by 20% above 7,500 units.
Fixed costs above 7,500 units are therefore 120% of fixed costs below 7,500 units.
Fixed costs below 7,500 units are therefore: $144,000 × (11/120) = $120,000.

(Note: Make sure that you understand the adjustment here. We do not subtract 20% from fixed costs above 7,500 units!)

(4) Using the cost analysis: Prepare a cost estimate

Cost estimate	Cost
	$
Fixed costs (below 7,500 units)	120,000
Variable cost (7,000 units × $12)	84,000
Estimated total costs	204,000

3.5 High/low analysis when there is a change in the variable cost per unit

High/low analysis can also be used when there is a change in the variable cost per unit between the 'high' and the 'low' levels of activity. The same approach is needed as for a step change in fixed costs, as described above.

The method of analysis to use depends on whether the step increase in the fixed cost is stated as a money amount of cost, or whether it is stated as a percentage increase.

The change in unit variable cost is given as a money amount

If the increase or reduction in variable cost per unit is given as a money amount, the total cost of the 'high' activity level should be adjusted by the amount of the increase or reduction, so that total costs for the 'high' and 'low' amounts have the same basis for total variable costs.

The high/low method can then be used in the normal way to obtain a variable cost per unit and a fixed cost at the 'low' activity level.

Example

A company has the following costs at three activity levels.

Activity	Total cost
units	$
21,000	276,000
30,000	327,000

The fixed costs are constant over this range of activity, but variable costs per unit fall by $0.50 above 24,000 units, but only for units above that level (i.e. not for all units).

Required

Using high/low analysis, calculate the total cost of 28,000 units.

a

Answer

The variable cost per unit falls by $0.50 per unit, but only for units above 24,000. This means that at the 30,000 level of activity, there are 6,000 units costing $0.50 less, which is $3,000 in total.

To carry out high/low analysis, we therefore need to add $3,000 to total costs for the high level of output. The variable cost per unit we calculate will be the variable cost before the $0.50 reduction.

(1) Steps 1 and 2: Calculate the variable cost per unit

	Units		$
High: Adjusted total cost $(327,000 + 3,000)	30,000 units	=	330,000
Low: Total cost	21,000 units	=	276,000
Difference: Variable cost of	9,000 units	=	54,000

Therefore variable cost per unit (up to 24,000 units) = $54,000/9,000 units = $6 per unit.
The variable cost per unit above 24,000 units is $6 - $0.50 = $5.50.

(2) Steps 3 and 4: Calculate fixed costs

Substitute in the 'low' equation	**Cost**
	$
Total cost of 21,000 units	276,000
Variable cost of 21,000 units (× $6 per unit)	126,000
Therefore fixed costs	150,000

(3) Using the cost analysis: Prepare a cost estimate

Cost estimate for 28,000 units	**Cost**
	$
Fixed costs	150,000
Variable cost	
First 24,000 units (× $6)	144,000
Next 4,000 units (× $5.50)	22,000
Estimated total costs	316,000

The change in unit variable cost is given as a percentage amount

When the change in the variable cost per unit is given as a percentage amount, a similar method is needed as for fixed costs. A third 'in between' estimate of costs should be used, and the variable cost per unit will be the same for:

- the 'in between' activity level and
- either the 'high' or the 'low' activity level.

High/low analysis should be applied to the two costs and activity levels for which unit variable costs are the same, to obtain an estimate for the variable cost per unit and the total fixed costs at these activity levels. The variable cost per unit at the third activity level can then be calculated making a suitable adjustment for the percentage change.

Example

A company has the following costs at three activity levels.

Activity	Total cost
units	$
20,000	300,000
25,000	320,000
30,000	356,000

The fixed costs are constant over this range of activity, but there is a 10% reduction in the variable cost per unit above 24,000 units of activity. This reduction applies to all units of activity, not just the additional units above 24,000.

Required
Estimate the expected total cost when the activity level is 22,000 units.

Answer

The variable cost per unit is the same for both 25,000 units and 30,000 units. High/low analysis should therefore be applied to these activity levels.

(1) Calculate the variable cost per unit above 24,000 units

	Units		$
High: Total cost	30,000 units	=	356,000
'In-between'	25,000 units	=	320,000
Difference: Variable cost of	5,000 units	=	36,000

Therefore variable cost per unit = $36,000/5,000 units = $7.20 per unit.

(2) Calculate the variable cost per unit below 24,000 units

The variable cost per unit above 24,000 units is 90% of the cost below 24,000 units. The variable cost per unit below 24,000 units is therefore (× 100/90) of the cost above 24,000 units.
Variable cost per unit below 24,000 units = $7.20 × 100/90 = $8

(3) Calculate fixed costs

Substitute in the 'low' equation	Cost
	$
Total cost of 20,000 units	300,000
Variable cost of 20,000 units (× $8 per unit)	160,000
Therefore fixed costs (above 7,500 units)	140,000

(4) Using the cost analysis: Prepare a cost estimate

Cost estimate for 22,000 units	Cost
	$
Fixed costs	140,000
Variable cost (22,000 units × $8)	176,000
Estimated total costs	316,000

Exercise and practice multiple choice questions

Exercise

A company has recorded the following costs in the past six months:

Month	Activity	Total cost
	Units of output	$
January	14,000	98,700
February	12,600	91,700
March	15,300	103,350
April	14,900	101,000
May	16,100	107,450
June	16,000	107,080

Required

Using high/low analysis, prepare an estimate of total costs in August if output is expected to be 15,000 units.

1 A company has the following costs at two activity levels.

Activity	Total cost
units	$
60,000	960,000
72,000	1,104,000

The variable cost per unit is constant over this range of activity, but there is a step fixed cost and total fixed costs increase by $36,000 when the activity level exceeds 64,000 units.

What is the expected total cost when the activity level is 70,000 units?

A $1,050,000
B $1,080,000
C $1,086,000
D $1,116,000

(2 marks)

2 A company has the following costs at three activity levels.

Activity	Total cost
units	$
60,000	960,000
72,000	1,104,000

The fixed cost is constant over this range of activity, but there is a reduction in the variable cost per unit by 10% when the activity level exceeds 15,000 units. This reduction applies to all units.

What is the expected total cost when the activity level is 14,000 units?

A $131,800
B $132,400
C $136,000
D $138,000

(2 marks)

CHAPTER 4

Business mathematics and computer spreadsheets

Contents

Dealing with uncertainty: expected values

- Decision-making and risk or uncertainty
- Probabilities and expected values
- How are expected values used?
- Limitations of the expected value technique

1 Expected values and decision-making

This chapter explains some of the mathematical techniques and computer models that might be used to provide cost and management accounting information. Mathematical techniques might be helpful with providing more reliable management information. Computer modelling with spreadsheets make it possible to use some mathematical models that might otherwise be impracticable (because of their complexity).

1.1 Decision-making and risk or uncertainty

Estimates of costs or profit are often needed by management to make a decision. Unfortunately, it is often impossible to predict with reasonable certainty what costs, revenues or profits will be. This is because there is considerable uncertainty about what might happen in the future.

- Sometimes, the uncertainty arises because the information needed to make an accurate forecast of costs or revenues is not sufficiently reliable. There isn't enough information to make an accurate prediction.
- There is also risk in most business decisions. The outcome of a decision might be favourable or unfavourable, depending on events and circumstances in the future. Several different possible outcomes might result from the decision, and managers take a risk hoping that the outcome will be favourable.

Decisions are therefore often made under conditions of uncertainty or risk. There are some mathematical techniques that can be used to analyse risk or uncertainty in business decisions. At this stage of your studies, you do not need to know all of them and you do not need to know any technique in great detail.

The main technique you need to understand is the use of expected values.

One way of analysing costs and revenues when there is risk or uncertainty is to:

- estimate the probability of different possible results or outcomes, and
- use these estimates to calculate an expected value, and
- base any decision on the expected value, or prepare a plan or budget on the basis of the expected value.

1.2 Probabilities and expected values

Probabilities

When there is risk or uncertainty about what will happen, it might be possible to estimate probabilities of the different possible outcomes. The total of the probabilities of different possible outcomes is always 100% or 1.0. For example:

- If it is estimated that there is an equal probability that the cost per unit of a product will be $5 and $6, there is a 0.50 probability of $5 and a 0.50 probability of $6.
- If a company thinks it might make either a profit of $20,000 from a venture or a loss of $15,000, and it is three times more likely that there will be a profit rather than a loss, there is a 0.75 probability of a profit and a 0.25 probability of a loss.

Estimates of the probabilities of different outcomes might be an 'educated guess' based on experience and judgement. Sometimes, probabilities can be estimated more reliably, using past experience as a guide to what is likely to happen in the future. For instance, probabilities for different possible outcomes in the future might be based on an analysis of historical records. An example might be an estimate of the rate of defective output from a manufacturing process: historical records might show that 0.5% of items produced in a manufacturing process are rejected as defective items. This historical record might be used to asses the probability that output will be defective in the future is 0.005 (= 0.5%) and the probability that units of output will be free from defects is 0.995.

Expected value (EV)

An expected value (EV) is a weighted average value of different possible outcomes, where the **probability** of each different possible outcome can be estimated. An expected value can also be described as the 'weighted average of a probability distribution'.

An EV can be calculated using the following formula.

Expected value (EV) = $\sum px$

where:

$\sum$ means 'the sum of'

p = the probability of the outcome occurring. When there is a 50% probability of an outcome, p = 0.50 and when the probability is 7%, p = 0.07, etc. The total of the probabilities of all possible outcomes is 1.0 or 100%.

x = the outcome for which the probability has been estimated

When there is risk or uncertainty, and there different possible outcomes, each possible outcome (x) has an associated probability (p). For each outcome and its associated probability, multiply x by p. Then add up the total these values for 'px' that you have calculated. This gives you the expected value of the future outcome – i.e. the weighted average expected outcome.

Example

A cost accountant, working for a firm of builders, has been asked to estimate the cost of building a new house, for which a customer has agreed a fixed price of $500,000. There is some uncertainty about the costs of the labour for the job. These will not be confirmed until after the building work begins. The cost accountant has estimated that there is a 50% chance that the cost will be $360,000 and a 50% chance that it will be $480,000.

One way of estimating the expected cost of building the house is to calculate the expected value of cost.

Cost (= outcome)	Probability	
x	p	px
$		$
360,000	0.50	180,000
480,000	0.50	240,000
	Expected value	420,000

Since the income from building the house will be $500,000, the expected value of profit from the job is $500,000 – $420,000 = $80,000.

This EV is a weighted average probability of the profit. The actual outcome might be $360,000 (in which case profit will be $140,000) or $480,000 (in which case profit will be $20,000). The weighted average of possible outcomes is $80,000.

Example

The chief accountant in a company is concerned about the very high level of input errors that the cost accountants are making when they enter transaction data into the cost accounting system.

An investigation into a sample of transactions entered into the system during the past two months has shown that 70% of entries were error-free, 20% had 1 error and 10% contained 2 errors. During a normal month, there are 10,000 entries into the system.

What would be the estimate of the total number of errors in transaction entries each month?

Answer

The estimate can be made by calculating an expected number of errors per transaction entry. This is simply a weighted average of the number of errors per entry. This is an expected value.

Errors (= outcome)	Probability	
x	p	px
0	0.7	0.0
1	0.2	0.2
2	0.1	0.2
	Expected value	0.4

The expected value is 0.4 errors per entry, so if there are 10,000 entries, the expected total number of errors per month is 10,000 × 0.4 = 400 errors.

1.3 How are expected values used?

Expected values are used to make forecasts or estimates, and to help management with decision-making.

Expected values and decision-making

A decision is choice between two or more alternatives. Companies are often faced with making decisions when the outcome is uncertain. There are two types of decision where EVs might be used.

- Making a choice between doing something and not doing it. For example, should we invest in this new equipment? The choice is between investing and not investing.
- Making a choice between two or more different possible options. For example, when a company has decided that it needs to replace an item of equipment, there might be a choice between buying a smaller model or a larger model.

The following rules apply to the use of expected values for decision-making, when there is risk or uncertainty and probabilities of different possible outcomes are estimated.

1 When the choice is between doing something and not doing it.

- If the expected value of profit is negative, the decision should be NO (do not do it).
- If the expected value of profit is positive, the decision should be YES (do it).

2 If there are two or more options and each has a positive expected value of profit, the option with the highest expected value of profit should be chosen in preference to the others.

Example

The management accountant of a company has estimated that if the company tries to sell a new product, Product X, there is a 60% probability that the product will make an annual profit of $25,000 and a 40% probability that it will make a loss of $15,000.

The EV of annual profit from the product is:

Profit ($)	Probability	
x	p	px
$		$
25,000	0.60	15,000
(15,000)	0.40	(6,000)
Expected value of annual profit		9,000

The expected value of profit is $9,000 per year. If the company makes its decisions on the basis of expected value, it will go ahead and try to sell the new product.

Example

A company is considering investing in one of two projects, A and B. It cannot invest in both of them. The profits and associated probabilities of each project are as follows.

Project A		Project B	
Monthly profit	Probability	Monthly profit	Probability
$		$	
15,000	0.1	(18,000)	0.05
25,000	0.2	16,000	0.30
65,000	0.4	80,000	0.35
75,000	0.3	95,000	0.30

Required

Using the expected value technique, decide which project should be undertaken and explain why.

Answer

The choice is between Option A and Option B. Using expected values, the option with the higher expected value of profit should be chosen. If the expected value for both options shows a loss, neither project should be undertaken.

	Option A			Option B	
Profit per month	Probability		Profit per month	Probability	
x	p	px	x	p	px
$		$	$		$
15,000	0.1	1,500	(18,000)	0.05	(900)
25,000	0.2	5,000	16,000	0.30	4,800
65,000	0.4	26,000	80,000	0.35	28,000
75,000	0.3	22,500	95,000	0.30	28,500
Expected value of profit		55,000		EV of unit cost	60,400

If EV is used to make the decision, Project B should be undertaken because it has a higher EV of profit.

However, Option B is more risky, because there is some chance (a 5% chance) of making a loss.

Note that the expected value is not equal to any of the possible monthly profit figures. The EV is a weighted average value, not a value that is actually expected to occur.

Exercise 1

There is a 70% chance that a company will make a profit of $800,000 next year and a 30% chance that it will make a loss of $150,000.

Required

Calculate the expected profit or loss for next year.

Exercise 2

A company that makes glassware products is considering a proposal to make and sell a batch of 10,000 special drinking glasses, to commemorate the 100th anniversary of the country's independence.

The sales director has estimated that there is a 60% probability that the glasses will sell for $5 each, and a 10% probability that a sales price of $6 can be achieved. However, there is a 30% probability that the selling price will be just $4.

The management accountant has estimated that for a batch of 10,000 units, there is a 75% probability that the unit cost will be $3.60 and a 35% probability that it will be $4.20.

Required

(a) Calculate the expected value of he sales price.

(b) Calculate the expected value of the unit cost.

(c) Calculate the expected value of the profit or loss on the 10,000 glasses, and recommend whether the company should make and sell the batch of glasses.

1.4 Limitations of the expected value method for decision-making

There are a number of limitations associated with using the expected value technique in decision-making situations.

- The probabilities used in calculating expected values are estimates. If these estimated probabilities are not reliable, then the expected values calculated from the probabilities will also be unreliable.

- An expected value might not be an 'actual value' of a possible outcome. For example if there is a 0.50 probability that the cost will be $2,000 and a 0.50 probability that the cost will be $5,000, the EV of cost is $3,500. However a cost of $3,500 will not happen: the cost will be either $2,000 or $5,000.
- Expected values don't normally take into account the attitude to risk of the person taking the decision. This will obviously vary from person to person. For example, a project might have an EV of profit of $50,000, but there might be a 20% probability of making a loss of $20,000. The company might be unwilling to take the risk of a $20,000 loss, even though the EV shows a profit.

Example

A company is considering investing in one of two projects, X and Y. It cannot invest in both of them. The profits and associated probabilities of each project are as follows.

Probability	Project X profit/(loss)	Project Y profit/(loss)
	$	$
0.6	15,000	40,000
0.4	(10,000)	(20,000)

Project X has an EV of profit of $5,000 and Project Y has an EV of profit of $16,000. (Workings are not shown but you should be able to calculate these expected values yourself.) Applying the normal rule, both projects would be worth undertaking. However, since only one project can be selected, Project Y should be preferred because it has a higher EV of profit.

The limitations of expected values should be apparent.

- Although both projects have an EV of profit, they each have a 40% probability of making a loss.
- Although Project Y has a higher EV of profit, the risk is greater, because the loss might be as high a $20,000, whereas with Project X it will not exceed $10,000.

It is important to remember that an expected value is a weighted average of the different expected results. Like all averages it is only 'accurate' when it is used for a large number of repetitive events or outcomes, where the actual results are likely to be close to the weighted average. For 'one off' events, expected values should not be used without giving careful consideration to the possible variations in the results that might occur, and the risk involved.

Regression analysis

- The purpose of linear regression analysis
- The linear regression formulae
- Applying the linear regression formulae

2 Regression analysis

2.1 The purpose of linear regression analysis

Linear regression analysis is a statistical technique for calculating a line of best fit from a set of data:

$y = a + bx$

The data is in 'pairs', which means that there are a number of different values for x, and for each value of x there is an associated value of y in the data.

Linear regression analysis can be used to estimate fixed costs and the variable cost per unit from historical data for mixed costs. For example, there might be historical data for the total monthly costs of operating a workshop. It might be assumed that total costs each month vary with the number of direct labour hours worked. Historical data can be collected about total monthly costs in the past (cost in each month = y) and the associated number of direct labour hours worked in that month (hours in each month = x). This data can then be used to estimate fixed costs per month and variable costs per direct labour hour, which can be expressed in a formula $y = a + bx$.

Linear regression analysis can also be used to predict future sales by projecting the historical sales trend into the future (on the assumption that sales growth is rising at a constant rate, in a 'straight line').

Regression analysis is an alternative technique to high-low analysis, which was described in the previous chapter. It can be used for all the same purposes in cost and management accounting that high-low analysis is used for.

Regression analysis and high-low analysis compared

Regression analysis and the high-low analysis are used for the same purposes. Regression analysis is therefore an alternative technique to high-low analysis, which was described in the previous chapter, but there are important differences between them.

- High-low analysis uses just two sets of data for x and y, the highest value for x and the lowest value for x. Regression analysis uses as many sets of data for x and y as are available.

- Because regression analysis calculates a line of best fit for all the available data, it is likely to provide a more reliable estimate than high-low analysis for the values of a and b.
- In addition, regression analysis can be used to assess the extent to which values of y depend on values of x. For example, if a line of best fit is calculated that estimates total costs for any volume of production, we can also calculate the extent to which total costs do seem to be linked (or 'correlated') to the volume of production. This is done by calculating a **correlation co-efficient**, which is explained later.
- Regression analysis uses more complex arithmetic than high-low analysis, and a calculator or small spreadsheet model is normally needed

In summary, linear regression analysis is a better technique than high-low analysis because:

- it is more reliable and
- its reliability can be measured.

High-low analysis has the benefit of simplicity and speed/ease of calculation.

2.2 The regression analysis formulae

The formulae for estimating costs using regression analysis are provided in a formulae sheet in your examination. You might be required to apply the formulae to data provided in an examination question.

Linear regression analysis is used to calculate values for a and b in the linear cost equation: y = a + bx.

The linear regression formulae for calculating a and b are shown below. The number of pairs of data that are used in the calculation is n.

The regression analysis formulae are as follows. They will be given to you in your examination:

$$a = \frac{\sum y}{n} - \frac{b\sum x}{n}$$

$$b = \frac{n\sum xy - \sum x\sum y}{n\sum x^2 - (\sum x)^2}$$

where:
n = the number of pairs of data used for x and y
x, y represent the values of x (volume of activity or output) and y (total cost)

The value of 'b' is an item in the formula for calculating 'a'. It is therefore necessary to calculate 'b' first before calculating 'a'.

Understanding the formulae

These formulae might seem very complicated, and in your examination you might be given a question that requires you to show your understanding of what the different items in the formulae mean.

- You should think of the pairs of data as a list of values set out in two columns, with one column for the values of x and the second column for the associated values of y.
- You should then prepare two more columns.
- There should be an additional column for x^2. Calculate the square of each value of x in the x column and write the answer in the x^2 column.
- The fourth column is for xy. For each pair of data for x and y, multiply the value of x by the value of y, and enter the answer in the xy column.
- You must then add up the totals for each of the four columns. $\sum x$ is the total of all the values in the x column. $\sum y$ is the total of all the values in the y column. $\sum x^2$ is the total of all the values in the x^2 column and $\sum xy$ is the total of all the values in the xy column.
- You now have all the values you need to calculate a value for b in the formula $y = a + bx$.
- The only other item you might not be sure about is $(\sum x)^2$. This is not the same as $\sum x^2$. It is the square of the value for $\sum x$.
- Having calculated a value for b, you can then use the formula for calculating the value of a: this includes the value for b, which is why you need to calculate b first.

2.3 Applying the regression analysis formulae

The formulae might seem complicated, but they are actually fairly straightforward provided that you understand the meaning of the $\sum$ items in the formulae, and remember that n is the number of pairs of data used to make the estimate. Study the following example carefully.

Example

The total costs and output volumes of a manufacturing company in the first six months of the year have been as follows.

Month	Output	Total cost
	000 units	$000
January	5	146
February	7	152
March	6	148
April	5	142
May	8	164
June	6	151

Required

Using regression analysis:

- estimate a value for fixed costs each month and a variable cost per unit
- estimate the expected costs in September if output volume is expected to be 8,000 units.

a

Answer

The starting point is to draw a table showing the values of x (output) and y (total cost). For each value of x and y, you should calculate the value of:

- x^2 and
- xy.

For reasons to be explained later, the value of y^2 will also be calculated here.

There are six pairs of data, so there should be six different values for x, y, x^2, xy and y^2.

Add the figures in each column to obtain totals for:

- Σx (= the sum of the values of x)
- Σy (= the sum of the values of y)
- Σx^2
- Σxy
- Σy^2. (The reason for calculating Σy^2 will be explained later.)

Month	Output	Total cost			
	000 units	$000			
	x	y	x^2	xy	y^2
January	5	146	25	730	21,316
February	7	152	49	1,064	23,104
March	6	148	36	888	21,904
April	5	142	25	710	20,164
May	8	164	64	1,312	26,896
June	6	151	36	906	22,801
	37	903	235	5,610	136,185
	$= \Sigma x$	$= \Sigma y$	$= \Sigma x^2$	$= \Sigma xy$	$= \Sigma y^2$

There are six pairs of data, so n = 6.

We now have all the figures we need to calculate values for 'a' and 'b, starting with 'b'.

$$b = \frac{n\Sigma xy - \Sigma x \Sigma y}{n\Sigma x^2 - (\Sigma x)^2}$$

$$b = \frac{6\,(5{,}610) - (37)(903)}{6\,(235) - (37)^2} = \frac{33{,}660 - 33{,}411}{1{,}410 - 1{,}369} = \frac{249}{41}$$

$$b = 6.07$$

This is the estimate of the variable cost per unit. The value of 'b' is used to calculate a value for 'a', as follows.

$$a = \frac{\sum y}{n} - \frac{b\sum x}{n}$$

$$a = \frac{903}{6} - \frac{6.07(37)}{6} = 150.5 - 37.4$$

a (in $000) = 113.1

Answer (a)

Estimated fixed costs each month = a = $113,100

Estimated variable cost per unit = b = $6.07

Therefore, linear cost function, y, is estimated to be:

y = 113,100 + 6.07x

For simplicity, this could be rounded to:

y = 113,000 + 6x.

Answer (b)

Using y = 113,100 + 6.07x, when monthly output is expected to be 8,000 units, the expected total costs will be:

	$
Fixed	113,100
Variable (8,000 × $6.07)	48,560
	161,660

Linear regression analysis and your examination

As you might appreciate, calculating a linear equation using linear regression analysis is a time-consuming process, unless you have a programmed calculator or spreadsheet. You will therefore not be required to use the full technique in your examination. However, you might be required to:

- comment on the meaning of items in the formulae, such as $\sum x^2$, $\sum xy$ and $(\sum x)^2$, or
- calculate a value for a or b, given values in the question for $\sum x$, $\sum y$, $\sum x^2$ and $\sum xy$.

Correlation and the correlation coefficient

- Correlation
- Degrees of correlation
- Correlation coefficient, r
- Coefficient of determination, r^2

3 Correlation and the correlation coefficient

3.1 Correlation

Linear regression analysis can be applied to any sets of data where the data is in pairs (x and y). It could be used, for example, to calculate a line of best fit for total weekly costs of an activity by taking pairs of data for total weekly costs (= y) and the associated values for the activity. However, the activity level might be any of the following:

- units of output each week, if it is assumed that weekly costs vary with the volume of output produced
- direct labour hours each week, if it is assumed that weekly costs vary with the number of direct labour hours worked
- machine hours operated each week, if it is assumed that weekly costs vary with the number of machine hours.

Which activity is the best one to choose as 'x'?

You could even use linear regression analysis to calculate a line of best fit between total weekly costs and the air temperature on the factory floor at midday, if you decided that total costs vary with the air temperature. (This might seem a ridiculous idea, but the point that you should try to understand is that linear regression analysis can be used to calculate a line of best fit for any two variables, given pairs of data, even when there is no actual connection between them.)

Since a line of best fit can be calculated between any two variables using regression analysis, important questions are:

- How can we assess the reliability of the line of best fit?'
- How do we know whether our choice of activity as 'x' is a good one?

The answer to both questions is that the reliability of the regression formula can be assessed using a statistic called the coefficient of correlation.

Correlation is a measure of the strength of the relationship between two variables. Variables are said to be correlated if a change in one variable results in a change in the other variable.

If you plot a graph of the data relating to two variables, you should be able to see if any visible relationship exists between them (such a graph is known as a scattergraph or scatterchart). If a visible relationship is seen to exist, the data on the graph can be plotted to show the 'line of best fit'. The 'line of best fit' is of the form $y = a + bx$ (linear cost function) and indicates that a 'possible' linear relationship exists between two variables.

3.2 Degrees of correlation

The following scattergraphs show the different degrees of correlation that may be seen to exist between two variables.

Perfect positive correlation

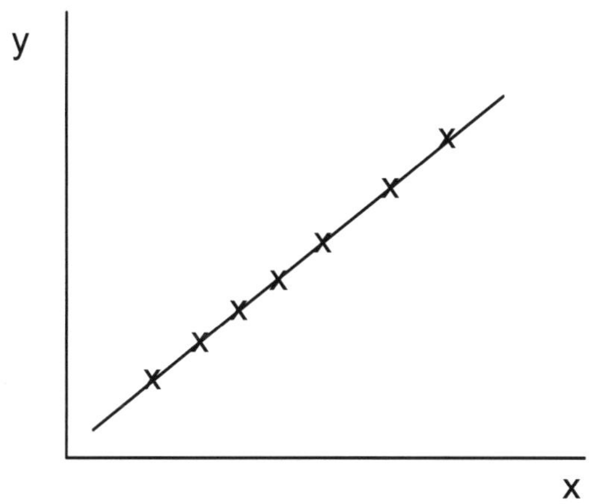

Perfect correlation is seen to exist when all the data points plotted lie in an exact straight line and a linear relationship exists between the two variables.

Perfect positive correlation means that high values of are variable are associated with high values of another variable. Alternatively, low values of one variable may be associated with low values of another variable.

Perfect negative correlation

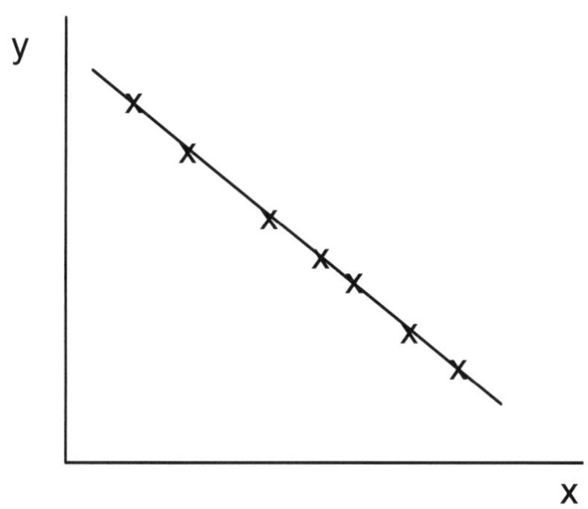

Perfect negative correlation is seen to exist when all the data points plotted lie in an exact straight line and that high values of one variable are associated with low values of another variable. Alternatively, low values of one variable may be associated with high value of another variable.

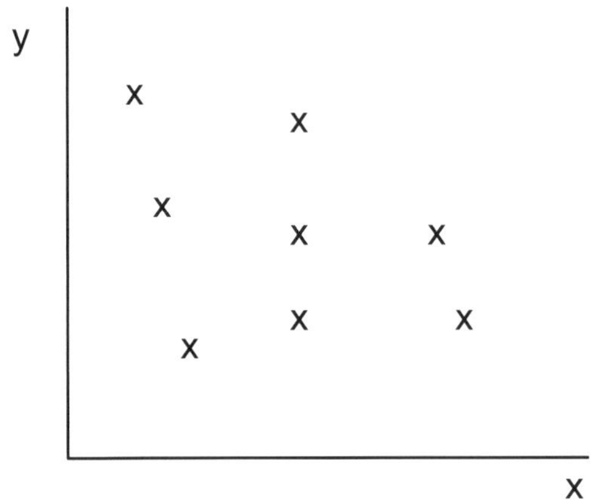

No correlation (uncorrelated)

'Uncorrelated' means that no correlation is seen to exist between the variables.

Positive correlation (but not perfect correlation)

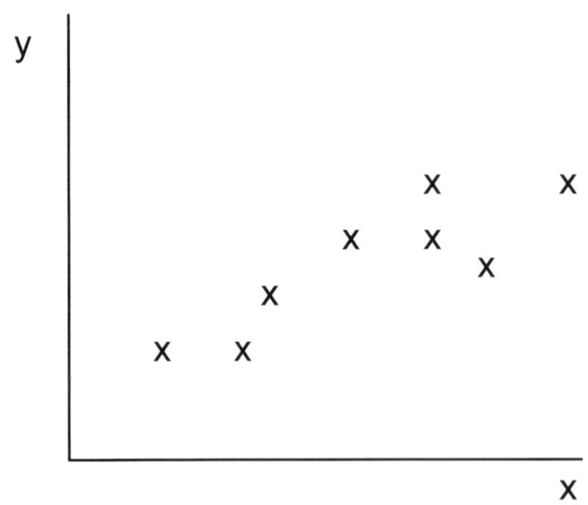

Positive correlation means that there appears to be some correlation between the values of y and x, and in general the value of y increases as the value of x increases. However, the correlation is not perfect because all the data does not lie exactly on a straight line on the scattergraph.

Negative correlation

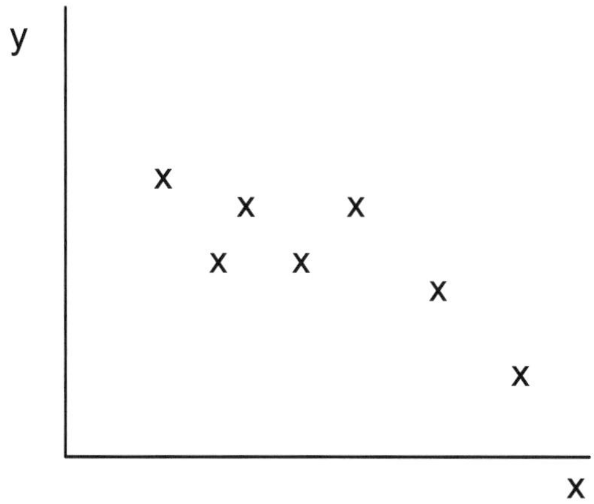

Negative correlation means that a relationship exists between two variables, and the value of y declines as the value of x increases. However, the correlation is not perfect.

As an alternative to drawing a scattergraph to see whether a visible relationship exists between the two variables x and y, the correlation between them can be measured by calculating a **correlation coefficient**.

3.3 Correlation coefficient r

An advantage of using the regression analysis method is that the reliability of the estimates can be assessed statistically, by calculating a correlation coefficient.

The formula for the correlation coefficient (r) will be given to you in the examination.

$$r = \frac{n\Sigma xy - \Sigma x \Sigma y}{\sqrt{\left(n\Sigma x^2 - (\Sigma x)^2\right)\left(n\Sigma y^2 - (\Sigma y)^2\right)}}$$

This formula might seem difficult, but it is fairly similar to the formula for calculating 'b' in the linear cost equation. The only additional value that we need to calculate the correlation coefficient is a value for $[n\Sigma y^2 - (\Sigma y)^2]$.

- If you look back at the previous example, you will see that the value for Σy^2 has already been calculated. In the example, there is a separate column for y^2. Calculate the square of each value of y in the y column and enter it in the same row in the y^2 column. Then add up all the values of y^2 in the y^2 column to get Σy^2.
- $(\Sigma y)^2$ is a different value. It is the square of the value for Σy.

The value of the correlation coefficient, r, in the example in paragraph 2.3 is therefore calculated as follows. Remember that most of the values for the formula have been calculated in paragraph 2.3 as parts of the formula for calculating the value of b.

$$r = \frac{249}{\sqrt{(41)\,[6(136{,}185) - (903)^2\,]}} = \frac{249}{\sqrt{(41)\,(1{,}701)}} = \frac{249}{264} = +0.94$$

The correlation coefficient is + 0.94.

Significance of the correlation coefficient

The value of the correlation coefficient must always be in the range – 1 to + 1.

- A value of – 1 indicates that there is perfect negative correlation between the values for y and the values for x that have been used in the regression analysis estimates. Perfect negative correlation means that all the values for x and y, plotted on a graph, would lie on a straight downward-sloping line.
- A value of + 1 indicates that there is perfect positive correlation between the values for y and the values for x that have been used in the regression analysis estimates. Perfect positive correlation means that all the values for x and y, plotted on a graph, would lie on a straight upward-sloping line.
- A value of r = 0 indicates no correlation at all between the values of x and y.

For cost estimation, a value for r close to + 1 would indicate that the cost estimates are likely to be very reliable.

As a general guide, a value for r between + 0.90 and + 1 indicates good correlation between the values of x and y, suggesting that the formula for costs can be used with reasonable confidence for cost estimation.

If you calculate a value for r that is more than +1 or is a greater negative value than – 1, your calculation will be wrong.

3.4 Coefficient of determination r^2

The square of the correlation coefficient, r^2, is called the coefficient of determination. The value of r^2 shows how much the variations in the value of y, in the data used to calculate the regression analysis formula, can be explained by variations in the value of x.

Significance of coefficient of determination

The value of the coefficient of determination must always be in the range 0 to +1.

- If the value of r is + 0.70, this means that on the basis of the data used in the regression analysis formula, 0.49 or 49% (= 0.70^2) of variations in the value of y can be explained by variations in the value of x.
- Similarly if the value of r is – 0.80, this means that on the basis of the data used in the regression analysis formula, 0.64 or 64% (= 0.80^2) of variations in the value of y can be explained by variations in the value of x. Since r is negative, this means that y falls in value as the value of x increases.

In the example above, where r = + 0.94, we can say that from the data used to produce a formula for total costs, 88.36% (0.94 × 0.94 = 0.8836) of the variations in total cost can be explained by variations in the volume of output. This would suggest that the formula obtained for total costs is likely to be fairly reliable for estimating future costs for any given (budgeted) volume of production.

The coefficient of correlation and the coefficient of determination can therefore be used to give a statistical measurement to the reliability of estimates of y from a given value for x, using a line of best fit that has been calculated by linear regression analysis. As you might imagine, this can be a very useful item of management information for the purpose of forecasting or planning.

Spreadsheet models

- Features of a spreadsheet
- Using spreadsheets
- Applications of spreadsheets in cost and management accounting
- 'What if' analysis: sensitivity analysis

4 Spreadsheet models

4.1 Features of a spreadsheet

Spreadsheets are used extensively in management accounting, because they enable accountants to make long and detailed calculations very quickly.

A spreadsheet program is a type of computer software. A spreadsheet is a table of rows and columns. Like any table, the rows and columns can contain words, figures or other symbols. A spreadsheet program is used to create spreadsheets.

A spreadsheet created by a spreadsheet program enables the user to prepare one or more tables of figures. Any table of figures, no matter how complex, can be prepared in a spreadsheet.

A blank spreadsheet is simply a huge table of rows and columns, with each row and having a unique identity number and each column having a unique letter code (A, B, C …AA, AB, etc). The table therefore consists of boxes or cells, and each cell can be identified by a unique combination of column letters and row number, such as B5, T28, AA4 and so on.

A description of the features of a spreadsheet system is given in an Appendix at the end of this text. If you are not familiar with spreadsheets, you should read the Appendix before continuing to read this chapter.

4.2 Using spreadsheets

A blank spreadsheet can be used to create a table of figures by entering words, figures and formulae. Figures are entered in the appropriate cells if their values are known. Otherwise a formula can be entered into a cell, and the spreadsheet model will convert the formula into a numerical value. The use of formulae in spreadsheets is the reason why they can be used to produce tables of figures so quickly. Formulae avoid the need to make calculations 'by hand' with a calculator.

Example

The example below is a very simple illustration of how spreadsheets are used to construct accounting calculations.

	All text in this column	Entered in the spreadsheet file as text of formulae	Shown in the spreadsheet on screen or printout
Column	F	G	G
Row			
6	**Year**	**Sales**	**Sales**
7		$	$
8	1	100,000	100,000
9	2	=G8*1.05	105,000
10	3	=G9*1.05	110,250
11	Total sales Years 1 - 3	=G8+G9+G10	315,250
12	Average annual sales	=G11/3	105,083

Column G is shown twice here. The left hand column for G shows the data as it has been entered into the spreadsheet as formulae. The left hand column for G shows the data that is displayed on the screen and in printouts.

The figures in the spreadsheet can be changed quickly simply by amending some of the data in the cells. For example, if the accountant wants to change the figures so that sales in Year 1 are $110,000 and annual sales growth in Years 2 and 3 is 4%, he can do this by amending the number in cell G8 to 110,000 and amending cells G9 and G10 to change 1.05 to 1.04.

Example

Here is another example of a simple accounting calculation entered as text, numbers and formulae in a spreadsheet.

Column	C	D	E	F
Row				
		1st 6 months	**2nd 6 months**	**Year**
4	Output (units)	10,000	15,000	= D4+E4
5		$	$	$
6	Variable costs	=D4*F11	=E*F11	=D6+E6
7	Fixed costs	40,000	=D7	=D7+E7
8	Total costs	=D6+D7	=E6+E7	=D8+E8
9				
10	Average cost/unit	=D8/D4	=E8/E4	=F8/F4
11	Variable cost/unit			3.00

This would appear on screen as follows:

Column	C	D	E	F
Row				
		1st 6 months	**2nd 6 months**	**Year**
4	Output (units)	10,000	15,000	25,000
5		$	$	$
6	Variable costs	30,000	45,000	75,000
7	Fixed costs	40,000	40,000	80,000
8	Total costs	70,000	85,000	155,000
9				
10	Average cost/unit	7.00	5.67	6.20
11	Variable cost/unit			3.00

The figures can be re-calculated using different figures for output in each half of the year, or different figures for fixed costs or the unit variable costs. All that is required is an alteration to the number in cells D4, E4, D7 or F11.

4.3 Applications of spreadsheets in cost and management accounting

Spreadsheets can be used for many tasks in cost and management accounting, where a large number of calculations are required. They are used to construct mathematical 'models' and to carry out a large number of calculations quickly and accurately.

Examples of applications of spreadsheets in management accounting include:

- Preparing forecasts of sales, and forecasts of profit or loss
- Cost estimation using linear regression analysis and the calculation of a correlation coefficient and coefficient of determination
- Preparing financial plans, such as budgets
- Comparing actual results with a plan or budget (control reporting).

Each table or set of related tables in a spreadsheet is held in a single file and accountants often carry a number of spreadsheet files on their lap top computer.

There are cost and management applications for which spreadsheets are not suitable. These include any application involving the recording and filing of large amounts of data. For these applications, involving the maintenance of records and large files, other types of software are more suitable, such as:

- A cost accounting software package for keeping cost accounting records (in a double entry 'book-keeping' system)
- An inventory control software package for maintaining records of inventory
- A database for maintaining and accessing other large files of data.

Graphical reproduction of spreadsheet data

Spreadsheets can be printed out and included in management reports. It is very common in practice to find tables of figures produced in a spreadsheet to be included as appendices in management reports.

In addition, the figures in a spreadsheet can be converted by the spreadsheet program into graphical display format, and shown as graphs, bar charts or pie charts. This facility can also be very useful for the preparation of management reports.

For example, if a spreadsheet is used for linear regression analysis, it can be used to show the line of best fit as a graph. Similarly, if a spreadsheet is used to prepare an estimate of costs, the percentage of total costs made up by different items of cost (direct materials, direct labour, production overheads etc) can be shown as a pie chart or a bar chart.

Applications of spreadsheets in management accounting include:

- Making forecasts, such as sales forecasts
- Preparing budgets and other financial plans
- Preparing flexible budgets for comparing actual and expected costs
- Preparing a complex income statement.

Some examples of spreadsheets are illustrated below. Don't worry about the detail in these examples. Cost-volume-profit analysis will be explained in a later chapter.

Example

Cost-volume-profit analysis is a technique in cost accounting that might be used to prepare profit forecasts or to estimate what the profit might be at different selling prices per unit or at different sales volumes. In this example, numbers might have been entered in cells C7, D7, F7 and G7. All the other cells, except for the text cells, will contain formulae.

The estimates for selling price, variable costs, budgeted sales units and fixed costs can be amended simply by changing the numbers in C7, D7, F7 and G7. (However, in this example, the text cells A8 – A12 might also need changing.

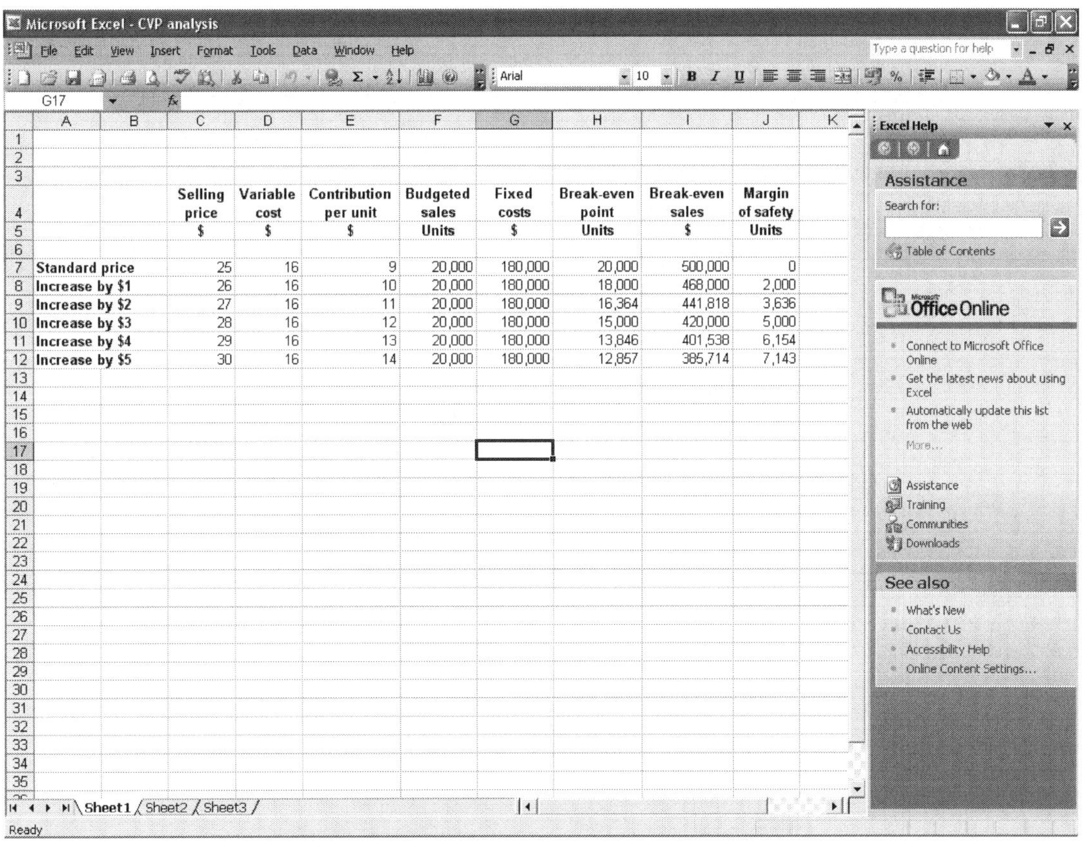

	Selling price $	Variable cost $	Contribution per unit $	Budgeted sales Units	Fixed costs $	Break-even point Units	Break-even sales $	Margin of safety Units
Standard price	25	16	9	20,000	180,000	20,000	500,000	0
Increase by $1	26	16	10	20,000	180,000	18,000	468,000	2,000
Increase by $2	27	16	11	20,000	180,000	16,364	441,818	3,636
Increase by $3	28	16	12	20,000	180,000	15,000	420,000	5,000
Increase by $4	29	16	13	20,000	180,000	13,846	401,538	6,154
Increase by $5	30	16	14	20,000	180,000	12,857	385,714	7,143

Graphical reproduction of spreadsheet data

Spreadsheets can be printed out and included in management reports. It is very common in practice to find tables of figures produced in a spreadsheet to be included as appendices in management reports.

In addition, the figures in a spreadsheet can be converted by the spreadsheet program into graphical display format, and shown as graphs, bar charts or pie charts. This facility can also be very useful for the preparation of management reports.

For example, if a spreadsheet is used for linear regression analysis, it can be used to show the line of best fit as a graph. Similarly, if a spreadsheet is used to prepare an estimate of costs, the percentage of total costs made up by different items of cost (direct materials, direct labour, production overheads etc) can be shown as a pie chart or a bar chart.

In the Microsoft Excel spreadsheet program, the facility to produce graphical displays is provided by the Chart Wizard facility. A Chart Wizard icon is on the menu bar and appears as follows:

The example below shows how the profits for six different companies can be shown in the form of a graph using 'Chart Wizard'.

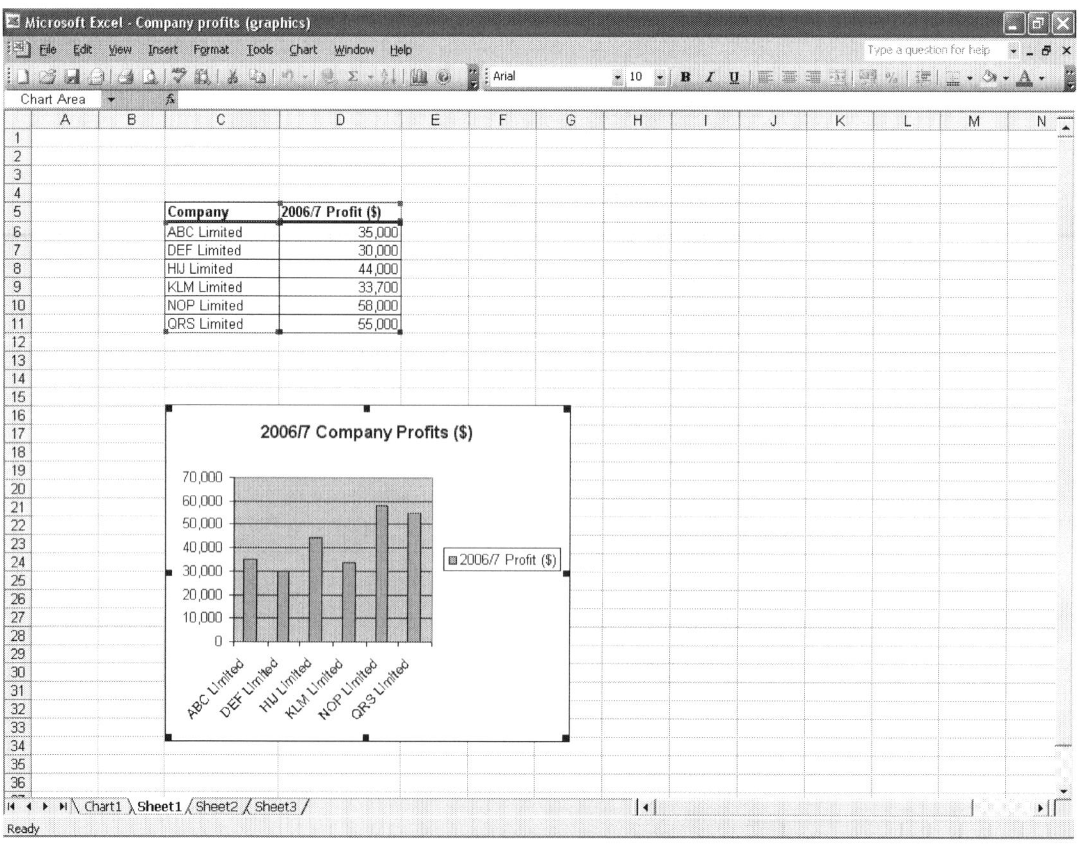

4.4 'What if' analysis: sensitivity analysis

An important feature of spreadsheets is the ability to re-calculate figures very quickly simply by changing the number or formula in one cell, or several cells.

For example if a spreadsheet is used to prepare a budget, the budget can be re-calculated changing the assumption about sales volume from, say, '50,000 units in month 1 and rising by 1,000 units each month' to '48,000 units in month 1 and rising by 800 units in each month' This would need amendments to just two cells In the spreadsheet.

Sensitivity analysis is a method of risk and uncertainty analysis. It analyses what the outcome will be if some factors are more favourable or more adverse than expected. For example, if a budget is prepared on the assumption that raw materials prices will increase by 3% compared with the previous year, sensitivity analysis could be used to estimate what the profit would be if raw material costs were higher, say 5% higher than the previous year.

By changing some key assumptions and seeing what happens to the profit, sensitivity analysis provides management with information about the sensitivity of the budget to changes in different assumptions about unit costs, sales volumes or selling prices.

The ability to carry out sensitivity analysis is improved enormously by using spreadsheets. Each analysis of the sensitivity of the outcome to changes in a key variable can be made quickly, by amending one or two items in the spreadsheet. A task that could take hours if done by hand can be finished in seconds (or possibly as much as a few minutes) using a spreadsheet.

Practice multiple choice questions

1 A company is assessing the expected profitability from a proposed business venture. It has been estimated that there is a 0.5 probability of making a profit of $64,000, a 25% probability of a profit of $10,000 and a 25% probability of a loss of $20,000. What is the expected value of the profit from the venture?

A $14,500

B $18,000

C $29,500

D $39,500. ***(2 marks)***

2 The following statements relate to the calculation of a line of best fit for $y = a + bx$ using the formulae in the formula sheet for your examination.

(i) n represents the number of pairs of data used
(ii) $\sum x^2$ is calculated as the square of $\sum x$
(iii) $\sum xy$ is calculated by multiplying $\sum x$ by $\sum y$.

Which of the statements is/are correct?

A (i) only

B (i) and (ii) only

C (ii) and (iii) only

D (i) and (iii) only

(2 marks)

3 Regression analysis is being used to estimate a line of best fit from five pairs of data. The following values have been calculated from the data.

$\sum x = 258$, $\sum y = 2{,}670$, $\sum xy = 138{,}546$, $\sum x^2 = 13{,}732$, $\sum y^2 = 269{,}361$.

What is the value of 'a' (to the nearest whole number) in the line of best fit calculated from this data?

A 439

B 457

C 629

D 734

(2 marks)

4 Which one of the following is a feasible value for a correlation coefficient?

A + 1.05

B - 0.78

C - 1.25

D + 2.0

(1 mark)

5 The following statements relate to the use of spreadsheets in cost and management accounting.

(i) a spreadsheet is suitable for storing large quantities of data as cost records

(ii) a spreadsheet can be used to calculate a line of best fit using linear regression analysis

(iii) figures in a spreadsheet table can be converted by a spreadsheet program into a bar chart form

Which of the statements are correct?

A (i) and (ii) only

B (i) and (iii) only

C (ii) and (iii) only

D (i), (ii) and (iii)

(2 marks)

CHAPTER

5

Accounting for materials and labour

Contents

Materials: procedures and documentation

- The need for procedures and documentation of materials
- The procedures and documents
- Monitoring physical inventory: comparison with the inventory records
- Entries and balances in a materials inventory account

1 Materials: procedures and documentation

1.1 The need for procedures and documentation of materials

When an entity purchases materials from a supplier, the purchasing process should be properly documented. There are several reasons for this.

Any purchase of materials from a supplier should be properly authorised and approved at the appropriate management level. Documentation of the purchasing process provides evidence that approval has been obtained.

The receipt of materials from a supplier should also be documented, to make sure that the goods that were ordered have actually been delivered.

There should be an invoice from the supplier for the goods that have been delivered. (In rare cases when goods are bought for cash, there should be a receipt from the supplier.) The amount payable for the materials provides documentary evidence about their cost.

When materials are received from a supplier, they might be held in a store or warehouse until needed. When they are issued from the store, there should be a documentary record of who has taken the materials and how many were taken. This is needed to provide a record of the cost of materials used by different departments or cost centres.

Documentation of materials is therefore needed:

- to ensure that the procedures for ordering, receiving and paying for materials has been conducted properly, and there is no error or fraud
- to provide a record of materials purchases for the financial accounts
- to provide a record of materials costs for the cost and management accounts.

1.2 The procedures and documents

The detailed procedures for purchasing materials and the documents used might differ according to the size and nature of the business. However the basic requirements should be the same for all types of business where material purchases are made.

Purchasing procedures and documents

In a large company with a purchasing department (a buying department) and a stores department, the procedures for purchasing materials might be as follows.

- The stores department identifies the need to re-order an item of raw materials for inventory. It produces a request to the purchasing department to buy a quantity of the materials. This request is called a **purchase requisition.** It should be properly authorised by a manager with the authority to approve any such requisition.
- A buyer in the purchasing department selects a supplier and provides the supplier with **a purchase order,** stating the identity of the item to be purchased, the quantity required and possibly also the price that the supplier has agreed.
- When the supplier delivers the goods, the goods are accompanied by a **delivery note** from the supplier. The delivery note is a statement of the identity and quantity of the items delivered, and it provides confirmation that the items have been delivered. One copy is kept with the stores department, and another copy is retained by the supplier (the driver of the delivery vehicle), as evidence of the delivery.
- The stores department prepares a **goods received note,** recording the details of the materials received. This should include the inventory identity code for the item, as well as the quantity received.
- Copies of the delivery note and goods received note are sent to the accounts department, where they are matched with a copy of the purchase order.
- A **purchase invoice** is received from the supplier, asking for payment. The accounts department checks the invoice details with the details on the purchase order and goods received note, to confirm that the correct items have been delivered in the correct quantities.
- The purchase invoice is used to record the purchase in the **accounting records**.
- In the cost accounting system, there should be **inventory records** to record the quantities and costs of materials received. Data for recording costs of purchases for each item of inventory is obtained from the goods received note (quantity and inventory code) and purchase invoice (cost).

The purchase process

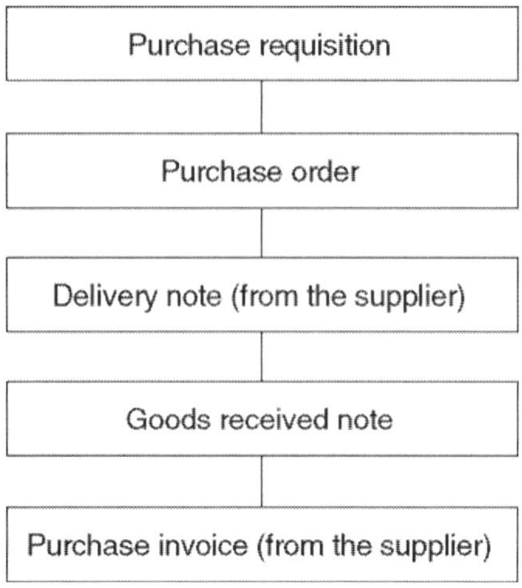

Inventory records

An entity should keep an up-to-date record of the materials that it is holding in inventory.

- **In the stores department**, the materials should be kept secure, and there should be systems, processes and controls to prevent loss, theft or damage. The stores department should keep a record of the quantity of each item of material currently held in inventory. For each item of material, there might therefore be an inventory record card, or 'bin card'. This card is used to keep an up-to-date record of the number of units of the material currently in the stores department, with records of each receipt and issue of the inventory item. This process of continuous record-keeping is known as **perpetual inventory**. The inventory record should be updated every time materials are delivered into store from a supplier, and every time that materials are issued to an operating department. Instead of having a 'physical' card for each stores item, there may be a computerised record containing similar information.
- **In the cost accounting department**, another separate record of inventory might be kept, with an **inventory ledger record** for each item of material. The inventory ledger record is a record of the quantity of the materials currently held in inventory, the quantities received into store from suppliers and the quantities issued to operational departments. In addition the inventory ledger record also records the **cost** of the materials currently held in inventory, the cost of new materials purchased and the cost of the materials issued to each operating department (cost centre).
- **In a computerised inventory control system**, the stores department and the cost accounting department should use the same computerised records for inventory.

Issues and returns of materials

A cost accounting system also needs to record the quantities and cost of items of materials that are issued to the user departments, and the quantities and cost of any items that are subsequently returned to store unused.

The documentation for the issue and returns of materials are:

- A **materials requisition note**: this is a formal request from a user department to the stores department for a quantity of an items of materials
- A materials return note: when items are returned to store unused, the stores department should record the return on a **materials return note**.

A materials requisition note is used to record:

- the details of the quantity of materials issued
- the department (cost centre) that receives them, and
- (in a cost accounting system) their cost.

The inventory records are updated from the requisitions notes and returns notes to record all issues and returns of materials.

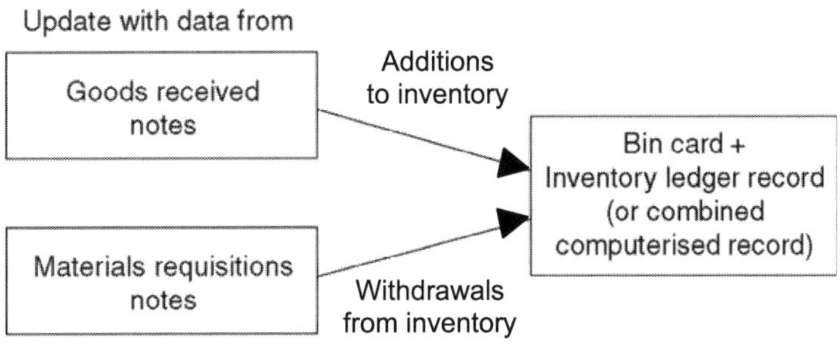

A simplified version of an inventory record for a perpetual inventory system is shown below, to demonstrate that inventory records can be used to record receipts and issues (and returns) of materials, and their cost or value. The record needs to identify the cost centres that have issued or returned materials, and will probably also record the number of the materials requisition note or materials returns note (although this data is not shown in the example below).

Inventory item **Code number** **1234**
Description

		Issues		Returns		Purchases		Balance	
		Quantity	Cost	Quantity	Cost	Quantity	Cost	Quantity	Cost
			$		$		$		$
Date	Department (code)								
March									
1								200	400
3						300	630	500	1,030
7	23	250	505					250	525
9	23			30	63			220	462
12	18	100	210					120	252

1.3 Monitoring physical inventory: comparison with the inventory records

For various reasons, the inventory records in the cost accounts might not agree with the physical quantities of materials actually held in store. There are several reasons for this.

- **Errors in recording receipts, issues and returns**. Mistakes might be made in recording transactions for materials received from the supplier, materials issued from store and returns to store. For example, an issue of material item 1234 from inventory might be recorded as an issue of item 1243. This would result in inaccurate inventory records for both item 1234 and item 1243.
- **Omissions**. Similarly, some purchases, issues and returns to store might not be recorded, due to mistakes.
- **Theft or physical loss**. Some inventory might be stolen or might get lost, and the theft or loss might not be noticed or recorded.
- **Damage to stores items** or **deterioration of items**. Stores items might deteriorate in quality when they are stored, particularly if they are stored in poor conditions. Damaged items might be thrown away, but the write-off might not be recorded.

Management should try to minimise these discrepancies between inventory records (in a perpetual inventory system) and physical inventory in the store.

- It is the responsibility of the stores manager to minimise losses due to theft, loss or deterioration and damage.
- Documentation and record keeping should be accurate and mistakes should be minimised. All movements of materials should be properly recorded in a document, and the data from the document should be transferred accurately into the inventory records.

Even so, good record keeping and goods stores management will not prevent some discrepancies between inventory records and physical inventory in store. This discrepancy should be checked from time to time. The stores department staff can do this by carrying out a **physical count** of the quantity of each material item currently held, and comparing this 'physical count' with the figures in the stores records. The records should then be adjusted to the correct quantities. (Quantities that are 'missing' will be recorded as a write-off of materials in the accounts.)

Minimising discrepancies and losses

When physical inventory is checked against the inventory records, there will often be some differences. When the differences are big, there could be a serious problem with either:

- Poor control over inventory. Some losses through theft, deterioration and breakages should be expected, but the losses should not be large.
- Poor inventory records. If the inventory records are inaccurate, the information prepared for management from inventory records will be unreliable.

Whichever failing is the reason for big discrepancies between physical inventory and inventory records, management should take measures to deal with the problem.

- Theft can be reduced by keeping inventory locked in a safe place. TV cameras can be used to monitor activity in the warehouse.
- Deterioration of inventory can be reduced by keeping the inventory in better storage condition.

- Poor procedures for recording inventory movements in and out of the store can be improved through better procedures and suitable controls, such as better supervision of the recording process and better staff training.

1.4 Entries and balances in a materials inventory account

In a system of cost accounting, a separate record is kept for each inventory item. This record – an inventory account – is used to maintain a record of all movements in the materials, in terms of both quantities and cost.

The main contents of an inventory record are shown in the previous example. An inventory record in the cost accounts provides a continual record of the following:

- Purchases/deliveries from suppliers: quantity and cost
- Returns to suppliers: quantity and cost
- Issues of the item to user departments: quantity, cost and department identity
- Returns from user departments to the stores: quantity, cost and department identity
- The balance held in inventory (quantity and cost or value).

The inventory records are combined into a total record for all inventory, which is used for reporting purposes such as the preparation of a costing statement or an income statement of the profit or loss made in a period. The system for recording inventory and materials costs might also be a part of a bigger cost accounting system.

A cost accounting system is a system for recording all costs and in large organisations it is maintained in the form of a double entry accounting system of cost records in a 'cost ledger'. These accounting aspects of recording materials costs are explained in a later chapter.

Material purchase quantities: Economic Order Quantity

- Minimising materials costs
- Holding costs and ordering costs
- Economic order quantity (EOQ)
- EOQ: changes in the variables in the formula

2 Material purchase quantities: Economic Order Quantity

2.1 Minimising materials costs

Organisations that purchase and consume large quantities of materials should try to minimise the total costs. Total materials costs, for any item of materials, consist of:

- the cost of materials purchased (the purchase price)
- the costs of making purchase orders to buy the material (ordering costs)
- the costs of holding inventory (this is often a cost of interest on the investment in inventory).

In most cases, the most significant cost is the purchase cost of the materials. However, ordering costs and holding costs might also be substantial.

2.2 Holding costs and ordering costs

It is useful to be aware of what holding costs and ordering costs consist of.

Holding costs for inventory include costs such as:

- the interest cost of the investment in inventory
- the costs of losses through holding inventory, due to obsolescence, deterioration in the condition of the inventory and theft of inventory items
- the costs of insurance of inventory.

Inventory has to be paid for, and when an organisation holds a quantity of inventory it must therefore obtain finance to pay for it. For example suppose that a company holds between 0 units and 1,000 unit of an item of material that costs $10 per unit to purchase. The cost of the materials held in store therefore varies between $0 and $10,000. On average the cost of the inventory in store is likely to be about $5,000. This inventory must be financed, and it is usual to assume (for simplicity) that it is financed by borrowing that has an interest cost. In this example, if the interest cost of holding inventory is 5% per year, the cost per year of holding the inventory would be $250 (= $5,000 × 5%).

There are other inventory holding costs too, such as the costs of operating a stores department – the rental cost of the stores, the wages or salaries of stores staff and other running costs.

Ordering costs are the costs of making an order to purchase a quantity of a material item from a supplier. They include costs such as:

- the cost of delivery of the purchased items, if these are paid for by the buyer
- the costs associated with placing an order, such as the costs of telephone calls
- costs associated with checking the inventory after delivery from the supplier.

2.3 Economic order quantity (EOQ)

If the price of materials is the same, no matter what the size of the purchase order, the purchase order quantity that minimises total costs is the quantity at which ordering costs plus the costs of holding inventory are minimised.

This order quantity or purchase quantity that minimises the total annual cost of ordering the item plus holding it in store is called the economic order quantity or EOQ.

- EOQ minimises Ordering costs + Holding costs
- Ordering costs each year = $\left(\frac{C_O \times D}{Q}\right)$
- Inventory holding costs each year = $\left(\frac{Q}{2}\right) \times C_H$

Where:

- Q = the quantity of materials purchased in each order (EOQ)
- D = the annual demand for the materials
- C_o = the cost of making an order for materials
- C_H = the cost of holding one unit of material in store for one year

Assumptions:

- There is a constant demand for the materials throughout the year. For example, if annual demand is 4,000 units of the item each year, the item is consumed at a constant rate throughout the year.
- There will be an immediate supply of new materials (Q units) as soon as existing as quantities in store run down to 0. The minimum quantity held in store is therefore 0 units and this always occurs just before a new purchase order quantity is received. The maximum quantity is Q units. The average amount of inventory held is therefore Q/2 and total holding costs each year are $(Q/2) \times C_H$.
- The number of orders each year is D/Q. Total ordering costs each year are therefore $(D/Q) \times C_O$.

The economic order quantity (EOQ) is the order size that will minimise the total of these costs during a period (normally one year), given the assumptions stated above.

The formula for the EOQ is as follows:

$$\text{Economic order quantity (EOQ)} = \sqrt{\frac{2C_oD}{C_H}}$$

This formula is given to you in the examination (on the formulae sheet), although you should be able to learn it.

A note on ordering costs and inventory holding costs. For the purpose of the EOQ formula, the costs that should be used in the formula are only those costs that are incurred as a **direct consequence** of ordering inventory or holding inventory. Costs that would be incurred anyway – such as the salary costs of the buyer or the costs of renting warehouse space – should not be used in the formula because they are not relevant costs for deciding the EOQ size. Relevant costs are explained in more detail in a later chapter.

Examination hint: annual demand and annual holding cost per unit

It is important to make sure that all the items in the EOQ formula are based on the same time period. The demand should be annual demand and the holding cost should be an annual holding cost per unit. You might be given an examination in which demand is stated as a quantity for each three-month period but the holding cost is given as an annual cost. You would therefore need to convert the three-monthly demand into an annual demand for using in the EOQ formula.

e

Example

A company uses 14,450 units of Material X each year, which costs $2 for each unit. The cost of placing an order is $125 for each order. The cost of holding inventory each year is 10% of the purchase cost.

What is the order quantity for Material X that will minimise annual costs?

a

Answer

$$\text{EOQ} = \sqrt{\frac{2C_oD}{C_H}}$$

Where:

$C_o = 125$

$D = 14{,}450$

$C_H = 10\% \times 2 = 0.2$

$$= \sqrt{\left(\frac{2 \times 14{,}450 \times 125}{0.2}\right)} = \sqrt{18{,}062{,}500} = 4{,}250 \text{ units}$$

The economic order quantity is 4,250 units, which means that the average number of orders placed with suppliers will be 3.4 orders each year (= 14,450/4,250).

EOQ: Annual holding costs = Annual ordering costs

It might be useful to know that the EOQ is also an order quantity where the total annual costs of ordering and the total annual holding costs are exactly the same. In the example above:

- EOQ = 4,250 units
- Annual ordering costs = $(C_O \times D)/Q$ = ($125 × 14,450)/4,250 = $425
- Annual holding costs = $(Q/2) \times C_H$ = (4,250/2) × $0.20 = $425.
- Ordering costs and holding costs each year are both $425.

Total annual ordering costs and annual holding costs are always the same whenever the purchase quantity for materials is the EOQ and the assumptions on which the EOQ is based (described earlier) apply.

Exercise 1

The purchase cost of an item of stock is $60 per unit. In each three-month period, 5,000 units of the item are used. Annual holding costs for this item are 8% of its cost. The cost of placing an order is $250.

What is the economic order quantity for this item, to the nearest whole unit?

2.4 EOQ: changes in the variables in the formula

You need to develop a good understanding of the EOQ formula. An examination question might test your ability to assess the consequences of a change in the value of any variable in the formula. For example, what would be the consequences of:

- an increase in the annual holding cost per unit
- a reduction in the annual holding cost per unit
- an increase or a reduction in the order cost
- an increase or a reduction in the annual order quantity.

A change in any of these variables will affect:

- the size of the EOQ, and because the EOQ changes
- total annual ordering costs, and
- total annual holding costs.

Example

A company uses the economic order quantity formula to decide the purchase quantities for its major items of material purchases. The holding cost of inventory is currently 6% of the purchase cost.

Required

What will be the effect of a reduction in the interest rate to 5% on:

(a) the EOQ

(b) total annual ordering costs

(c) total annual holding costs?

Answer

$$EOQ = \sqrt{\frac{2C_oD}{C_H}}$$

A fall in interest rates will reduce the value of C_H.

(a) C_H is below the line in the EOQ formula and if it falls in value, the EOQ will increase.

(b) An increase in the EOQ will result in a reduction in ordering costs. Since the EOQ is higher, the number of orders each year (= D/Q) will fall, and given no change in the cost of each order, total ordering costs must therefore fall.

(c) If the order quantity is EOQ, total annual ordering costs and total annual holding costs are the same. If total annual ordering costs fall, it follows that total annual holding costs will fall too.

Example

A company uses the economic order quantity formula to decide the purchase quantities for its major items of material purchases. The cost of an order increases by 10%.

Required

What will be the effect of the increase in order cost on:

(a) the EOQ

(b) total annual ordering costs

(c) total annual holding costs?

Answer

$$EOQ = \sqrt{\frac{2C_oD}{C_H}}$$

The approach to a solution is similar to the previous example.

An increase in the order cost means an increase in C_O.

(a) C_O is above the line in the EOQ formula and if it increases in value, the EOQ will increase.

(b) An increase in the EOQ will result in a higher average inventory quantity (Q/2 will be higher). Given no change in the annual holding cost per unit, total holding costs must therefore increase.

(c) If the order quantity is EOQ, total annual ordering costs and total annual holding costs are the same. If total annual holding costs increase, it follows that total annual ordering costs will also rise.

Material purchase quantities: purchase discounts and gradual replenishment

- Order quantity with price discounts for large orders
- Economic batch quantity (EBQ): gradual replenishment of inventory

3 Material purchase quantities: purchase discounts and gradual replenishment

3.1 Order quantity with price discounts for large orders

The optimum purchase quantity is the order size that minimises the total costs of:

- Annual purchase costs = (D × price per unit)
- Ordering costs each year = $\frac{(C_O \times D)}{Q}$
- Inventory holding costs each year = $\left(\frac{Q}{2}\right) \times C_H$

When the EOQ formula is used to calculate the purchase quantity, it is assumed that the purchase cost per unit of material is a constant amount, regardless of the order quantity.

In some cases, however, a supplier might offer a discount on the purchase price for orders above a certain quantity. When this situation arises, the order quantity that minimises total costs will be either:

- the economic order quantity, or
- the **minimum** order quantity necessary to obtain the price discount.

To identify the order quantity that minimises costs, you need to calculate the total costs each year of purchases, ordering costs and holding costs, for both order quantities (the EOQ and the minimum order quantity to obtain the discount).

(If a supplier offers a discount for order quantities above a certain amount and an larger discount orders above an even larger quantity, you need to compare total costs for the EOQ and for each minimum quantity at which a different purchase discount applies.)

Example

A company uses 14,450 units of Material X each year, which costs $2 for each unit before discount. The costs of making an order are $125 for each order. The annual cost of holding inventory is 10% of the purchase cost. The supplier will offer a price discount of $0.10 per unit for orders of 6,000 up to 10,000 units, and a discount of

$0.20 per unit for orders of 10,000 units or more.

What is the order quantity that will minimise total costs?

a

Answer

The economic order quantity, ignoring discounts, is 4,250 units (see earlier example). The order quantity that will minimise costs is therefore one of the following:

- 4,250 units, the economic order quantity
- 6,000 units, the smallest quantity required above the EOQ to get a discount of $0.10 per unit
- 10,000 units, the smallest quantity required above the EOQ to get a discount of $0.20 per unit.

	Order quantity		
	4,250 units	**6,000 units**	**10,000 units**
	$	$	$
Annual purchase costs (14,450 units) (W1)	28,900	27,455	26,010
Annual ordering costs $\frac{(Co \times D)}{Q}$ (W2)	425	301	181
Holding costs $\left(\frac{Q}{2}\right) \times C_H$ (W3)	425	570	900
Total costs	29,750	28,326	27,091

Conclusion

The order quantity that minimises total costs is 10,000 units.

Workings

(W1) Annual purchase costs

Order quantity		**Annual purchase cost**
Units		$
4,250 (= EOQ)	14,450 × $2	28,900
6,000	14,450 × $(2 – 0.10)	27,455
10,000	14,450 × $(2 – 0.20)	26,010

(W2) Annual ordering costs

Order quantity		**Annual ordering costs**
Units		$
4,250 (= EOQ)	(14,450/4,250) × $125	425
6,000	(14,450/6,000) × $125	301
10,000	(14,450/10,000) × $125	181

(W3) Annual holding costs

Order quantity		Annual holding costs
Units		$
4,250 (= EOQ)	(4,250/2) × $2	425
6,000	(6,000/2) × $1.90	570
10,000	(10,000/2) × $1.80	900

3.5 Economic batch quantity (EBQ): gradual replenishment of inventory

Batch production

The EOQ formula is based on the assumption that when inventory is replenished with a new delivery, the full order quantity is received into store immediately. The inventory level therefore ranges between 0 units and Q units. The economic order quantity is used when materials are purchased from external suppliers.

A similar situation arises when an entity manufactures items itself in batches and holds them as inventory until they are sold or used for further processing. For example, a company might produce finished goods in batches, and on completion of production, the materials are transferred to finished goods inventory until they are sold.

However, when it takes some time to produce a batch of items the items might be delivered into store gradually, whilst production is still in progress. The first units are therefore received into store before production of the batch is complete.

If we assume that the first items from a new production batch are received into store when the inventory level falls to 0 units, and if we assume that the order quantity (or 'batch quantity') is Q units, the maximum inventory level will be less than Q. This is because by the time that the full batch has been delivered into store, some of the units have already been used.

Economic batch quantity (EBQ)

The economic batch quantity (EBQ) is similar to the economic order quantity. It is used to calculate the order quantity that minimises total annual costs. If it is assumed that the cost per unit produced is the same regardless of the batch size, the economic batch size is the quantity that minimises the total annual costs of:

- getting each batch production run ready ('set-up costs') and
- inventory holding costs for the finished goods inventory.

Set-up costs. Set-up costs occur in production when items are manufactured in batches. These are the costs incurred in cleaning up the machinery and equipment from the previous batch and getting the machinery ready for making the new batch. (In the context of the EBQ formula, they are similar to order costs in the EOQ formula.)

Set-up costs each year = $\frac{(C_o \times D)}{Q}$

Inventory holding costs. As stated earlier, it is assumed that inventory is replenished as soon as it reaches 0. However, the replenishment of inventory continues throughout the time that the batch of units is still being manufactured. New units are produced continually throughout the batch production process.

For example, suppose that a factory has the capacity to make 8,000 units of an item each year, but it only needs 4,000 units a year. It therefore produces the units in batches. Suppose the batch size is 2,000 units. This is a quarter of the factory capacity, so it would take at least three months to complete one batch. As the units are produced, they are transferred to inventory. There is no need to wait until the end of the batch production run before transferring any of the units to inventory.

This means that the maximum inventory level is not Q. It is a smaller amount:

$Q\,(1 - D/R)$

where:

Q = the quantity of materials produced in each batch

D = the annual demand for the material item

R = the annual rate at which the materials can be produced

In the example above, the maximum inventory level will be 2,000(1 – 4,000/8,000) = 2,000 × 0.5 = 1,000 units. If this is the maximum inventory level, average inventory is 500 units.

Give an annual holding cost per unit of C_H:

Inventory holding costs each year = $\frac{Q\left(1-\frac{D}{R}\right)}{2} \times C_H$

This is similar to the economic order quantity formula, with the exception that average inventory is not $\frac{Q}{2}$ units, but $\frac{Q\left(1-\frac{D}{R}\right)}{2}$ units.

Economic batch production quantity: formula

The formula for the economic batch quantity is

Economic batch quantity (EBQ) = $\sqrt{\frac{2C_oD}{C_H\left(1-\frac{D}{R}\right)}}$

This formula is also given to you in the examination, in the formulae sheet. It is identical to the EOQ formula, except for the assumption about the maximum inventory quantity – due to the gradual replenishment of inventory during the batch production process.

Example

A company uses 9,000 units of product A23 each year, in batches. The annual production rate at which Product A23 could be made is 30,000 units each year. The cost of preparing for the production of a new batch is $405. The annual cost of holding inventory of finished goods is $5.71 per unit.

What is the batch quantity size for Product A23 that will minimise annual costs?

Answer

$$\text{Economic batch quantity} = \sqrt{\frac{2 \times 405 \times 9{,}000}{5.71\left(1 - \dfrac{9{,}000}{30{,}000}\right)}} = \sqrt{\left(\frac{7{,}290{,}000}{4}\right)}$$

$$= \sqrt{1{,}822{,}500}$$

$$= 1{,}350 \text{ units}$$

EBQ: total holding costs and total set-up costs

When the batch production quantity is the EBQ and the assumptions of the EBQ model apply, total annual holding costs and total annual set-up costs will be the same. This is the same situation that applies to the EOQ for total holding costs and total ordering costs.

In the example above:

- If the EBQ is 1,350 units:
- Average inventory will be 1,350(1 – 9,000/30,000) = 945 units
- Total annual holding costs will be (945/2) × $5.71 = $2,698 – say $2,700
- Total set-up costs per year will be (9,000/1,350) × $405 = $2,700

Allowing for a small rounding error of $2, it can be seen that total annual holding costs and total annual set-up costs are the same when the batch production quantity is calculated by the EBQ formula.

You might be tested in your examination on the effect on the EBQ, annual holding costs and annual set-up costs of a change in any variable in the EBQ formula. The approach to analysis should be the same as for changes invariables in the EOQ formula (explained earlier), but the EBQ formula is bit more complex and you should be careful when analysing the effect of any change.

Example

A company uses the economic batch quantity formula to decide the batch production quantities for an item of material. Due to improvements in efficiency in the factory, the production capacity (speed of production) is increased.

Required

What will be the effect of the increase in order cost on:

(a) the economic batch quantity (EBQ)

(b) total annual set-up costs

(c) total annual holding costs?

Answer

Economic batch quantity (EBQ) = $\sqrt{\dfrac{2C_oD}{C_H\left(1-\dfrac{D}{R}\right)}}$

An increase in output capacity means an increase in the value of R.
An increase in the value of R increases the value of (1 – D/R).
An increase in the value of (1 – D/R) increases the value below the line in the EBQ formula
The EBQ will therefore become smaller.

(a) A reduction in the EBQ will result in an increase in set-up costs, because there will be more batches each year. Given no change in the set-up cost per batch, total set-up costs must therefore be higher.

(b) If the order quantity is the EBQ, total annual set-up costs and total annual holding costs are the same. If total annual set-up costs increase, it follows that total annual holding costs will also rise. Although the batch quantity is lower, the maximum inventory level (Q (1 – D/R) is higher.

Inventory reorder level and other warning levels

- Reorder level
- Maximum inventory level
- Minimum inventory level

4 Inventory reorder level and other warning levels

So far, it has been assumed that when an item of materials is purchased from a supplier, the delivery from the supplier will happen immediately. In practice, however, there is likely to be some uncertainty about when to make a new order for materials in order to avoid the risk of running out of inventory before the new order arrives from the supplier. There are two reasons for this.

- There is **a supply 'lead time'**. This is the period of time between placing a new order with a supplier and receiving the delivery of the purchased items. The length of this supply lead time might be uncertain and might be several days, weeks or even months.
- The daily or weekly usage of the material may not be a constant amount. During the supply lead time, the actual usage of the material may be more than or less than the average usage.

However, the examination syllabus specifies that you will only be examined about situations where the demand during the lead time is constant; therefore only the length of the supply lead time might be uncertain.

Running out of an item of inventory (or stock) is called a **stock-out**. (However, you might come across the unusual term 'inventory-out' in your examination.)

When there is a stock-out of a key item of materials, there might be a hold-up in production and a disruption to the production schedules. This in turn may lead to a loss of sales and profits.

Management responsible for inventory control might to know:

- when a new order for each item of materials should be made, in order to avoid any stock-out.
- whether the inventory level for each item of materials appears to be too high or too low.

In an inventory control system, there may be warning levels for inventory, warning management that:

- the materials item should now be reordered (the reorder level)
- the inventory level is too high (a maximum inventory level) or
- the inventory level is getting dangerously low (a minimum inventory level).

It is assumed that it is management policy to avoid running out of any item of inventory. In other words, it is assumed that there will be no stock-out of any material item.

- The material item must be re-ordered when the inventory level falls to the reorder quantity: If the item is not reordered at this point there will be some risk of a stock-out during the supply lead time, before the new purchase quantity is received.
- If the inventory level is higher than the maximum inventory level, something unusual must have happened. For example the supplier might have delivered a new order quantity much sooner than usual (and much sooner than expected) or demand for the item must be below even the expected minimum.
- If the inventory level falls below the minimum level, this should act as a warning to the stores manager that there might be a stock-out. The stores manager might need to check with the supplier about why there is a delay in the delivery, and how soon a new delivery of the material item can be expected.

4.1 Reorder level

A new quantity of materials should be ordered when current inventory reaches the reorder level for that material.

- If the supply lead time (time between placing an order and receiving delivery) is constant or certain, the reorder level is:

  [Demand for the material item per day/week] × [Lead time in days/weeks]

- If the supply lead time is uncertain or not constant, but demand during the lead time is constant, there should be a safety level of inventory. The **reorder level should be**:

  [Demand for the material item per day/week] × [Maximum supply lead time in days/weeks]

Safety inventory

The reorder level is therefore set at the maximum expected consumption of the material item during the supply lead time. This is more than the average usage during the supply lead time. As a result, more inventory is held that is needed on average.

If the order quantity is Q, the average inventory level is Q/2 + 'safety inventory'.

Safety inventory is the average amount of inventory held in excess of average requirements in order to remove the risk of a stock-out (or 'inventory out'). The size of the safety inventory is calculated as follows:

		Units
Reorder level	(Demand per day × Maximum lead time)	A
Average usage in the lead time period	(Demand per day × Average lead time)	B
Safety inventory		(A – B)

The cost of holding safety inventory is the size of the safety inventor multiplied by the holding cost per unit.

4.2 Maximum inventory level

The inventory level should never exceed a maximum level. If it does, something unusual has happened to either the supply lead time or demand during the supply lead time.

When demand during the supply lead time is constant, the maximum inventory level is:

Reorder level + Reorder quantity – [Demand for the material item per day/week × Minimum supply lead time in days/weeks]

This maximum level should occur at the time that a new delivery of the item has been received from the supplier. The supply lead time is short; therefore there are still some units of inventory when the new delivery is received.

4.3 Minimum inventory level

The inventory level could be dangerously low if it falls below a minimum warning level. When inventory falls below this amount, management should check that a new supply will be delivered before all the inventory is used up, so that there will be no stock-out.

When demand during the supply lead time is constant, the minimum (warning) level for inventory is:

Reorder level – [Demand for the material item per day/week × Average lead time in days/weeks]

Example

A company uses material item BC56. The reorder quantity for this material is 12,000 units. Weekly usage of the item is 1,500 units per week, but there is some uncertainty about the length of the lead time between ordering more materials and receiving delivery from the supplier.

	Supply lead time (weeks)
Average	2.5
Maximum	3
Minimum	1

Required

Calculate the reorder level, the maximum inventory level and the minimum inventory level for material item BC56.

Answer

Re-order level = [Demand for the material item per day/week] × [Maximum lead time in days/weeks]

Demand per week	1,500 units
Maximum lead time (weeks)	3 weeks
Re-order level	**4,500 units**

Maximum inventory level = Reorder level + Reorder quantity - [Demand for the material item per day/week × Minimum lead time in days/weeks]

		Units
Re-order level		6,000
Reorder quantity		12,000
Demand per week	1,500 units	
Minimum lead time (weeks)	× 1 week	
		(1,500)
Maximum inventory level		**16,500**

Minimum inventory level = Reorder level - [Demand for the material item per day/week × Average lead time in days/weeks]

		Units
Re-order level		6,000
Demand per week	1,500 units	
Average lead time (weeks)	× 2.5 weeks	
Subtract:		(3,750)
Minimum inventory level		**2,250**

Labour costs: direct and indirect labour costs

- Elements of labour costs
- Direct and indirect labour costs
- Recording labour costs

5 Labour costs: direct and indirect labour costs

5.1 Elements of labour costs

Labour costs consist of:

- the basic wages and salaries of employees
- additional payments for overtime working
- bonuses and other payments on top of basic pay and overtime (such as contributions paid by the employer into a pension scheme for its employees).

5.2 Direct and indirect labour costs

In an earlier chapter, it was explained that a distinction is made in cost accounting between direct labour employees and indirect labour employees. Direct labour employees are those who work directly on the goods or services produced by the entity.

The general rule is that direct labour costs are the costs of direct labour employees and indirect labour costs are the costs of indirect labour employees. However, there are some exceptions to this general rule, and some costs of direct labour employees are treated as indirect labour costs. Two exceptions are:

- the cost of idle time
- the cost of overtime premium.

Idle time

Idle time is time when employees are paid and are available to work, but are not doing any active work The cause of idle time could be a breakdown in production equipment or a delay in the delivery of materials from a supplier. Idle time might also occur when there are no orders from customers, and there will be no more work until the next order arrives.

Idle time should be treated as an indirect labour cost. However, in order to treat idle time as an indirect cost, the cost accounting system must be able to identify the amount of time that is lost as idle time. To do this, idle time must be recorded on labour time sheets (which are often used to document the use of labour time, for the purpose of cost accounting).

Overtime premium

When hourly-paid employees work hours in excess of their normal working hours, they are usually paid 'overtime' at a higher rate of pay per hour than the basic rate.

- The total rate of pay per hour is the basic rate per hour plus an overtime 'premium'.
- Total overtime hourly rate = Basic hourly rate + Overtime premium.

For example, if the basic rate of pay is $20 per hour and overtime is paid at time and a half (100% + 50% = 150% of the basic rate), the overtime premium is $10 per hour and the total overtime pay is $30 per hour.

In costing systems, it is usual to separate the labour cost at the basic rate per hour from the cost of the overtime premium. This is because overtime premium costs are usually treated as an indirect labour cost (an overhead cost) and should be measured separately.

Example

During one week, Masha works 46 hours. This includes 8 hours of overtime working. Her basic rate of pay is $10 per hour and overtime is paid at time and a half, the overtime rate per hour is $10 × 150% = $15, consisting of the $10 basic rate plus a premium of $5 per hour.

Her weekly cost is calculated as follows, keeping the overtime premium separate from the basic pay for the hours worked.

	$
Basic pay – 46 hours × $10	460
Overtime premium (8 hours × $10 × 50%)	40
Total weekly pay	500

The reason why overtime premium is usually treated as an indirect labour cost is that when employees are paid for working hours of overtime, it is a matter of chance what work they are doing in normal hours and what work they do in overtime. It is therefore 'unfair' to charge the work done in overtime directly with the overtime premium.

The main rules about whether production labour costs should be treated as a direct labour cost or as an indirect labour cost can be summarised as follows.

	Direct labour costs	Indirect labour costs
Direct labour employees	Basic wage or salary for hours worked	
	Overtime premium only if the overtime hours are worked specifically at a customer's request	In most cases, the overtime premium cost of hours worked in overtime

	Direct labour costs	Indirect labour costs
		In most cases, all other costs of direct labour employees. This includes: • the cost of all hours recorded as 'idle time' – time spent doing nothing • the cost of other hours spent away from direct production work, such as time spent on training courses.
Indirect labour employees		All labour costs of indirect labour employees

5.3 Recording labour costs

In a cost accounting system, there must be a system for relating the cost of labour to work that is done. There are various ways in which labour time might be recorded, but the main methods are:

- payroll records
- time sheets or similar time records

Payroll records can be used to:

- identify employees as direct labour or indirect labour employees
- charge the labour costs of each employee to the department (cost centre) where he or she is employed.

Time sheets or similar time recording systems can be used within a cost centre to record the time spent by each employee on different activities or tasks (or as idle time). Time sheets are not necessary if an employee does the same work all the time. For example, it is not necessary to prepare time sheets for a machine worker if the employee spends all his time working at the same machine producing the same items of output.

However, time sheets are needed if employees spend time on more than one cost item, so that their labour cost has to be allocated to the different cost items. For example, a manufacturing centre might product two products, Product A and Product B, and a direct labour employee might spend time working on both products. Time sheets can be used to record the time spent on each product, so that the labour cost can be allocated to each product according to the amount of time spent on each. Similarly time sheets are needed to work out the labour cost of specific jobs or contracts: the time spent by employees on each job or contract should be recorded, so that the cost of the time can be allocated and the labour cost for each job or contract can be calculated.

Accounting for labour costs

Within a cost accounting system, indirect and direct labour costs are recorded and charged to the appropriate cost centres and cost units. The records of labour costs are included within the double-entry cost accounting system (where such a costing system is used).

Accounting for labour costs with 'ledger entries' in a cost accounting system is explained in a later chapter.

Labour costs: remuneration methods

- Calculating the cost of labour
- Time-based systems
- Piecework systems
- Incentive schemes

6 Labour costs: remuneration methods

6.1 Calculating the cost of labour

The labour cost of a product, service, job or activity is calculated as the cost of paying the employees to do the work. Labour costs are allocated between different jobs or activities on the basis of the time spent working on each job or activity.

Many employees are paid a fixed salary each month. Their costs are allocated to the departments they work in and to the activities they perform on a time basis. For example, if an employee spends half his time on one type of activity and half of his time on another activity, the cost of his labour will be divided 50:50 between the two activities.

Some employees are paid by the hour, and a few are paid a piecework rate. The labour costs of these employees can be measured and charged to the units of work they produce.

6.2 Time-based systems

When employees are paid an hourly rate, their basic pay (per week or month) is calculated as follows:

Basic pay = Hours worked × Rate of pay per hour

Production records should kept of the time spent by these employees on specific jobs or batches of production, so that the labour cost for this work can be measured accurately.

As explained earlier, any overtime premium for overtime working is usually treated as an indirect labour cost. (Overtime premium is charged as a direct cost only when the overtime is worked for a specific purpose, for example to meet specific demands by a customer for meeting a delivery date.)

6.3 Piecework systems

In piecework systems, employees are usually paid a certain amount for the number of units of output produced:

Basic pay = Units produced × Rate paid per unit produced

Example

A worker in a textile company sews buttons on shirts. She is paid $0.20 for each shirt that she completes. During one week, she completes 800 shirts.

Her pay for the week, and the labour cost of sewing buttons on the 800 shirts, is: 800 × $0.20 = $160.

Differential piecework systems

Differential piecework systems encourage employees to increase the number of units they produce by paying higher rates per unit when more units are produced.

It is quite common for employees involved in piecework schemes to be paid a guaranteed minimum wage so that their earnings do not suffer too much when production levels are low because of circumstances outside of their control.

For example, as employee is paid the following rates of pay:

Production	Rate of pay per unit
Units	$
0 – 100	1.50
101 – 200	1.75
201 – 300	2.00

The company pays a guaranteed minimum ways of $300 per week. In a week, the employee produces 220 units. How much are his earnings for the week?

Production	Rate of pay per unit	Earnings
Units	$	$
0 – 100	1.50	150
101 – 200	1.75	175
201 – 300	2.00	40
		365

Don't forget that if the employee had earned less than $300, he still would have been paid the guaranteed minimum wage of $300 per week.

6.4 Incentive schemes

Employees might be offered an incentive or bonus payment for improving their productivity, or for achieving certain production targets during a period. The purpose of an incentive scheme for greater productivity should be to:

- increase total production output with the same number of employees, or
- achieve the same total output volume, but in fewer hours of work.

Some of the benefits of the productivity improvement are given to the employees, in the form of a bonus. This should give them an incentive to achieve the productivity improvement. Incentive schemes may be based on:

- an individual's performance or
- the performance of a work group as a whole.

Individual incentive schemes and group incentive schemes are similar for the purpose of cost accounting.

(If the cost of a bonus payment can be traced directly to a cost unit it should be treated as a direct labour cost. If it is difficult to trace the cost of a bonus payment to a specific cost unit, for example because it is paid at a much later date, it will be recorded as an indirect labour cost.)

The employer (company) also benefits from the productivity improvements, because the unit cost of production should be reduced. If the total reduction in costs is greater than the additional amount paid to employees, the company will benefit.

Example

A manufacturing company produces 1,000 units of a product each week. This requires 900 direct labour hours. Direct labour employees are paid $12 per hour.

The company introduces an incentive scheme, in which it will pay a bonus of 5% of the basic rate per hour worked if productivity can be improved by 10%, and either:

- the employees can make 10% more units each week in 900 hours, or
- the employees can produce 1,000 units each week in 10% fewer hours.

Does this bonus scheme benefit the company? If so, by how much?

Answer

At the moment the weekly cost of direct labour is 900 hours × $12 = $10,800, and the direct labour cost per unit is $10,800/1,000 = $10.80.

(a) If 10% more units are made each week in the same number of hours (900 hours), the labour cost will be (including the bonus of 5%):

- 900 hours × $12 × 1.05 = $11,340.
- The cost per unit will be $11,340/1,100 = $10.31.
- The cost per unit will fall by $0.49 or 4.5%.

(b) If 1,000 units are made each week in only 810 hours (90% x 900), the direct labour cost will be (including the bonus of 5%):

- 810 hours × $12 × 1.05 = $10,206.
- The cost per unit will be $10,206/1,000 = $10.21.
- The cost per unit will fall by $0.59 or 5.5%.

Labour efficiency and labour turnover

- Labour efficiency ratio (productivity ratio)
- Capacity utilisation ratio
- Production volume ratio
- Labour turnover rate
- Costs and causes of labour turnover

7 Labour efficiency and labour turnover

7.1 Labour efficiency ratio (productivity ratio)

Non-financial information might be provided to management about labour performance. Performance measurements include the labour efficiency ratio or productivity ratio:

$$\text{Labour efficiency ratio} = \frac{\text{Expected time to produce the output (in hours)}}{\text{Actual time to produce the output (in hours)}} \times 100\%$$

When output is produced in exactly the time expected, the efficiency ratio is 100%. When output is produced more quickly than expected, the efficiency ratio is above 100%.

Example

During July, a factory produced 3,600 units of a product. The expected production time is 3 direct labour hours for each unit. The actual number of direct labour hours worked in the month was 10,000 hours.

$$\text{Efficiency ratio} = \left[\frac{(3{,}600 \times 3 \text{ hours})}{10{,}000 \text{ hours}}\right] \times 100\% = 108\%$$

Efficiency ratio and idle time

When a labour efficiency ratio is calculated, the actual hours worked should **exclude** any hours recorded as idle time.

7.2 Capacity utilisation ratio

Employees are not always engaged in active work during the time they attend the work place. Employees might be 'idle' for several reasons, such as waiting for the next work to come along, or because of a halt in production due to a machine breakdown.

A capacity utilisation ratio is a ratio that measures the actual hours actively working as a percentage of the actual hours that were available for working.

$$\text{Capacity utilisation ratio} = \frac{\text{Hours spent in active working}}{\text{Total hours available for work}} \times 100\%$$

Example

A production department has 6 employees who each work 40 hours a week. In a particular week, the recorded idle time was 25 hours.

Total hours available for work = 6 employees × 40 hours = 240 hours.

Capacity utilisation ratio = [(240 – 25)/240] × 100% = 89.6%

7.3 Production volume ratio

Labour activity can also be measured by a production volume ratio which is calculated as follows:

$$\text{Production volume ratio} = \frac{\text{Expected time to produce the output}}{\text{Total hours available for work}} \times 100\%$$

The production volume ratio can be calculated as follows:

Production volume ratio = Labour efficiency ratio × Capacity utilisation ratio

Example

During May there were 21 working days of 8 hours per day. The workforce consists of 10 employees, who all do the same work.

Due to problems in the production system and a machine breakdown, 240 hours were recorded as idle time during the month.

During May, the workforce produced 5,400 units of output. The expected time per unit of output is 15 minutes (= 0.25 hours).

Required

Calculate, for May:

(a) the efficiency ratio

(b) the capacity utilisation ratio

(c) the production volume ratio

Answer

To calculate the efficiency ratio, the hours worked should exclude idle time. Hours worked = (21 days × 8 hours × 10 employees) – 240 hours idle time = 1,680 – 240 = 1,440 hours.

(a) **Efficiency ratio**
Expected time to produce 5,400 units = 5,400 × 0.25 hours = 1,350 hours.
Efficiency ratio = (1,350/1,440) × 100% = 93.75%

(b) **Capacity utilisation ratio**
Active hours worked/Hours available
= (1,440 hours/1,680 hours) × 100% = 85.71%

(c) **Production volume ratio**
Expected time to produce 5,400 units/Total hours available
= (1,350 hours/1,680 hours) × 100% = 80.35%.

Efficiency ratio × Capacity utilisation ratio = Production volume ratio
93.75% × 85.71% = 80.35%.

7.4 Labour turnover rate

Labour turnover occurs when employees leave their job and have to be replaced. The labour turnover rate is a measure of the rate at which employees are leaving and have to be replaced.

$$\frac{\text{Number of employees leaving/being replaced each year}}{\text{Average number of employee positions in the year}} \times 100\%$$

Example

A company employs 4,800 employees. During the past 12 months, 660 employees left the company and had to be replaced.

$$\text{Labour turnover rate} = 100\% \times \left(\frac{660}{4{,}800}\right) = 13.75\%$$

Example

A company employed 2,800 people at the beginning of the year. During the year 420 people left and 450 were recruited. There were 2,830 employees at the end of the year.

Average number of employees = (2,800 + 2,830)/2 = 2,815
Labour turnover rate = (420/2,815) × 100% = 14.9%.

Exercise 2

A company employed 600 employees at the beginning of the year and 630 employees at the end of the year. During the past 12 months, 35 employees left the company and had to be replaced.

What was the labour turnover rate?

7.5 Costs and causes of labour turnover

The main cause of labour turnover is when employees leave one company to go and work for another.

Labour turnover can be very costly for an employer, and result in higher costs.

- When employees leave, their experience is lost. New employees taking their place are less experienced, and will be less efficient until they learn how to do the job. A high labour turnover, by reducing efficiency, increases costs.
- New employees might make many more mistakes, and so there will be additional costs of correcting faulty work.
- New employees might have to be trained, and there will be additional training costs.
- A very high labour turnover rate could have an adverse effect on the morale and efficiency of the employees who remain in their jobs.

Practice multiple choice questions

1 The demand for an item of material is 8,000 units each year. The cost of making an order is $240. The purchase cost per unit is $9 and the holding cost of inventory is 6% per annum of the purchase cost. Using the economic order quantity formula, what quantity of the item should be purchased in each order (to the nearest unit)?

A 800

B 843

C 1,886

D 2,667 ***(1 mark)***

2 A manufacturing company uses the economic order quantity (EOQ) formula to decide the purchase quantities for its main items of raw materials. Due to an increase in interest rates, the cost of holding inventory has increased. What will be the effect of this cost increase on the EOQ for each raw material item and on annual ordering costs?

A The EOQ will be lower and annual ordering costs higher.

B The EOQ will be lower and annual ordering costs will not be affected.

C The EOQ will be higher and annual ordering costs lower.

D The EOQ will be higher and annual ordering costs higher. ***(2 marks)***

3 A company uses the economic order quantity formula to decide the purchase quantity for materials. The purchase cost of item 1234 is $25 per unit. Annual demand is 10,000 units. The annual holding cost is $2.50 per unit and ordering costs are $500 per order. The supplier is offering a reduction is the purchase price to $23 per unit on all orders of 5,000 units or more.

Which one of the following statements is correct?

A The company will minimise its total annual costs if it continues to purchase in the economic order quantity of 1,000 units per order.

B The company will minimise its total annual costs if it continues to purchase in the economic order quantity of 2,000 units per order.

C The company will minimise its total annual costs if it takes the large order discount and purchases in quantities of 5,000 units per order.

D The company will minimise its total annual costs if it takes the large order discount and purchases in quantities of 10,000 units per order. ***(2 marks)***

4 A company manufactures Product Z in batches. Output capacity is 1,000 units of Product Z per week but demand is only 200 units per week. There are 50 weeks in each year. The annual cost of holding finished units o Product Z in store is $2 per unit per year. Set-up costs for a batch of Product Z are $800 per batch.

What batch production quantity for Product Z will minimise total annual costs, to the nearest 100 units?

A 400 units

B 2,800 units

C 3,200 units

D 7,100 units ***(2 marks)***

5 A production department uses Component P to manufacture a product. This component is purchased from an external supplier in quantities of 3,000 units per order. Daily usage is 150 units of the component each day. The supply lead time is normally 6 days, but might be as little as 4 days or as much as 10 days.

To avoid the risk of running out of inventory of Component P, what should be the reorder level for this item?

A 3,900 units

B 1,500 units

C 900 units

D 600 units ***(2 marks)***

6 A production department consists of 15 direct labour employees who each work 36 hours per week. Output from the department is expected to be 4 units of product per direct labour hour worked. During a particular week, the department recorded 500 hours of time spent working on production and actual output was 2,100 units of the product.

What was the production volume ratio for the department for the week?

A 92.5%

B 97.2%

C 102.9%

D 105.0% ***(2 marks)***

7 A company employed 5,700 employees at the end of a financial year. During the year 600 employees left the company and 360 were recruited.

What was the rate of labour turnover in the year?

A 10.3%

B 10.5%

C 10.8%

D 16.5% ***(2 marks)***

CHAPTER 6

Accounting for overheads

Contents

Definition and purpose of absorption costing

- Introduction to absorption costing
- The treatment of direct and indirect expenses
- Definition of absorption costing
- The purpose of absorption costing

1 Definition and purpose of absorption costing

1.1 Introduction to absorption costing

This chapter describes the basic principles and methods of absorption costing. Absorption costing is a method of costing in which overhead costs are added to the cost of cost units, and a 'full cost' is calculated. The full cost of an item is the prime cost plus a share of overhead costs.

The absorption costing method can be used in either manufacturing industries or service industries, but it is more commonly associated with costing for manufacturing. This is because in manufacturing there are usually large quantities of inventory, and work-in-progress and finished goods are normally valued (or 'costed') to include some production overhead costs.

The absorption costing method therefore focuses mainly on production costs and the treatment of production overheads.

1.2 The treatment of direct and indirect expenses

In cost accounting, direct and indirect costs are treated differently.

- Direct costs are charged directly to the cost of production. They are directly identified with cost units, batches of production, a production process or a job or a contract.
- **Overheads are indirect costs**, and cannot be identified directly with specific cost units, jobs or processes etc. They are therefore recorded as overhead costs, and a distinction is made between production overheads, administration overheads and sales and distribution (marketing) overheads.

Overhead costs can then be treated in either of two ways.

- **Method 1 – Marginal costing**. They might be treated as period costs, and charged as an expense against the period in which they are incurred, without any attempt to add a share of the overhead costs to the cost of units of production.
- **Method 2 – Absorption costing**. They might be shared out between cost units or processes. Overhead costs might be charged to cost units in addition to direct costs, so that the cost of goods sold (the cost of cost units) includes a fair share of overhead costs.

	\$ per unit
Direct material costs	A
Direct production labour cost	B
Production overheads	C
Full production cost	(A + B + C) = D
Administration overhead	E
Sales and distribution overhead	F
Full cost of sale	D + E + F

This chapter deals with absorption costing. In absorption costing, a share of overhead costs is added to direct costs, to obtain a 'full cost' or a 'fully absorbed cost' for cost units. This chapter explains the methods that are used to calculate the amount of overhead costs to add to unit costs in order to obtain a full cost per unit. Marginal costing is explained in a later chapter.

1.3 Definition of absorption costing

Absorption costing is based on the idea that the cost of a product or a service should be:

- its direct costs (direct materials, direct labour and sometimes direct expenses)
- plus a share of overhead costs.

Absorption costing is therefore a system of costing in which a share of overhead costs is added to direct costs, to obtain a full cost. This might be:

- a full production cost, or
- a full cost of sale.

An absorption costing system might be used to decide the **full production cost** of the product, so that only a share of production overheads is added to product costs. Administration overheads and selling and distribution overheads are simply charged as an expense to the period in which they occur.

Income statement: absorption costing	\$000	\$000	\$000
Sales			950
Cost of inventory at the beginning of the period		80	
Production cost of items manufactured in the period:			
Direct materials	280		
Direct labour	120		
Direct expenses (if any)	0		
Production overhead added to cost ('absorbed')	240		
		640	
		720	
Less: Cost of inventory at the end of the period		(120)	
Production cost of items sold			600
Gross profit			350
Administration overhead		100	
Selling and distribution overhead		200	
			300
Net operating profit			50

Inventory valuation is an important feature of absorption costing, because the cost of production in any period depends partly on the valuation of opening and closing inventory, including work-in-progress and finished goods inventory.

In some costing systems, a share of administration overhead and selling and distribution overhead might be added to the full production cost, to obtain a **full cost of sale**. However, it is not common practice to calculate a full cost of sale, because it has only limited value as management information.

1.4 The purpose of absorption costing

There are several reasons why absorption costing is sometimes used, and production overhead costs are added to direct costs to calculate the full production cost of products (or services).

- There is a view that inventory should include a fair share of production overhead cost. This view is applied in financial accounting and financial reporting. It can therefore be argued that inventory should be valued in a similar way in the cost accounting system. (However, inventory valuations may differ between the cost accounts and the financial accounts.)
- There is also a view that in order to assess the profitability of products or services, it is appropriate to charge products and services with a fair share of overhead costs. Unless products contribute sufficiently to covering indirect costs, its 'profitability' might be too low, and the business as a whole might not be profitable.

Criticisms of absorption costing

There are criticisms of absorption costing. The main criticisms are as follows:

- Absorption costing does not provide reliable information about profitability. Methods of charging overhead costs to products, as we shall see, are not 'scientific', and rely on fairly arbitrary assump[illegible]
- There are better methods of measuring profitability, such as marginal costing. There are also better ways of providing cost information to help managers make decisions (relevant costs). Marginal costing and relevant costs are explained in later chapters.

When absorption costing was first used in manufacturing, well over 100 years ago, total overhead costs were fairly small compared with direct costs. Manufacturing was labour-intensive, and direct labour costs were a significant proportion of total costs. Adding a share of overheads to product costs, usually in proportion to the cost of direct labour or direct labour time, was therefore a reasonable method of dealing with overhead costs.

In a modern manufacturing environment, however, direct labour is a fairly small proportion of total costs. Most work in production now consists of the 'support' activities of indirect labour employees, and the cost of this labour is an overhead cost. Overhead costs are high compared to direct labour costs. As a consequence, it is often argued that a costing system should use a different approach to overhead costing, and try to present overhead costs in a way that is more useful to management for information purposes. One such technique, activity based costing, is outside the scope of the syllabus.

Stages in absorption costing

- Cost centres and general expenses
- Allocation, apportionment and absorption (recovery)
- Overhead cost allocation

2 Stages in absorption costing

2.1 Cost centres and general expenses

In a system of absorption costing, each item of overhead cost is charged either:

- to a cost centre, or
- as a general expense.

The cost centres might be:

- a cost centre in the production function (production overhead)
- a cost centre in administration (= administration overhead)
- a cost centre in sales and distribution (= sales and distribution overhead).

The cost centres in the production function might be:

- a department engaged directly in production work (a production department), or
- a department or service section engaged in support activities, such as inventory management, production planning and control, quality control, repairs and maintenance, and so on (= '**service departments**').

In a system of absorption costing, overheads are charged to products or services on the basis of this structure of cost centres and general expenses.

2.2 Allocation, apportionment and absorption (recovery)

There are three main stages in absorption costing for charging overhead costs to the cost of production and cost units:

- **Allocation.** Overheads are allocated to cost centres. If a cost centre is responsible for the entire cost of an item of expenditure, the entire cost is charged directly to the cost centre.
- **Apportionment.** Many overhead costs are costs that cannot be allocated directly to one cost centre, because they are shared by two or more cost centres. These costs are apportioned between the cost centres. 'Apportionment' means sharing on a fair basis.
- **Absorption** (also called overhead **'recovery'**). When overheads have been allocated and apportioned to production cost centres, they are charged to the cost of products manufactured in the cost centre. The method of charging

overheads to cost units is to establish a charging rate (an absorption rate or recovery rate) and to apply this rate to all items of production.

Allocation	Overhead costs are recorded. Initially they are allocated to a cost centre or recorded as a general expense
Apportionment	Overhead costs are shared between the departments or activities that benefit from them
Absorption (Overhead recovery)	Overheads are added to the cost of cost units, using a fair basis for charging (absorption costing only)

2.3 Overhead cost allocation

Many items of indirect cost cannot be charged directly to a cost unit (a unit of product or service), but they can be charged directly to a cost centre (for example, a department or work group). Items of expense that can be identified with a specific cost centre should be charged in full as a cost to the cost centre. The process of charging costs directly to cost centres is called cost **allocation.**

In absorption costing for a manufacturing company, overhead costs may be allocated to:

- **production departments** or production centres: these are cost centres that are directly engaged in manufacturing the products
- **service departments** or service centres: these are cost centres that provide support to the production departments, but are not directly engaged in production, such as engineering, repairs and maintenance, the production stores and materials handling department (raw materials inventory), production planning and control, and so on
- administration departments
- selling departments and distribution departments.

Production overheads are the overhead costs of both the production departments and the service departments.

Overhead costs that cannot be directly allocated to a cost centre must be shared (apportioned) between two or more cost centres.

For example:

- The salary of the manager of the production planning department can be allocated directly as a cost of the production planning cost centre, which is a service department cost centre within production.

- Similarly the rental cost of equipment used by engineers in the maintenance department can be allocated directly as a cost of the maintenance department, which is also a service department cost centre within production.
- If the machining department has its own electricity power supply, electricity charges for the machining department can be allocated directly to the department, which is a production department cost centre.
- The salary of a supervisor in the finishing department can be allocated directly to the finishing department, which is also a production department cost centre.
- The cost of security guards for the manufacturing site cannot be allocated to any specific department or cost centre; therefore security guard services are likely to be recorded as a general production overhead expense, and the cost is allocated to 'security services'.

Overhead apportionment

- The apportionment of shared costs between cost centres
- The basis of apportionment

3 Overhead apportionment

3.1 The apportionment of shared costs between cost centres

Some costs cannot be allocated in full to a cost centre, because they are shared by two or more cost centres. These are divided between the cost centres on a fair basis. The process of dividing the shared costs is called **apportionment.**

Shared costs may be divided between administration cost centres and selling and distribution cost centres, as well as production centres and service centres. However, examination questions on absorption costing will usually concentrate on production overhead costs.

The apportionment of production overhead costs might be in two stages:

- sharing (or dividing) general costs between production centres and service centres
- then sharing the costs of the service centres between the production centres.

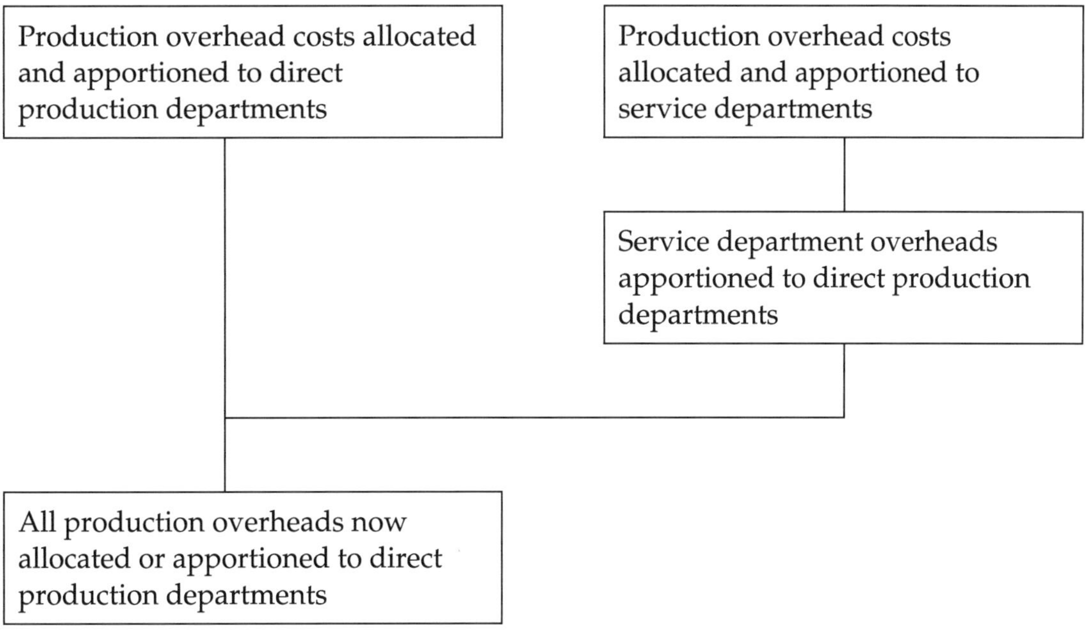

After this has been done, all the production overhead costs have been allocated or apportioned to the production centres. The total overhead costs of each production centre should be:

(1) costs allocated directly to the production centre, plus

(2) shared costs apportioned to the production centre, plus

(3) a share of the costs of each service department, apportioned to the production centre.

3.2 The basis of apportionment

Shared overhead costs should be apportioned on a fair basis between cost centres. For each item of shared expense, a 'fair' basis for apportionment must be selected.

Choosing the basis of apportionment for each cost is a matter of judgement, but there is often an 'obvious' basis to choose. For example, the rental cost of a building and the insurance costs for the building will be apportioned between the cost centres that use the building. The basis of apportionment will probably be to share the costs in relation to the floor space used by each cost centre.

In some cases, however, it might not be clear what the most suitable basis of apportionment should be, and the choice is then simply a matter of judgement and preference.

At the end of the apportionment process, all overhead costs should be allocated or apportioned to a cost centre.

Example: apportionment of shared costs

A manufacturing company has two production departments, Machining and Assembly, and two service departments, Repairs and Quality Control. The following information is available about production overhead costs.

	Total	Machining	Assembly	Repairs	Quality control
	$	$	$	$	$
Indirect labour cost	15,500	5,000	5,000	3,500	2,000
Indirect materials	5,300	1,500	2,400	1,000	400
Factory rental	14,400				
Power costs	4,800				
Depreciation (note 1)	14,000				
Building insurance	1,800				
Equipment insurance	4,200				
	60,000				

Note: Depreciation is a charge for the use of items of plant and equipment, such as machinery.

Indirect labour and indirect material costs have been allocated directly to these four cost centres. The other overhead costs are shared between the cost centres and so cannot be allocated directly.

Other information

	Total	Machining	Assembly	Repairs	Quality control
Cost of plant/equipment ($)	70,000	40,000	15,000	5,000	10,000
Floor area (square metres)	1,800	500	900	100	300
Kilowatt hours (000s)	800	600	100	50	50

Required

How should overheads be allocated and apportioned between the four cost centres?

Answer

The indirect labour costs and indirect materials costs are allocated directly to the cost centres. The basis of apportionment chosen for each of the other shared costs will be as follows:

Item of cost	Basis of apportionment	Rate of apportionment	
Factory rental	Floor area	$14,400/1,800 =	$8 per square metre
Power costs	Kilowatt hours	$4,800/800 =	$6 per kilowatt hour
Depreciation	Cost of plant and equipment	$14,000/$70,000 =	20% of cost
Building insurance	Floor area	$1,800/1,800 =	$1 per square metre
Equipment insurance	Cost of plant and equipment	$4,200/70,000 =	6% of cost

Make sure that you understand how the apportionment of costs is calculated. The rate of apportionment ensures that the total cost can be shared out in full between the cost centres.

These apportionment rates can be used to establish the amount of overheads to apportion to each of the four departments.

	Total	Machining	Assembly	Repairs	Quality control
	$	$	$	$	$
Indirect labour cost	15,500	5,000	5,000	3,500	2,000
Indirect materials	5,300	1,500	2,400	1,000	400
Factory rental	14,400	4,000	7,200	800	2,400
Power costs	4,800	3,600	600	300	300
Depreciation (note 1)	14,000	8,000	3,000	1,000	2,000
Building insurance	1,800	500	900	100	300
Equipment insurance	4,200	2,400	900	300	600
	60,000	25,000	20,000	7,000	8,000

If you are not sure how these figures are obtained, the workings for the machining department are shown below.

	Absorption rate		Machining
	$		$
Indirect labour cost: allocated	-		5,000
Indirect materials: allocated	-		1,500
Factory rental	$8 per square metre	× 500	4,000
Power costs	$6 per kilowatt hour	× 600	3,600
Depreciation (note 1)	20% of cost	× 40,000	8,000
Building insurance	$1 per square metre	× 500	500
Equipment insurance	6% of cost	× 40,000	2,400
Totasa overheads			25,000

Apportionment of service department costs

- The reciprocal method of apportioning service department costs
- Simple application of the reciprocal method
- Reciprocal method: repeated distribution technique
- Reciprocal method: simultaneous equations technique

4 Apportionment of service department costs

After production overheads have been allocated and apportioned to production departments and service departments, the costs of the service departments must then be apportioned to the production departments. When this has been done, all production overhead costs will have been allocated or apportioned to the production departments.

The purpose of doing this is to calculate an absorption rate for each production department. Absorption rates are used to add overhead costs to the costs of production (the cost of the cost units produced in the production department).

4.1 The reciprocal method of apportioning service department costs

There are several methods of apportionment of service department costs. Each method uses an **estimate of the proportion of its work** that each service department does for the other departments.

The only method of apportionment of service department costs that you need to know for your examination is called the **reciprocal method** of cost apportionment.

A feature of the reciprocal method is that when service department overheads are apportioned, the apportionment method allows for the work that each service department does for other service departments, as well as production departments. An example might help to illustrate this point.

Example

A manufacturing company has two production departments, Department 1 and Department 2. It also has two service departments, the factory canteen and the repairs department.

Allocated overhead costs and apportioned general overhead costs for each cost centre are as follows:

Department 1:	$100,000
Department 2:	$200,000
Canteen:	$150,000
Repairs:	$220,000

The repairs department does no work for the canteen: 75% of its time is spent on repair work for Department 1 and 25% of its time is spent on repair work for Department 2. There are 10 employees in Department 1, 20 employees in Department 2 and 20 employees in the repairs department.

How should the service department costs be apportioned between the production departments?

The costs of the canteen are $150,000 and a fair basis for apportioning these costs is the number of employees in each department. If we ignored the repairs department, the costs of the canteen would be divided between Department 1 and Department 2 in the ratio 10:20 respectively. However the repairs department has 20 employees, and it would be more fair to recognise the use that the repairs department makes of the factory canteen. The canteen costs should therefore be divided between Departments 1 and 2 and also the repairs department in the ratio 10:20:20.

The repairs department costs can be apportioned between Department 1 and Department 2 (since it does no work for the canteen) in the ratio 75:25 respectively. You might recognise that as a consequence of charging some canteen costs to the repairs department, Department 1 will lend up with a larger share of total production overhead costs than if the canteen costs had been charged directly to Departments 1 and 2.

The apportionment of overheads using the reciprocal method will therefore be as follows:

	Basis of apportionment	Department 1	Department 2	Canteen	Repairs
		$	$	$	$
Initial costs		100,000	200,000	150,000	220,000
Apportion canteen	(10:20:20)	30,000	60,000	(150,000)	60,000
					280,000
Apportion repairs	(75:25)	210,000	70,000	-	(280,000)
		340,000	330,000		

After the apportionment of the service department costs, Department 1 has overhead costs of $340,000 and Department 2 has overhead costs of $330,000. These add up to the total of all production overhead costs.

4.2 Simple application of the reciprocal method

In your examination, you are unlikely to be given a question with more than two service departments. This is because with three or more service departments, the computations to apportion the service centre costs can become lengthy – and too long for a 1 mark or 2 mark question.

The simplest application of the reciprocal method is in a situation where:

- there are two service centres
- one service centre does work for the production departments and also the other service centre

- the second service centre does work for the production departments, but not for the other service centre.

In this situation, the reciprocal method of service centre overhead apportionment is as follows:

- Begin by apportioning the overhead costs of the service centre that does work for the other service centre as well as the production departments, using a basis for apportionment that seems appropriate.
- Next, apportion the overheads of the service centre that does work only for the production departments. The overheads of this service centre will now include the overheads apportioned from the other service centre.
- Having done this, all overhead costs will be apportioned to the production departments.

The sequence in which the service centre costs are apportioned is important. With the reciprocal method, the costs of the service centre that does work for the other service centre must be apportioned first.

Example

A manufacturing company has two production departments, P1 and P2 and two service departments, S1 and S2. The following information is available.

	P1	P2	S1	S2
Allocated and apportioned production overheads	$200,000	$250,000	$195,000	$180,000
Work done by service department for other departments				
S1	40%	60%	-	-
S2	50%	25%	25%	-

The service centre costs should be apportioned using the reciprocal method, because this method fully recognises any work done by one service centre for another.

The service centre costs should be apportioned by apportioning the costs of S2 first. This is because S2 does work for S1 as well as the production departments

	Basis of apportionment	**P1**	**P2**	**S1**	**S2**
		$	$	$	$
Initial costs		200,000	250,000	195,000	180,000
Apportion S2	(50:25:25)	90,000	45,000	45,000	(180,000)
				240,000	
Apportion S1	(40:60)	96,000	144,000	(240,000)	
		386,000	439,000		

4.3 Reciprocal method: repeated distribution technique

It is quite possible that if you are given a question in your examination on service centre overhead cost apportionment, the situation will be as described in the previous examples, where only one service department does work for the other service department.

A situation may arise where both service departments do work for the other service department, as well as the production departments. When this happens, the process of apportioning service centre costs is more lengthy – possibly too lengthy for an examination question. Even so, it is useful to be aware of how to deal with a situation where each of two service departments does some work for the other service department.

In this type of situation, reciprocal apportionment can be done in either of two ways. Both give the same result:

- repeated distribution method
- simultaneous equations method.

The repeated distribution method is probably easier, but takes a bit longer. The simultaneous equations method is quicker, but it is important to get the arithmetic correct.

With the repeated distribution method, you should take each service department in turn. It does not matter which service department you take first. (However, you will probably complete the calculations more quickly if you start by selecting the service department that does the least amount of its work for the other service department.)

Taking each service department in turn, you should apportion all the allocated and apportioned overheads of the service department. The overheads should be apportioned to the other service department as well as to the production departments.

When you apportion the costs of each service department you will be apportioning some of the overhead costs apportioned from other service department(s).

When you have apportioned the costs of each service department once, repeat the process again. Keep on repeating the process until all the overheads have been apportioned to the production departments only, and the overheads of each service department are 0.

The repetitive nature of the overhead apportionment process explains the name of the technique – 'repeated distribution'.

Example

A manufacturing company has two production departments, Machining and Assembly, and two service departments, Repairs and Quality Control. The following information is available.

	Total	Machining	Assembly	Repairs	Quality control
Allocated/apportioned overhead costs	\$60,000	\$25,000	\$20,000	\$7,000	\$8,000
Work done by the service departments:					
Repairs	100%	60%	10%	-	30%
Quality Control	100%	30%	50%	20%	-

Required

The costs of the two service departments should be apportioned to the production departments, to establish the total overhead costs for each production department.

Answer

	Total	Machining	Assembly	Repairs	Quality control
	$	$	$	$	$
Allocated/apportioned overhead costs	60,000	25,000	20,000	7,000	8,000
Apportion costs of service departments:					
Repairs (60:10:30)		4,200	700	(7,000)	2,100
				0	10,100
Quality Control (30:50:20)		3,030	5,050	2,020	(10,100)
Now repeat:					
Repairs (60:10:30)		1,212	202	(2,020)	606
Quality Control (30:50:20)		182	303	121	(606)
Repeat again					
Repairs (60:10:30)		73	12	(121)	36
Quality Control (30:50:20)		11	18	7	(36)
Repeat again					
Repairs (60:10:30)		4	1	(7)	2
Quality Control (30:50:20)		1	1	0	(2)
	60,000	33,713	26,287	0	0

Comment

The total overhead costs of $60,000 have been apportioned. ($33,713 + $26,287 = $60,000).

4.5 Reciprocal method: simultaneous equations technique

This technique is an alternative to the repeated distribution technique, and should produce exactly the same final apportionment of overhead costs between the production departments.

The method is to create two equations for the apportionment of service department overheads. These are simultaneous equations, which must then be solved. The solutions to the simultaneous equations can then be used to calculate the overhead apportionment to each production department.

The technique will be illustrated using the previous example.

Example

The information is as follows:

	Total	Machining	Assembly	Repairs	Quality control
Allocated/apportioned overhead costs	$60,000	$25,000	$20,000	$7,000	$8,000
Work done by the service departments:					
Repairs	100%	60%	10%	-	30%
Quality Control	100%	30%	50%	20%	-

Step 1: formulate the simultaneous equations

The first step is to establish two simultaneous equations. There should be one equation for each service department.

Each equation should state the total amount of overheads that will be apportioned from the service department. This total overhead is the original overhead cost allocation/apportionment for the service department, plus the proportion of the costs of the other service department that will be apportioned to it.

Using the example, the two equations are formulated as follows.

- Let the total overheads apportioned from the Repairs department be X.
- Let the total overheads apportioned from the Quality Control department be Y.

X = Original overheads of Repairs department + 20% of Quality Control costs.
Y = Original overheads of Quality Control department + 30% of Repair costs.

This gives us:

- $X = 7{,}000 + 0.20Y$
- $Y = 8{,}000 + 0.30X$

Make sure that you understand these formulae. It is easy to get them wrong and confuse the percentage figure that goes into each equation. Here, the first equation (for overheads apportioned from the Repairs department) includes 20% of Quality Control costs because 20% of the costs of this service department are apportioned to Repairs.

Step 2

The next step is to solve these simultaneous equations.

Re-arrange the two equations:

$$\begin{array}{rcrcll} X & - & 0.2Y & = & 7{,}000 & \text{.........(1)} \\ -0.3X & + & Y & = & 8{,}000 & \text{.........(2)} \end{array}$$

Solve to find values for X and Y.

(You need to know how to solve simultaneous equations. The aim should be to multiply one of the equations – or both equations if necessary – so that the coefficient for either X or Y is the same in both equations. Then add the equations, or subtract one from the other, in order to get a value for either X or Y. Having obtained a value for X or Y, substitute this value in one of the simultaneous equations, in order to obtain the remaining unknown value, for Y or X.)

In this example, the easiest method of solution is to multiply equation (1) by 5, so that the coefficient for Y is -1. This matches the coefficient of + 1 in equation (2). Add the two equations to obtain a value for X.

$$\begin{array}{rcrcll} 5X & - & Y & = & 35{,}000 & \text{.........(1)} \times 5 = (3) \\ -0.3X & + & Y & = & 8{,}000 & \text{.........(2)} \\ \hline 4.7X & & & = & 43{,}000 & \text{.........(2)} + (3) \end{array}$$

$$X = 9{,}149 \quad (= 43{,}000/4.7)$$

Now substitute this value for X in equation (2)

$$-0.3X + Y = 8{,}000$$
$$Y = 8{,}000 + 0.3\,(9{,}149)$$
$$Y = 10{,}745$$

Step 3

Use the values for X and Y that you have calculated to establish the total costs to apportion from the service department to each production department.

In this example:

- Of the total value of X, 60% is apportioned to Machining and 10% to Assembly
- Of the total value of Y, 30% is apportioned to Machining and 50% to Assembly.

	Machining	Assembly
	$	$
Allocated/apportioned overhead costs	25,000	20,000
Apportion costs of service departments:		
Repairs (60% and 10% of X = 9,149)	5,489	915
Quality Control (30% and 50% of Y =10,745)	3,224	5,372
Final apportionment	33,713	26,287

This is the same as with the repeated distribution method.

e 1

Exercise 1: reciprocal method of cost apportionment of service department costs

A manufacturing company has two production departments P1 and P2, and two service departments S1 and S2. The allocated and apportioned production overheads for each of the four departments are shown below, together with the proportion of the work of each service department that is done for the other departments.

	Total	P1	P2	S1	S2
Allocated/apportioned overhead costs	$92,000	$32,520	$22,000	$15,000	$22,480
Work done by the service departments:					
S1	100%	20%	60%	-	20%
S2	100%	70%	20%	10%	-

Required

Using the reciprocal method of cost apportionment for service department overheads:

- apportion the service department costs to production departments P1 and P2 and

- calculate the total allocated and apportioned overheads for each production department.

Overhead absorption

- Full production cost
- Overhead absorption rate (recovery rate)
- Departmental absorption rates or a factory-wide absorption rate?
- The treatment of non-production overheads

5 Overhead absorption

5.1 Full production cost

When all production overheads have been allocated or apportioned to the production departments, a rate can be calculated for absorbing the overheads into the cost of the cost units manufactured in each department. This is the **overhead absorption rate** or **overhead recovery rate**.

Cost unit	$
Direct materials cost	A
Direct labour cost	B
Production overheads absorbed	C
Full production cost	A + B + C

5.2 Overhead absorption rate (recovery rate)

The overhead absorption rate for a production department is calculated as follows:

$$\frac{\text{Total allocated and apportioned overheads}}{\text{Volume of activity in the period}}$$

The volume of activity can be any of the following:

Activity basis (volume of activity)	**Absorption rate**
Units produced in the period, but only if all units are identical	Absorption rate per unit. Not practical where units are not identical. However, used in standard costing.
Direct labour hours worked in the period	Absorption rate per direct labour hour. Commonly-used method.
Direct labour cost in the period	Overhead absorbed as a percentage of direct labour cost. Could be used when there are no records for direct labour hours worked.
Machine hours operated in the period	Absorption rate per machine hour. Commonly-used method in *machine-intensive* production departments.
Prime costs of production in the period (direct materials plus direct labour costs)	Overhead absorbed as a percentage of prime cost. This is uncommon.

The basis of activity selected for an absorption rate should be one that charges overhead costs to cost units on a fair basis. A rate per direct labour hour and a rate per machine hour are the most common methods, although a rate per unit is used in standard costing or where a single identical unit of product is manufactured..

Example: absorption rate

The allocated and apportioned overhead costs of Production Department X are $24,000 during a period when the department produces the following units of product:

	Product A	Product B	Product C
Units produced (quantity)	3,000	4,000	1,000
Prime cost per unit	$3	$4	$5
Direct labour hours per unit	0.1	0.2	0.4
Direct labour cost	$3,500	$8,000	$4,500
Machine hours per unit	0.2	0.1	0.2

It has been decided that production overheads will be absorbed on a direct labour hour basis.

The overhead absorption rate is calculated as follows.

Step 1: Calculate the total number of direct labour hours

	Direct labour hours
Product A: (3,000 units × 0.1 hours)	300
Product B: (4,000 units × 0.2 hours)	800
Product C: (1,000 units × 0.4 hours)	400
Total direct labour hours	1,500

Step 2: Calculate an absorption rate per direct labour hour

Production overhead expenditure	$24,000
Number of labour hours	1,500
Absorption rate per direct labour hour	$16

Step 3: Use this absorption rate to charge overhead costs to products

Overheads absorbed by each product:	$
Product A: (300 hours × $16)	4,800
Product B: (800 hours × $16)	12,800
Product C: (400 hours × $16)	6,400
Total	24,000

	Product A	Product B	Product C
	$	$	$
Prime cost per unit	3.00	4.00	5.00
Overhead at $16/direct labour hour	1.60	3.20	6.40
Full production cost/unit	4.60	7.20	11.40

The choice of the basis for absorbing overheads can have a significant effect on the overheads charged to each product or cost unit.

Exercise 2

(a) Calculate the overhead absorption rate and the full production cost per unit in the example above, if overheads are absorbed on a machine hour basis.

(b) Calculate the overhead absorption rate in the example above, if overheads are absorbed as a percentage of direct labour costs, and show how much overhead would be absorbed into the cost of each of the three products A, B and C.

5.3 Departmental absorption rates or a factory-wide absorption rate?

An overhead absorption rate can be calculated for each production department separately.

Alternatively, a single overhead absorption rate might be used for all the production departments in the factory. Calculating a single factory-wide rate involves less time and effort than calculating separate absorption rates for each production department within the factory. However, it might be argued that a single-factory wide absorption rate is less 'exact' or less 'fair' in sharing overhead costs between products or cost units.

Example: absorption rate

A manufacturing company has two production departments. Each department is involved in making two products, X and Y. Information about costs and production volume in the year is shown below:

	Production departments		**Products**	
	Department P1	**Department P2**	**Product X**	**Product Y**
Overhead costs	$60,000	$90,000		
Direct labour hours/unit:				
Product X	0.5 hours	2 hours		
Product Y	3.5 hours	1.5 hours		
Units produced			2,000	4,000

Required

Calculate the total production overhead cost/unit for Product X and Product Y using:

(1) separate departmental overhead rates for departments P1 and P2

(2) a single absorption rate for the entire factory.

Answer

Separate departmental rates

	Department P1		Department P2	
Direct labour hours		**hours**		**hours**
Product X	(2,000 × 0.5)	1,000	(2,000 × 2)	4,000
Product Y	(4,000 × 3.5)	14,000	(4,000 × 1.5)	6,000
		15,000		10,000
Overhead expenditure		$60,000		$90,000
Absorption rate/direct labour hour		$4		$9

Production overhead cost/unit	**Product X**	**Product Y**
	$	$
Department P1 (at $4/hour)	2	14.00
Department P2 (at $9/hour)	18	13.50
Total production overhead cost/unit	20	27.50

Single departmental rate

$$\frac{(\$60{,}000 + \$90{,}000)}{(15{,}000 + 10{,}000)\text{ hours}} = \$6 \text{ per direct labour hour}$$

Production overhead costs

- Product X: (0.5 hours + 2 hours) × $6 = $15 per unit of Product X.
- Product Y: (3.5 hours + 1.5 hours) × $6 = $30 per unit of Product Y.

In your examination, if you are given a question about overhead absorption rates, with two production departments, you should normally assume that you are required to calculate separate overhead absorption rates for each department.

5.4 The treatment of non-production overheads

In many costing systems, administration overheads and sales and distribution overheads are not absorbed into product costs. Instead, they are treated in full as an expense in the financial period to which they relate.

Non-production overhead costs are never added to the value of inventory. The main reason for absorbing production overheads is normally to calculate a value for inventory, for the purpose of measuring profit.

However, it is possible to add non-production overheads to the full production cost of units produced, to obtain a full cost of sale. When this happens, the basis for absorbing the overhead costs should be 'fair'.

- Administration overheads might be added as a percentage of production costs.
- Sales and distribution overheads might also be added as a percentage of production costs. Alternatively, they might be added as a percentage of the value of sales.

Example: non-production overheads

A company has budgeted to make and sell 100,000 units of Product X and 50,000 units of Product Y. Product X will sell for $5 per unit and Product Y will sell for $6 per unit.

The following costs have been budgeted.

	$
Full production cost, Product X	200,000
Full production cost, Product Y	100,000
Administration overheads	120,000
Sales and distribution overheads	200,000

Administration overheads will be absorbed into product costs as a percentage of full production costs. Selling and distribution overheads will be absorbed as a percentage of sales revenue.

Required

Calculate the cost of sales for each product and the budgeted profit for each product.

Answer

Budgeted administration overheads = $120,000
Budgeted production costs ($200,000 + $100,000) = $300,000.
Absorption rate for administration overheads = (120,000/300,000) × 100% = 40% of production cost.

	$
Budgeted sales revenue, Product X (100,000 × $5)	500,000
Budgeted sales revenue, Product Y: (50,000 × $6)	300,000
Total budgeted sales revenue	800,000
Budgeted sales and distribution costs	200,000

Absorption rate for sales and distribution overheads = (200,000/800,000) × 100% = 25% of budgeted sales revenue.

	Product X		Product Y	
	$	$	$	$
Sales		500,000		300,000
Production costs	200,000		100,000	
Administration costs (40% of production cost)	80,000		40,000	
Sales and distribution costs (25% of sales revenue)	125,000		75,000	
Full cost of sale		405,000		215,000
Profit		95,000		85,000

Under-absorbed and over-absorbed overheads

- Problem with calculating actual overhead costs
- Calculating a predetermined overhead rate
- Under-absorption or over-absorption of overheads
- The reasons for under- or over-absorption: expenditure and volume variances

6 Under-absorbed and over-absorbed overheads

6.1 Problem with calculating actual overhead costs

There is a serious problem with calculating production overhead absorption rates using actual overhead expenditure and actual activity levels (actual production volume).

Overhead rates are normally calculated for the entire financial year, and the same absorption rate is used throughout the year. If overhead rates are based on actual overhead expenditure and actual direct labour hours or machine hours, it would be necessary to wait until the end of the financial year to calculate any overhead absorption rates and product costs. This is unacceptable, because of the delay in providing management information about costs and profitability.

The cost accountant needs to know what the overhead absorption rate is in order to calculate product costs as soon as the products are manufactured. For this to be possible, the absorption rate must be decided in advance, for the entire financial year.

Predetermined absorption rates are therefore calculated and used. The absorption rates are calculated in advance using estimates for cost and production volume in the annual financial plan or **budget.**

6.2 Calculating a predetermined overhead rate

The predetermined overhead absorption rates are calculated from:

- budgeted (planned) overhead expenditure, and
- the budgeted volume or activity levels (planned labour hours or machine hours).

The method of calculating a predetermined overhead rate, either for separate production departments or as a factory-wide rate, are the processes of allocation, apportionment and absorption that have already been described. Budgeted data is used, rather than data about actual costs and output.

6.3 Under absorption or over absorption of overheads

Actual overhead expenditure and actual production volume will almost certainly be different from the planned expenditure and production volume. This means that the production overheads absorbed into product costs will be higher or lower than the actual production overhead expenditure.

- **Over-absorption**. If the amount of production overheads absorbed into product costs is more than the actual production overhead expenditure, there **is over-absorbed overhead.** Too much overhead cost has been charged to production costs, because actual costs were lower. The over-absorbed overhead is accounted for as an adjustment to the profit in the period, and is added to profit in the cost accounting income statement.
- **Under-absorption**. If the amount of production overheads absorbed into product costs is less than the actual production overhead expenditure, there is **under-absorbed overhead.** Not enough overhead cost has been charged to production costs, because actual costs were higher. Under-absorbed overhead is accounted for as an adjustment to the profit in the period, and is deducted from profit.

There is no adjustment to the value of closing inventory to allow for any over-absorption or under-absorption of overhead in the cost accounting income statement.

Example

A company manufactures and sells a range of products in a single factory. Its budgeted production overheads for Year 6 were $150,000, and budgeted direct labour hours were 50,000 hours.

Actual results in Year 6 were as follows:

	$	
Sales	630,000	
Direct materials costs	130,000	
Direct labour costs	160,000	
Production overhead	140,000	(40,000 hours)
Administration overhead	70,000	
Selling and distribution overhead	90,000	

There was no opening or closing inventory at the beginning or end of Year 6.
The company uses an absorption costing system, and production overhead is absorbed using a direct labour hour rate.

Required

(a) Calculate the production overhead absorption rate.

(b) Calculate the cost per unit produced

(c) Show how the profit or loss for the year will be reported.

a

Answer

The predetermined absorption rate is $150,000/50,000 hours = $3 per direct labour hour.

The full production cost per unit produced is:

	$
Direct materials costs	130,000
Direct labour costs	160,000
Production overhead absorbed (40,000 hours × $3)	120,000
Full production cost (= cost of sales in this example)	410,000

The profit for the year is reported as follows. Notice that under-absorbed overhead is an adjustment that reduces the reported profit. Over-absorbed overhead would be an adjustment that increases profit.

	$	$
Sales		630,000
Full production cost of sales		(410,000)
		220,000
Overhead absorbed	120,000	
Actual overhead expenditure	140,000	
Under-absorbed overhead		(20,000)
		200,000
Administration overhead	70,000	
Selling and distribution overhead	90,000	
		(160,000)
Profit for Year 6		40,000

e 3

Exercise 3

A manufacturing company uses absorption costing and absorbs overhead costs on a direct labour hour basis.

For Year 7, budgeted production overheads were $240,000, and 30,000 direct labour hours were budgeted.

Actual production overhead costs in Year 7 were $258,000 and 33,000 direct labour hours were worked.

Required

(a) How much production overhead was charged to the cost of production in year 7?

(b) What was the under- or over-absorbed overhead in Year 7?

6.4 The reasons for under- or over-absorption: expenditure and volume variances

There are two reasons for over-absorbed or under-absorbed overheads. These can be measured as:

- an overhead expenditure variance, and
- an overhead volume variance.

The predetermined overhead absorption rate is based on budgeted overhead expenditure and budgeted production volume. What was expected in the budget might not actually happen. When there are differences between actual and budget fixed overhead expenditure, and actual and budgeted activity volume, an under- or over-absorption of overheads occurs.

An overhead variance is reported as either favourable (F) or adverse (A).

- When an overhead variance causes **over-absorption of overhead**, it is a **favourable variance**. The over-absorption is an adjustment that increases profit.
- When an overhead variance causes **under-absorption of overhead**, it is an **adverse variance**. The under-absorption is an adjustment that reduces profit.

Expenditure variance

Actual overhead expenditure might be different from the budgeted expenditure. Therefore there will be some under-absorbed or over-absorbed overheads because actual overhead expenditure differs from the budgeted expenditure.

	$	
Expected overhead expenditure	E	
Actual overhead expenditure	A	
Expenditure variance	(E – A)	(favourable or adverse)

When actual fixed overhead expenditure exceeds the budget, there is an 'adverse' variance, and this will result in some under-absorption of fixed overheads. When actual fixed overhead expenditure is less than budget, there is a 'favourable' variance and this will result in over-absorption of fixed overhead.

The reasons for an expenditure variance might be either:

- excessive spending on overhead items, or
- under-estimating fixed overhead expenditure in the budget.

Volume variance

The second reason for under- or over-absorption of fixed overhead is difference between the actual and budgeted volume of activity (= the volume of activity on which the pre-determined overhead absorption rate was calculated).

	Units or hours	
Expected production volume	E	
Actual production volume	A	
Volume variance (in units or hours)	(E – A)	(favourable or adverse)
× Absorption rate per unit	$X	
Volume variance (in $)	$X × (E – A)	

When actual activity volume exceeds the budget, there will be over-absorption of fixed overheads, which is a 'favourable' variance. When actual activity volume is less than budget, there will be under-absorption of fixed overhead, which is an 'adverse' variance.

When overheads are absorbed on the basis of direct labour hours or machine hours, the actual hours worked might be higher or lower than budgeted. The reasons for a favourable or an adverse volume variance might therefore be any of the following.

- Working more hours than budgeted might be caused by working overtime, or taking on additional direct labour employees.
- Working fewer hours than budgeted might be caused by staff shortages (due to employees leaving or absence from work), hold-ups in production or lack of customer orders.

e

Example

In its annual financial plan for Year 1, a manufacturing company budgets that production overhead expenditure will be $800,000 and that there will be 100,000 direct labour hours of work. It uses a single absorption rate, which is a rate per direct labour hour.

Actual production overhead during Year 1 was $805,000 and 105,000 direct labour hours were worked.

a

Answer

The total under- or over-absorbed overhead

The production overhead absorption rate for the year is $800,000/100,000 = $8 per direct labour hour. All cost units produced during the year are charged with production overheads at the rate of $8 for each direct labour hour.

	$
Overheads absorbed (105,000 hours × $8)	840,000
(Overheads included in product costs)	
Actual overhead expenditure	805,000
Over-absorbed overheads	35,000

This is added to profit when calculating the actual profit for Year 1.

Explaining the over-absorbed overhead

The over-absorbed overhead of $35,000 can be explained by a combination of an expenditure variance and a volume variance.

	$	
Budgeted overhead expenditure	800,000	
Actual overhead expenditure	805,000	
Expenditure variance	5,000	Adverse

The expenditure **variance is adverse** because actual expenditure was more than planned expenditure, and this has resulted in some **under-absorption** of overhead.

	Hours	
Budgeted volume (direct labour hours)	100,000	
Actual volume (direct labour hours)	105,000	
Volume variance (direct labour hours)	5,000	Favourable
Absorption rate/direct labour hour	$8	
Volume variance in $	$40,000	Favourable

The volume **variance is favourable** because actual hours worked exceeded the planned hours, and this has resulted in some **over-absorption** of overhead.

Summary	$	
Expenditure variance	5,000	Adverse
Volume variance	40,000	Favourable
Total over-absorbed overhead	35,000	Favourable

e 4

Exercise 4

In its annual financial plan for Year 2, a manufacturing company budgets that production overhead expenditure will be $720,000 and that there will be 120,000 direct labour hours of work. It uses a single absorption rate, which is a direct labour hour rate.

Actual production overhead during Year 2 was $704,000 and 106,000 direct labour hours were worked. The company worked on two jobs during the year, Job 123 and Job 124. 50,000 hours were worked on Job number 123, which had a prime cost in total of $270,000 and 56,000 hours were worked on Job number 124, which had prime costs in total of $360,000. Job 123 and Job 124 were both started at the beginning of Year 2 and were completed on the final day of Year 2.

Required

(a) Calculate the under- or over-absorbed overhead in Year 2, and analyse this into an expenditure variance and a volume variance.

(b) Calculate the full production cost of Job 123 and Job 124.

Fixed and variable overheads

- Definition of fixed and variable overheads
- Absorption rates for fixed and variable production overheads
- Calculating under- or over-absorbed overhead with fixed and variable overheads

7 Fixed and variable overheads

7.1 Definition of fixed and variable overheads

Most overhead is usually fixed, but some overhead might be a variable cost.

- **Fixed overhead** is overhead expenditure that should be a fixed amount in total during a given period of time, and will not change if more or less production work is done.
- **Variable overhead** is overhead that increases as more production work is done. Total variable overhead expenditure therefore depends on the volume of production. Variable overhead is usually calculated as an amount for each direct labour hour worked.

7.2 Absorption rates for fixed and variable production overheads

When an absorption costing system identifies fixed and variable overhead costs separately, there will be separate absorption rates for fixed overheads and variable overheads.

Example

The budgeted production overhead expenditure for Year 1 is $2,400,000 of fixed overheads plus variable overheads of $3 per direct labour hour. The budgeted direct labour hours are 100,000 for the year.

	$
Budgeted fixed overhead	2,400,000
Budgeted variable overhead (100,000 × $3)	300,000
Total budgeted overhead expenditure	2,700,000

The overhead absorption rate per direct labour hour is calculated as a separate rate for fixed and variable overheads:

	$
Fixed overhead absorption rate ($2,400,000/100,000)	24
Variable overhead absorption rate	3
Total absorption rate per direct labour hour	27

Total overhead expenditure

The total fixed overhead **expenditure** is unaffected by changes in production volume. However, total variable overhead expenditure increases or falls with increases or falls in production volume.

Unit overhead cost and overhead absorption rate

The budgeted fixed overhead cost per unit or per direct labour hour decreases as the planned production volume increases. The variable overhead absorption rate and spending rate is the same, regardless of the volume of production.

Example

Suppose that in the previous example, the budget is amended, and the new plan is to work 120,000 direct labour hours, rather than 100,000 hours. The new budget for overhead expenditure will be as follows:

	$
Budgeted fixed overhead	2,400,000
Budgeted variable overhead (120,000 × $3)	360,000
Total budgeted overhead expenditure	2,760,000

The overhead absorption rate per direct labour hour would be calculated as follows, with the fixed overhead absorption rate lower due to the higher budgeted direct labour hours, but the variable overhead absorption rate unchanged.

	$
Fixed overhead absorption rate ($2,400,000/120,000)	20
Variable overhead absorption rate	3
Total absorption rate/direct labour hour	23

7.3 Calculating under- or over-absorbed overhead with fixed and variable overheads

When there is some variable overhead, the method of calculating under- or over-absorbed overhead is slightly different from the calculation when all overheads are fixed. This is because variable overhead expenditure is expected to vary with the actual volume of activity.

Example

A company has budgeted fixed production overheads of $600,000 for Year 3, and a variable overhead cost of $2 per direct labour hour. The budgeted production volume is 60,000 direct labour hours of work. Actual production in Year 3 was 62,000 direct labour hours, and actual overhead expenditure (fixed and variable) was $790,000 in total.

Required

Calculate the under- or over-absorbed overhead in the year, and analyse this into an expenditure and a volume variance.

a

Answer

The fixed overhead absorption rate is $600,000/60,000 hours = $10 per direct labour hour.

Absorbed overheads	$
Fixed overheads (62,000 hours × $10)	620,000
Variable overheads (62,000 hours × $2)	124,000
Total absorbed overheads	744,000
Actual overhead expenditure	790,000
Under-absorbed overheads	46,000

Explaining the under-absorbed overhead

This under-absorbed overhead of $46,000 can be analysed into an expenditure and a volume variance. There are two important points to note.

- The expected overhead expenditure is the budgeted fixed overhead expenditure plus the expected variable overhead expenditure for the hours actually worked.
- The volume variance affects fixed overheads only, not variable overheads.

Expected overhead expenditure	$	
Expected fixed overheads (= Budgeted fixed overhead)	600,000	
Expected variable overheads (62,000 × $2)	124,000	
Total expected overhead expenditure	724,000	
Actual overhead expenditure	790,000	
Expenditure variance	66,000	Adverse

	Hours	
Budgeted volume (direct labour hours)	60,000	
Actual volume (direct labour hours)	62,000	
Volume variance (direct labour hours)	2,000	Favourable
Fixed overhead absorption rate/direct labour hour	$10	
Volume variance in $ (fixed overhead only)	$20,000	Favourable

Summary	$	
Expenditure variance	66,000	Adverse
Volume variance	20,000	Favourable
Total under-absorbed overhead	46,000	Adverse

Exercise 5

A company has budgeted fixed production overheads of $800,000 for Year 4, and a variable overhead cost of $4 per direct labour hour. The budgeted production volume is 100,000 direct labour hours of work. Actual production in Year 4 was 97,000 direct labour hours, and actual overhead expenditure (fixed and variable) was $1,120,000 in total.

Required

Calculate the under- or over-absorbed overhead in the year, and analyse this into an expenditure and a volume variance.

Practice multiple choice questions

1 A factory consists of two production centres P1 and P2, and two service centres S1 and S2. The total overheads allocated and apportioned to each of these cost centres is as follows.

	P1	**P2**	**S1**	**S2**
Total overheads	$300,000	$450,000	$320,000	$350,000

The work done by the service centres for each of the other centres has been estimated as follows:

	P1	**P2**	**S1**	**S2**
% of service centre S1 to:	30%	70%	-	-
% of service centre S2 to:	30%	40%	30%	-

The costs of the service centres are apportioned to production cost centres using a method that fully recognises any work done by one service cost centre for another.

What are the total overheads for production cost centre P2 after the re-apportionment of all service centre costs?

A $814,000

B $874,000

C $887,500

D $947,500 ***(2 marks)***

2 A company manufactures two products Y and Z in a factory that has two production cost centres, CC1 and CC2. The following budgeted data are available.

	Product Y	**Product Z**	**Allocated and apportioned fixed overheads**
	hours per unit	hours per unit	
Cost centre			
CC1	4	2	$660,000
CC2	5	4	$540,000

Budgeted output is 20,000 units of each product. Fixed overhead costs are absorbed on a direct labour hour basis.

What is the budgeted fixed overhead cost per unit for Product Z?

A $23.00

B $24.00

C $37.00

D $39.50 ***(2 marks)***

3 A company manufactures two products P and Q in a factory that has two production cost centres, C1 and C2. The following budgeted data are available.

	Cost centre	
	C1	**C2**
Allocated and apportioned fixed overheads	$324,000	$583,200
Direct labour hours per unit:		
Product P	2	5
Product Q	4	3

Budgeted output is 15,000 units of each product. Fixed overhead costs are absorbed on a direct labour hour basis.

What is the budgeted fixed overhead cost per unit for Product Q?

A $28.98

B $30.24

C $31.50

D $32.58 ***(2 marks)***

4 A manufacturing company uses absorption costing with a predetermined fixed overhead absorption rate based on direct labour hours worked. The following situations occurred in the previous three months.

(i) Budgeted direct labour hours were more than the actual direct labour hours worked.

(ii) Actual fixed overhead expenditure was higher than the planned expenditure.

Which one of the following statements is correct?

A Situation (i) would cause overheads to be over-absorbed and situation (ii) would cause overheads to be under-absorbed.

B Situation (i) would cause overheads to be under-absorbed and situation (ii) would cause overheads to be over-absorbed.

C Both situations would cause overheads to be over-absorbed.

D Both situations would cause overheads to be under-absorbed. ***(2 marks)***

5 A manufacturing company budgeted 36,000 direct labour hours of work and overhead spending of $144,000. It uses absorption costing, and absorbs overhead costs on the basis of direct labour hours. During the period, overhead spending was $157,500 and 37,500 direct labour hours were worked.

What was the amount of overheads under- or over-absorbed?

A Under-absorbed $13,500

B Over-absorbed $13,500

C Over-absorbed $6,000

D Under-absorbed $7,500 ***(2 marks)***

6 A manufacturing company budgeted 24,000 direct labour hours of work and production overhead spending of $300,000. It uses absorption costing, and absorbs overhead costs on the basis of direct labour hours. During the period, overhead spending was $318,500 and 26,000 direct labour hours were worked.

What was the amount of overheads under- or over-absorbed?

A Over-absorbed $6,500

B Over-absorbed $24,500

C Over-absorbed $25,000

D Under-absorbed $18,500 ***(2 marks)***

CHAPTER

7

Accounting for costs: ledger entries

Contents

The cost ledger

- The nature and purpose of the cost ledger
- Accounts in the cost ledger
- Double entry cost accounting system

1 The cost ledger

1.1 The nature and purpose of the cost ledger

An accounting system is needed to record costs of production and sales. One way of doing this is to record transactions relating to costs in a set of cost accounts. Cost accounts are held in the cost ledger. (A ledger is a word meaning 'a collection of related accounts'.)

If you already know about double entry ledger accounting, you will find this chapter easier to follow than if you are reading about double entry accounting systems for the first time. If you do not know anything about double entry accounting systems (debits and credits) you should be able to learn what you need to know by reading this chapter carefully.

1.2 Accounts in the cost ledger

The accounts in the cost ledger are used to record transactions relating to:

- the costs of materials, labour and expenses
- overhead costs
- the costs of production
- sales and the cost of sales
- profit or loss.

There are other accounts in the cost ledger, such as an account for recording the under-absorbed or over-absorbed production overhead within a system of absorption costing.

There might also be accounts for recording the cost of abnormal losses (process costing) or variances (standard costing). These accounts will be explained in later chapters dealing with process costing and standard costing.

The inventory accounts

There are accounts in the cost ledger for recording work as it progresses through the production process. In a simple cost accounting system, there are accounts for raw materials, work-in-progress and finished goods:

- **Raw materials.** A costing system keeps a continuous record of transactions involving receipts into stores and issues from stores. The raw materials inventory account, or stores account, is used to record the cost of materials purchased, and the cost of materials issued from the stores department to other departments. The balance on the raw materials inventory account shows the cost of the raw materials currently held as inventory

- **Work-in-progress (WIP).** A costing system keeps a continuous record of costs of production. In an absorption costing system, the WIP account records the costs of direct materials, direct labour and direct expenses (if any), and absorbed production overhead costs. It also records the cost of finished production. (Finished production is either transferred to a finished goods store or sold directly to the customer.) The balance on the WIP inventory account shows the cost of production still in progress and not yet completed. This inventory of unfinished production is called 'work–in-progress'.
- **Finished goods.** The finished goods account is a stores account for completed production that has not yet been sold. It records the production cost of completed units transferred from production into the finished goods store, and the production cost of goods that are then transferred from the store and sold to customers. The balance on the finished goods inventory account shows the production cost of finished output held in store.

1.3 Double entry cost accounting system

A cost accounting system, like the financial accounting book-keeping system, uses a double entry system for recording transactions. With double entry, every transaction is recorded twice in the accounts:

- as a debit entry in one account, and
- as a credit entry in a different account.

The total of debit entries and the total of credit entries must always be equal. It is useful to think of an account as having a T shape, with a debit side and a credit side, as follows:

Name of the account

Debit side	$	**Credit side**	$

The **balance on an account** is the difference between the total value of entries in the debit side and the total value of entries on the credit side.

- When the total value of debit entries is higher than the total value of credit entries, there is a debit balance.
- When the total value of credit entries is higher than the total value of debit entries, there is a credit balance.

The **balance on the three inventory accounts** should always be either zero (= no inventory) or a debit balance (= the cost of the inventory that is currently held).

Double entry accounting for costs: basic rules

- Recording costs incurred
- Costs of production and the WIP account
- From raw materials to cost of sales
- Non-production overheads
- Opening and closing inventory
- The costing system income statement
- The financial ledger control account

2 Double entry accounting for costs: basic rules

There are some basic rules that need to be remembered when recording costs in the cost accounting system.

2.1 Recording costs incurred

Some accounts are used to record costs that are incurred.

- The **raw materials account** records the cost of materials purchased.
- The **wages and salaries cost account** records the cost of labour. (Sometimes, you might come across a direct labour cost account, which records the wages and salary costs of direct labour only.)
- **Overhead cost accounts** record the overhead costs incurred.
- The **work-in-progress account** records the production costs of items produced. It records the cost of direct materials, direct labour and production overheads absorbed. These costs are transferred to work in progress from the raw materials account, wages and salaries cost account and production overheads account.
- The **finished goods account** records the production cost of completed production that is transferred from work in progress to the store of finished goods inventory.
- The **cost of sales account** records the total cost of sales, which consists of production costs, administration costs and sales and distribution costs.

Costs incurred are recorded as debit entries in these accounts.

2.2 Costs of production and the WIP account

The WIP account is used to record the costs of production – direct materials, direct labour and production overheads absorbed. These costs are recorded in a double entry cost accounting system as follows:

	Debit	Credit
1) Direct materials issued from stores to production	WIP account	Raw materials account (stores account)
2) Direct labour costs in production	WIP account	Wages and salaries account
3) Production overheads absorbed into production costs	WIP account	Production overheads account

Example

Raw materials costing $6,000 are transferred from the stores account into production. Direct labour costs of $12,500 were incurred and overheads of $25,000 were absorbed into production costs

In a cost ledger system these items would be accounted for as follows.

Work in Progress

(Debit side)	$	(Credit side)	$
Raw materials (stores) account	6,000		
Wages account	12,500		
Production overhead account	25,000		

The balance on this account is now a debit balance of $43,500.

Stores account

(Debit side)	$	(Credit side)	$
		Work in progress	6,000

Wages account

(Debit side)	$	(Credit side)	$
		Work in Progress	12,500

Production overhead account

(Debit side)	$	(Credit side)	$
		Work in Progress	25,000

2.3 From raw materials to cost of sales

Materials progress through the production system, from raw materials to work in progress, from work in progress to finished goods, and from finished goods to cost of sales. This is recorded in the double entry system as follows:

		Debit	Credit
1)	Direct materials issued from stores to production (work in progress)	WIP account	Raw materials account (stores account)
2)	Completed production transferred from WIP to finished goods (at production cost)	Finished goods account	WIP account
3)	Finished goods sold to customers	Cost of sales account	Finished goods account (production cost of sales)

Example

Continuing the previous example, the cost of finished output is $40,000. This is transferred to the finished goods warehouse, and finished goods costing $35,000 are sold.

In a cost ledger system these items would be accounted for as follows.

Work in Progress

(Debit side)	$	(Credit side)	$
Raw materials (stores) account	6,000	Finished goods account	40,000
Wages account	12,500		
Production overhead account	25,000		

The balance on this account is now a debit balance of $3,500. This means that unfinished work-in-progress has a cost of $3,500.

Finished goods account

(Debit side)	$	(Credit side)	$
Work in progress	40,000	Cost of sales account	35,000

The balance on this account is now a debit balance of $5,000. This means that finished goods held in the finished goods warehouse has a cost of $5,000.

Cost of sales account

(Debit side)	$	(Credit side)	$
Finished goods account	35,000		

2.4 Non-production overheads

Non-production overheads are recorded initially in an administration overheads account and a sales and distribution overheads account. They are transferred from these accounts to the cost of sales account. The cost of sales account therefore records the production cost of finished goods sold, administration overheads costs and sales and distribution overheads costs.

	Debit	Credit
1) Administration overheads	Cost of sales account	Administration overheads account (administration overheads for the period)
2) Sales and distribution overheads	Cost of sales account	Sales and distribution overheads account (sales and distribution overheads for the period)

Example

Continuing the previous example, finished goods with a production cost of $35,000 are sold. Administration overhead costs are $15,000 and sales and distribution overheads are $20,000.

In a cost ledger system these items would be accounted for as follows.

Cost of sales account

(Debit side)	$	(Credit side)	$
Finished goods account	35,000		
Administration overhead	15,000		
Sales and distribution overhead	20,000		

The total cost of sales is $70,000.

Administration overhead account

(Debit side)	$	(Credit side)	$
		Cost of sales	15,000

Sales and distribution overhead account

(Debit side)	$	(Credit side)	$
		Cost of sales	20,000

2.5 Opening and closing inventory

The raw materials account, work-in-progress account (incomplete production) and finished goods account provide a record of the cost of opening and closing inventory at the beginning and end of each accounting period.

The value of the inventory is the current balance on the inventory account. This is always either 0 or a debit balance.

However, at the end of an accounting period, an account is 'closed off' for the period, and the balance on the account is:

- carried forward as a closing balance for the period that has just ended, and
- an opening balance at the beginning of the new period.

An example of a materials account is shown below, to illustrate how the opening and closing inventory are recorded:

Materials account

Period 1	$	*Period 1*	$
Opening inventory b/f	5,000	Work in progress (direct materials)	35,000
Purchases	46,000	Production overheads (indirect materials)	9,000
		Closing inventory c/f	7,000
	51,000		51,000
Period 2			
Opening inventory b/f	7,000		

The closing inventory at the end of a period is entered on the credit side 'above the line' and the corresponding double entry is a debit entry 'below the line' as opening inventory at the beginning of the next period.

'b/f' means 'brought forward'. You might also see the letters 'b/fwd' or 'b/d' (meaning 'brought down'). Similarly, 'c/f' means carried forward. You might also see the letters 'c/fwd' or c/d (for 'carried down').

The opening inventory brought forward is called the 'balance' on the account at the beginning of the period. In the example above, the opening balance of $7,000 at the beginning of period 2 could be calculated as (Opening inventory + Purchases) – Materials issued. Here this is $5,000 + 46,000 - $(35,000 + 9,000) = $7,000.

2.6 The costing system income statement

There is an income statement in the cost ledger, for recording the profit or loss in each accounting period. This is a part of the double entry cost accounting system. The credit side of the income statement records sales. The debit side of the income statement records the cost of sales.

There might also be other items in this account, such as under- or over-absorbed overheads (in an absorption costing system) or variances (in a standard costing system) or abnormal loss or abnormal gain (in a process costing system). The basic rules of double entry, however, are as follows:

	Debit	Credit
Sales	Sales account	Income statement account
Cost of sales	Income statement account	Cost of sales account

The balance on this income statement account is:

- a credit balance when sales are higher than the cost of sales, and there is a profit.
- a debit balance when sales are less than the cost of sales, and there is a loss.

The profit or loss for the period is then transferred to a retained profits account, so that the balance on the income statement becomes 0.

Example

Continuing the previous example, finished goods with a production cost of $35,000 are sold. Administration overhead costs are $15,000 and sales and distribution overheads are $20,000. Sales in the period are $82,000.

In a cost ledger system these items would be accounted for as follows.

Cost of sales account

(Debit side)	$	(Credit side)	$
Finished goods account	35,000	Income statement	70,000
Administration overhead	15,000		
Sales and distribution overhead	20,000		
	70,000		70,000

Cost accounting income statement

(Debit side)	$	(Credit side)	$
Cost of sales account	70,000	Sales account	82,000

The profit of $12,000 is shown by the credit balance on the costing income statement account.

	Debit	Credit
Profit	Income statement account	Accumulated profit account, or financial ledger control account
Loss	Accumulated profit account, or financial ledger control account	Income statement account

2.7 The financial ledger control account

The cost ledger includes accounts relating to costs. There are many other accounts that are not specifically related to costs, such as the bank account, the account for trade receivables, the account for trade payables, an account for accumulated profits, and so on. In the cost ledger, a special account called the financial ledger control account (or the cost ledger control account) may be used to record one of the double entry transactions required when the appropriate account does not exist in the cost ledger.

Examples

- A company buys raw materials on credit from a supplier, at a cost of $2,000. It has an addition to its materials, and owes the supplier. The double entry is:

  Debit: Materials account $2,000
  Credit: Financial ledger control account $2,000.

- A company pays wages of $3,000 to its work force. It has incurred labour costs, and paid for them out of its bank account. The double entry is:

  Debit: Wages and salaries cost account $3,000
  Credit: Financial ledger control account $3,000.

- A company incurs production overhead expenses, such as factory rental costs, and either pays for them out of its bank account or obtains the items on credit from a supplier. The double entry is:

  Debit: Production overheads account
  Credit: Financial ledger control account.

Exercise 1

A company incurs the following costs:

(a) Purchases of raw materials $20,000

(b) Costs of wages and salaries $25,000

(c) Cost of production overhead expenses $4,000

(d) Cost of other overhead expenses (administration overheads and selling and distribution overheads) $7,000

(e) The opening inventory in the materials account is a balance of $1,000 and in the work-in-progress account the opening balance is $4,000. The opening balance on the financial ledger control account is $5,000.

(f) The company also had sales of $90,000.

Required

Record these transactions in the following cost accounts:

- Materials account
- Wages and salaries account
- Production overheads account
- Other overheads account
- Sales account

- Financial ledger control account.

(You are not required to show the WIP account, although you can do so if you want to see that all the debit entries and all the credit entries add up to the same total amount.)

Double entry accounting for costs: overheads

- Accounting for direct and indirect materials and labour costs
- Absorbed production overheads

3 Double entry accounting for costs: overheads

3.1 Accounting for direct and indirect materials and labour costs

Direct materials costs and direct labour costs are direct costs of production and are charged to the work-in-progress account.

Indirect materials costs and indirect labour costs are overhead costs of production and are charged to the production overhead account, administration overhead account or selling and distribution overheads account, as appropriate.

	Debit	**Credit**
Direct materials issued from stores to production	WIP account	Raw materials account (inventory account)
Direct labour costs in production	WIP account	Wages and salaries account
Indirect materials		
Indirect materials issued from stores to production cost centres	Production overheads account	Raw materials account (inventory account)
Indirect materials issued from stores to administration cost centres	Administration overheads account	Raw materials account (inventory account)
Indirect materials issued from stores to sales and distribution cost centres	Sales and distribution overheads account	Raw materials account (inventory account)
Indirect labour		
Indirect labour production cost	Production overheads account	Wages and salaries account
Administration costs of labour	Administration overheads account	Wages and salaries account
Sales and distribution labour costs	Sales and distribution overheads account	Wages and salaries account

3.2 Absorbed production overheads

Production overheads are absorbed into the cost of production. This is accounted for as follows:

	Debit	Credit
Production overheads absorbed	WIP account (Absorbed overheads are added to the cost of production)	Production overheads account

The balance on the production overhead account is the under-absorbed overhead or over-absorbed overhead. At the end of each accounting period, this balance is transferred to an under- or over-absorbed overhead account.

Example

During an accounting period, a company recorded the following transactions:

(a) Opening inventory: raw materials $5,000; WIP $3,000

(b) Purchased raw materials costing $23,000

(c) Used $14,000 of direct materials in production and $5,000 of indirect production materials.

(d) Incurred total labour costs of $25,000. Of this total, $12,000 were direct labour costs, $6,000 were indirect production labour costs and $7,000 were other overhead labour costs.

(e) Production overhead expenses were $18,000.

(f) Absorbed $27,000 of production overheads into the cost of production.

These transactions are accounted for as follows. Work through the accounting entries carefully, and make sure that you can see how each item is accounted for. 'Balance' in some of the accounts here means 'balancing item': this is the entry required to complete the account, which is calculated from the other figures in the account.

Raw materials

	$		$
Opening inventory b/f	5,000	Work-in-progress	14,000
Purchases (financial ledger control account)	23,000	Production overheads	5,000
		Closing inventory c/f (balance)	9,000
	28,000		28,000
Opening inventory b/f	9,000		

Wages and salaries

	$		$
Costs incurred (financial ledger control account)	25,000	Work-in-progress	12,000
		Production overheads	6,000
		Other overhead	7,000
	25,000		25,000

Production overheads

	$		$
Expenses (fin. ledger control)	18,000	Work-in-progress (absorbed)	27,000
Raw materials	5,000	Under-absorbed o'head (balance)	2,000
Wages and salaries	6,000		
	29,000		29,000

Work-in-progress

	$		$
Opening inventory b/f	3,000		
Materials	14,000		
Wages and salaries	12,000		
Production overhead	27,000		

Other overheads

	$		$
Wages and salaries	7,000		

Under-absorbed overhead account

	$		$
Production overhead	2,000		

Completing the cost accounting income statement

- The finished goods account
- The cost of sales account and the sales account
- The cost accounting income statement

4 Completing the cost accounting income statement

The cost ledger includes an income statement where sales are matched with the cost of sales. Other adjustments, such as an adjustment for under- or over-absorbed overheads, are also recorded in the income statement, and the balance on the account is the profit or loss for the period.

4.1 The finished goods account

The finished goods account records the production cost of finished goods completed in the period, and the production cost of goods sold in the period.

Finished goods account

	$		$
Opening inventory b/f	18,000	Cost of sales	95,000
Work-in-progress (= cost of completed production)	87,000	Closing inventory c/f	10,000
	105,000		105,000
Opening inventory b/f	10,000		

4.2 The cost of sales account and the sales account

The cost of sales account records the total cost of sales in the period – the production cost of sales and administration and sales and distribution overheads.

Cost of sales account

	$		$
Finished goods (= production cost of goods sold)	95,000	Income statement (= cost of sales)	155,000
Administration overheads	20,000		
Sales and distribution overheads	40,000		
	155,000		155,000

Sales are recorded in a sales account, and then transferred to the income statement at the end of each costing period.

Sales account

	$		$
Income statement	200,000	Financial ledger control account (= sales in the period)	200,000
	200,000		200,000

4.3 The cost accounting income statement

The profit or loss is recorded in a cost accounting income statement. The income statement also includes any other adjustments to profit, such as under- or over-absorbed overhead, abnormal loss or gain, or standard cost variances.

The balance on the income statement is the profit or loss for the period. The matching double entry is in the financial ledger control account (accumulated profits).

Cost accounting income statement

	$		$
Cost of sales	155,000	Sales	200,000
Under-absorbed overheads	3,000		
Profit	42,000		
	200,000		200,000

Exercise 2

Record the following transactions in the cost ledger accounts.

Prepare a statement of the closing balances.

	$
Opening balances:	
Materials	7,000
Work-in-progress	3,000
Finished goods	4,000
Financial ledger control account	14,000
Transactions in the period	
Material purchases	50,000
Direct materials used in production	33,000
Indirect production materials	17,000
Indirect materials: other overheads	2,000
Wages and salaries costs	45,000
Direct labour costs	28,000
Indirect production labour	7,000
Indirect labour: other overheads	10,000
Expenses: production overheads	24,000
Expenses: other overheads	15,000
Production overheads absorbed	50,000
Closing inventory, work-in-progress	8,000
Production cost of goods sold	109,000
Sales	160,000

CHAPTER

8

Marginal costing and absorption costing

Contents

Marginal cost and marginal costing

- Marginal cost
- Marginal costing and its uses
- Assumptions in marginal costing
- Contribution

1 Marginal cost and marginal costing

1.1 Marginal cost

The marginal cost of an item is its variable cost.

- **Marginal production cost** = Direct materials + Direct labour + Variable production overhead.
- **Marginal cost of sale** for a **product** = Direct materials + Direct labour + Variable production overhead + Other variable overhead (for example, variable selling and distribution overhead).
- **Marginal cost of sale** for a **service** = Direct materials + Direct labour + Variable overhead.

It is usually assumed that **direct labour costs** are variable (marginal) costs, but in some situations, direct labour costs might be fixed costs, and so would not be included in marginal cost.

Variable overhead costs might be difficult to identify. In practice, variable overheads might be measured using a technique such as high/low analysis or linear regression analysis, to separate total overhead costs into fixed costs and a variable cost per unit of activity.

- For variable production overheads, the unit of activity is often either direct labour hours or machine hours, although another measure of activity might be used.
- For variable selling and distribution costs, the unit of activity might be sales volume or sales revenue.
- Administration overheads are usually considered to be fixed costs, and it is very unusual to come across variable administration overheads.

Marginal costs and total costs

When marginal costing is used, total costs are the sum of variable costs (marginal costs) and fixed costs. It is important in marginal costing that you should separate variable costs from fixed costs, and identify them separately. Remember that there might be some variable selling and distribution costs. The table below shows how variable and fixed costs might be separated in a marginal costing analysis.

	$	$
Direct materials		60,000
Direct labour		40,000
Direct expenses		5,000
Prime cost		105,000
Variable production overheads		15,000
Variable selling and distribution overheads		10,000
Total variable costs (marginal cost)		**130,000**
Fixed costs		
Fixed production overheads	60,000	
Fixed administration overheads	40,000	
Fixed selling and distribution overheads	50,000	
Fixed costs		**150,000**
Total costs		280,000

1.2 Marginal costing and its uses

Marginal costing is a method of costing with marginal costs. It is an alternative to absorption costing as a method of costing. In marginal costing, fixed production overheads are not absorbed into product costs.

There are several reasons for using marginal costing:

- To measure profit (or loss), as an alternative to absorption costing
- To forecast what future profits will be
- To calculate what the minimum sales volume must be in order to make a profit

It can also be used to provide management with information for decision making.

This chapter looks at using marginal costing to measure profit, as an alternative to absorption costing.

Its main uses, however, are for planning (for example, budgeting), forecasting and decision making.

1.3 Assumptions in marginal costing

For the purpose of marginal costing, the following assumptions are normally made:

- Every additional unit of output or sale, or every additional unit of activity, has the same variable cost as every other unit. In other words, the variable cost per unit is a constant value.
- Fixed costs are costs that remain the same in total in each period, regardless of how many units are produced and sold.
- Costs are either fixed or variable, or a mixture of fixed and variable costs. Mixed costs can be separated into a variable cost per unit and a fixed cost per period. Techniques such as high/low analysis or linear regression analysis should be used to do this.
- The marginal cost of an item is therefore the extra cost that would be incurred by making and selling one extra unit of the item.

1.4 Contribution

Contribution is a key concept in marginal costing.

Contribution = Sales – Variable costs

Fixed costs are a constant total amount in each period. To make a profit, an entity must first make enough contribution to cover its fixed costs. Contribution therefore means: 'contribution towards covering fixed costs and making a profit'.

Total contribution – Fixed costs = Profit

- When fixed costs have been covered, any additional contribution adds directly to profit.
- If total contribution fails to cover fixed costs, there is a loss.

Reporting profit with marginal costing

- Total contribution minus fixed costs
- A marginal costing income statement with opening and closing inventory

2 Reporting profit with marginal costing

2.1 Total contribution minus fixed costs

With marginal costing, profit is measured as follows (illustrative figures are shown):

When you are measuring profits using marginal costing, it is usual to identify contribution, and then to subtract fixed costs from the total contribution in order to get to the profit figure. An simplified example of a marginal costing income statement is shown below.

	$	$
Sales		360,000
Direct costs	105,000	
Variable production costs	15,000	
Variable sales and distribution costs	10,000	
Total marginal costs		130,000
Total contribution		230,000
Total fixed costs		150,000
Profit		80,000

Total contribution and contribution per unit

In marginal costing, it is assumed that the variable cost per unit of product (or per unit of service) is constant. If the selling price per unit is also constant, this means that the contribution earned from selling each unit of product is the same.

Total contribution can therefore be calculates as: Units of sale × Contribution per unit.

Example

A company manufactures and sells two products, A and B. Product A has a variable cost of $6 and sells for $10, and product B has a variable cost of $8 and sells for $15. During the period, 20,000 units of Product A and 30,000 units of Product B were sold. Fixed costs were $260,000. What was the profit or loss for the period?

a

Answer

Contribution per unit:

- Product A: $10 – $6 = $4
- Product B: $15 – $8 = $7

	$
Contribution from Product A: (20,000 × $4)	80,000
Contribution from Product B: (30,000 × $7)	210,000
Total contribution for the period	290,000
Fixed costs for the period	(260,000)
Profit for the period	30,000

e 1

Exercise 1

An entity sells two products, X and Y. Product X sells for $8 per unit and has a variable cost of $3. Product Y sells for $6 per unit and has a variable cost of $2. Fixed costs each month are $250,000.

Monthly sales are 40,000 units of Product X and 30,000 units of Product Y. There is no inventory of either product.

Required

Using marginal costing, calculate the profit for the month.

2.2 A marginal costing income statement with opening and closing inventory

The explanation of marginal costing has so far ignored opening and closing inventory.

In absorption costing, the production cost of sales is calculated as 'opening inventory value + production costs incurred in the period – closing inventory value'.

The same principle applies in marginal costing. The variable production cost of sales is calculated as 'opening inventory value + 'opening inventory value + variable production costs incurred in the period – closing inventory value'.

When marginal costing is used, inventory is valued at its **marginal cost of production** (= variable production cost), without any absorbed fixed production overheads.

If an income statement is prepared using marginal costing, the opening and closing inventory might be shown, as follows:

Income statement for the period ended [date]	$	$
Sales		440,000
Opening inventory at variable production cost	5,000	
Variable production costs		
Direct materials	60,000	
Direct labour	30,000	
Variable production overheads	15,000	
	110,000	
Less: Closing inventory at variable production cost	(8,000)	
Variable production cost of sales	102,000	
Variable selling and distribution costs	18,000	
Variable cost of sales		120,000
Contribution		320,000
Fixed costs:		
Production fixed costs	120,000	
Administration costs (usually 100% fixed costs)	70,000	
Selling and distribution fixed costs	90,000	
Total fixed costs		280,000
Profit		40,000

However, when the variable production cost per unit is a constant amount, there is no need to show the opening and closing inventory valuations, and the income statement could be presented more simply as follows:

Income statement for the period ended [date]	$	$
Sales		440,000
Variable production cost of sales	102,000	
Variable selling and distribution costs	18,000	
Variable cost of sales		120,000
Total contribution		320,000
Fixed costs:		
Production fixed costs	120,000	
Administration costs	70,000	
Selling and distribution fixed costs	90,000	
Total fixed costs		280,000
Profit		40,000

Marginal costing and absorption costing compared

- Reporting profit with absorption costing
- The difference in profit between marginal costing and absorption costing
- Calculating the difference in profit: increase in inventory during a period
- Calculating the difference in profit: reduction in inventory during a period
- Summary: comparing marginal and absorption costing profit

3 Marginal costing and absorption costing compared

3.1 Reporting profit with absorption costing

Absorption costing is the 'traditional' way of measuring profit in a manufacturing company. Inventory is valued at the full cost of production, which consists of direct materials and direct labour cost plus absorbed production overheads (fixed and variable production overheads).

The absorption rate for variable production overheads should be the same as the variable overhead rate of expenditure. However in absorption costing variable and fixed production overheads might not be separated.

In absorption costing, there is some under- or over-absorbed overhead, which occurs because the absorption rate is a predetermined rate.

The full presentation of an absorption costing income statement might therefore be as follows (illustrative figures included):

Income statement for the period ended [date]	$	$
Sales		430,000
Opening inventory at full production cost	8,000	
Production costs		
Direct materials	60,000	
Direct labour	30,000	
Production overheads absorbed	100,000	
	198,000	
Less: Closing inventory at full production cost	(14,000)	
Full production cost of sales		184,000
		246,000
Production overheads absorbed	100,000	
Production overheads incurred	95,000	
Over-absorbed overheads		5,000
		251,000
Administration costs	70,000	
Selling and distribution costs (fixed + variable)	108,000	
		178,000
Profit		73,000

3.2 The difference in profit between marginal costing and absorption costing

The profit for an accounting period calculated with marginal costing is different from the profit calculated with absorption costing. The difference in profit is due **entirely** to the differences in inventory valuation.

When there is no opening or closing inventory, exactly the same profit will be reported using marginal costing and absorption costing.

The main difference between absorption costing and marginal costing is that:

- in absorption costing, inventory cost includes a share of fixed production overhead costs
- in marginal costing, inventory cost contains no fixed production overhead costs.

The following rules may be applied to calculate the difference in the profit for a period calculated with marginal costing and with absorption costing.

3.3 Calculating the difference in profit: increase in inventory during a period

Look at the difference between the quantity of opening inventory and closing inventory. Establish whether:

- closing inventory is larger than opening inventory, or
- closing inventory is less than opening inventory.

Closing inventory is higher than opening inventory when the quantity produced in the period is more than the quantity sold. If the cost per unit is a constant amount, using marginal costing or absorption costing, when the production quantity exceeds the sales quantity:

- There is an increase in inventory during a period
- Closing inventory is therefore higher in value than opening inventory
- The increase in inventory will be greater with absorption costing, by the amount of the increase in fixed production costs in the inventory value
- The production cost of sales is therefore lower with absorption costing than with marginal costing, and the difference is this increase in fixed costs in the inventory value
- Therefore the profit is higher with absorption costing than with marginal costing, by the amount of the increase in fixed costs in the inventory value.

Basic rule: comparing marginal costing and absorption costing profit

Production volume bigger than sales volume

Increase in inventory (closing – opening inventory)

Absorption costing profit higher than marginal costing profit

Difference in profit = amount of fixed production overhead in the increase in inventory

Example

A company uses marginal costing. In the financial period that has just ended, opening inventory was $8,000 and closing inventory was $15,000. The reported profit for the year was $96,000.

If the company had used absorption costing, opening inventory would have been $16,000 and closing inventory would have been $34,000.

Required
What would have been the profit for the year if absorption costing had been used?

Answer

There was an increase in inventory. It was $7,000 using marginal costing (= $15,000 – $8,000). It would have been $19,000 using absorption costing.

	$
Increase in inventory, marginal costing	7,000
Increase in inventory, absorption costing	19,000
Difference (profit higher with absorption costing)	12,000
Profit with marginal costing	96,000
Profit with absorption costing	108,000

The profit is higher with absorption costing because there has been an increase in inventory (production volume has been more than sales volume.)

3.4 Calculating the difference in profit: reduction in inventory during a period

When there is a reduction in inventory during a period, and closing inventory is lower in value than opening inventory, the reverse situation applies.

Closing inventory is lower than opening inventory when the quantity sold exceeds the quantity produced in the period. If the cost per unit is a constant amount, using marginal costing or absorption costing, when the sales quantity exceeds the production quantity:

- There is a reduction in inventory during a period.
- Closing inventory is therefore lower in value than opening inventory
- The reduction in inventory will be greater with absorption costing, by the fixed production costs in the amount by which inventory has been reduced.
- The production cost of sales is therefore higher with absorption costing than with marginal costing, and the difference is the amount of fixed production costs in the reduction in inventory value.
- Therefore the profit is lower with absorption costing than with marginal costing, by the amount of the fixed costs in the fall in inventory value.

Basic rule: comparing marginal costing and absorption costing profit

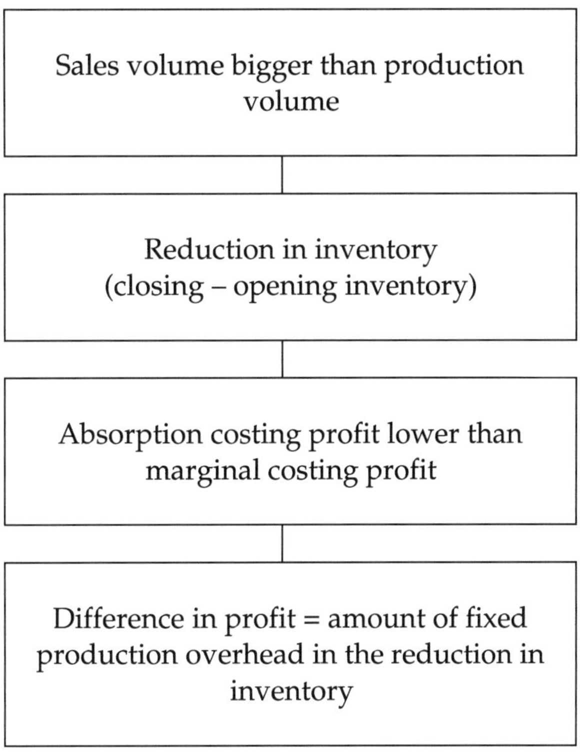

Example

A company uses absorption costing. In the financial period that has just ended, opening inventory was $76,000 and closing inventory was $49,000. The reported profit for the year was $183,000.

If the company had used marginal costing, opening inventory would have been $40,000 and closing inventory would have been $28,000.

Required
What would have been the profit for the year if marginal costing had been used?

Answer

There was a reduction in inventory. It was $27,000 using absorption costing (= $76,000 – $49,000). It would have been $12,000 using marginal costing.

	$
Reduction in inventory, absorption costing	27,000
Reduction in inventory, marginal costing	12,000
Difference (profit higher with marginal costing)	15,000
Profit with absorption costing	183,000
Profit with marginal costing	198,000

Profit is higher with marginal costing because there has been a reduction in inventory during the period.

3.5 Summary: comparing marginal and absorption costing profit

An examination might test your ability to calculate the difference between the reported profit using marginal costing and the reported profit using absorption costing. To calculate the difference, you might need to make the following simple calculations.

- Calculate the increase or decrease in inventory during the period, in units.
- Calculate the fixed production overhead cost per unit.
- The difference in profit is the increase or decrease in inventory quantity multiplied by the fixed production overhead cost per unit.
- If there has been an increase in inventory, the absorption costing profit is higher. If there has been a reduction in inventory, the absorption costing profit is lower.
- You should **ignore fixed selling overhead or fixed administration overhead**. These are written off in full as a period cost in both absorption costing and marginal costing, and only fixed production overheads are included in inventory values.

e

Example

The following information relates to a manufacturing company for the next costing period.

Production	16,000 units	Fixed production costs	\$80,000
Sales	14,000 units	Fixed selling costs	\$28,000

Using absorption costing, the profit for this period would be \$60,000

Required
What would have been the profit for the year if marginal costing had been used?

a

Answer

Ignore the fixed selling overheads. These are irrelevant since they do not affect the difference in profit between marginal and absorption costing.

- There is an increase in inventory by 2,000 units, since production volume (16,000 units) is higher than sales volume (14,000 units).
- If absorption costing is used, the fixed production overhead cost per unit is \$5 (= \$80,000/16,000 units).
- The difference between the absorption costing profit and marginal costing profit is therefore \$10,000 (= 2,000 units × \$5).
- Absorption costing profit is higher, because there has been an increase in inventory.
- Marginal costing profit would therefore be \$60,000 – \$10,000 = \$50,000.

e
2

Exercise 2

A company budgets to make 37,000 units of a product and fixed production costs are expected to be \$111,000.

The budgeted direct costs of production are \$5 per unit, and there are no variable overhead costs. Budgeted sales are 40,000 units and the sales price is \$11 per unit.

Budgeted administration overheads and selling and distribution overheads are \$80,000 (all fixed costs).

Required

(a) Calculate the expected profit for the period using marginal costing.

(b) Having calculated the marginal costing profit, calculate what the absorption costing profit would be for the period. (Assume that the cost per unit of opening inventory is the same as the cost per unit of closing inventory.)

Advantages and disadvantages of absorption and marginal costing

- Advantages and disadvantages of absorption costing
- Advantages and disadvantages of marginal costing

4 Advantages and disadvantages of absorption and marginal costing

The previous sections of this chapter have explained the differences between marginal costing and absorption costing as methods of measuring profit in a period. Some conclusions can be made from these differences.

- The amount of profit reported in the cost accounts for a financial period will depend on the method of costing used.
- Since the reported profit differs according to the method of costing used, there are presumably reasons why one method of costing might be used in preference to the other. In other words, there must be some advantages (and disadvantages) of using either method.

4.1 Advantages and disadvantages of absorption costing

Absorption costing has a number of advantages and disadvantages.

Advantages of absorption costing

- Inventory values include an element of fixed production overheads. This is consistent with the requirement in financial accounting that (for the purpose of financial reporting) inventory should include production overhead costs.
- Calculating under/over absorption of overheads may be useful in controlling fixed overhead expenditure.
- By calculating the full cost of sale for a product and comparing it will the selling price, it should be possible to identify which products are profitable and which are being sold at a loss.

Disadvantages of absorption costing

- Absorption costing is a more complex costing system than marginal costing.
- Absorption costing does not provide information that is useful for decision making (like marginal costing does).

4.2 Advantages and disadvantages of marginal costing

Marginal costing has a number of advantages and disadvantages.

Advantages of marginal costing

- It is easy to account for fixed overheads using marginal costing. Instead of being apportioned they are treated as period costs and written off in full as an expense the income statement for the period when they occur.
- There is no under/over-absorption of overheads with marginal costing, and therefore no adjustment necessary in the income statement at the end of an accounting period.
- Marginal costing provides useful information for decision making.
- Contribution per unit is constant, unlike profit per unit which varies as the volume of activity varies.

Disadvantages of marginal costing

- Marginal costing does not value inventory in accordance with the requirements of financial reporting. (However, for the purpose of cost accounting and providing management information, there is no reason why inventory values should include fixed production overhead, other than consistency with the financial accounts.)
- Marginal costing can be used to measure the contribution per unit of product, or the total contribution earned by a product, but this is not sufficient to decide whether the product is profitable enough. Total contribution has to be big enough to cover fixed costs and make a profit.

Practice multiple choice questions

1 The costs and sales revenue in a period are as follows.

	$000
Direct materials	24
Direct labour	36
Direct expenses	5
Variable production overheads	6
Fixed production overheads	70
Administration overheads	30
Variable selling overheads	8
Fixed selling overheads	35
Sales	250

What is the total contribution for the period?

A $171,000

B $176,000

C $179,000

D $184,000

(2 marks)

2 The following information relates to a manufacturing company for the next costing period.

Production	24,000 units	Fixed production costs	$96,000
Sales	25,000 units	Fixed selling costs	$75,000

Using marginal costing, the profit for this period would be $65,000

Required

What would have been the profit for the year if absorption costing had been used?

A $58,000

B $61,000

C $69,000

D $72,000 ***(2 marks)***

3 The following information relates to a manufacturing company for the next costing period.

Production	32,000 units	Fixed production costs	$160,000
Sales	30,000 units	Fixed selling costs	$30,000

Using absorption costing, the profit for this period would be $101,000

Required

What would have been the profit for the year if marginal costing had been used?

A $89,000

B $91,000

C $111,000

D $113,000 ***(2 marks)***

4 The following information relates to a manufacturing company for the next costing period.

Fixed production costs	$125,000
Fixed selling costs	$25,000
Production	25,000 units

The profit for the period using absorption costing would be $15,000 less than if marginal costing were used.

Required

What is the expected sales volume in the period?

A 22,000 units

B 23,000 units

C 27,000 units

D 28,000 units ***(2 marks)***

CHAPTER

9

Job costing, batch costing and service costing

Contents

Job costing

- The nature of job costing
- The cost of a job
- Cost records and accounts for job costing

1 Job costing

Costing systems are used to record total costs. They are also used to record the costs of individual cost units. The method used to measure the cost of cost units depends on the production system and how the products are made.

1.1 The nature of job costing

Job costing is used when a business entity carries out tasks or jobs to meet specific customer orders. Although each job might involve similar work, they are all different and are carried out to the customer's specific instructions or requirements.

Examples of 'jobs' include work done for customers by builders or electricians, audit work done for clients by a firm of auditors, and repair work on motor vehicles by a repair firm.

Job costing is similar to contract costing, in the sense that each job is usually different and carried out to the customer's specification or particular requirements. However, jobs are short-term and the work is usually carried out in a fairly short period of time. Contracts are usually long-term and might take several months or even years to complete.

1.2 The cost of a job

A cost is calculated for each individual job, and this cost can be used to establish the profit or loss from doing the job.

Job costing differs from most other types of costing system because each cost unit is a job, and no two jobs are exactly the same. Each job is costed separately.

- The expected cost of a job has to be estimated so that a price for the job can be quoted to a customer.
- A costing system should also calculate the actual cost of each job that has been carried out.

A job costing system is usually based on absorption costing principles, and in addition a cost is included for non-production overheads, as follows.

Job cost

	$
Direct materials	500
Direct labour	300
Direct expenses	200
Prime cost	1,000
Production overhead absorbed	750
Production cost of the job	1,750
Non-production overheads	400
Total job cost	2,150

In many cases, job costs include not just direct materials costs and direct labour costs, but also **direct expenses**, such as:

- the rental cost of equipment hired for the job
- the cost of work done for the job by sub-contractors
- the depreciation cost of equipment used exclusively on the job.

Production overheads might be absorbed on a direct labour hour basis, or on any other suitable basis.

Non-production overheads might be added to the cost of the job:

- as a percentage of the prime cost of the job, or
- as a percentage of the production cost of the job.

Example

The following cost information has been gathered about Job number 453.

The direct materials cost is $100, the direct labour cost is $60 and direct expenses are $40. Direct labour costs $20 per hour. Production overheads are charged at the rate of $30 per direct labour hour and non-production overheads are charged at the rate of 40% of prime cost.

The job cost for Job 453 is calculated as follows:

Job cost: Job 453

	$
Direct materials	100
Direct labour (3 hours at $20)	60
Direct expenses	40
Prime cost	100
Production overhead (3 hours at $30)	90
Production cost of the job	190
Non-production overheads (40% of prime cost)	40
Total job cost	230

1.3 Cost records and accounts for job costing

In order to establish the cost of each individual job in a costing system, it is necessary to have procedures for recording direct costs in such a way that they can be allocated to specific jobs. Production overheads and non-production overheads can be charged using overhead absorption rates within a system of absorption costing.

Each job is given a unique identity number, or job number. The costs for individual jobs are recorded as follows.

- The direct materials costs for a job are issued directly from stores to the job. The materials requisition note should specify the job number and the costs of the materials are charged to the job.
- The labour time spent on a job is recorded on time sheets or job sheets. The time sheets for each individual employee identify the jobs he has worked on and the time that he spent on each job. These can be converted into a cost for the job at the employee's hourly rate.
- A system is needed for recording direct expenses to specific jobs. Costs might be obtained from purchase invoices from suppliers, and recorded in the job cost record (the 'job sheet') for the job.
- Production overheads are charged to the job (absorbed, in an absorption costing system) at the appropriate absorption rate, when the job has been completed.
- Similarly, non-production overheads can be charged when the job has been finished by charging them at the appropriate absorption rate.

Direct costs and overheads are recorded on a job sheet or job card for the job. At one time, a job card used to be an actual card or sheet of paper, although job costing systems are now likely to be computerised.

In a costing system, a job account is similar to a work in progress account, except that it is for one job only. In a company that specialises in jobbing work, the work in progress account is the total of all the individual job accounts.

Job account: Job 12345

	$		$
Direct materials	1,800	Cost of sales	7,300
Direct wages	2,500		
Direct expenses			
Production overhead	3,000		
	7,300		7,300

When the job is finished, the total cost of the job is transferred to the cost of sales.

Batch costing

- The nature of batch production
- The nature of batch costing
- Cost records and accounts for batch costing

2 Batch costing

2.1 The nature of batch production

As the name might suggest, batch costing is a system of costing for items that are produced in batches rather than individually. A batch might also be called a 'production run'.

Batch costing is used when production units are manufactured in batches or production runs.

Batch production is used in manufacturing in the following circumstances:

- The capacity of a factory to make a product exceeds the sales demand for the product. The factory is therefore not required to make the product continuously. Instead it makes the product in occasional 'production runs' or batches.
- The factory makes several different products using the same equipment or machinery. The machinery must therefore switch between making the different products, which means that the products will not be manufactured continuously. Instead the products are made in occasional 'production runs' or batches. For example, a company might manufacture a range of wooden furniture items on the same machinery. It might manufacture a batch of 100 tables, followed by a batch of 400 chairs, followed by a batch of 200 bookshelves, and so on.
- In some industries, it might be impractical to manufacture items except by making them several units at a time, in batches. An example is the manufacture of bread rolls and other products in a bakery. Several bread rolls are put into the baking oven on the same tray and they are made at the same time, all in the same batch.

The products are therefore made in batches, several units at a time. The finished units are transferred to finished goods inventory. The product is not manufactured again until the finished goods inventory is sold and more units are required. Another batch of the product is then manufactured.

2.2 The nature of batch costing

In **batch costing**, the total cost is established for each individual batch, where each batch consists of a large number of similar units or items.

Unlike job costing, however, it is less common to include non-production overhead costs within the total batch cost, although it is certainly possible to do so.

To establish the cost per unit, the total batch cost is divided by the number of units produced in the batch.

In all other respects, batch costing is very similar to job costing.

Batch number 123	$
Direct materials	550
Direct labour	300
Production overhead absorbed	750
Total production cost, batch 123	1,600
Number of units made in the batch	2,000
Production cost per unit	$0.80

To prepare for the next batch production run, there might be set-up costs. If so, set-up costs can be charged directly to the cost of the batch.

2.3 Cost records and accounts for batch costing

In job costing, it is necessary to record the direct costs of each job. In the same way, in a system of batch costing there must be a system for charging costs directly to individual batches or production runs.

- Each batch or production run should be given a unique identity code.
- When direct materials are issued from store, the materials requisition note should specify the batch for which the materials will be used.
- Direct labour time spent on each production run or batch can be recorded on time sheets within each production cost centre.

Service costing

- The nature of services and operations
- Service costing, product costing and job costing compared
- Cost units in service costing: composite cost units
- Calculating the cost per unit of service (or operation)

3 Service costing

3.1 The nature of services and operations

It is usual to explain costing in terms of how to calculate and record the costs of manufactured products. However, many business entities do not make and sell products: they provide services. Hotel services, consultancy services, legal and accounting services, providers of telephone services (telecommunications companies), providers of television and radio channels, entertainment services, postal services, medical services, and so on.

Operations are activities. Like services, they do not result in a finished product to sell to customers. Examples of operations include a customer service centre taking telephone calls and e-mails from customers, and the staff canteen providing meals to employees.

Costs can be established for services, such as hotel accommodation, telephone calls, auditing work, holidays and travel, and so on. The costs of a service are the sum of direct materials, direct labour, direct expenses (if any) and a share of operational overheads.

Costs can also be established for operations, in a similar way.

3.2 Service costing , product costing and job costing compared

Service costing differs from costing in manufacturing industries in several ways.

- There is no production system; therefore there are no production overheads.
- Direct materials costs are often a fairly small proportion of total costs (for example, the direct materials costs to a telecommunications company of providing telephone services are very small).
- In some service industries, direct labour costs are high (for example, in the film-making industry, accountancy and investment banking).
- General overhead costs can be a very high proportion of total costs.
- Inventory is usually very small; therefore absorption costing is usually of little or no value for management information purposes.

Not all entities that provide services will use service costing. The purpose of service costing is to provide information to management about the costs of different services that the entity provides, and the profitability of each of the different services. Each service should be fairly standard. If they are not standard services, it is more sensible to use job costing to calculate the cost of each 'job' of service. For example:

- Service costing might be used by a hospital to record or calculate the cost of each of the different services provided by the hospital, such as the cost of treating a patient for a particular condition.
- Job costing might be used by a professional firm such as a firm of accountants or solicitors, where the cost of each job depends largely on the amount of time spent on each job by the professional staff.

3.3 Cost units in service costing: composite cost units

One of the main problems with service costing is that it can be difficult to identify a suitable cost unit for the service. It is often appropriate to use a composite cost unit in service costing. This is a cost that is made up from two variables, such as a cost per man per day (a cost per 'man/day'). Here, the two variables are 'men' (the number of employees) and 'days'.

Examples of composite **cost units used in service costing** are as follows:

- The cost per room per day. This is a useful unit cost in the hotel services industry.
- The cost per passenger mile or the cost per passenger kilometre (= the average cost of transporting a passenger for one mile or one kilometre). This unit measure of cost is used by transport companies that provide bus or train services.
- The cost per tonne mile delivered (= the average cost of transporting one tonne of goods for one mile). This unit cost is commonly used for costing freight services and delivery operations.
- The cost per patient/day (= the average cost of treating one patient for one day) or the cost per hospital bed/day (= the cost of maintaining one hospital bed in a hospital for one day). These costs are used by health service providers.
- The cost per man day. This unit cost is widely used in professional services, such as auditing, legal services and consultancy services.

Composite cost units can be used in addition to a 'job costing' type of service costing system. For example, a firm of accountants might calculate the cost of each job performed for a client. In addition, it might calculate average the cost per man day for the professional services that it provides.

- The cost of each service 'job' enables management to monitor costs and profits on individual jobs for a customer.
- The composite cost, which is an average cost for all 'jobs' allows management to monitor the general level of costs.

3.4 Calculating the cost per unit of service (or operation)

The cost of a service unit is (or composite cost unit) is calculated as follows.

$$\text{Cost per unit of service} = \frac{\text{Total costs of the service}}{\text{Number of units of service}}$$

Total costs are the costs of direct materials, direct labour and direct expenses, plus a charge for overheads (unless marginal costing is used to cost the services).

The total number of service units might be a bit more difficult to calculate. Here are a few examples.

Example

A hotel has 80 standard twin-bedded rooms. The hotel is fully-occupied for each of the 350 days in each year that it is open. The total costs of running the hotel each year are $3,360,000.

What would be a useful measure of the cost of providing the hotel services?

Answer

A useful unit cost is the cost per room/day. This is the average cost of maintaining one room in the hotel for one day.

Room/days per year = 80 rooms × 350 days = 28,000
Cost per room/day = $3,360,000/28,000 = $120.

Example

A train company operates a service between two cities, Southtown and Northtown. The distance between the cities is 400 miles. During the previous year, the company transported 200,000 passengers from Southtown to Northtown and 175,000 passengers from Northtown to Southtown. The total costs of operating the service were $60 million.

What would be a useful measure of the cost of providing the train service between the two cities?

Answer

A useful unit cost is the cost per passenger/mile. This is the average cost of transporting one passenger for one mile.

Passenger/miles per year = (200,000 × 400) + (175,000 × 400) = 150 million.
Cost per passenger/mile = $60,000,000/150,000,000 = $0.40.

Practice multiple choice questions

1 A company does jobbing work for customers. Job 947 has direct materials costs of \$125, direct labour costs of \$80 and direct expenses of \$25. Direct labour is paid \$20 per hour. Production overheads are charged at the rate of \$35 per hour and non-production overheads are charged as 60% of prime cost.

What is the cost for Job 947?

A \$493

B \$508

C \$514

D \$592

(2 marks)

2 Which one of the following firms is most likely to use a system of job costing?

A A company that manufactures motor cars on a production line

B A telephone company that provides mobile telecommunications services

C A chemical manufacturer that produces processed chemicals

D A company that installs elevators in office buildings ***(2 marks)***

3 A road haulage company transports goods. It operates two trucks. During a particular period, the two trucks travelled a total of 80,000 kilometres carrying goods. The average load was 3 tonnes per journey. In total they made 200 journeys. Total costs were \$720,000.

What is the average cost per tonne-kilometre transported?

A \$3

B \$4.50

C \$6

D \$12 ***(2 marks)***

CHAPTER

10

Process costing

Contents

Introduction to process costing

- The characteristics of process costing
- Situations where process costing might be appropriate

1 Introduction to process costing

1.1 The characteristics of process costing

Process costing is a system of costing output from a production process. There are several characteristics that make process costing different from other types of costing, such as unit costing, job costing and batch costing. (Process costing provides a system of costing where any or all of these characteristics occur.)

- There is a manufacturing process in which output is continually produced from the process and output is normally measured in total quantities, such as tonnes or litres produced, or in very large quantities of small units (such as the number of cans or tins).
- In the production process, materials might be added in full at the start of a process, or might be added gradually throughout the process. The materials are processed to produce the final output. In a process costing system, it is usual to distinguish between:
  - direct materials and
  - conversion costs, which are direct labour costs and production overheads.
- There might be losses in the process, due to evaporation or chemical reaction and the quantity of output might therefore be less than the quantity of materials input. Process costing provides a system of costing that allows for expected losses in the manufacturing process.
- When there is a continuous production process, it is difficult to measure the quantity of work-in-process (incomplete production) at the end of a financial period. Process costing provides a method of measuring and costing incomplete WIP.
- In some processes, more than one product might be output from the same process. When more than one product is output, they might be called joint products or a by-product. Process costing offers methods of costing each of the different products.
- In some process manufacturing systems, there is a series of sequential processes. For example a manufacturing system might consist of three consecutive processes: raw materials are input to Process 1, then the output from Process 1 goes onto the next process (Process 2) and the output from Process 2 then goes into a final process, Process 3. The output from Process 3 is the final product.

Processes are different, and all these characteristics do not occur in all processes. For the purpose of your examination, processes will not include all these characteristics. For example, you might be given a question in which there are losses in process but no opening or closing WIP; or you might be given a question in which there is opening or closing WIP but no losses in process.

Even so, process costing can be fairly complex, and you need to study this chapter carefully.

1.2 Situations where process costing might be appropriate

Process costing is used when output is produced in a continuous process system, and it is difficult to separate individual units of output. Examples of manufacturing where process costing is used are:

- chemicals manufacture
- the manufacture of liquids
- the continuous manufacture of high volumes of low-cost food items such as tins of peas or beans, or bottles of tomato ketchup.

In these types of production process, losses in process might occur and there are often problems in measuring exactly the amount of unfinished work-in-process at the end of a period.

The basic principle of costing is the same as for other types of costing. The cost of output from a process is measured as:

$$\frac{\text{Total costs of the process}}{\text{Total units produced}}$$

However, in process costing there are special methods for costing loss in process and for dealing with process costs when there is opening and closing WIP.

Process costing: losses

- Process costing and normal loss
- Accounting for normal loss
- Process costing: accounting for normal loss when loss has a scrap value
- Introduction to abnormal loss
- Accounting for abnormal loss
- Process costing: abnormal loss and loss with a scrap value

2 Process costing: losses

2.1 Process costing and normal loss

A feature of process manufacturing is that there is often some loss or wastage in production, and output quantities are less than input quantities of materials.

- **Normal loss** is the expected loss in processing. Normal loss is usually expressed as a percentage of the input units of materials.
- **Expected output** = Input materials quantities – Normal loss

2.2 Accounting for normal loss

Normal loss is not given a value if it does not have a scrap value. This is logical, because if there will always be some loss in a process, it makes no sense to give a cost to the expected loss. It makes more sense to calculate the cost of the expected output by making an allowance for the expected loss.

The cost per unit of output =

$$\frac{\text{Total costs of the process}}{\text{Expected units of output}}$$

For example, suppose that input to a process is 100 units and expected loss is 10% of the input quantity. The process costs are $4,500. Expected output is 90 units.

- We could calculate the cost of production as $45 per unit of input, so that the cost of output is $4,050 (= 90 units × $45) and the expected loss has a cost of $450 (= 10 units × $45). This is not appropriate, however, because the loss is expected to happen and giving it a cost serves no useful purpose and certainly does not provide useful management information.
- We could calculate the cost of output as $50 per unit, which is the cost of the process divided by the expected output (= $4,500/90 units). This is the method of costing used when there is normal loss. Output is costed in a way that recognises the loss that should be expected to occur.

e

Example

The following information relates to a production process:

Input quantities of materials: 2,000 litres
Direct materials cost: $3,600
Direct labour cost: $300
Production overhead absorbed: $600
Normal loss as % of input: 10%
Actual output is 1,800 litres, and actual loss = expected loss (normal loss)

The cost per unit produced can be calculated as follows:

	$
Direct materials	3,600
Direct labour	300
Production overheads	600
Total production cost	4,500
Expected output (90% of 2,000)	1,800 litres
Cost per litre (= production cost/expected output)	$2.50

Accounting for normal loss: cost ledger

These costs could be set out in a process cost account. This is a work-in-progress account for the process. The debit side of the account records direct materials and direct labour costs, and production overheads absorbed. (= a work-in-progress account for the process) as follows. The credit side of the WIP account records the cost of the finished output.

The account also includes memorandum columns for the quantities of direct materials input and the quantities of output and loss. Normal loss is shown so that the quantities columns add up to the same amount on the debit or credit sides, but the normal loss has no cost.

Process account

	litres	$		litres	$
Direct materials	2,000	3,600	Cost of sales	1,800	4,500
Direct labour	-	300	(at $2.50 each)		
Overhead	-	600	Normal loss	200	-
	2,000	4,500		2,000	4,500

2.3 Process costing: accounting for normal loss when loss has a scrap value

In some cases, losses in a process have a scrap value. When loss has a scrap value, the **scrap value of the normal loss** is deducted from the cost of the process. A cost per unit of output is calculated as:

$$\frac{\text{Total costs of the process minus the scrap value of normal loss}}{\text{Expected units of output}}$$

Example: scrap value of normal loss

The following information relates to a production process:

Input quantities of materials: 2,000 litres
Direct materials cost: $3,600
Direct labour cost: $300
Production overhead absorbed: $600
Normal loss as % of input: 10%
Actual output is 1,800 units, and actual loss = expected loss (normal loss)
Loss has a scrap value of $0.90 per litre.
The cost per unit produced can be calculated as follows:

	$
Direct materials	3,600
Direct labour	300
Production overheads	600
	4,500
Less: scrap value of normal loss (200 x $0.90)	180
	4,320
Expected output (90% of 2,000)	1,800 litres
Cost per litre	$2.40

These costs could be set out in a process cost account as follows.

Process account

	litres	$		litres	$
Direct materials	2,000	3,600	Cost of sales (at $2.40 each)	1,800	4,320
Direct labour	-	300			
Overhead	-	600	Normal loss (at $0.90): scrap account	200	180
	2,000	4,500		2,000	4,500

This is exactly the same as the previous process account showing normal loss, with the exception that the scrap value of the normal loss is shown as a value for the normal loss in the credit side of the account.

2.4 Introduction to abnormal loss

Normal loss is the expected amount of loss in a process. Actual loss might be more than the expected or normal loss. When actual loss exceeds normal loss, there is abnormal loss. The difference between total actual loss and normal loss is abnormal loss.

Abnormal loss = Actual loss – Expected (normal) loss, when actual loss is higher than expected loss.

Alternatively:
Total loss = Normal loss + Abnormal loss.

Abnormal loss is not expected and should not happen. It therefore makes sense to give it a cost. By giving a cost to abnormal loss, management information about the loss can be provided, and management can be made aware of the extent of any problem that might exist with excessive losses in process.

2.5 Accounting for abnormal loss

Units of abnormal loss are given a cost. If it is assumed that all losses in process occur at the end of the process, units of abnormal loss are costed in exactly the same way in the as units of finished output.

The cost of actual output units and the cost of abnormal loss units = the cost of an expected unit of output. The cost per unit of abnormal loss is therefore:

$$\frac{\text{Total costs of the process}}{\text{Expected units of output}}$$

The cost of units of abnormal loss is treated as an expense for the period, and charged as an expense in the income statement for the period.

Example: abnormal loss

The following information relates to a production process:

Input quantities of materials: 2,000 litres
Direct materials cost: $3,600
Direct labour cost: $300
Production overhead absorbed: $600
Normal loss as % of input: 10%
Actual output is 1,700 units.

Actual loss is 300 units in total (= 2,000 – 1,700). Normal loss = 200 litres (= 10% of 2,000); therefore abnormal loss = 100 litres.

The cost per unit produced can be calculated as follows:

	$
Direct materials	3,600
Direct labour	300
Production overheads	600
	4,500
Expected output (90% of 2,000 = actual output + abnormal loss)	1,800 litres
Cost per litre	$2.50

Cost of finished output = 1,700 units × $2.50 = $4,250.
Cost of abnormal loss = 100 units × $2.50 = $250.

Accounting for abnormal loss: ledger entries

These costs could be set out in a process cost account as follows.

Process account

	litres	$		litres	$
Direct materials	2,000	3,600	Cost of sales (at $2.50)	1,700	4,250
Direct labour	-	300	Normal loss	200	0
Overhead	-	600	Abnormal loss (at $2.50)	100	250
	2,000	4,500		2,000	4,500

Notice that abnormal loss is included in the credit side of the account, in the same way that normal loss is shown on the credit side. However whereas normal loss has no value/cost, abnormal loss has a cost. The appropriate double entry in the cost ledger is:
Debit: Abnormal loss account
Credit: Work-in-process account

Abnormal loss account

	litres	$		$
WIP account	100	250		

At the end of the financial period, the balance on the abnormal loss account is written off as a cost in the costin gincome statement.

2.5 Process costing: abnormal loss and loss with a scrap value

When loss has a scrap value, the scrap value of **normal loss** is deducted from the process cost, as explained earlier.

Any abnormal loss will also have a scrap value. However, the scrap value of abnormal loss is treated differently from the scrap value of normal loss.

- The cost of expected units of output is calculated in the usual way.

- In the WIP account the cost of abnormal loss = units of abnormal loss × cost per expected unit of output.

- The scrap value of abnormal loss is set off against the cost of abnormal loss in the abnormal loss account, not the process account (WIP).
  - Debit: Cash (= scrap value: money from sale of the scrapped units)
  - Credit: Abnormal loss account (abnormal loss units × scrap value per unit)
- The net cost of abnormal loss (= cost of abnormal loss minus its scrap value) is then transferred as a cost to the cost accounting income statement at the end of the accounting period.

Example: abnormal loss when loss has a scrap value

The following information relates to a production process:

Input quantities of materials: 2,000 litres
Direct materials cost: $3,600
Direct labour cost: $300
Production overhead absorbed: $600
Normal loss as % of input: 10%
Loss has a scrap value of $0.90 per litre.

Actual output is 1,700 litres. and actual loss is 300 litres. Normal loss = 200 litres; therefore abnormal loss = 100 litres.

Actual loss is 300 units. Normal loss is 200 units; therefore abnormal loss is 100 units.

	$
Direct materials	3,600
Direct labour	300
Production overheads	600
	4,500
Scrap value of **normal loss** (200 × $0.90)	180
	4,320

Expected output (1,700 litres + 100 litres)	1,800 litres
Cost per litre	$2.40

These costs would be set out in a process cost account as follows:

Process account

	litres	$		litres	$
Direct materials	2,000	3,600	Cost of sales (at $2.40)	1,700	4,080
Direct labour	-	300	Normal loss (at $0.90)	200	180
Overhead	-	600	Abnormal loss (at $2.40)	100	240
	2,000	4,500		2,000	4,500

Abnormal loss account

	litres	$		litres	$
WIP	100	240	Scrap (at $0.90)	100	90

At the end of the financial period, the balance on this account should be written off in the costing income statement as a cost for the period.

Scrap account

	litres	$		litres	$
WIP: normal loss	200	180	Bank (or financial ledger control account)	300	270
Abnormal loss	100	90			
		270			270

Process costing: abnormal gain

- Definition of abnormal gain
- Accounting for abnormal gain: no scrap value for loss
- Accounting for abnormal gain: where loss has a scrap value

3 Process costing: abnormal gain

3.1 Definition of abnormal gain

Abnormal loss occurs when actual loss is more than the expected (normal) loss. **Abnormal gain** occurs when the actual loss is less than normal loss. Abnormal gain is the difference between the normal loss (expected loss) and the actual loss.

Abnormal gain = Expected (normal) loss – Actual loss, when actual loss is less than expected loss.

Alternatively:
Actual loss = Normal loss – Abnormal gain

3.2 Accounting for abnormal gain: no scrap value for loss

The method of costing for abnormal gain is the same in principle as for abnormal loss. If it is assumed that all losses occur at the end of the process, the cost per unit of finished output and the value/cost of abnormal gain are calculated as the cost per expected unit of output.

When loss has no scrap value, the cost/value per unit of abnormal loss is therefore:

$$\frac{\text{Total costs of the process}}{\text{Expected units of output}}$$

The differences between costing for abnormal loss and costing for abnormal gain are that:

- Abnormal gain is a benefit rather than a cost: whereas abnormal loss is written off as a cost at the end of the financial period, abnormal gain is an adjustment that increases the profit for the period.
- Abnormal gain is recorded as a debit entry in the process account, because it is a benefit.
- The other half of the double entry is recorded in an abnormal gain account. At the end of the period, the balance on the abnormal gain account is then transferred to the income statement as a benefit for the period, adding to profit.

Example: abnormal gain

The following information relates to a production process:

Input quantities of materials: 2,000 litres
Direct materials cost: $3,600
Conversion costs (= direct labour + production overheads): $900
Normal loss as % of input: 10%
Actual output is 1,850 litres, and actual loss is 150 litres.

Normal loss = 200 litres (= 10% of 2,000) and actual loss is 150 units. There is abnormal gain of 50 litres.

The cost per unit produced can be calculated as follows:

	$
Direct materials	3,600
Conversion costs	900
	4,500
Expected output	1,800 litres
Cost per litre	$2.50

Cost of actual finished output = 1,850 units × $2.50 = $4,625
Value of abnormal gain = 50 units × $2.50 = $125.

Accounting for abnormal gain: ledger entries

These costs could be set out in a process cost account as follows:

Process account

	litres	$		litres	$
Direct materials	2,000	3,600	Cost of sales (at $2.50)	1,850	4,625
Conversion costs	-	900	Normal loss	200	0
Abnormal gain (at $2.50)	50	125			
	2,050	4,625		2,050	4,625

Notice that the abnormal gain is shown on the debit side of the account, and the total number of units in the memorandum column for quantities (2,050) is larger than the actual quantity of units input to the process (2,000).

Abnormal gain account

	litres	$		litres	$
			WIP	50	125

The balance on this account should be taken to the costing income statement at the end of the period, and will add to the reported profit.

3.3 Accounting for abnormal gain: where loss has a scrap value

When loss has a scrap value, the value of abnormal gain is actually less than the amount shown in the WIP account. This is because actual revenue from scrap will be less than the expected revenue, due to the fact that actual loss is less than the expected loss.

Accounting for the scrap value of abnormal gain is similar to accounting for the scrap value of abnormal loss.

- In the process account (WIP), abnormal gain is valued at the cost per expected unit of output.
- The scrap value of normal loss is normal loss units × scrap value per unit.
- The scrap value of abnormal gain is the scrap revenue that has been 'lost' because actual loss is less than expected loss. This is abnormal gain units × scrap value per unit.
- The scrap value of abnormal gain is recorded as a debit entry in the abnormal gain account (in a similar way to recoding the scrap value of abnormal loss as a credit entry in the abnormal loss account).
- The scrap value of the abnormal gain is set off against the value of the abnormal gain in the abnormal gain account, not the process account.
- The balance on the abnormal gain account is the net value of abnormal gain (= value of abnormal gain minus the scrap value not earned). This balance is transferred as a net benefit to the cost accounting income statement at the end of the accounting period.

e

Example

The following information relates to a production process:

Input quantities of materials: 2,000 litres
Direct materials cost: $3,600
Conversion costs (= direct labour + production overhead): $900
Normal loss as % of input: 10%
Loss has a scrap value of $0.90 per litre.

Actual output is 1,850 litres, and actual loss is 150 litres. Normal loss = 200 litres; therefore abnormal gain = 50 litres.

	$
Direct materials	3,600
Conversion costs	900
	4,500
Scrap value of normal loss (200 × $0.90)	180
	4,320

Expected output	1,800 litres
Cost per litre	$2.40

Cost of actual finished output = 1,850 units × $2.40 = $4,440
Value of abnormal gain = 50 units × $2.40 = $120.

These costs could be set out in a process cost account as follows:

Process (WIP) account

	litres	$		litres	$
Direct materials	2,000	3,600	Cost of sales (at $2.40)	1,850	4,440
Conversion costs	-	900	Normal loss (at $0.90 scrap value)	200	180
Abnormal gain (at $2.40)	50	120			
	2,050	4,620		2,050	4,620

Abnormal gain account

	litres	$		litres	$
Scrap (at $0.90)	50	45	WIP	50	120
					120

The balance on this account is $75. This is treated as an addition to profit in the cost accounting income statement for the period.

Exercise 1: process costing and losses

From the following information, prepare:

- the process account,
- the abnormal loss or abnormal gain account.

Process: Input 6,000 units

Normal loss: 5% of input

Direct materials: $21,600

Direct labour: $8,000

Production overhead: $16,000

Actual output: 5,500 units

Loss has a scrap value per unit of $3.80.

Exercise 2: process costing and losses

- From the following information, prepare the process account.

Process: Input 10,000 units

Normal loss: 4% of input

Direct materials: $35,200

Conversion costs: $29,600

Actual output: 9,750 units

Loss has no scrap value.

Process costing: inventory valuation and equivalent units

- Sharing out process costs between finished units and unfinished inventory
- Equivalent units
- A three-stage calculation
- Weighted average cost and FIFO valuation methods

4 Process costing: inventory valuation and equivalent units

4.1 Sharing out process costs between finished units and unfinished inventory

When manufacturing is a continuous process, there may be unfinished work-in-progress ('work-in-process') at the beginning of an accounting period and at the end of the period. Since inventory is unfinished, its cost or value is less than the cost of a unit of completed output. The common costs of the process must be shared between finished output and unfinished work-in-process on a fair basis. The basis of apportionment used in process costing is equivalent units.

4.2 Equivalent units

An equivalent unit means 'equal to one finished unit of output'.

- One fully-finished unit of production = 1 equivalent unit
- One unit 50% complete = 0.50 equivalent units. 400 units 50% complete = 200 equivalent units.
- One unit 20% complete = 0.20 equivalent units. 400 units 20% complete = 80 equivalent units.

Costs are shared between finished units and inventory by calculating a cost per equivalent unit:

$$\text{Cost per equivalent unit} = \frac{\text{Costs of the process}}{\text{Number of equivalent units produced}}$$

Equivalent units of closing inventory

It is normally assumed that direct materials are added to the production process at the beginning of the process and that direct labour operations are carried out throughout the process. When this assumption is used, units of closing inventory are:

- 100% complete for direct material costs added at the beginning of the process, but

- only partly-complete for direct labour and production overhead costs, and only partly complete for additional materials that are added throughout the process.

The number of equivalent units of direct materials cost in a period will therefore differ from the number of equivalent units of conversion costs (direct labour and production overhead).

A cost per equivalent unit is therefore calculated separately for:

- direct materials
- conversion costs.

Costs for finished output and closing inventory can be calculated from the number of equivalent units and the cost per equivalent unit.

4.3 A three-stage calculation

We recommend a three-stage calculation:

- Prepare a **statement of equivalent units**. This should calculate the equivalent units (direct materials and conversion costs) for output from the process and for closing WIP
- Next, prepare a **statement of cost per equivalent unit**. There should be a separate cost per equivalent unit of direct materials and a cost per cost per equivalent unit of conversion costs.
- Third, prepare a **statement of evaluation**. This is a statement of the cost of finished output and closing WIP, which is prepared from your statement of equivalent units and statement of cost per equivalent unit.

Example

At the beginning of a financial period, there were no units of opening work-in-process. During the period, input to the process was 4,000 units. During the period 3,500 units were output from the process and closing WIP was 500 units.

All the direct materials are added to production at the beginning of the process.

Closing inventory of 500 units was therefore 100% complete for materials, and production was 40% complete.

Costs incurred during the period were:

Direct materials: $24,000

Conversion costs: $7,400

Required: calculate the cost of the finished output and the value of closing WIP.

a

Answer

Statement of equivalent units

Output	Total units	Direct materials		Conversion costs	
		Degree of completion	Equivalent units	Degree of completion	Equivalent units
Finished output	3,500	100%	3,500	100%	3,500
Closing WIP	500	100%	500	40%	200
	4,000		4,000		3,700

Statement of cost per equivalent unit

	Direct materials	Conversion costs
Total costs	$24,000	$47,400
Equivalent units	4,000	3,700
Cost per equivalent unit	$6	$2

Statement of evaluation

		Finished output		Closing WIP
		$		$
Direct materials	(3,500 × $6)	21,000	(500 × $6)	3,000
Conversion costs	(3,500 × $2)	7,000	(200 × $2)	400
Total cost		28,000		3,400

These costs would be recorded in the process account as follows.

Process (WIP) account

	units	$		units	$
Direct materials	4,000	24,000	Finished goods	3,500	28,000
Conversion costs	-	7,400	Closing WIP	500	3,400
	4,000	31,400		4,000	31,400

4.4 Weighted average cost and FIFO valuation methods

Another problem with establishing the cost of finished output and inventory in process costing is the problem of how to work out costs when there is opening inventory at the beginning of the period. When there is opening WIP, output from a process(and closing WIP) can be valued on either of the following bases:

- weighted average cost method
- first-in, first-out (FIFO) method

You need to know how to apply each of these different valuation methods.

Equivalent units: weighted average cost method

- The underlying principle
- The three-stage calculation
- Weighted average cost method: summary

5 Equivalent units: weighted average cost method

5.1 The underlying principle

When the weighted average cost method is used, the assumption is that all units produced during the period and all units of closing inventory should be valued at the same cost per equivalent unit for materials and the same cost per equivalent unit for conversion costs.

An average cost per equivalent unit is therefore calculated for all units of output and closing inventory. This includes the units that were partly-completed at the beginning of the period (and which were therefore valued as closing WIP at the end of the previous period).

5.2 The three-stage calculation

The costs are worked out in a similar way to the previous example (where there was no opening WIP).

- **Statement of equivalent units**. Prepare a statement of equivalent units for finished output (1 equivalent unit of direct materials and 1 equivalent unit of conversion costs each) and for closing WIP.
- **Statement of cost per equivalent unit**. Calculate the cost per equivalent unit for direct materials and the cost per equivalent unit for conversion costs. However, remember to include the cost of the opening WIP. The materials cost of the opening WIP should be included in the total direct materials cost, and the conversion costs in the opening WIP should be added to the conversion costs for the current period.

$$\text{Cost per equivalent unit} = \frac{\text{Cost of opening inventory} + \text{Costs incurred in the period}}{\text{Equivalent units of output and closing inventory}}$$

  Remember that you will normally have to calculate a separate cost per equivalent units for materials and for conversion costs. This is because the equivalent units of closing inventory will be different for materials and conversion costs.

- **Statement of evaluation**. Having calculated the equivalent units and a cost per equivalent unit, prepare a statement of evaluation.

Example

From the following information relating to a production process in March, calculate the cost of finished output in the month and the value of the closing inventory, using the weighted average cost valuation method:

Opening inventory on 1 March: 3,000 units

100% complete for direct materials

30% complete for conversion costs

Cost = $13,570 (= direct materials $12,600 + conversion costs $970)

Costs incurred during March:

Direct materials: 7,000 units input, cost $28,000

Conversion costs: $17,430

Units completed in the month (finished goods): 8,000 units

Closing inventory:

2,000 units: 100% complete for direct materials and 60% complete for conversion costs.

Answer

Equivalent units	Total	Direct materials		Conversion costs
	Total units	Equivalent units		Equivalent units
Completed units	8,000	8,000		8,000
Closing inventory	2,000	2,000	(2,000 x 60%)	1,200
Total equivalent units	10,000	10,000		9,200

Statement of cost per equivalent unit

Costs	Direct materials	Conversion costs
	$	$
Opening inventory	12,600	970
Costs incurred in the period	28,000	17,430
Total costs	40,600	18,400
Equivalent units	10,000	9,200
Cost per equivalent unit	$4.06	$2

Statement of evaluation

		Finished output		Closing WIP
		$		$
Direct materials	(8,000 × $4.06)	32,480	(2,000 × 4.06)	8,120
Conversion costs	(8,000 × $2)	16,000	(1,200 × $2)	2,400
Total cost		48,480		10,520

These costs would be recorded in the process account as follows.

Process (WIP) account

	units	$		units	$
Opening WIP	3,000	13,570	Finished goods	8,000	48,480
Direct materials	7,000	28,000			
Conversion costs	-	17,430	Closing WIP	2,000	10,520
	10,000	59,000		10,000	59,000

5.3 Weighted average cost method: summary

The weighted average cost method for process costing with opening WIP can be summarised as follows.

- All output and closing inventory is valued at the same cost per equivalent unit
- Cost of opening inventory + Costs in the period = Total costs
- Units of closing inventory + Units of output in the period = Total equivalent units
- Cost per equivalent unit = Total costs/Total equivalent units

	Direct materials	Conversion costs
Cost of opening inventory	M_1	C_1
Costs incurred in the period	M_2	C_2
Total costs	$M_1 + M_2$	$C_1 + C_2$
Number of units output	P	P
Equivalent units of closing inventory	I_m	I_c
Total equivalent units	$P + I_m$	$P + I_c$
Cost per equivalent unit	$(M_1 + M_2) \div (P + I_m)$	$(C_1 + C_2) \div (P + I_c)$

e
3

Exercise 3: weighted average cost method

From the following information relating to Process 2 in April:

(a) calculate the cost of finished output in the month and the value of the closing inventory, using the weighted average cost valuation method

(b) prepare the process account for the period.

Opening inventory on 1 April: 2,000 units:

100% complete for direct materials

80% complete for conversion costs

Cost $20,900 (= direct materials $14,800 + conversion costs $6,100)

Costs incurred during April:

Direct materials: 14,000 units input, cost $70,000

Conversion costs: $34,200

Completed units in the month: 11,000 units

Closing inventory on 30 April:

5,000 units: 100% complete for direct materials and 40% complete for conversion costs.

Equivalent units: FIFO method

6 Equivalent units: FIFO method

6.1 Assumption with the FIFO method of process costing

With the weighted average cost method of costing, it is assumed that all units of output in a period have the same cost per unit.

With the first-in, first-out (FIFO) method of process costing, it is assumed that the opening units of work-in-process at the beginning of the month will be the first units completed. The cost of these units is their value at the beginning of the period plus the cost to complete them in the current period.

6.2 Equivalent units of work done in the current period

It is necessary to calculate the number of equivalent units of work done in the period. This consists of:

- The equivalent units of direct materials and conversion costs required to complete the opening WIP. These are the first units completed in the period.
- The equivalent units of finished output in the period that was started as well as finished in the period. These have one equivalent unit of direct materials and one equivalent unit of conversion costs. The total number of these units is:
  - the total finished output in the period
  - **minus** the quantity of opening WIP (which are completed first)
- The equivalent units of closing WIP (calculated in the normal way).

A cost per equivalent unit, for direct materials and conversion costs, is now calculated as:

$$\frac{\text{Costs of the process in the current period (exclude opening WIP value)}}{\text{Number of equivalent units of work done in the period}}$$

The equivalent units in the current period to complete the opening WIP are calculated using the following percentage value:

- 100%
- minus the degree of completion at the beginning of the period.

For example, suppose that opening WIP is 1,000 units which is 100% complete for direct materials and 70% complete for conversion costs. The number of equivalent units in the current period to complete the opening WIP is 0 for direct materials (= 1,000 × (100 – 100)%) and 300 for conversion costs (= 1,000 × (100 – 70)%).

6.3 The three-stage calculation

The three-stage calculation with the FIFO method is similar to the calculation method previously described, with the exception that in the statement of evaluation, the cost of finished output consists of:

- the finished cost of opening WIP (completed first) plus
- the cost of finished output started as well as finished in the period.

The finished cost of opening WIP is the sum of:

- the costs in the opening WIP value at the start of the period
- the costs in the current period to complete these units.

Study the following example carefully.

Example: FIFO method of process costing

From the following information relating to Process 1 in March, calculate the cost of finished output in the month and the value of the closing inventory, using the FIFO cost valuation method:

Opening inventory on 1 March: 3,000 units

100% complete for direct materials

30% complete for conversion costs

Cost $13,570 (= direct materials $12,600 + conversion costs $970)

Costs incurred during March:

Direct materials: 7,000 units input, cost $28,000

Conversion costs: $17,430

Completed units in the month: 8,000 units

Closing inventory: 2,000 units 100% complete for direct materials and 60% complete for conversion costs.

Answer

Statement of equivalent units (work done in the current period)

Equivalent units	Total units		Direct materials Equivalent units		Conversion costs Equivalent units
To complete opening inventory, finished first	3,000	(0%)	0	(70% × 3,000)	2,100
Units started and completed in the current period (8,000 – 3,000)	5,000		5,000		5,000
Finished output	8,000		5,000		7,100
Closing inventory	2,000		2,000	(2,000 × 60%)	1,200
Total equivalent units	10,000		7,000		8,300

Statement of cost per equivalent unit in the current period

Cost per equivalent unit	Direct materials	Conversion costs
Total cost in current period	$28,000	$17,430
Total equivalent units in the current period	7,000	8,300
Cost per equivalent unit (current period)	$4.00	$2.10

Statement of evaluation

		Direct materials		Conversion costs	Total cost
		$		$	$
Finished units:					
1. Opening WIP					
Cost b/f		12,600		970	13,570
Cost to complete		0	(2,100 × $2.1)	4,410	4,410
		12,600		5,380	17,980
2. Units started and finished	(5,000 × $4)	20,000	(5,000 × $2.1)	10,500	30,500
Finished units		32,600		15,880	48,480
Closing inventory	(2,000 × $4)	8,000	(1,200 × $2.1)	2,520	10,520
		40,600		18,400	59,000

These costs would be recorded in the process account as follows.

Process (WIP) account

	units	$		units	$
Opening WIP	3,000	13,570	Finished goods	8,000	48,480
Direct materials	7,000	28,000			
Conversion costs	-	17,430	Closing WIP	2,000	10,520
	10,000	59,000		10,000	59,000

(**Tutorial note**: If you compare this example using FIFO with the previous example using the weighted average cost method, you might notice that the cost of finished output and value of closing WIP is the same in each case. This is a coincidence. Normally, the two methods provide different costs for finished output and different closing WIP valuations.)

6.4 FIFO method: summary

The first-in, first-out method for process costing with opening WIP can be summarised as follows.

- The cost of the opening units completed in the current period is calculated separately from the cost of the units that are started and finished in the current period.
- A cost per equivalent unit is calculated **for the current period**, as follows:

	Direct materials	**Conversion costs**
Costs incurred in the current period	TC_m	TC_c
Equivalent units of work in the current period to complete opening WIP	A	D
Number of units started and finished in the current period	B	E
Equivalent units of closing inventory at the end of the current period	C	F
Total equivalent units of work in this period	(A + B + C)	(D + E + F)
Cost per equivalent unit in the current period	TC_m /(A + B + C)	TC_c /(D + E + F)

- These costs are used to apportion the process costs in the current period between:
  - the cost of completing the opening WIP
  - the cost of units started and finished in the current period
  - the value of closing inventory.

- Having calculated costs for the current period, the valuation of output from the process is calculated as follows:

	Direct materials	**Conversion costs**	**Total costs**
Value of opening inventory b/f	M_1	C_1	$M_1 + C_1$
Costs to complete in the current period	M_2	C_2	$M_2 + C_2$
Total cost of opening inventory, finished first	$M_1 + M_2 = M_3$	$C_1 + C_2 = C_3$	$M_3 + C_3$
Units started and completed in the current period	M_4	C_4	$M_4 + C_4$
Total cost of finished output	$M_3 + M_4 = M_5$	$C_3 + C_4 = C_5$	$M_5 + C_5$

Exercise 4: FIFO cost method

From the following information relating to Process 2 in April:

(a) calculate the cost of finished output in the month and the value of the closing inventory, using the FIFO cost valuation method

(b) prepare the Process 2 account for the month.

Opening inventory on 1 April: 2,000 units:

100% complete for direct materials

80% complete for conversion costs

Cost $20,900 (= direct materials $14,800 + conversion costs $6,100)

Costs incurred during April:

Direct materials: 14,000 units input, cost $70,000

Conversion costs: $34,200

Completed units in the month: 11,000 units

Closing inventory: 5,000 units 100% complete for direct materials and 40% complete for conversion costs.

Losses and gains at different stages of the process

- Assumptions about when loss occurs
- Equivalent units and abnormal loss part-way through the process
- Equivalent units and abnormal gain part-way through the process

7 Losses and gains at different stages of the process

7.1 Assumptions about when loss occurs

In the earlier explanation of accounting for abnormal loss and abnormal gain, it was assumed that losses occur at the end of the production process. This assumption is not relevant for normal loss, but it is relevant for abnormal loss and abnormal gain, because these are given a value.

If it is assumed that losses occur at the end of a process, units of abnormal loss or gain are given a cost or value as if they are fully completed units – and so one equivalent unit each.

If losses occur at a different stage in the process, this assumption should not be applied. Instead, the concept of equivalent units should be used to decide the cost of the abnormal loss or the value of the abnormal gain. Equivalent units can be used provided that an estimate is made of the degree of completion of units at the time that loss occurs in the process. Differing degrees of completion might be used for direct materials and conversion costs.

7.2 Equivalent units and abnormal loss part-way through the process

When loss occurs part-way through a process, the cost of any abnormal loss should be calculated by:

- establishing the equivalent units of direct materials and conversion costs for the loss
- calculating a cost per equivalent units
- using the calculations of equivalent units and cost per equivalent unit to obtain a cost for finished output and abnormal loss in the period.

Example: abnormal loss and loss part-way through a process

The following information relates to a production process:

Input quantities of materials: 10,000 units
Direct materials cost: $27,000
Conversion costs: $13,200
Normal loss as % of input: 10%
Direct materials are added in full at the beginning of the process, and loss occurs

60% of the way through the process.

Actual output is 8,500 units.

Actual loss is 1,500 units. Normal loss is 1,000 units (= 10% of 10,000); therefore abnormal loss is 500 units.

The cost of finished output and abnormal loss can be calculated as follows.

Statement of equivalent units

Output	Direct materials		Conversion costs	
	Degree of completion	Equivalent units	Degree of completion	Equivalent units
Finished output	100%	8,500	100%	8,500
Abnormal loss	100%	500	60%	300
		9,000		8,800

Statement of cost per equivalent unit

	Direct materials	Conversion costs
Total costs	$27,000	$13,200
Equivalent units	9,000	8,800
Cost per equivalent unit	$3	$1.50

Statement of evaluation

		Finished output		Abnormal loss
		$		$
Direct materials	(8,500 × $3)	25,500	(500 × $3)	1,500
Conversion costs	(8,500 × $1.50)	12,750	(300 × $1.50)	450
Total cost		38,250		1,950

These costs would be recorded in the process account as follows.

Process (WIP) account

	units	$		units	$
Direct materials	10,000	27,000	Finished goods	8,500	38,250
Conversion costs	-	13,200	Normal loss	1,000	-
			Abnormal loss	500	1,950
	10,000	40,200		10,000	40,200

7.3 Equivalent units and abnormal gain part-way through the process

The same principles apply to the valuation of abnormal gain where the loss/gain occurs part-way through the process. However, there is one important difference. **Equivalent units of abnormal gain** are given a **negative value** and are **subtracted** from the total equivalent units of output in the period.

Perhaps the easiest way to think of the reason for this is that abnormal gain is on the opposite side of the process account (the debit side) from actual finished output (credit side) and abnormal gain equivalent units are subtracted because they offset the cost of the finished output.

Example: abnormal gain part-way through a process

The following information relates to a production process:

Input quantities of materials: 6,000 units
Direct materials cost: $27,000
Conversion costs: $11,040
Normal loss as % of input: 10%
Direct materials are added in full at the beginning of the process, and loss occurs 40% of the way through the process.

Actual output is 5,600 units.

Actual loss is 400 units. Normal loss is 600 units (= 10% of 6,000); therefore there is abnormal gain of 200 units.

The cost of finished output and abnormal loss can be calculated as follows. Note in particular that abnormal gain is given a negative value for equivalent units.

Statement of equivalent units

Output	Total units	Direct materials		Conversion costs	
		Degree of completion	Equivalent units	Degree of completion	Equivalent units
Finished output	5,600	100%	5,600	100%	5,600
Abnormal gain	200	100%	(200)	40%	(80)
			5,400		5,520

Statement of cost per equivalent unit

	Direct materials	Conversion costs
Total costs	$27,000	$11,040
Equivalent units	5,400	5,520
Cost per equivalent unit	$5	$2

Statement of evaluation

Abnormal gain is given a value in the usual way based on equivalent units and cost per equivalent unit.

		Finished output		Abnormal gain
		$		$
Direct materials	(5,600 × $5)	28,000	(200 × $5)	1,000
Conversion costs	(5,600 × $2)	11,200	(80 × $2)	160
Total cost		39,200		1,160

These costs would be recorded in the process account as follows.

Process (WIP) account

	units	$		units	$
Direct materials	6,000	27,000	Finished goods	5,600	39,200
Conversion costs	-	11,040	Normal loss	600	-
Abnormal gain	200	1,160			
	6,200	39,200		6,200	39,200

Process costing: joint products and by-products

- Definition of joint products
- Apportioning common processing costs between joint products
- Definition of by-products
- Cost accounting treatment of by-products

8 Process costing: joint products and by-products

8.1 Definition of joint products

In some process manufacturing systems, two or more different products are produced. These are called **joint products** if they have a **substantial sales value** (or a substantial sales value after further processing).

Until the joint products are produced in the manufacturing process, they cannot be distinguished from each other. The same input materials and processing operation produces all the joint products together.

8.2 Apportioning common processing costs between joint products

The costs of the common process that produces the joint products are common costs. In order to calculate a cost for each joint product, these common costs must be shared (apportioned) between the joint products. The common costs of the process must be apportioned between the joint products on a fair basis, in much the same way that overhead costs are apportioned between cost centres.

One of the following three methods of apportionment is normally used:

- **Units basis**: Common costs are apportioned on the basis of the total number of units produced. the cost per unit is the same for all the joint products.
- **Sales value at the split-off point basis**: Common costs are apportioned on the basis of the sales value of the joint products produced, at the point where they are separated in the process (the 'split off point').
- **Sales value less further processing costs basis:** common costs are apportioned on the basis of their eventual sales value after they have gone through further processing to get them ready for sale.

Example

Two joint products JP1 and JP2, are produced from a common process. During March, 8,000 units of materials were input to the process. Total costs of processing (direct materials and conversion costs) were $135,880.

Output was 5,000 units of JP1 and 3,000 units of JP2.

JP1 has a sales value of $40 per unit when it is output from the process.

JP2 does not have a sales value at the split-off point, but can be sold for $80 per unit after further processing costs of $15 per unit.

Required

Apportion the process costs between the joint products on the basis of:

- units produced
- sales value.

Answer

Units basis

$$\text{Process cost per unit} = \frac{\text{Process costs}}{\text{Number of units produced}} = \frac{\$135,880}{(5,000 + 3,000)} = \$16.985$$

Costs:	$
JP1: 5,000 units × $16.985	84,925
JP2: 3,000 units × $16.985	50,955
	135,880

Sales value basis (or sales value minus further processing costs)

	Sales value per unit	**Sales value less further processing cost**	**Units**	**Total value**
	$	$		$
JP1	40		5,000	200,000
JP2		65	3,000	195,000
				395,000
Common process costs				$135,880
Apportionment of overhead as % of sales value				34.4%

Costs:	**Total cost**	**Units**	**Cost per unit**
	$		$
JP1: $200,000 × 34.4%	68,800	5,000	13.76
JP2: $195,000 × 34.4%	67,080	3,000	22.36
	135,880		

7.3 Definition of by-products

In some process manufacturing systems, when two or more different products are produced, any product that **does not have a substantial sales value** is called a **by-product.**

7.4 Cost accounting treatment of by-products

Since a by-product does not have any substantial value, there is no sense in charging it with a share of the common processing costs.

- Instead, the sales value of the by-product is deducted from the common processing costs.
- If there are joint products, the common processing costs are apportioned after deducting the sales value of the by-product from the total costs of the process.
- The sales value of the by-product is recorded as a credit entry in the process account, together with the cost of the finished joint products.

Example: by-product and joint products

Two joint products JP1 and JP2, are produced from a common process. During March, 9,000 units of materials were input to the process. Total costs of processing (direct materials and conversion costs) were $135,880.

- Output was 5,000 units of JP1 and 3,000 units of JP2 and 1,000 units of by-product BP3.
- JP1 has a sales value of $40 per unit when it is output from the process.
- JP2 does not have a sales value at the split-off point, but can be sold for $80 per unit after further processing costs of $15 per unit.
- BP3 has a sales value of $1.58 per unit.

Required

Apportion the process costs between the joint products on the basis of sales value.

Answer

Common process costs	$
Total process costs	135,880
Deduct: Sales value of by-product (1,000 × $1.58)	(1,580)
	134,300

Apportionment of cost between joint products on a sales value basis

	Sales value per unit	**Sales value less further processing cost**	**Units**	**Total value**
	$	$		$
JP1	40		5,000	200,000
JP2		65	3,000	195,000
				395,000

Common process costs	$134,300
Apportionment of overhead as % of sales value	34.0%

Costs:	Total cost	Units	Cost per unit
	$		$
JP1: $200,000 × 34%	68,000	5,000	13.60
JP2: $195,000 × 34%	66,300	3,000	22.10
	134,300		

These costs would be shown in a process account as follows.

Process account

	Units	$		Units	$
Input costs	9,000	135,880	By-product (Bank account)	1,000	1,580
			JP1	5,000	68,000
	-	-	JP2	3,000	66,300
	9,000	135,880		9,000	135,880

Practice multiple choice questions

1 The input to a production process in one-month period was 12,000 units. There was no opening inventory. Output during the period was 11,000 units. Direct materials costs were $60,000 and conversion costs were $15,240. What was the cost of the abnormal loss in the month?

A $2,508

B $2,640

C $3,960

D $4,104 *(2 marks)*

2 The input to a production process in one-month period was 3,600 units. There was no opening inventory. Output during the period was 3,200 units. Direct materials costs were $15,000 and conversion costs were $5,160. Normal loss is one-sixth of the quantity input. What was the value of the abnormal gain in the month?

A $1,120

B $1,260

C $1,344

D $1,440 *(2 marks)*

3 A company has a manufacturing process and uses the weighted average cost method of inventory valuation. In one month, opening inventory consisted of 500 units, 100% complete for direct materials and 60% complete for conversion costs. Its total value was $8,955, consisting of direct materials of $7,935 and conversion costs of $1,020.

During the month, a further 1,500 units of direct materials were input to the process, costing $25,605, and conversion costs in the month were $5,440. Direct materials are added in full at the start of the process. Closing work in process was 400 units, 100% complete for direct materials and 25% complete for conversion costs.

What was the value of the closing work-in-process at the end of the month?

A $7,048

B $7,088

C $7,168

D $10,000 ***(2 marks)***

4 A company has a manufacturing process and uses the FIFO method of inventory valuation. In one month, opening inventory consisted of 400 units, 100% complete for direct materials and 75% complete for conversion costs. Its total value was $2,920, consisting of direct materials of $2,200 and conversion costs of $720.

During the month, a further 2,000 units of direct materials were input to the process, costing $12,200, and conversion costs in the month were $3,060. Direct materials are added in full at the start of the process. Closing work in process was 500 units, 100% complete for direct materials and 40% complete for conversion costs.

What was the value of the finished output from the process during the month?

A $14,365

B $14,620

C $14,790

D $14,820 ***(2 marks)***

5 The input to a production process in one-month period was 8,000 units. There was no opening inventory. Output during the period was 7,000 units. Direct materials costs were $30,400 and conversion costs were $11,040. Normal loss is 5% of input. All direct materials are input at the beginning of the process, and loss occurs 60% of the way into the process. What was the cost of the abnormal loss in the month?

A $2,940

B $3,272

C $3,300

D $5,672 ***(2 marks)***

6 Two joint products JP1 and JP" are output from a common process, and a by-product BP1 is also produced from the same process. The by-product has a sales value of $1.50 per unit. Data for the current month are as follows:

Input 6,000 units: cost $57,000 (direct materials $42,000, conversion costs $15,000)

Output: 3,000 units of JP1, 2,000 units of JP2 and 1,000 units of BP1.

Common processing costs are shared on the basis of the quantities of joint products produced.

What is the cost of the output of JP2 in the month?

A $18,500

B $19,000

C $22,200

D $22,800 ***(2 marks)***

CHAPTER 11

Budgeting

Contents

The budgeting process

- The nature of budgets
- Purposes of budgeting
- Preparing the budget
- The master budget
- Functional budgets
- Principal budget factor
- Stages in the budget process

1 The budgeting process

1.1 The nature of budgets

A budget is a formal plan, expressed mainly in financial terms and covering all the activities of the entity. It is for a specific period of time, typically one year. When budgets are prepared annually, they are for the next financial year.

The total budget period (one year) may be sub-divided into shorter control periods of one month or one quarter (three months).

1.2 Purposes of budgeting

Budgets have several purposes.

- To convert long-term plans (strategic plans) into more detailed shorter-term (annual) plans.
- To ensure that planning is linked to the long-term objectives and strategies of the organisation.
- To co-ordinate the actions of all the different parts of the organisation, so that they all work towards the same goals. (This is known as 'goal congruence'.) One of the benefits of budgeting is that is covers all activities, so the plan should try to ensure that all the different activities are properly co-ordinated and working towards the same objective.
- To communicate the company's plans to the individuals (managers and other employees) who have to put the plans into action.
- To motivate managers and employees, by setting targets for achievement, and possibly motivating them with the incentive of bonuses or other rewards if the targets are met.
- To provide guidelines for authorising expenditure. Expenditure might not be permitted unless it has been planned in the budget or unless it is within the budgeted expenditure limits for the department.

- To identify areas of responsibility for implementing the plans. For each part of the budget, an individual manager should be made responsible for achieving the budget targets for performance.
- To provide a benchmark against which actual performance can be measured.
- To control costs. Costs can be controlled by comparing budgets with actual results and investigating any differences (or variances) between the two. This is known as **budgetary control**.

1.3 Preparing the budget

Preparing the annual budget is a major activity for many entities. In many medium-sized and large companies, there is a well-defined process for budget preparation, because a large number of individuals have to co-ordinate their efforts to prepare the budget plans. The budgeting process may take several months, from beginning to eventual approval by the board of directors.

The budget process might be supervised and controlled by a special committee (the **budget committee**). This consists of senior managers from all the main areas of the business. The committee co-ordinates the various functional budgets submitted to it for review, and gives instructions for changes to be made when the draft budgets are unsatisfactory or the functional budgets are not consistent with each other.

Although the budget committee manages the budget process, the functional budgets are usually prepared by the managers with responsibility for the particular aspect of operations covered by that functional budget.

Budget manual

To guide everyone involved in the budgeting process, there should be a budget manual or budget handbook. This should set out:

- the key objectives of the budget
- the planning procedures and the timetables to follow when preparing the budget
- instructions about the budget details that must be included in the functional budgets
- responsibilities for preparing the functional budgets (sales budget, production budget, materials budgets, labour budget and overhead expenditure budgets)
- details of the budget approval process. The budget must be approved by the budget committee and then by the board of directors.

1.4 The master budget

The 'master budget' is the final approved budget. It is usually presented in the form of financial statements - a budgeted income statement and a budgeted balance sheet for the end of the financial year.

However the master budget is the result of a large number of detailed plans, many of them prepared at a departmental or functional level. To prepare the master budget, it is therefore necessary to prepare functional budgets first.

1.5 Functional budgets

A functional budget is a budget for a particular aspect of the entity's operations. The functional budgets that are prepared vary with the type of business and industry. In a manufacturing company, functional budgets should include:

- a sales budget
- a production budget
- a budget for production resources and resource costs (such as a materials cost budget and a labour cost budget)
- a materials purchasing budget
- expenditure budgets for every overhead cost centre and general overhead costs.

1.5 Principal budget factor

The budgeting process begins with the preparation of functional budgets, which must be co-ordinated and consistent with each other. To make sure that functional budgets are co-ordinated and consistent, the first functional budget that should be prepared is the budget for the principal budget factor.

The principal budget factor (also called the key budget factor) is the factor in the budget that will set a limit to the volume and scale of operations.

Sales demand (sales volume) as the principal budget factor

Normally, the principal budget factor is the expected sales demand. When this happens, the expected sales demand should set a limit on the volume of production (or volume of services). A company might have the capacity to increase its production and output, but producing larger quantities has no purpose unless the extra quantities can be sold.

A company will therefore prepare a budget on the basis of the sales volumes that it hopes or expects to achieve. When sales demand is the principal budget factor, the sales budget is the first functional budget that should be prepared.

A principal budget factor other than sales volume

Sometimes, there is a different limitation on budgeted activity. There might be a shortage of a key resource, such as machine time or the availability of skilled labour. When there is a shortage of a resource that will set a limit on budgeted production volume or budgeted activity, the first functional budget to prepare should be the budget for that resource.

In government, the principal budget factor for each government department is often an expenditure limit for the department. The department must then prepare a budget for the year that keeps the activities and spending plans of the department within the total expenditure limit for the department as a whole.

1.6 Stages in the budget process

The budgeting process for a manufacturing company is probably more complex than for many other types of organisation, and manufacturing company budgets are more likely to be the subject of an examination question than budgets for companies in other industries. This chapter therefore describes the budgeting process for a manufacturing company.

The stages in setting the budget might be as follows.

- **Stage 1**: Identify the principal budget factor (or key budget factor). The principal budget factor is normally sales volume.
- **Stage 2**: Prepare the functional budget or plan for the principal budget factor. Usually, this means that the first functional budget to prepare is the sales budget.
- All the other functional budgets should be prepared within the limitation of the principal budget factor. For example, even if the company has the capacity to produce more output, it should not produce more than it can sell (unless it formally decides to increase the size of the finished goods inventory, in which case the production volume will be higher than the sales volume).
- **Stage 3**: Prepare the other functional budgets, in logical sequence where necessary. When the sales budget has been prepared, a manufacturing organisation can then prepare budgets for inventories (= plans to increase or reduce the size o fits inventories), a production budget, labour budgets and materials usage and purchasing budgets. Expenditure budgets should also be prepared for overhead costs (production overheads, administration overheads and sales and distribution overheads). Overhead costs are usually prepared for each cost centre individually.
- **Stage 4**: Submit the functional budgets to the budget committee for review and approval. The functional budgets are co-ordinated by the budget committee, which must make sure that they are both realistic and consistent with each other.
- **Stage 5**: Prepare the 'master budget'. This is the budget statement that summarises the plans for the budget period. The master budget might be presented in the form of:
  - a budgeted income statement for the next financial year
  - a budgeted balance sheet as at the end of the next financial year
  - a cash budget or cash flow forecast for the next financial year.
- It should be possible to prepare the master budget statements from the functional budgets.
- **Stage 6**: The master budget and the supporting functional budgets should be submitted to board of directors for approval. The board approves and authorises the budget.
- **Stage 7**: The detailed budgets are communicated to the managers responsible for their implementation.
- **Stage 8**: Control process. After the budget has been approved, actual performance should be monitored by comparing it with the budget. Actual

results for the period should be recorded and reported to management. These results should be compared with the budget, and significant differences should be investigated. The reasons for the differences ('variances') should be established, and where appropriate control measures should be taken. Comparing actual results with the budget therefore provides a system of control. The managers responsible for activities where actual results differ significantly from the budget will be held responsible and accountable.

The planning process (budgeting) should therefore lead on to a management monitoring and control process (budgetary control).

Preparing functional budgets

- The sales budget
- The production budget
- The materials usage budget
- The materials purchases budget
- The labour budget
- Overheads budgets

2 Preparing functional budgets

This section describes the approach that can normally be used to prepare functional budgets for a manufacturing organisation. In practice, budgets are usually prepared with a computer model, such as a **spreadsheet**. However, you need to understand the logic of budget preparation.

2.1 The sales budget

The sales budget is the plan for the volume and value of sales in the budget period. It is prepared for each product individually, in units of sale and sales revenue, and for sales revenue in total.

It is calculated for each product simply by multiplying the volume of sales in units by the budgeted sales price per unit.

Example

A company makes and sells two products, Product P and Product Q.

The sales price and expected sales volume for each product next year are as follows:

	Product P	**Product Q**
Sales price per unit	$20	$30
Budgeted sales volume	20,000 units	30,000 units

A sales budget can be prepared as follows.

Product	**Budgeted sales quantity**	**Budgeted sales price**	**Budgeted sales revenue**
	units	$	$
P	20,000	20	400,000
Q	30,000	30	900,000
Total			1,300,000

Sometimes, a sales budget is prepared by making adjustments to actual sales in the current financial year.

Example

A company is preparing its sales budget for the year. In the current financial year it expects that total sales will be $2.6 million. Next year it hopes to raise its selling prices by 3% and to increase sales volume by 5%.

The sales budget for next year is therefore: $2.6 million × 1.03 × 1.05 = $2.8 million (to the nearest $100,000).

2.2 The production budget

The production budget is calculated initially in units of output, although a budget for production costs can be prepared when production quantities have been decided. The production budget in units is prepared for each product, as follows:

	Units
Sales budget in units	S
Plus: Budgeted closing inventory	C
Minus: Opening inventory	(O)
Production budget	(S + C – O)

In other words, the production budget for each product in units is:

- the sales budget in units
- plus any planned increase in finished goods inventories (and work-in-progress inventories)
- or minus the opening inventories of finished goods (and work in progress).

Example

A company makes and sells two products, Product P and Product Q. Its sales budget for next year is to sell 20,000 units of Product P and 30,000 units of Product Q.

It expects opening inventory of finished goods to be 4,000 units of Product P and 500 units of Product Q. It has been decided that inventory of Product P should be reduced to 2,000 units by the end of the budget period, and inventory of Product Q should be increased to 1,500 units.

A production budget can be prepared as follows.

	Product P	Product Q
	units	units
Sales budget	20,000	30,000
Plus: Budgeted closing inventory	2,000	1,500
Minus: Opening inventory	(4,000)	(500)
Production budget	18,000	31,000

2.3 The materials usage budget

After the production budget has been prepared, budgets can be prepared for the resources required to achieve the production targets. Production resources budgets will include a materials usage budget, a direct labour budget and possibly a machine hours budget.

Separate budgets can be prepared for each production centre, and these can be added together to create the total production budget. For example, if a manufacturing process consists of a machining department, a finishing department and an assembly department, production budgets will be prepared for each department separately, and these will then be combined to produce a total production department.

The materials usage budget is a budget for the quantities of materials that will be used. It is a statement of the quantities of direct materials required for production, and their cost. The usage budget is prepared for each item of material separately, and a total cost of the materials used should also be shown.

Example

A company makes and sells two products, Product S and Product T. Its production budget for next year is to make 40,000 units of Product S and 10,000 units of Product T.

The materials required to make one unit of each product, and their cost, are as follows.

	Product S	**Product T**	**Cost per kilo**
	kilos	kilos	
Material M1	2.0	3.0	$0.4
Material M 2	2.5	1.5	$0.6

A materials usage budget can be prepared as follows.

	Material M1	**Material M2**	**Total**
	kilos	kilos	
To make 40,000 S	80,000	100,000	
To make 10,000 T	30,000	15,000	
Total quantities	110,000	115,000	
Price per kilo	$0.4	$0.6	
Total cost	$44,000	$69,000	$113,000

2.4 The materials purchases budget

The budgeted cost of materials for use in production is not the same as the quantity and cost of materials that will be purchased. Material purchases and material usage will be different if there are plans to increase or reduce raw materials inventories.

The materials purchases budget is the budget for the purchase cost of materials that will be purchased in the budget period. The materials purchases budget might be prepared for all materials, direct and indirect, or for direct materials only.

The purchases budget differs from the materials usage budget by the amount of the planned increase or decrease in inventory levels of materials in the budget period.

The purchase quantities are calculated first. Purchase quantities are calculated as follows, for each item of material:

	Units
Material usage budget in units	M
Plus budgeted closing inventory	C
Minus opening inventory	(O)
Purchases budget, in units	(M + C – O)

The purchase quantities for each item of material are converted into a purchases cost at the budgeted purchase price for the item of material.

The total material purchases budget (in $) is the sum of the purchases budget for each of the individual items of material.

Example

A company makes and sells two products, Product X and Product Y. Its production budget for next year is to make 20,000 units of Product X and 15,000 units of Product Y.

The materials required to make one unit of each product, and their cost, are as follows.

	Product X	Product Y	Cost per litre
	litres	litres	
Material M3	0.5	1.5	$3
Material M 4	1.0	2.0	$4

The company expects to have opening inventory of 3,000 litres of Material M3 and 2,000 litres of Material M4. It plans to have closing inventory of 3,500 litres of Material M3 and 1,200 litres of Material M4

The materials purchases budget can be calculated as follows, after a production budget has been established.

	Material M3	Material M4	Total
	litres	litres	
To make 20,000 X	10,000	30,000	
To make 15,000 Y	15,000	30,000	
Material usage quantities	25,000	60,000	
Closing inventory	3,500	1,200	
Opening inventory	(3,000)	(2,000)	
	25,500	59,200	
Price per litre	$3	$4	
Total cost	$76,500	$236,800	$313,300

2.5 The labour budget

Direct labour budget

The direct labour budget is prepared in a similar way to the materials usage budget. It is a statement of the quantities of direct labour required for production, and its cost.

The budget is prepared for different grades of labour separately, but the total labour cost should also be shown.

For each grade of labour, the expected hours of work should be calculated, for making the budgeted production quantities of product individually and then for all the products in total. The total budget in hours for each grade of labour is converted into a cost at the standard/budgeted rate per hour for the grade of labour.

Example

A company makes and sells two products, Product S and Product T. Its sales budget is to sell 40,000 units of Product S and 10,000 units of Product T. The expected opening inventories of finished goods are 500 units of Product S and 1,000 units of Product T, and the plan is to double finished goods inventories by the end of the budget period.

The direct labour hours required to make one unit of each product, and their cost, are as follows.

	Product S	Product T	Cost per hour
	hours	hours	
Grade G1 labour	0.2	0.6	$20
Grade G2 labour	0.3	0.8	$16

A direct labour budget can be prepared as follows, after a production budget has been established.

	Product S	Product T
	units	units
Sales budget	40,000	10,000
Plus: Budgeted closing inventory	1,000	2,000
Minus: Opening inventory	(500)	(1,000)
Production budget	40,500	11,000

	Grade G1	Grade G2	Total
	hours	hours	
To make 40,500 S	8,100	24,300	
To make 11,000 T	3,300	8,800	
Total labour hours	11,400	33,100	
Rate of pay per hour	$20	$16	
Total direct labour cost	$228,000	$529,600	$757,600

Indirect labour costs

Budgets must also be prepared for indirect labour employees. It is usual to include indirect labour costs within the budget for the overhead cost centre or department where the employees work.

2.6 Overheads budgets

Overheads budgets are prepared for each department or cost centre, in production, administration and sales and distribution.

- To prepare expenditure budgets for each overhead cost centre, overhead expenditure is allocated and apportioned, using the methods described in the earlier chapter on overhead costs.
- In an absorption costing system, an overhead absorption rate should then be calculated from the total budgeted expenditure and the budgeted volume of activity.

When flexed budgets are prepared, overhead costs might be divided into variable and fixed costs.

Example

A company makes and sells one product, Product Z. The production budget is to make and sell 5,000 units of Product Z, but there is a possibility that sales demand might be less than expected; therefore management have decided to prepare a budget for 4,000 units of production and sales.

Production overhead costs are expected to be fixed costs of $360,000 plus variable overheads of $1.50 per direct labour hour. Product Z takes 2 hours to produce.

A production overheads budget can be prepared at production volumes of both 4,000 and 5,000 units, as follows.

	4,000 units	5,000 units
	$	$
Variable overheads (2 hours × $1.50 = $3 per unit)	12,000	15,000
Fixed overheads	360,000	360,000
Total overheads	372,000	375,000
Overhead cost per unit	$93	$75

Exercise 1

A company produces Products A and B and the budgeted production in the coming year is 5,000 units of A and 10,000 units of B. Products A and B require the following quantities of raw materials to produce one unit.

	Product A	Product B
	per unit	per unit
Raw material X	5 kg	4 kg
Raw material Y	7 kg	3 kg

Raw material X costs $10 per kg and raw material Y costs $20 per kg.

Data relating to opening and closing inventory is as follows.

	Raw material	
	X	Y
Closing inventory	10,000	8,000
Opening inventory	8,000	4,000

Required

Prepare the materials usage and purchases budget for the year.

Fixed, flexible and flexed budgets

- Budgetary control
- Fixed budgets
- Flexed budgets
- Flexible budgets

3 Fixed, flexible and flexed budgets

3.1 Budgetary control

One of the main purposes of budgeting is budgetary control and the control of costs. Costs can be controlled by comparing budgets with the results actually achieved.

Differences between expected results and actual results are known as variances. Variances can be either favourable (F) or adverse (A) depending on whether the results achieved are better or worse than expected. Favourable variances increase profits and adverse variances decrease profits.

There are three different types of budget that you need to know about.

- fixed budgets
- flexed budgets
- flexible budgets.

3.2 Fixed budgets

The original budget prepared at the beginning of a budget period is known as the fixed budget. A fixed budget is a budget for a specific volume of output and sales activity, and it is the 'master plan' for the financial year that the company tries to achieve.

The term 'fixed' in 'fixed budget' means that the output and sales volumes are for a fixed amount or quantity.

A fixed budget might be suitable as a plan, provided that the business environment is fairly stable and sales and production volumes should be predictable with reasonable accuracy. However, a fixed budget is not suitable for the purpose of budgetary control – reporting differences between actual costs and profits and what costs and profits should have been. Fixed budgets are not suitable for budgetary control reporting because the variances calculated with a fixed budget can provide misleading information

Example

A company makes and sells a single product. Its budget for the year was to make and sell 10,000 units of the product. Actual sales and production were 15,000 units.

The expected results in the fixed budget and actual results are set out and compared in the table below.

	Fixed budget	Actual results	Difference
Units	10,000	15,000	
	$	$	
Sales revenue	200,000	286,000	$86,000 Favourable
Materials costs	60,000	94,000	$34,000 Adverse
Labour costs	70,000	97,000	$27,000 Adverse
Variable overheads	20,000	23,000	$3,000 Adverse
Fixed costs	30,000	34,000	$4,000 Adverse
Total costs	180,000	248,000	

The total differences calculated in this way, comparing the fixed budget for 10,000 units with the actual results for 15,000 units, do not provide useful information for management. The differences do not compare 'like with like'. It should be expected that when sales and production volumes are higher than the budgeted quantities, sales revenues and costs will be higher, and profit will be higher.

Much more useful information would be provided by producing a revised budget based on the actual quantities produced and sold.

3.3 Flexed budgets

A flexed budget is a budget prepared to show the revenue, costs and profits that should have been expected from the actual volumes of production and sale. A flexed budget is prepared for the actual volume of sales and output, and it allows for the fact that sales revenues and variable costs should be expected to increase or fall with increases or falls in sales and output.

A flexed budget is prepared at the end of the budget period when the actual results are known. It is used to compare:

- the actual results with the flexed budget
- the fixed budget with the flexed budget.

If a flexed budget is compared with the actual results for a period, the differences between the two (variances) are much more meaningful than if the fixed budget and actual results are compared.

Example

Taking the previous example which shows a fixed budget and actual results, a flexed budget would be prepared as follows.

	Fixed budget	Flexed budget	Actual results	Difference
Units	10,000	15,000	15,000	
	$	$	$	
Sales revenue	200,000	300,000	286,000	$14,000 Adverse
Materials costs	60,000	90,000	94,000	$4,000 Adverse
Labour costs	70,000	105,000	97,000	$8,000 Favourable
Variable overheads	20,000	30,000	23,000	$7,000 Favourable
Fixed costs	30,000	30,000	34,000	$4,000 Adverse
Total costs	180,000	255,000	248,000	
Profit	20,000	45,000	38,000	

In the flexed budget, the expected sales revenue and all the expected variable costs are shown for output and sales of 15,000 units, which is the actual volume. A comparison of the flexed budget and actual results shows the differences (variances) between the actual performance and the results that should have been expected for the actual volume of output and sales.

The table also shows the expected profit in the fixed budget, the expected profit in the flexed budget and the actual profit obtained in the period.

- The expected profit n the fixed budget is $20,000 but in the flexed budget it is $5,000. By increasing sales from 10,000 units to 15,000 units, the company would have been expected to earn an additional profit of $25,000.
- However, actual profit was only $38,000, which is $7,000 less than in the flexed budget. This difference is explained by the sum of the variances in the right-hand column of the table. These variances add up to $7,000 Adverse.

A budgetary control report can be prepared as follows from this information. (F) represents a favourable variance and (A) represents and adverse variance.

	$		$	
Original budgeted profit (fixed budget)			20,000	
Sales volume variance			25,000	(F)
Flexed budget profit			45,000	
Sales price variance			14,000	(A)
Actual sales minus flexed budget costs			31,000	
Materials cost variance	4,000	(A)		
Labour cost variance	8,000	(F)		
Variable overhead cost variance	7,000	(F)		
Fixed overhead expenditure variance	4,000	(A)		
Total cost variances			7,000	(F)
Actual profit			38,000	

Variances are explained in more detail in the next chapter.

3.4 Flexible budgets

Flexible budgets are not the same as flexed budgets, although they are similar.

- **Flexed budgets** are prepared at the end of a budget period and look back at what costs, revenues and profits should have been in a period (based on actual activity levels). They are used to calculate variances for the purpose of management control and control reporting (**budgetary control**).
- **Flexible budgets**, on the other hand, are forward-looking and are prepared at the beginning of a budget period when the fixed (original) budget is prepared. Flexible budgets are prepared to show the results that would be expected at different levels of activity, for example, at 75%, 80% and 85% of the full capacity. They might be prepared when there is uncertainty about what the actual volumes of sales and production will be, and several budgets are therefore prepared for a number of different possible outcomes.

Flexible budget		**Level of activity**		
	75%	**80%**	**85%**	**100%**
	$	$	$	$
Direct materials	7,500	8,000	8,500	10,000
Direct labour	22,500	24,000	25,500	30,000
Production overheads	27,500	28,000	28,500	30,000
Other overheads	8,000	8,000	8,000	8,000
Total cost	65,500	68,000	70,500	78,000

Practice multiple choice questions

1 In the budgeting process, what is usually considered to be the principal budget factor?

A Sales volume

B Sales price

C Machine capacity

D Skilled labour capacity *(1 mark)*

2 A manufacturing company makes and sells a single product, product X. Budgeted sales next year are 20,000 units of product X. Each unit of product X consumes 3 kilos of material. A decision has been taken that inventory of material B will be increased from 9,000 kilos to 18,000 kilos by the end of the year, and inventory product X will be reduced from 5,000 to 4,000 units during the year.

What is the budgeted materials purchase quantity for material B?

A 57,000 kilos

B 66,000 kilos

C 69,000 kilos

D 72,000 kilos ***(2 marks)***

3 Which one of the following statements most accurately defines a fixed budget?

A fixed budget is a plan for the entire entity:

A in which no changes are permitted to the plan

B in which there is a specific quantity of output and sales volume

C that can be adjusted for changes in the expected activity level

D that provides useful control information through comparison of budget and actual results. ***(1 mark)***

4 A company manufactures Product Z. The sales budget for Product Z is 19,000 units. Each unit of product Z uses 2 kilos of a raw material, material T. The materials purchase budget for material T, which is used only in the manufacture of Product Z, is 40,000 kilos. The budget plans for a reduction in the inventory level of material T by 4,000 kilos during the year.

What is the planned change in inventory of Product Z during the year?

A Reduction by 1,000 units

B No change

C Increase by 1,000 units

D Increase by 3,000 units ***(2 marks)***

5 A company manufactures two products, Product A and Product B, using the same team of direct labour employees. The sales budget for Product A is 12,000 units and budgeted sales of Product B are 15,000 units. The company plans to reduce inventory of Product A from 2,000 units to 1,000 units by the end of the budget period, and to increase inventory of Product B during the same period from 3,000 to 5,000 units. Each unit of Product A requires 2 hours of direct labour and each unit of Product B requires 1.5 hours. Direct labour is paid $18 per hour.

What is the direct labour budget for the year?

A $747,000

B $819,000

C $855,000

D $927,000 ***(2 marks)***

CHAPTER 12

Standard costing and variance analysis

Contents

Standard costs

- Standard units of product or service
- Standard cost defined and standard costing
- Who sets standard costs?
- The purposes of standard costing
- Establishing a standard cost

1 Standard costs

1.1 Standard units of product or service

A standard costing system might be used when an organisation produces standard units of a product or service that are identical to all other similar units produced. Standard costing is usually associated with standard products, but can be applied to standard services too (for example standard costs of burgers and other items in a fast-food restaurant).

A standard unit should have exactly the same input resources (direct materials, direct labour time) as all other similar units, and these resources should cost exactly the same. Standard units should therefore have exactly the same cost. This is the standard cost for the item.

1.2 Standard cost defined and standard costing

A **standard cost is a predetermined unit cost** based on expected direct materials quantities and expected direct labour time, and priced at a predetermined rate per unit of direct materials and rate per direct labour hour and rate per hour of overhead.

- Standard costs are usually restricted to production costs only, not administration and selling and distribution overheads. This is because traditionally, standard costing has been used in manufacturing industries but much less so in service industries.
- Standard costing can be based on either absorption costing or marginal costing. When absorption costing is used with standard costs, Overheads are normally absorbed into the standard cost per unit at a rate per direct labour hour.

Example

The standard cost of Product XYZ might be:

	$	$
Direct materials:		
Material A: 2 litres at $4.50 per litre	9.00	
Material B: 3 kilos at $2 per kilo	6.00	
		15.00

Direct labour		
Grade 1 labour: 0.5 hours at $10 per hour	5.00	
Grade 2 labour: 0.75 hours at $8 per hour	6.00	
		11.00
Variable production overheads: 1.25 hours at $4 per hour		5.00
Fixed production overheads: 1.25 hours at $20 per hour		25.00
Standard (production) cost per unit		56.00

Standard costing

Standard costing is a system of costing in which:

- all units of product (or service) are recorded in the cost accounts at their standard cost, and
- the value of inventory is based on standard production cost.

In the cost ledger, production costs are recorded at their standard cost. Differences between actual costs and standard costs are recorded as variances, which may be either favourable or adverse. Variances that occur during a costing period are used to adjust the reported profit at the end of the period.

When a standard cost system is used:

- finished goods inventory is always valued at standard production cost (which may be either a full cost with absorption costing or a variable cost only with marginal costing)
- raw materials inventory may be valued at either actual cost or standard cost: there is no 'rule' that either standard cost or actual cost should be used.

1.3 Who sets standard costs?

Standard costs are set by managers with the expertise to assess what the standard prices and rates should be. Standard costs are normally reviewed regularly, typically once a year as part of the annual budgeting process.

- Standard prices for direct materials should be set by managers with expertise in the purchase costs of materials. This is likely to be a senior manager in the purchasing department (buying department).
- Standard rates for direct labour should be set by managers with expertise in labour rates. This is likely to be a senior manager in the human resources department (personnel department).
- Standard usage rates for direct materials and standard efficiency rates for direct labour should be set by managers with expertise in operational activities. This may be a senior manager in the production or operations department, or a manager in the technical department.
- Standard overhead rates should be identified by a senior management accountant, from budgeted overhead costs and budgeted activity levels that have been agreed in the annual budgeting process.

1.4 The purposes of standard costing

Standard costing has three main purposes:

- It is an alternative system of cost accounting. In a standard costing system, all units produced are recorded in the cost ledger at their standard cost of production.
- It is a system of performance measurement. The differences between standard costs (= expected costs) and actual costs can be measured as variances. Variances can be reported regularly to management, in order to identify areas of good performance or poor performance.
- It is also a system of control reporting. When differences between actual results and expected results (the budget and standard costs) are large, this could indicate that operational performance is not as it should be, and that the causes of the variance should be investigated.

Management can therefore use variance reports to identify whether control measures might be needed, to improve poor performances or continue with good performances.

- When there are large adverse (unfavourable) variances, this might indicate that actual performance is poor, and control action is needed to deal with the weaknesses.
- When there are large favourable variances, and actual results are much better than expected, management should investigate to find out why this has happened, and whether any action is needed to ensure that the favourable results continue in the future.

1.5 Establishing a standard cost

A standard variable cost is established by building up the standard materials, labour and variable overhead costs for each standard unit.

In a standard absorption costing system, the standard fixed overhead cost is a standard cost per unit, based on budgeted data about fixed costs and the budgeted production volume. ('Normal' annual production volume is used as the volume of activity for deciding the absorption rate for overheads.)

Exercise 1

A company manufactures two products, X and Y. In Year 1 it budgets to make 2,000 units of Product X and 1,000 units of Product Y. The standard quantity of resources per unit are as follows:

	Product X	**Product Y**
Direct materials per unit:		
Material A	2 units of material	1.5 units of material
Material B	1 unit of material	3 units of material
Direct labour hours per unit	1.5 hours	2 hours

Standard rates and prices are as follows.

Direct material A	\$4 per unit
Direct material B	\$3 per unit
Direct labour	\$10 per hour
Variable production overhead	\$2 per direct labour hour

Fixed production overheads per unit are calculated by applying a direct labour hour absorption rate to the standard labour hours per unit, using the budgeted fixed production overhead costs of \$60,000 for the year.

Required

Calculate the standard full production cost per unit of:

(a) Product X, and

(b) Product Y

Cost variances

- Adverse and favourable cost variances
- Cost variances and measuring profit
- Variances and performance reporting
- Calculating cost variances
- Total variable cost variances

2 Cost variances

2.1 Adverse and favourable cost variances

In a standard costing system, all units of output are valued at their standard cost. Cost of production and cost of sales are therefore valued at standard cost.

Actual costs will differ from standard costs. A cost variance is the difference between an actual cost and a standard cost.

- When actual cost is higher than standard cost, the cost variance is adverse [(A)] or unfavourable [(U)].
- When actual cost is less than standard cost, the cost variance is favourable [(F)].

Several different variances are calculated, relating to direct materials, direct labour, variable production overhead and fixed production overhead. (There are also some sales variances. These are explained in a later section.)

2.2 Cost variances and measuring profit

In a cost accounting system, cost variances are adjustments to the profit in an accounting period.

- Favourable variances increase the reported profit.
- Adverse variances reduce the reported profit.

2.3 Variances and performance reporting

Variance reports are produced at the end of each control period (say, at the end of each month).

- Large adverse variances indicate poor performance and the need for control action by management.

- Large favourable variances indicate unexpected good performance. Management might wish to consider how this good performance can be maintained in the future.

Variances might be reported in a statement for the accounting period that reconciles the budgeted profit with the actual profit for the period. This statement is known as an **operating statement**.

2.4 Calculating cost variances

The method of calculating cost variances is similar for all variable production cost items (direct materials, direct labour and variable production overhead).

A different method of calculating cost variances is required for fixed production overhead.

There are several different techniques that can be used to calculate variances. Some people learn variances as formulae. The approach taken here is to present variance calculations in tables. The advantages of this approach are that:

- Presenting variances in tables helps to explain the logic of variances – both what they mean and how they are calculated
- Learning how to calculate variances in tables also teaches you how to work out a standard cost when you are given a variance and an actual cost, and how to work out an actual cost when you are given a variance and a standard cost. (This is a specific learning requirement in the syllabus!)

2.5 Total variable cost variances

In standard costing, variable cost variances can be calculated for all items of variable cost – direct materials, direct labour and variable production overhead. The method of calculating the variances is similar for each variable cost item.

- The total cost variance for the variable cost item is the difference between the actual variable cost of production and the standard variable cost of producing the items.
- However, the total cost variance is not usually calculated. Instead, the total variance is calculated in two parts, that add up to the total cost variance:
  - a price variance or rate variance or expenditure per hour variance.
  - a usage or efficiency variance.

However, if you are asked to calculate a total variable cost variance, the method to apply is as follows (for a variable production cost).

When Q units have been produced:

	$	**(F) or (A)**
Q units of output should cost (= Q units × Standard cost per unit)		
Q units of output did cost		
Difference = Total cost variance for the variable cost item		(F) or (A)

The variance is adverse (A) if actual cost is higher than the standard cost, and favourable (F) if actual cost is less than the standard cost.

Example

A unit of Product P123 has a standard cost of 5 litres of Material A at $3 per litre. The standard direct material cost per unit of Product 123 is therefore $15.

In a particular month, 2,000 units of Product 123 were manufactured. These used 10,400 litres of Material A, which cost $33,600.
The total direct material cost variance is calculated as follows:

	$
2,000 units of output should cost (× $15)	30,000
They did cost	33,600
Total direct materials cost variance	3,600 (A)

The variance is adverse, because actual costs were higher than the standard cost.

Exercise 2

The standard variable production overhead for Product Z is $3, representing 1.5 direct labour hours at $2 per hour. During September, 4,000 units of Product Z were produced in 5,500 hours. The variable production overhead cost was $11,700.

Required

Calculate the total variable production overhead variance for September.

Direct materials: price and usage variances

- Direct materials price variance
- Direct materials usage variance
- Direct materials: possible causes of variances

3 Direct materials: price and usage variances

The direct materials total cost variance can be analysed into a price variance and a usage variance.

- A price variance measures the difference between the actual price paid for materials and the price that should have been paid (the standard price).
- A usage variance measures the difference between the materials that were used in production and the materials that should have been used (the standard usage).

3.1 Direct materials price variance

The price variance is calculated by taking the **actual quantity** of:

- materials purchased or
- materials used.

For your examination, it is unlikely that you will need to decide whether to use the quantity purchased or the quantity used. Briefly, however:

- the price variance is calculated from the **quantities purchased** when closing inventory of direct materials is valued at standard cost
- the price variance is calculated from the **quantities used** when closing inventory of direct materials is valued at actual cost.

An examination question will often state that quantities of materials purchased and materials used were the same. However, if a question states that raw materials are valued at standard cost, the price variance must be calculated using actual quantities of materials purchased.

The actual cost of the actual quantity of materials is compared with the standard purchase price of the materials. The difference is the materials price variance.

A direct materials price variance is calculated as follows:

	$	
Units of materials purchased/used should cost (× standard price per unit of material)	A	
They did cost	B	
Material price variance	A – B	(F) or (A)

If there are two or more direct materials, a price variance is calculated separately for each material.

Example

A unit of Product P123 has a standard cost of 5 litres of Material A at $3 per litre. The standard direct material cost per unit of Product 123 is therefore $15. In a particular month, 2,000 units of Product 123 were manufactured. These used 10,400 litres of Material A, which cost $33,600.
The direct materials price variance is calculated as follows.

The price variance is calculated on the quantity of materials purchased/used.

Materials price variance		
	$	
10,400 litres of materials should cost (× $3)	31,200	
They did cost	33,600	
Material price variance	2,400	(A)

The price variance is adverse because the materials cost more to purchase than they should have done (i.e. actual cost was higher than the standard or expected cost).

3.2 Direct materials usage variance

The usage variance is calculated by taking the **actual quantity of units produced**.

For the actual number of units produced, the actual usage of materials is compared with the standard usage. The difference is the usage variance, measured as a quantity of materials. This is converted into a money value at the **standard price** for the material.

A direct materials usage variance is calculated as follows:

	Units of material	
Units produced should use (output × standard material usage per unit)	X	
They did use	Y	
Material usage variance in quantities	X – Y	(F) or (A)
× Standard price per unit of material	x $P	
Material price variance in $	(X – Y) x $P	(F) or (A)

Example

A unit of Product P123 has a standard cost of 5 litres of Material A at $3 per litre. The standard direct material cost per unit of Product 123 is therefore $15. In a particular month, 2,000 units of Product 123 were manufactured. These used 10,400 litres of Material A, which cost $33,600.

The direct materials price variance is calculated as follows.

The usage variance is calculated by taking the actual quantity of units produced. The usage variance in material quantities is then converted into a money value at the standard price per unit of the raw material.

Materials usage variance		
	litres	
2,000 units of Product P123 should use (× 5 litres)	10,000	
They did use	10,400	
Material usage variance in litres	400	(A)
Standard price per litre of Material A	$3	
Material usage variance in $	$1,200	(A)

The usage variance is adverse because more materials were used than expected, which has added to costs.

Exercise 3

The standard direct materials cost of Product P44 is:

2 kilos of material L at $3 per kilo: $6.

During February, 6,000 units of Product P44 were produced. These used 12,800 kilos of material L, which cost $35,900.

Required

(a) Calculate the direct materials total cost variance for the month.

(b) Analyse this total variance into a direct material price variance and a direct material usage variance.

3.3 Direct materials: possible causes of variances

When variances occur and they appear to be significant, management should investigate the reason for the variance. If the cause of the variance is something within the control of management, control action should be taken. Some of the possible causes of materials variances are listed below.

Materials price variance: causes

- Suppliers increased their prices by more than expected. (Higher prices might be caused by an unexpected increase in the rate of inflation.)
- Different suppliers were used, and these charged a higher price (adverse price variance) or lower price (favourable price variance) than the usual supplier.

- Materials were purchased in sufficient quantities to obtain a bulk purchase discount (a quantity discount), resulting in a favourable price variance.
- Materials were bought that were of lower quality than standard (and so cheaper than expected) or better quality than standard (and more expensive than expected).
- There was a severe shortage of the materials, so that prices in the market were much higher than expected.

Materials usage variance: causes

- Poor materials handling resulted in a large amount of breakages (adverse usage variance). Breakages mean that a quantity of materials input to the production proves are wasted.
- Improvements in production methods resulted in more efficient usage of materials (favourable usage variance).
- Wastage rates were higher or lower than expected.
- Materials used were of cheaper quality than standard, with the result that more materials had to be thrown away as waste.

Direct labour: rate and efficiency variances

- Direct labour rate variance
- Direct labour efficiency variance
- Direct labour: possible causes of variances

4 Direct labour: rate and efficiency variances

The direct labour total cost variance can be analysed into a rate variance and an efficiency variance. These are calculated in a similar way to the direct materials price and usage variances.

- A rate variance measures the difference between the actual wage rate paid to per labour hour and the rate that should have been paid (the standard rate of pay).
- An efficiency variance (or productivity variance) measures the difference between the time taken to make the production output and the time that should have been taken (the standard time).

4.1 Direct labour rate variance

The direct labour rate variance is calculated by taking the actual number of hours worked and paid for.

The actual labour cost of the actual hours worked is compared with the standard cost for those hours. The difference is the labour rate variance.

A direct labour rate variance is calculated as follows.

	$	
Hours worked/paid for should cost (× standard rate per hour)	A	
They did cost	B	
Direct labour rate variance	A – B	(F) or (A)

If there are two or more different types or grades of labour, each paid a different standard rate per hour, a rate variance is calculated separately for each labour grade.

4.2 Direct labour efficiency variance

The direct labour efficiency variance is calculated by taking the actual quantity of units produced.

For the actual number of standard units produced, the actual hours worked is compared with the standard number of hours that should have been worked to produce the actual output. The difference is the efficiency variance, measured in hours. This is converted into a money value at the standard direct labour rate per hour.

A direct labour efficiency variance is calculated as follows.

	Hours	
Units produced should take (× standard hours per unit)	X	
They did take	Y	
Efficiency variance in hours	X – Y	(F) or (A)
× Standard direct labour rate per hour	$P	
Direct labour efficiency variance in $	(X – Y) x $P	(F) or (A)

Example

Product P234 has a standard direct labour cost per unit of:

0.5 hours × $12 per direct labour hour = $6 per unit.

During a particular month, 3,000 units of Product 234 were manufactured. These took 1,400 hours to make and the direct labour cost was $16,200.

Required

Calculate for the month:

- the total direct labour cost variance
- the direct labour rate variance
- the direct labour efficiency variance.

Answer

Total direct labour cost variance	$	
3,000 units of output should cost (× $6)	18,000	
They did cost	16,200	
Direct labour total cost variance	1,800	(F)

The variance is favourable, because actual costs were less than the standard cost.

The direct labour rate variance is calculated by taking the actual number of hours worked (and paid for).

Direct labour rate variance	$	
1,400 hours should cost (× $12)	16,800	
They did cost	16,200	
Direct labour rate variance	600	(F)

The rate variance is favourable because the labour hours worked cost less than they should have done.

The labour efficiency variance, like a materials usage variance, is calculated for the actual number of units produced. The variance in hours is converted into a money value at the standard rate of pay per hour.

Direct labour efficiency variance		
	hours	
3,000 units of Product P234 should take (× 0.5 hours)	1,500	
They did take	1,400	
Efficiency variance in hours	100	(F)
Standard direct labour rate per hour	$12	
Direct labour efficiency variance in $	$1,200	(F)

The efficiency variance is favourable because production took less time than expected, which has reduced costs.

Labour cost variances: summary	$	
Labour rate variance	600	(F)
Labour efficiency variance	1,200	(F)
Total direct labour cost variance	1,800	(F)

4.3 Direct labour: possible causes of variance

When labour variances appear significant, management should investigate the reason why they occurred, and take control measures where appropriate to improve the situation in the future. Possible causes of labour variances include the following.

Labour rate variance

- An increase in pay for employees.
- Working overtime hours, when overtime is paid at a premium above the basic rate.
- Using direct labour employees who were more skilled and experienced than the 'normal' and who are paid more than the standard rate per hour (adverse rate variance).
- Using direct labour employees who were relatively inexperienced and new to the job (favourable rate variance, because these employees would be paid less than 'normal').

Labour efficiency variance

- More efficient methods of working.
- Good morale amongst the workforce and good management with the result that the work force is more productive.
- If incentive schemes are introduced to the workforce, this may encourage employees to work more quickly and therefore give rise to a favourable efficiency variance.

- Using employees who are more experienced or less experienced than 'standard', resulting in favourable or adverse efficiency variances. Experienced employees might be able to complete their work more quickly than less-experienced colleagues.

Variable production overheads: expenditure and efficiency variances

- Variable production overhead expenditure variance
- Variable production overhead efficiency variance
- Variable production overheads: possible causes of variances

5 Variable production overheads: expenditure and efficiency variances

The variable production overhead total cost variance can be analysed, if required, into an expenditure variance (= spending rate per hour variance) and an efficiency variance.

- The expenditure variance is similar to a materials price variance or a labour rate variance. It is the difference between actual variable overhead spending in the hours worked and what the spending should have been (the standard rate).
- The variable overhead efficiency variance in hours is the same as the labour efficiency variance in hours (excluding any idle time variance), and is calculated in a very similar way. It is the variable overhead cost or benefit from adverse or favourable direct labour efficiency variances.

5.1 Variable production overhead expenditure variance

It is normally assumed that variable production overheads are incurred during hours actively worked, but not during any hours of idle time.

- The variable production overhead expenditure variance is calculated by taking the actual number of hours worked.
- The actual variable production overhead cost of the actual hours worked is compared with the standard cost for those hours. The difference is the variable production overhead expenditure variance.

A variable production overhead expenditure variance is calculated as follows. Like the direct labour rate variance, it is calculated by taking the actual number of labour hours worked, since it is assumed that variable overhead expenditure varies with hours worked..

	$	
Hours worked should cost (active hours of work × standard rate per hour)	A	
They did cost	B	
Variable production overhead expenditure variance	A – B	(F) or (A)

5.2 Variable production overhead efficiency variance

The variable production overhead efficiency variance in hours is exactly the same as the direct labour efficiency variance in hours.

It is converted into a money value at the standard variable production overhead rate per hour.

Example

Product P123 has a standard variable production overhead cost per unit of:

1.5 hours × $2 per direct labour hour = $3 per unit.

During a particular month, 2,000 units of Product 123 were manufactured. These took 2,780 hours to make and the variable production overhead cost was $6,550.

Required

Calculate for the month:

- the total variable production overhead cost variance
- the variable production overhead expenditure variance
- the variable production overhead efficiency variance.

Answer

Total variable production overhead cost variance	$	
2,000 units of output should cost (× $3)	6,000	
They did cost	6,550	
Total variable production overhead cost variance	550	(A)

Variable production overhead expenditure variance	$	
2,780 hours should cost (× $2)	5,560	
They did cost	6,550	
Variable production overhead expenditure variance	990	(A)

The expenditure variance is adverse because the expenditure on variable overhead in the hours worked was more than it should have been.

Variable production overhead efficiency variance		
	hours	
2,000 units of Product P123 should take (× 1.5 hours)	3,000	
They did take	2,780	
Efficiency variance in hours	220	(F)
Standard variable production overhead rate per hour	$2	
Variable production overhead efficiency variance in	$440	(F)

The efficiency variance is favourable because production took less time than expected, which has reduced costs.

Variable production overhead cost variances: summary

	$	
Variable production overhead expenditure variance	990	(A)
Variable production overhead efficiency variance	440	(F)
Total variable production overhead cost variance	550	(A)

5.3 Variable production overhead: possible causes of variances

Source of the possible causes of variable production overhead variances including the following.

- Incorrect budgets being set at the beginning of the year may give rise to expenditure variances.
- Variable production overhead efficiency variances arise for the same reasons as labour efficiency variances, for example: substituting one grade of labour for another; introducing incentive schemes; and the learning curve effect.

Fixed production overhead cost variances: absorption costing

- Total fixed production overhead cost variance
- Fixed production overhead expenditure variance
- Fixed production overhead volume variance
- Fixed production overhead efficiency and capacity variances
- Fixed production overheads: possible causes of variances

6 Fixed production overhead cost variances: absorption costing

Variances for fixed production overheads are different from variances for variable costs. The variances reported differ according to whether standard absorption costing or standard marginal costing is used.

With standard absorption costing, the standard cost per unit is a full production cost, including an amount for absorbed fixed production overhead. Every unit produced is valued at standard cost.

This means that **production overheads are absorbed into production costs at a standard cost per unit produced**. This standard fixed cost per unit is derived from a standard number of direct labour hours per unit and a fixed overhead rate per hour.

- The **total fixed overhead cost variance** is the **total amount of under-absorbed or over-absorbed overheads**, where overheads are absorbed at the standard fixed overhead cost per unit.
- It was explained in an earlier chapter that the total under- or over-absorption of fixed overheads can be analysed into an **expenditure variance** and a **volume variance**. This applies to standard costing as well as to ordinary absorption costing.
- The total volume variance can be analysed even further in standard absorption costing, into a fixed overhead **capacity variance** and a fixed overhead **efficiency variance**.

Fixed overhead variances are as follows:

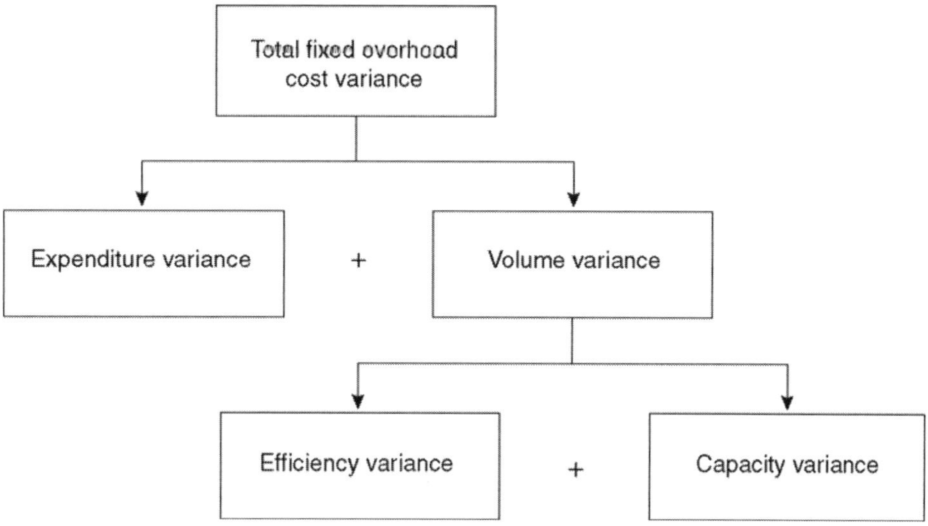

6.1 Total fixed production overhead cost variance

The total fixed overhead cost variance is rarely calculated, because it is more usual to calculate the expenditure and volume variances.

However, the total fixed overhead cost variance is the amount of:

- under-absorbed fixed production overhead (= adverse variance) or
- over-absorbed fixed production overhead (= favourable variance).

Overheads are absorbed at a standard fixed cost per unit produced, not at standard rate per hour.

In standard absorption costing, the total fixed production overhead cost variance can be analysed into an expenditure variance and a volume variance. Together, these variances explain the reasons for the under- or over-absorption.

6.2 Fixed production overhead expenditure variance

A fixed production overhead expenditure variance is the difference between:

- budgeted fixed production overhead expenditure, and
- actual fixed production overhead expenditure.

Actual fixed overheads are expected to be the budgeted fixed expenditure. If actual fixed cost expenditure differs from the budget, there is an expenditure variance.

- An **adverse** expenditure variance occurs when actual fixed overhead expenditure exceeds the budgeted fixed overhead expenditure.
- A **favourable** expenditure variance occurs when actual fixed overhead expenditure is less than budget.

	$	
Budgeted fixed production overhead expenditure	X	
Actual fixed production overhead expenditure	Y	
Fixed production overhead expenditure variance	X – Y	(F) or (A)

Fixed overhead expenditure variances can be calculated, for control reporting, for other overheads as well as production overheads. For example:

- an administration fixed overheads expenditure variance is the difference between budgeted and actual fixed administration overhead costs
- a sales and distribution fixed overheads expenditure variance is the difference between budgeted and actual fixed sales and distribution overhead costs.

6.3 Fixed production overhead volume variance

In a system of standard absorption costing, the total cost variance for fixed overheads can be analysed as the sum of the fixed overhead expenditure variance and a fixed overhead volume variance.

The fixed production overhead volume variance measures the amount of fixed overheads under- or over-absorbed because of the fact that actual production volume differs from the budgeted production volume.

The volume variance is measured first of all in either:

- units of output or
- standard hours of the output units.

These are the same amount.

The volume variance in units (or standard hours of those units) is converted into a money value, as appropriate, at the standard fixed overhead cost per unit (or the standard fixed overhead rate per standard hour produced).

Fixed overhead volume variance	**Units produced** **	
Actual number of units produced **	X	
Budgeted production (units)	Y	
Volume variance in units **	X – Y	(F) or (A)
× Standard fixed overhead cost per unit	× $P	
Fixed production volume variance in $	(X – Y) x $P	(F) or (A)

** Instead of units, these measurements could be in **standard hours produced**. Standard hours produced = Actual units produced × Standard hours per unit.

Example

A company budgeted to make 5,000 units of a single standard product in Year 1. Budgeted direct labour hours are 10,000 hours. Budgeted fixed production overhead is $40,000. Actual production in Year 1 was 5,200 units, and fixed production overhead was $40,500.

Required

Calculate for Year 1:

- the total fixed production overhead cost variance
- the fixed overhead expenditure variance
- the fixed overhead volume variance

Answer

Standard fixed overhead cost per unit = $8 ($40,000/$5,000 units)

Fixed production overhead total cost variance

	$	
5,200 units: standard fixed cost (× $8) = fixed overhead absorbed	41,600	
Actual fixed overhead cost expenditure	40,500	
Fixed production overhead total cost variance	1,100	(F)

The variance is favourable, because fixed overhead costs have been over absorbed.

Fixed overhead expenditure variance

	$	
Budgeted fixed production overhead expenditure	40,000	
Actual fixed production overhead expenditure	40,500	
Fixed overhead expenditure variance	500	(A)

This variance is adverse because actual expenditure exceeds the budgeted expenditure.

Fixed overhead volume variance

	units of production	
Budgeted production volume in units	5,000	
Actual production volume in units	5,200	
Fixed overhead volume variance in units	200	(F)
Standard fixed production overhead cost per unit	$8	
Fixed overhead volume variance in $	$1,600	(F)

This variance is favourable because actual production volume exceeded the budgeted volume.

Summary	$	
Fixed overhead expenditure variance	500	(A)
Fixed overhead volume variance	1,600	(F)
Fixed overhead total cost variance	1,100	(F)

Exercise 4

A company has budgeted to make 6,000 units of Product P345 in Year 2. Total budgeted fixed production costs are $72,000. Each unit of Product P345 has a standard direct labour time of 0.5 hours.

Actual output in Year 2 was 5,600 units of Product P345 and actual fixed production overhead expenditure was $71,200.

Required

Calculate for Year 2:

- the fixed production overhead expenditure variance
- the fixed production overhead volume variance.

6.4 Fixed production overhead efficiency and capacity variances

A fixed production overhead volume variance can be analysed, if required, into a fixed overhead efficiency variance and a fixed overhead capacity variance.

There are two reasons why actual production volume might differ from the budgeted production volume:

- Production operations were either more or less efficient than budgeted, so that more units or less units than expected were produced in the available time. This causes an **efficiency variance**.
- Actual hours worked were either more or less than budgeted, which means that either more units or less units than budgeted should be expected. This causes a **capacity variance**. (It might help you to think of the capacity variance as an 'hours worked' variance.)

Fixed production overhead efficiency variance

This is exactly the same, in hours, as the direct labour efficiency variance and the variable production overhead efficiency variance.

It is converted into a money value at the standard fixed overhead rate per hour.

Fixed production overhead capacity variance

This is the difference between the budgeted and actual hours worked (excluding any idle time hours). It is converted into a money value at the standard fixed overhead rate per hour.

Fixed overhead capacity variance	hours	
Actual number of hours worked	AH	
Budgeted hours	BH	
Capacity variance in hours	AH – BH	(F) or (A)
× Standard fixed overhead rate per hour	× $P	
Fixed production capacity variance in $	(AH – BH) × $P	(F) or (A)

Example

A company budgeted to make 5,000 units of a single standard product in Year 1. Budgeted direct labour hours are 10,000 hours. Budgeted fixed production overhead is $40,000. Actual production in Year 1 was 5,200 units in 10,250 hours of work, and fixed production overhead was $40,500.

This same example was used earlier to calculate the fixed overhead volume variance, which is $1,600 (F).

Required

Calculate for Year 1:

- the fixed overhead efficiency variance
- the fixed overhead capacity variance.

Answer

The standard direct labour hours per unit = 10,000 hours/5,000 units = 2 hours per unit.

The standard fixed overhead rate per hour = $40,000/10,000 hours = $4 per hour.

The standard fixed overhead cost per unit is 2 hours × $4 per hour = $8 (or $40,000/5,000 units).

Fixed overhead efficiency variance		
	hours	
5,200 units should take (× 2 hours)	10,400	
They did take	10,250	
Efficiency variance in hours	150	(F)
Standard fixed overhead rate per hour	$4	
Fixed overhead efficiency variance in $	$600	(F)

Fixed overhead capacity variance		
	hours	
Budgeted hours of work	10,000	
Actual hours of work	10,250	
Capacity variance in hours	250	(F)
Standard fixed overhead rate per hour	$4	
Fixed overhead capacity variance in $	$1,000	(F)

The capacity variance is favourable because actual hours worked exceeded the budgeted hours (therefore more units should have been produced).

Summary	$	
Fixed overhead efficiency variance	600	(F)
Fixed overhead capacity variance	1,000	(F)
Fixed overhead volume variance	1,600	(F)

Exercise 5

A company manufactures widgets. These are expected to take 0.25 hours each to make.

Budgeted production volume in Year 3 was 16,000 units and budgeted fixed production costs were $96,000.

Actual production volume in Year 3 was 15,700 units in 4,200 hours of work. Actual fixed overhead expenditure was $98,500.

Required

(a) For Year 3, calculate:

- the fixed overhead expenditure variance
- the fixed overhead volume variance.

(b) Analyse the volume variance into an efficiency and a capacity variance.

6.5 Fixed production overheads: possible causes of variances

Some of the possible causes of fixed production overhead variances include the following.

Fixed overhead expenditure variance

- Poor control over overhead spending (adverse variance) or good control over spending (favourable variance).
- Poor budgeting for overhead spending. If the budget for overhead expenditure is unrealistic, there will be an expenditure variance due to poor planning rather than poor expenditure control.

- Unplanned increases or decreases in items of expenditure for fixed production overheads, for example, an unexpected increase in factory rent.

Fixed overhead volume variance

A fixed overhead volume variance can be explained by anything that made actual output volume different from the budgeted volume. The reasons could be:

- Efficient working by direct labour: a favourable labour efficiency variance results in a favourable fixed overhead efficiency variance.
- Working more hours or less hours than budgeted (capacity variance).
- An unexpected increase or decrease in demand for a product, with the result that longer hours were worked.
- Strike action by the workforce, resulting in a fall in output below budget.
- Extensive breakdowns in machinery, resulting in lost production.

Sales variances: sales price and sales volume variances

- Sales price variance
- Sales volume variance
- Sales: possible causes of variances

7 Sales variances: sales price and sales volume variances

Sales variances, unlike cost variances, are not recorded in a standard costing system of cost accounts (in the cost ledger). However, sales variances are included in variance reports to management.

- They help to reconcile actual profit with budgeted profit.
- They help management to assess the sales performance.

There are two sales variances:

- a sales price variance, and
- a sales volume variance.

7.1 Sales price variance

A sales price variance shows the difference between:

- the actual sales prices achieved for items that were sold, and
- their standard sales price.

To calculate this variance, you should take the **actual items sold**, and compare the actual sales revenue with the standard selling prices for the items.

	$	
Actual units sold should sell for (units sold × standard sales price/unit)	A	
They did sell for (actual sales revenue)	B	
Sales price variance	A – B	(F) or (A)

There is a favourable sales price variance if units were sold for more than their standard sales price, and an adverse variance if sales prices were below the standard price.

7.2 Sales volume variance

A sales volume variance shows the effect on profit of the difference between the actual sales volume and the budgeted sales volume. The sales volume variance is calculated differently in standard absorption costing compared with standard marginal costing.

In a **standard absorption costing system**, the sales volume variance might be called a sales volume **profit** variance. A method for calculating the sales volume variance is as follows:

Sales volume variance: usual method of calculation		
	units of sale	
Actual sales volume (units)	AV	
Budgeted sales volume (units)	BV	
Sales volume variance in units	AV – BV	(F) or (A)
× Standard profit per unit	× $P	
Sales volume variance in $	(AV – BV) × $P	(F) or (A)

The volume variance is favourable if actual sales volume is higher than the budgeted volume, and adverse if the actual sales volume is below budget.

There is an alternative method of calculating the sales volume variance, which produces exactly the same figure for the variance.

Sales volume variance: alternative method of calculation		
	$	
Actual sales at standard selling price	A	
Budgeted sales revenue	B	
Sales volume variance in $ revenue	(A – B)	(F) or (A)
Standard profit/sales price ratio	P%	
Sales volume variance (profit variance)	(A – B) × P%	(F) or (A)

Example

A company budgets to sell 7,000 units of Product P456. It uses a standard absorption costing system. The standard sales price of Product P456 is $50 per unit and the standard cost per unit is $42.

Actual sales were 7,200 units, which sold for $351,400.

The sales price variance and sales volume variance would be calculated as follows.

Sales price variance	$	
7,200 units should sell for (× $50)	360,000	
They did sell for	351,400	
Sales price variance	8,600	(A)

The sales price variance is adverse because actual sales revenue from the units sold was less than expected.

Sales volume variance: usual method of calculation

	units	
Actual sales volume (units)	7,200	
Budgeted sales volume (units)	7,000	
Sales volume variance in units	200	(F)
Standard profit per unit ($50 – $42 = $8)	$8	
Sales volume variance (profit variance)	$1,600	(F)

The sales volume variance is favourable because actual sales exceeded budgeted sales.

Sales volume variance: alternative method of calculation

	$	
Actual sales at standard selling price (7,200 × $50)	360,000	
Budgeted sales (7,000 units × $50)	350,000	
Sales volume variance in $ revenue	10,000	(F)
Standard profit/sales price ratio ($8/$50)	16%	
Sales volume variance (profit variance)	$1,600	(F)

Both methods of calculating the sales volume variance produce the same answer.

6

Exercise 6

A company budgets to sell 42,000 units of Product P567. The standard sales price of Product P567 is $20 per unit and the standard cost per unit is $16. Actual sales were 39,200 units, which sold for $802,300.

Required

Calculate the sales price variance and the sales volume variance (profit variance) for the period. The company uses a standard absorption costing system.

7.3 Sales: possible causes of variances

Possible causes of sales variances include the following:

Sales price variance

- Actual increases in prices charged for products were higher or less than expected due to market conditions.
- Actual sales prices were less than standard because major customers were given an unplanned price discount.
- Competitors reduced their prices, forcing the company to reduce the prices of its own products.

Sales volume variance

- Actual sales demand was more or less than expected.
- The sales force worked well and achieved more sales than budgeted.
- An advertising campaign had more success than expected.
- A competitor went into liquidation, and the company attracted some of the former competitor's customers.
- The products that the company makes and sells are going out of fashion earlier than expected; therefore the sales volume variance was adverse.

Interrelationships between variances

- The nature of interrelationships between variances
- Sales price and sales volume
- Materials price and usage
- Labour rate and efficiency
- Footnote: the importance of reliable standard costs

8 Interrelationships between variances

8.1 The nature of interrelationships between variances

In your examination, you might be required to show an understanding of the possible causes of variances. Some causes of individual variances have already been listed.

The reasons for variances might also be connected, and two or more variances might arise from the same cause. This is known as an interrelationship between two variances.

For example, one variance might be favourable and another variance might be adverse. Taking each variance separately, the favourable variance might suggest good performance and the adverse variance might suggest bad performance. However, the two variances might be inter-related, and the favourable variance and the adverse variance might have the same cause. When this happens, management should look at the two variances together, in order to assess their significance and decide whether control action is needed.

Examples of interrelationships between variances are given below.

8.2 Sales price and sales volume

A favourable sales price variance and an adverse sales volume variance might have the same cause. If a company increases its selling prices above the standard price, the sales price variance will be favourable, but sales demand might fall and the sales volume variance would be adverse.

Similarly, in order to sell more products a company might decide to reduce its selling prices. There would be an adverse sales price variance due to the reduction in selling prices, but there should also be an increase in sales and a favourable sales volume variance.

8.3 Materials price and usage

A materials price variance and usage variance might be inter-related. For example, if a company decides to use a material for production that is more expensive than the normal or standard material, but easier to use and better in quality, there will be an adverse price variance. However a consequence of using better materials might be lower wastage. If there is less wastage, there will be a favourable material usage variance. Therefore, using a different quality of material can result in an adverse price variance and a favourable usage variance.

8.4 Labour rate and efficiency

If there is a change in the grade of workers used to do some work, both the rate and efficiency variances may be affected.

For example, if a lower grade of labour is used instead of the normal higher grade:

- there should be a favourable rate variance because the workers will be paid less than the standard rate
- however the lower grade of labour may work less efficiently and take longer to produce goods than the normal higher grade of labour would usually take. If the lower grade of labour takes longer, then this will give rise to an adverse efficiency variance.

Therefore the change in the grade of labour used results in two 'opposite' variances, an adverse efficiency variance and a favourable rate variance.

When inexperienced employees are used, they might also waste more materials than more experienced employees would, due to mistakes that they make in their work. The result might be not only adverse labour efficiency, but also **adverse materials usage**.

8.5 Footnote: the importance of reliable standard costs

It is important to remember that the value of variances as control information for management depends on the reliability and accuracy of the standard costs. If the standard costs are inaccurate, comparisons between actual cost and standard cost will have no meaning. Adverse or favourable variances might be caused by inaccurate standard costs rather than by inefficient or efficient working.

Reconciling budgeted and actual profit: standard absorption costing

- Purpose of an operating statement
- Format of an operating statement

9 Reconciling budgeted and actual profit: standard absorption costing

9.1 Purpose of an operating statement

A management report called an operating statement might be prepared, showing how the difference between budgeted and actual profit is explained by the sales variances and cost variances. An operating statement reconciles the profit that was expected in the budget with the actual profit that was achieved.

The purpose of an operating statement is to report all variances to management, so that management can assess the effect they are having on profitability. Senior management can also use an operating statement to assess the success of junior managers in controlling costs and achieving sales.

9.2 Format of an operating statement

In a standard absorption costing system, an operating statement can be set out as follows. You should try to familiarise yourself with this type of statement.

Operating statement (standard absorption costing)

			$	
Budgeted profit			BP	
Sales price variance			X	(F) or (A)
Sales volume variance			X	(F) or (A)
Actual sales minus the standard production cost of sales			X	
	(F)	(A)		
Cost variances	$	$		
Direct materials price	X			
Direct materials usage		X		
Direct labour rate		X		
Direct labour efficiency	X			
Variable production o'head expenditure	X			
Variable production o'head efficiency	X			
Fixed production overhead expenditure		X		
Fixed production overhead efficiency	X			
Fixed production overhead capacity		X		
Other overhead expenditure variances (see note)		X		
Total cost variances	Totals		X	(F) or (A)
Actual profit			AP	

Note: Other overhead expenditure variances, assuming administration overheads and selling and distribution overheads are all fixed costs, are the difference between:

- budgeted other overheads expenditure, and
- actual other overheads expenditure.

In a system of absorption costing:

- The operating statement begins with the budgeted profit.
- The sales variances are shown next. These are added to (favourable variances) or subtracted from (adverse variances), and the resulting figure is shown as a sub-total. This figure is the actual sales revenue in the period minus the standard production cost of sales.
- The cost variances are listed next. They can be listed in any format, but showing separate columns for favourable variances and adverse variances helps to make the statement clear to the reader. Adverse variances reduce the profit and favourable variances add to profit.
- The cost variances are added up and then shown as a total.
- The actual profit is shown as the final figure, at the bottom of the operating statement.

Standard marginal costing

- Standard marginal costing and standard absorption costing compared
- Fixed production overhead variances in standard marginal costing
- Sales volume variance in standard marginal costing
- Standard marginal costing operating statement
- Standard absorption costing and standard marginal costing: differences in profit

10 Standard marginal costing

10.1 Standard marginal costing and standard absorption costing compared

When a company uses standard marginal costing rather than standard absorption costing:

- units produced and finished goods inventory are valued at standard variable production cost, not standard full production cost
- variances are calculated and presented in exactly the same way as for standard absorption costing, but with two important differences:
  - fixed production overhead variances
  - sales volume variances.

10.2 Fixed production overhead variances in standard marginal costing

In standard marginal costing, there is a fixed production overhead expenditure variance, but no fixed production overhead volume variance.

The fixed production overhead expenditure variance is calculated in the way already described and is the same amount in a standard marginal costing system as in a standard absorption costing system.

10.3 Sales volume variance in standard marginal costing

In standard absorption costing, the sales volume variance is calculated by applying the standard profit per unit to the volume variance in units.

In standard marginal costing, the sales volume variance is calculated using standard contribution, and the variance might be called the sales volume contribution variance. Contribution is the difference between the selling price and the variable cost.

- Standard contribution is therefore the difference between the standard selling price per unit and the standard variable cost.

- Standard contribution can also be expressed as a contribution to sales ratio, which is the ratio of the standard contribution per unit to the standard selling price per unit. The standard contribution to sales ratio is a constant value.

A sales volume contribution variance is calculated in either of the following ways. (Both methods produce the same variance).

Sales volume variance: usual method of calculation

	units	
Actual sales volume (units)	AV	
Budgeted sales volume (units)	BV	
Sales volume variance in units	AV – BV	(F) or (A)
Standard contribution per unit	\$C	
Sales volume variance (contribution variance)	(AV – BV) × \$C	(F) or (A)

Sales volume variance: alternative method of calculation

	\$	
Actual sales at standard selling price	A	
Budgeted sales	B	
Sales volume variance in \$ revenue	(A – B)	(F) or (A)
Standard contribution /sales ratio	C%	
Sales volume variance (contribution variance)	\$(A – B) × C%	(F) or (A)

Both methods of calculating the sales volume (contribution) variance produce the same answer.

10.4 Standard marginal costing operating statement

With standard marginal costing, an operating statement is presented in a different way from an operating statement with standard absorption costing. Budgeted contribution can be reconciled with actual contribution, by means of the sales price variance, sales volume variance and variable cost variances. Fixed cost expenditure variances should be presented in a separate part of the operating statement.

Operating statement: standard marginal costing

	\$	
Budgeted profit	BP	
Add budgeted fixed costs	BF	
Budgeted contribution (BP + BF)	BC	
Sales price variance	X	(F) or (A)
Sales volume variance	X	(F) or (A)
Sales less standard variable cost of sales	X	

Variable cost variances	(F)	(A)		
	$	$		
Direct materials price	X			
Direct materials usage		X		
Direct labour rate		X		
Direct labour efficiency	X			
Variable production overhead rate	X			
Variable production o'head efficiency	X			
Total variable cost variances	Totals		X	(F) or (A)
Actual contribution			AC	
Budgeted fixed overhead expenditure	BF			
Fixed overhead expenditure variance	X	(F) or (A)		
Actual fixed production overheads			AF	
Actual profit (= AC – AF)			AP	

Try to familiarise yourself with the format of an operating statement with standard marginal costing.

- The operating statement begins with budgeted profit. However, most variances in standard marginal costing should show the effect of variances on total contribution. The budgeted profit should therefore be 'converted' into budgeted contribution, by adding the budgeted fixed costs.
- The sales variances are shown next, which is the same as in an operating statement with standard absorption costing.
- The variances for variable costs only are listed next, and the total of all variances for variable cost items is shown.
- The actual contribution is the difference between the budgeted contribution and the sum of the sales variances and the variable cost variances. Adverse variances reduce the profit and favourable variances add to profit.
- Actual fixed costs are deducted from actual contribution to arrive at the actual profit at the bottom of the operating statement. Actual fixed cost expenditure should be shown as the budgeted fixed overheads plus the adverse fixed overhead expenditure variance or minus the favourable fixed overhead expenditure variance.

10.5 Standard absorption costing and standard marginal costing: differences in profit

A previous chapter explains the difference in the reported profit using absorption costing compared with marginal costing. The same principles apply in standard costing.

The reported profit using standard absorption costing will differ from the reported profit using standard marginal costing, and the difference in the reported profit can be explained entirely by differences in the increase or decrease in inventory valuation during the period.

Example

A company uses standard absorption costing. It manufactures a single product, which has a standard full production cost of $20 per unit. This consists of $12 of standard variable costs and $8 per unit of fixed production costs.

During a financial period, the company made 25,000 units of the product and sold 23,000 units. The actual reported profit for the period, using standard absorption costing, was $55,000.

If standard marginal costing had been used, the reported profit would have been different.

- There was an increase in inventory of 2,000 units. When finished goods inventory increases, the reported profit with absorption costing is higher than with marginal costing.
- The difference in profit is the amount of fixed overhead in the increase (or reduction) in inventory. In this example, this is $16,000 (= 2,000 units × $8).
- Reported profit would therefore be $16,000 lower using standard marginal costing – i.e. the reported profit would be $39,000 (= $55,000 - $16,000).

Calculating actual costs or standard costs from variances

- Calculating actual cost from variances and standard cost
- Calculating standard cost from variances and actual cost

11 Calculating actual costs or standard costs from variances

In your examination, you might be given a question where you are required to:

- calculate actual costs, given information about variances and standard costs, or
- calculate a standard cost, given information about variances and actual costs.

This type of problem does not occur in practice, but it is a useful way of testing knowledge of variances.

11.1 Calculating actual cost from variances and standard cost

This type of problem can be solved by using the tables to calculate variances, described in this chapter. You can enter into a table all the data given by the question. The 'missing figure' for actual cost or standard cost can then be calculated.

Some examples will be used to illustrate the technique.

Example

The standard direct materials cost of making Product B is $20, consisting of 4 kilos of material at $5 per kilo. During one period, 1,250 kilos of the material were purchased and the direct materials price variance was $250 (A).

Required

Calculate the actual costs of direct materials purchased and used in the period.

Answer

A table should be prepared showing how the total materials cost variance is calculated, and the figures that are available should be entered in the table.

	$	
1,250 kilos of material should cost (× $5)	6,250	
The materials did cost	?	
Total materials cost variance	250	(A)

Actual purchase costs were higher than standard cost because the price variance is adverse. Actual purchase costs were therefore $6,250 + $250 = $6,500.

Example

The standard direct material cost of Product C is $21 (6 kilos of material at $3.50 per kilo). During a period when 400 units of Product C were made, the direct material usage variance was $630 (F).

Required

Calculate the actual quantity of direct materials used in the period.

Answer

A table should be prepared showing how the materials usage variance is calculated, and the figures that are available should be entered in the table.

Materials usage variance		
	kilos	
400 units of Product C should use (× 6 kilos)	2,400	
They did use	?	
Material usage variance in kilos	?	
Standard price per kilo	$3.50	
Material usage variance in $	$630	(F)

From this information we can **calculate the material usage variance in kilos**. A usage variance is valued at the standard cost per unit of material; therefore the usage variance in $ can be converted into a usage variance in kilos:
Usage variance = $630(F)/$3.50 per kilo = 180 kilos (F).

The variance is favourable, which means that actual usage was less than the standard (expected) usage. We know that the standard usage is 2,400 kilos.
Actual material usage was therefore:
2,400 kilos – 180 kilos = 2,220 kilos.

Example

In the standard cost of Product D, the cost of Grade A labour is $24 per unit (= 1.5 hours per unit at $16 per hour). During a month when 500 units of Product D were made and 780 hours were worked, the labour rate variance for Grade A labour was $1,500 (F).

Required

Calculate the actual cost of Grade A labour in the month.

Answer

A table should be prepared showing how the labour rate variance is calculated, and the figures that are available should be entered in the table.

Direct labour rate variance	$	
780 hours should cost (× $16)	12,480	
They did cost	?	
Direct labour rate variance	1,500	(F)

The rate variance was favourable, which means that actual costs were less than standard.

Actual cost of Grade A labour = $12,480 – $1,500 = $10,980.

Example

In a standard absorption costing system, the standard fixed production overhead cost per unit of Product E is $36. This represents 3 direct hours at $12 per hour.

The budgeted production volume in the period was 6,000 units of Product E. The fixed production overhead volume variance was $12,600 (F).

Required

Calculate the actual quantity of Product E that was produced.

Answer

A table should be prepared showing how the production overhead volume variance is calculated, and the figures that are available should be entered in the table.

Fixed overhead volume variance		
	units of production	
Budgeted production volume in units	6,000	
Actual production volume in units	?	
Fixed overhead volume variance in units	?	(F)
Standard fixed production overhead cost per unit	$36	
Fixed overhead volume variance in $	$12,600	(F)

We know the volume variance in $. The volume variance is valued at the standard fixed overhead cost per unit. The volume variance in $ can therefore be converted into a volume variance in units as follows:
$12,600(F)/$36 per unit = 350 units (F).

Actual production volume is higher than the budgeted volume, because the volume variance is favourable. The budgeted production volume was 6,000 units.

Actual production volume = 6,000 units + 350 units = 6,350 units.

11.2 Calculating standard cost from variances and actual cost

The same approach can be used to calculate a standard cost or budget amount if you are given a variance and data about actual costs (or sales revenues). Some further examples will illustrate the technique.

Example

Product F uses a direct material, material M. The standard price of material M is $4 per kilo. During one month, 2,500 units of Product F were manufactured. These required 12,000 kilos of material M and the material usage variance was $2,000 (A).

Required

Calculate the standard direct material cost per unit of Product F.

Answer

We know the standard price of material M, but we need to calculate the standard material usage. This can be obtained from the data provided. A table should be prepared showing how the material usage variance is calculated, and the figures that are available should be entered in the table.

Materials usage variance

	kilos	
2,500 units of Product F should use	?	
They did use	12,000	
Material usage variance in kilos	?	
Standard price per kilo	$4	
Material usage variance in $	2,000	(A)

We know the material usage variance in $. The variance is valued at the standard price per unit of material. From the information provided we can therefore calculate the material usage variance in kilos:
Usage variance = $2,000(A)/$4 per kilo = 500 kilos (A).

The variance is adverse, which means that actual usage was more than the standard (expected) usage. The standard material usage is therefore:
12,000 kilos – 500 kilos = 11,500 kilos.

This is the standard usage for 2,500 units of Product F, so the standard usage per unit is 11,500/2,500 = 4.60 kilos per unit.

The standard material cost for Product F is therefore:
4.6 kilos of material M at $4 per kilo = $18.40.

Example

The standard time required to make one unit of Product G is 1.25 hours of direct labour. During one month, total direct labour costs were $119,000. The company made 6,800 units of Product G. These took 9,100 direct labour hours and the direct labour rate variance was $8,400 (F).

Required

Calculate the standard direct labour cost per unit of Product G.

Answer

We know the standard direct labour time, which is 1.25 hours per unit, but we need to calculate the standard direct labour rate per hour. This can be obtained from the data provided. A table should be prepared showing how the labour rate variance is calculated, and the figures that are available should be entered in the table.

Direct labour rate variance	$	
9,100 hours should cost	?	
They did cost	119,000	
Direct labour rate variance	8,400	(F)

The rate variance is favourable, which means that actual costs were lower than standard costs. The actual labour cost for the 9,100 hours was $119,000. Expected costs are higher.

The 9,100 hours should therefore cost $119,000 + $8,400 = $127,400.
The standard rate per hour is $127,400/9,100 hours = $14 per hour.

The standard direct labour cost of Product G is:
1.25 hours at $14 per hour = $17.50

Tutorial note

It is easy to get confused about whether variances should be added or subtracted in this type of calculation. You need to think carefully and logically, to avoid making a mistake.

Exercise 7

A company makes a single product. The standard direct labour cost of one unit of the product is $24 (= 1.5 hours at $16 per hour).

During a month when 900 units of the product were manufactured, 1,240 hours were worked and the direct labour rate variance was $1,700 (F).

Required

Calculate actual cost of direct labour during the month.

Exercise 8

During one month, a factory produced 3,200 units of Product H and these took 5,150 direct labour hours. The standard direct labour rate per hour is $18 per unit, and the direct labour efficiency variance for the month was $8,100 (F).

Required

Calculate the standard direct labour cost per unit of Product H.

Practice multiple choice questions

1 A company uses standard costing. Last month 18,000 direct labour hours were worked at an actual cost of $328,500. The production output measured in standard hours was 17,700 standard hours. The standard direct labour cost per hour was $18.50.

What was the direct labour rate variance?

A $1,050 (A)

B $1,050 (F)

C $4,500 (A)

D $4,500 (F). ***(2 marks)***

2 A company uses standard costing. It makes a single product, and it should take 2 direct labour hours to make each unit. Last month 18,000 direct labour hours were worked at an actual cost of $18 per hour. Actual output measured was 8,800 units of product. The standard direct labour cost per hour is $18.50.

What was the direct labour efficiency variance?

A $7,200 (A)

B $7,200 (F)

C $7,400 (A)

D $7,400 (F). ***(2 marks)***

3 A company uses standard marginal costing. Last month, the budgeted sales were 6,000 units. The standard sales price is $15 per unit and the contribution to sales ratio is 80%. Actual sales in the month were 6,450 units and total sales revenue was $92,880.

What were the adverse sales price and favourable sales volume contribution variances?

	Sales price	Sales volume contribution
	$	$
A	1,800	5,400
B	3,870	5,400
C	1,800	6,750
D	3,870	6,750

(2 marks)

4 A company uses standard marginal costing. Last month, actual fixed overhead expenditure was 3% below budget and the fixed overhead expenditure variance was $2,400.

What was the actual fixed overhead expenditure last month?

A $155,200

B $159,856

C $160,000

D $164,800 ***(2 marks)***

5 A company uses standard absorption costing. The following data relates to the previous costing period.

	Budget	**Actual**
Sales and production (units)	1,500	1,600
	Standard	**Actual**
	$	$
Selling price per unit	48	46
Total production cost per unit	34	33

What was the favourable sales volume profit variance for the period?

A $1,200

B $1,300

C $1,400

D $1,500 ***(2 marks)***

6 Who should a materials price variance be reported to?

A Factory department manager

B Senior buying manager

C Human resources department manager ***(1 mark)***

7 A company manufactures a single product. The standard material cost of the product is 0.5 kilos of direct material at $8 per kilo. During last month 20,000 units of the product were made and these used 10,500 kilos of material. Purchases and usage of materials were the same quantity and purchases cost $82,500.

What was the direct materials price variance for the month?

A $1,500 (F)

B $1,500 (A)

C $2,500 (F)

D $2,500 (A) ***(2 marks)***

8 A company uses standard absorption costing. It manufactures a single product and the standard fixed production cost is $36 per unit, consisting of 3 hours per unit at a fixed overhead rate of $12 per hour. The following data relates to the previous costing period.

	Budget	**Actual**
Sales and production (units)	35,000	36,000

The fixed overhead capacity variance for the month was $7,200 favourable.

How many hours were worked in the month?

A 104,400

B 105,600

C 107,400

D 108,600 ***(2 marks)***

CHAPTER 13

Cost-volume-profit (CVP) analysis

Contents

The nature of CVP analysis

- Costing methods for planning and decision-making systems
- Assumptions in CVP analysis
- Calculating fixed and variable costs

1 The nature of CVP analysis

1.1 Costing methods for planning and decision-making

Previous chapters have described the use of costing systems to:

- record costs
- measure the cost of products, services and activities
- measure profitability using either absorption costing or marginal costing
- prepare functional budgets and a master budget
- produce budgetary control reports and calculate variances for control purposes in a system of standard costing.

Many of the costing methods described so far are concerned with measuring and analysing historical costs and they are not used for forward planning and decision-making. (Budgeting is an exception, but functional budgets are of only limited value as management information.)

However there are some costing or management accounting techniques that can be used to prepare forward-looking information and to help management to make planning decisions and 'one-off' decisions. These include:

- CVP analysis
- relevant costs.

CVP analysis stands for '**cost-volume-profit analysis**'. It is used to analyse how costs and profits will change with changes in the volume of activity, such as the volume of production and the volume of sales. It is an application of marginal costing concepts.

This chapter explains CVP analysis and some of its applications. Relevant costs are described in a later chapter.

1.2 Assumptions in CVP analysis

The normal assumptions in CVP analysis are the assumptions used in marginal costing, but they are applied to **future costs**.

- Costs are either fixed or variable. The variable cost per unit is the same at all levels of activity (output and sales). Total fixed costs are a constant amount in each period.

- Profit is measured as contribution (sales revenue minus variable costs) minus fixed costs.

	$
Sales	S
Variable costs	V
Contribution	(S – V) = C
Fixed costs	F
Profit	(C – F)

Some additional assumptions are normally used in CVP analysis.

- Since fixed costs are normally assumed to remain unchanged at all levels of output and sales, **profit is maximised by maximising total contribution**.
- The contribution per unit is constant for each unit sold (of the same product).
- The sales price per unit is also constant for every unit of product sold; therefore the contribution to sales ratio is also a constant value at all levels of sales.
- When marginal costing is used to report profits, changes in the level of finished goods inventory is important. With CVP analysis, inventory levels are irrelevant.

Example

A company makes and sells a single product. The product has a variable production cost of $8 per unit and a variable selling cost of $1per unit. Total fixed costs (production, administration and sales and distribution fixed costs) are expected to be $500,000. The selling price of the product is $16.

The contribution per unit is $16 – $8 – $1 = $7.

CVP analysis can be used to estimate what the profit will be at different volumes of sales. The table below shows how the profit or loss would be calculated for 70,000 units, 80,000 units and 90,000 units of sale.

	70,000 units	**80,000 units**	**90,000 units**
	$	$	$
Contribution ($7 per unit)	490,000	560,000	630,000
Fixed costs	(500,000)	(500,000)	(500,000)
Profit/(loss)	(10,000)	60,000	130,000

A loss is incurred at 70,000 units of sales because total contribution is not large enough to cover fixed costs. Profit increases as sales volume increases, and the increase in profit is due to the increase in total contribution as sales volume increases.

1.3 Calculating fixed and variable costs

A key to using CVP analysis is to identify fixed and variable costs, so that a contribution per unit sold or a contribution/sales ratio can be calculated and applied.

If necessary mixed costs should divided into a variable cost per unit and fixed costs, using techniques such as high/low analysis or linear regression analysis.

Example

A company has estimated that if it operates at 80% capacity, it will achieve the following results:

	$
Sales	800,000
Total production cost of sales	300,000
	500,000
Other costs (in total)	400,000
Profit	100,000

It has been estimated that at this activity level, 60% of production costs and 70% of other costs are fixed, and the rest are variable.

What is the expected profit at a 90% capacity level?

Answer

The first step is to identify the variable costs. We cannot calculate a variable cost per unit, because there is no information about the number of units produced. However, we can calculate the amount of variable costs as a percentage of sales revenue, using the information provided about costs at the 80% capacity level.

	$	$
Sales		800,000
Variable costs		
Production variable costs (40% × $300,000)	120,000	
Other variable costs (30% × $400,000)	120,000	
Total variable costs	240,000	

Variable costs are equal to 30% of sales revenue (= $240,000/$800,000).

Sales at 80% capacity level are $800,000. At a 90% capacity level, the sales will be $800,000 × 90%/80% = $900,000. The expected profit will be:

	$	$
Sales		900,000
Variable costs (30% of sales)		270,000
Contribution		630,000
Fixed production costs (60% × $300,000)	180,000	
Other fixed costs (70% × $400,000)	280,000	
Total fixed costs		460,000
Profit		170,000

Contribution and the C/S ratio

- The importance of contribution
- Contribution/sales ratio (C/S ratio)
- Calculating the sales price from the C/S ratio and variable cost
- Calculating fixed costs with CVP analysis

2 Contribution and the C/S ratio

2.1 The importance of contribution

In marginal costing analysis, contribution is a key concept:

Total profit is total contribution (S – V) minus fixed costs (F).
If the selling price per unit of product is a fixed amount, it follows that:

- The contribution per unit (= sales price minus variable cost) is a constant amount.
- Total contribution = Contribution per unit × Number of units sold.

2.2 Contribution/sales ratio (C/S ratio)

The contribution/sales ratio or C/S ratio is the ratio of the contribution per unit to the sales price per unit. If the sales price is a fixed amount per unit, and the contribution per unit is a constant amount, it follows that **the contribution/sales ratio is** also **a constant value at all levels of output and sales**.

The C/S ratio is a measure of the contribution earned per $1 of sales, expressed as a percentage.

The C/S ratio is an important concept in CVP analysis.

Example

An entity expects to achieve sales of $5,000,000 next year. Fixed costs will be $3,000,000 and variable costs $1,500,000.

How would the profit be affected if actual sales are 10% higher than the expected amount?

Answer

Contribution = Sales – Variable costs.

When sales are $5 million, contribution = $3.5 million (= $5 million – $1.5 million).

C/S ratio = \$3.5 million/\$5 million = 0.70 or 70%.

If sales are \$500,000 higher than expected, total contribution and total profit will be higher by: 70% × \$500,000 = \$350,000.

2.3 Calculating the sales price from the C/S ratio and variable cost

If you are given the C/S ratio for a product and the variable cost per unit, you can calculate the selling price per unit.

Example

A company makes and sells a product that has a variable cost of \$18 per unit and a contribution/sales ratio of 60%.

Since the contribution/sales ratio is 60%, it follows that the variable cost/sales ratio is 40% (since variable cost + contribution must add up to 100%).

	$
Variable cost (40% of sales price)	18
Therefore contribution (60% of sales price) = \$18 × 60/40	27
Sales price per unit	45

An alternative calculation would be as follows:
Variable cost/sales ratio = 40%
Therefore selling price = \$18/0.40 = \$45
Therefore contribution per unit = \$45 - \$18 = \$27.

2.4 Calculating fixed costs with CVP analysis

Examination questions on CVP analysis might require you to calculate a 'missing figure' from available information, by applying CVP analysis techniques.

For example, it is possible to calculate the fixed costs for a period given information about the profit at a particular level of sales, the variable cost per unit and the C/S ratio.

Example

A company makes and sells a product that has a variable cost of \$12 per unit and a contribution/sales ratio of 25%. At a volume of 30,000 units of sales, total profit would be \$25,000.

What are the fixed costs for the period?

Answer

The contribution per unit can be calculated from the variable cost per unit and the C/S ratio. The C/S ratio is 25%; therefore the variable cost is 75% of the sales price.

	$
Variable cost (75% of sales price)	12
Therefore contribution (25% of sales price) = $12 × 25/75	4

We know the total profit at 30,000 units of sale. We can also calculate the total contribution at this sales level. Fixed costs are the difference between total contribution and profit.

	$
Total contribution at 30,000 units of sale: 30,000 × $4	120,000
Total profit at 30,000 units of sale: given	25,000
Therefore total fixed costs	95,000

Break-even analysis

- Break-even analysis
- Calculating the break-even point
- Margin of safety
- Target profit

3 Break-even analysis

3.1 Break-even analysis

CVP analysis can be used to calculate a break-even point for sales.

Break-even point is the volume of sales required in a period (such as the financial year) to 'break even' and make neither a profit nor a loss. At the break-even point, profit is 0.

Management might want to know what the break-even point is in order to:

- assess the probability of avoiding a loss, or
- identify the minimum volume of sales that must be achieved in order to avoid a loss, or
- assess the amount of risk in the budget, by comparing the budgeted volume of sales with the break-even volume.

3.2 Calculating the break-even point

The break-even point can be calculated using simple CVP analysis.

At the break-even point, the profit is \$0. If the profit is \$0, **total contribution is exactly equal to total fixed costs**.

We therefore need to establish the volume of sales at which fixed costs and total contribution are the same amount.

Two methods of calculating the break-even point

There are two methods of calculating the break-even point, if the total fixed costs for the period are known:

Method 1

The first method is to calculate the break-even point using the contribution per unit. This method can be used where a company makes and sells just one product.

$$\text{Break-even point in sales units} = \frac{\text{Total fixed costs}}{\text{Contribution per unit}}$$

Total fixed costs are the same as the total contribution required to break even, and the break-even point can therefore be calculated by dividing the total contribution required (= total fixed costs) by the contribution per unit. Remember to include any variable selling and distribution costs in the calculation of the variable cost per unit and contribution per unit.

Method 2

The second method calculates the break-even point in sales revenue.

$$\text{Break - even sales volume in \$ revenue} = \frac{\text{Fixed costs}}{\text{C/S ratio}}$$

Having calculated the sales revenue required to break even , the break-even point can be converted into units of sales required to break even if the sales price per unit is known.

Example

A company makes a single product that has a variable cost of sales of $12 and a selling price of $20 per unit. Budgeted fixed costs are $600,000. What volume of sales is required to break even?

Answer

Method 1

$$\text{Break - even point in units of sales} = \frac{\text{Fixed costs (= Total contribution to break even)}}{\text{Contribution per unit}}$$

Contribution per unit = $20 – $12 = $8.

Therefore break-even point = $600,000/$8 per unit = 75,000 units of sales.

In sales revenue, the break-even point is 75,000 units × $20 per unit = $1,500,000 of sales.

Method 2

$$\text{Break - even sales volume in \$ revenue} = \frac{\text{Fixed costs}}{\text{C/S ratio}}$$

C/S ratio = $8/$20 = 40%

Therefore break-even point in sales revenue = $600,000/0.40 = $1,500,000 in sales revenue.

Break-even point in units = $1,500,000/sales price of $20 per unit = 75,000 units of sale.

Example

A company sells a range of products. If it sells its products in the budgeted proportions, it expects to achieve an average contribution/sales ratio of 60%. Its budgeted fixed costs for the year are $1,500,000.

What volume of sales (sales revenue in $) will be required to break even?

Answer

Break-even point = $1,500,000/60% = $2,500,000 of sales revenue.

Exercise 1

A company sells widgets. These cost $7.50 per unit and sell for $12 each. Budgeted fixed costs are $1,350,000.

What is the break-even point?

3.3 Margin of safety

The margin of safety is the difference between:

- the budgeted sales (in units or $) and
- the break-even amount of sales (in units or $).

It is usually expressed as a **percentage of the budgeted sales**. However, it may also be measured as:

- a quantity of units (= the difference between the budgeted sales volume in units and the breakeven sales volume), or
- an amount of sales revenue (= the difference between the budgeted sales revenue and the total sales revenue required to break even)

It is called the margin of safety because it is the maximum amount by which actual sales can be lower than budgeted sales without incurring a loss for the period. A high margin of safety therefore indicates a low risk of making a loss.

Example

A company budgets to sell 25,000 units of its product. This has a selling price of $16 and a variable cost of $4. Fixed costs for the period are expected to be $240,000.

The break-even point = $240,000/($16 – 4) = 20,000 units.

The budgeted sales are 25,000 units.

Margin of safety	= Budgeted sales – break-even sales
	= 25,000 – 20,000 = 5,000

The margin of safety is often expressed as a percentage of budgeted sales.
The margin of safety = 5,000 units = 20% of budgeted sales (= 5,000 units/25,000 units).

This means that sales volume could be up to 20% below budget, and the company should still expect to make a profit.

e 2

Exercise 2

A company budgets sales of $4,000,000 for the next financial year. Fixed costs are $2,100,000 and the C/S ratio is 60%.

What is the margin of safety?

3.4 Target profit

Management might want to know what the volume of sales must be in order to achieve a target profit. CVP analysis can be used to calculate the volume of sales required. To do the calculation, you need to establish:

- the total contribution required to achieve the target profit and
- the contribution per unit or the C/S ratio.

The volume of sales required must be sufficient to earn a total contribution that covers the fixed costs and makes the target amount of profit.

e

Example

A company makes and sells a product that has a variable cost of $5 per unit and sells for $9 per unit. Budgeted fixed costs are $600,000 for the year, and the company wishes to make a profit of at least $100,000. What is the volume of sales required to achieve the minimum profit target?

a

Answer

Contribution per unit = $9 – $5 = $4.
The total contribution must cover fixed costs and make the target profit.

	$
Fixed costs	600,000
Target profit	100,000
Total contribution required	700,000

Sales required to make a profit of $100,000 = $700,000/$4 per unit = 175,000 units.
Sales revenue required to achieve target profit = 175,000 units × $9 = $1,575,000.
Alternatively:
C/S ratio = 4/9
Sales required to make a profit of $100,000 = $700,000 ÷ (4/9) = $1,575,000.

e 3

Exercise 3

A company achieves a contribution/sales ratio from its sales of 75%. Its annual fixed costs are $3,200,000. What annual sales must it achieve to make an annual profit of $400,000?

Break-even charts and profit-volume charts

- Break-even charts
- Profit-volume charts

4 Break-even charts and profit-volume charts

4.1 Break-even chart

A break-even chart is a chart or graph showing, for all volumes of output and sales:

- total costs, analysed between variable costs and fixed costs
- sales
- profit (= the difference between total sales and total costs)
- the break-even point (where total costs = total sales revenue, and profit = 0).

The concept of a break-even chart is similar to a cost behaviour chart, but with sales revenue shown as well.

If the chart also indicates the budgeted volume of sales, the margin of safety can be shown as the difference between the budgeted volume and the break-even volume of sales.

Two examples of break-even charts are shown below. The only difference between them is the way in which variable costs and fixed costs are shown.

- In the first diagram, variable costs are shown on top of fixed costs. Fixed costs are represented by the horizontal line of dashes. Fixed costs are the same amount at all volumes of sales. Variable costs are shown on top of fixed costs, rising in a straight line from sales of $0. Total costs are shown as the sum of fixed costs and variable costs.
- In the second diagram (a more unusual presentation), fixed costs are shown on top of variable costs. An advantage of this method of presentation is that total contribution is shown. This is the difference between the total sales line and the total variable costs line.
- Total costs are exactly the same in both diagrams.

Because the sales price per unit is constant, the total sales revenue line rises in a straight line from the origin of the graph (i.e. from x = 0, y = 0).

First break-even chart: variable costs on top of fixed costs

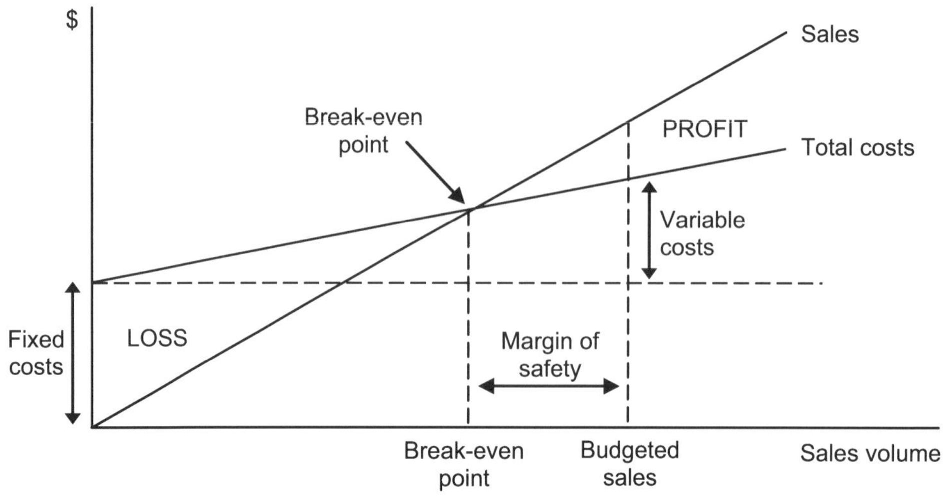

Second break-even chart: fixed costs on top of variable costs

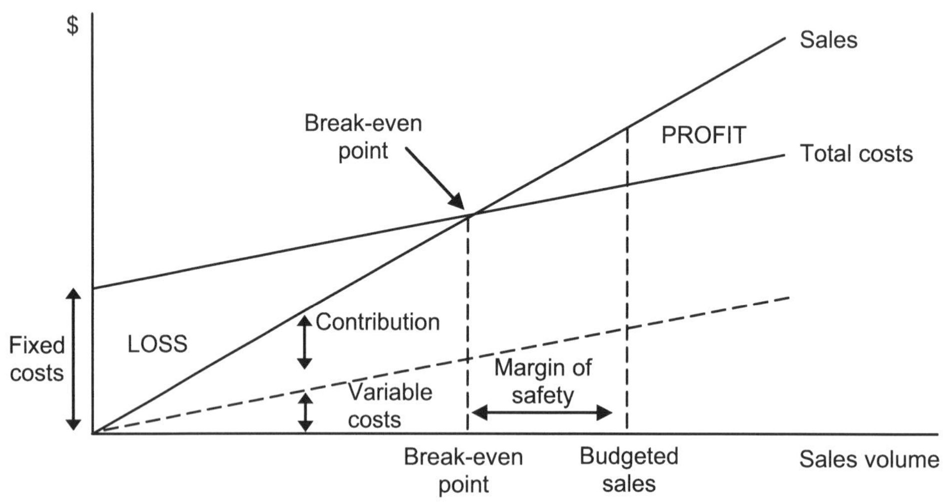

Points to note

You should be able to identify the following points on these charts.

- The break-even point is shown on both charts as the volume of sales at which total revenue equals total costs.
- In the second chart, total contribution at the break-even point is shown as exactly equal to fixed costs.
- If budgeted sales are shown on the chart, the margin of safety can also be show, as the difference between budgeted sales and the break-even point.

4.2 Profit/volume chart (P/V chart)

A profit volume chart (or P/V chart) is an alternative to a break-even chart for presenting CVP information. It is a chart that shows the profit or loss at all levels of output and sales.

An example is shown below.

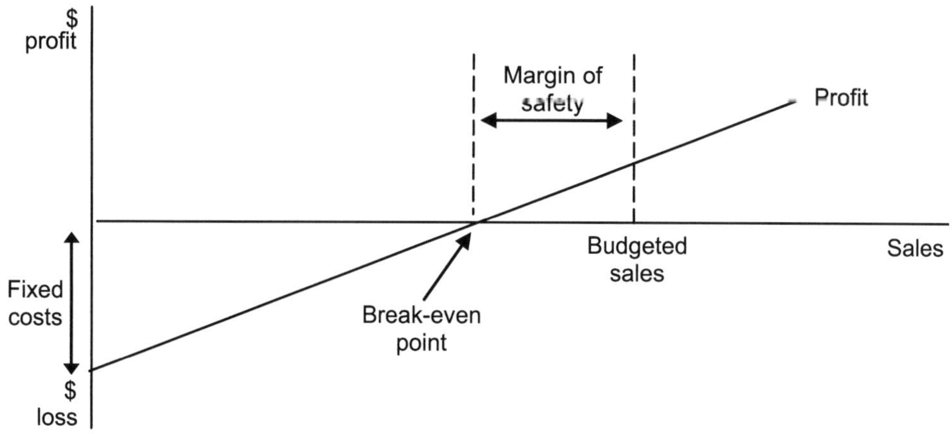

At $0 sales, there is a loss equal to the total amount of fixed costs. The loss becomes smaller as sales volume increases, due to the higher contribution as sales volume increases. Break-even point is then reached and profits are made at sales volumes above the break-even point.

We could draw a line on the graph to show fixed costs. This line should be drawn parallel to the x axis, starting at the loss (= total fixed costs) at $0 sales. By drawing this line for fixed costs, total contribution would be shown as the difference between the line showing the profit (or loss) and the line for the fixed costs.

Practice multiple choice questions

1 A product has the following full cost of sale.

	$
Direct materials	4
Direct labour	3
Variable production overhead	1
Fixed production overhead	6
Variable sales and distribution overhead	2
Fixed sales and distribution overhead	5
Administration overhead (fixed)	3
Full cost of sale	24

The sales price per unit is $32.

What is the contribution/sales ratio (C/S ratio)?

A 25%

B 31.25%

C 68.75%

D 75% *(2 marks)*

2 A company makes and sells a single product, whose variable cost is $12. Fixed costs are expected to be $360,000. The C/S ratio for the product is 40%.

What is the break-even point in units?

A 18,000

B 30,000

C 45,000

D 75,000 ***(2 marks)***

3 A company makes and sells a single product, whose variable cost is $48. Fixed costs are expected to be $234,000. The C/S ratio for the product is 60%. The company expects to sell 5,100 units in the period.

What is the margin of safety in units?

A The company will make a loss; therefore there is no margin of safety

B 225

C 1,850

D 3,250 ***(2 marks)***

4 A company makes and sells a single product, whose variable cost is $36. Fixed costs are expected to be $810,000. The C/S ratio for the product is 60%.

What is the break-even point in units?

A 9,000

B 15,000

C 22,500

D 33,750 ***(2 marks)***

5 A company makes and sells a single product for which the C/S ratio is 40%. Fixed costs for the next period are expected to be $1,440,000.

What volume of sales (in $) is required to achieve a target profit of $300,000?

A $2,700,000

B $2,900,000

C $3,900,000

D $4,350,000 ***(2 marks)***

CHAPTER

14

Relevant costs

Contents

The concept of relevant costing

- Information for decision making
- Marginal costing and decision making
- Relevant costs and decision making
- Terms used in relevant costing
- Opportunity costs

1 The concept of relevant costing

1.1 Information for decision making

Managers make decisions about the future. When they make decisions for economic or financial reasons, the objective is usually to increase profitability or the value of the business, or to reduce costs and improve productivity.

Costing information should help managers to make well-informed decisions about the best course of action to take.

- Decisions affect the future, but cannot change what has already happened. Decision making should therefore look at the future consequences of a decision, and should not be influenced by historical events and historical costs.
- Decisions should consider what can be changed in the future. They should not be influenced by what will happen in the future that is unavoidable, possibly due to commitments that have been made in the past.

Managers therefore need information about the likely consequences of their decisions, and how their decisions might change costs and profits.

It was suggested in the previous chapter that traditional cost accounting information is not intended to help managers look forward and plan for the future, which is why CVP analysis can be so useful.

However, CVP analysis has some limitations, and cannot be used in every situation to identify what the consequences of a decision might be. Accounting information for decision-making should be based on the 'relevant costs' in the situation. Relevant costs are concerned with the effect of decisions on cash flow:

- the extra cash spending that might have to be incurred as a result of a decision
- the savings in cash expenditure that might result from a decision and
- the increase or reduction in cash income that might be expected from a decision.

Relevant costs are used as information for decision-making because traditional cost accounting or financial accounting measures of cost are inadequate for the purpose of decision-making. Economic or financial decisions should be based on future cash flows, not future accounting measurements of costs or profits. Accounting conventions, such as the accruals concept of accounting and the depreciation of non-current assets, do not reflect economic reality. Cash flows, on the other hand, do reflect the economic reality of decisions. Managers should therefore consider the effect that their decisions will have on future cash flows, not reported accounting profits.

1.2 Marginal costing and decision making

Marginal costing might be used for decision making. As explained in the previous chapter, marginal costing is used for planning decisions (CVP analysis), and can be used to identify the sales volume required to break even or make a minimum target level of profit.

It is normally appropriate to use CVP analysis for decision making when it can be assumed that future fixed costs will be the same, no matter what decision is taken, and that all variable costs represent future cash flows that will be incurred as a consequence of any decision that is taken.

These assumptions about fixed and variable costs are not always valid. When they are not valid, relevant costs should be used to evaluate the economic/financial consequences of a decision.

1.3 Relevant costs and decision making

Relevant costs should be used for assessing the economic or financial consequences of any decision by management. Only relevant costs and benefits should be taken into consideration when evaluating a decision.

A relevant cost is a future cash flow that will occur as a direct consequence of making a particular decision.

The key concepts in this definition of relevant costs are as follows:

- Relevant costs are **costs that will occur in the future**. They cannot include any costs that have already occurred in the past.
- Relevant costs of a decision are **costs that will occur as a direct consequence of making the decision**. Costs that will occur anyway, no matter what decision is taken, cannot be relevant to the decision.
- Relevant costs are **cash flows**. Notional costs, such as depreciation charges, notional interest costs and absorbed fixed costs, cannot be relevant to a decision.
- The concept of relevant costs also applies to revenue (i.e. the changes in cash revenue arising as a direct consequence of a decision), but the main focus of this chapter is on the measurement of relevant costs.

1.4 Terms used in relevant costing

Several terms are used in relevant costing, to indicate how certain costs might be relevant or not relevant to a decision.

Incremental cost

An incremental cost is an additional cost that will occur if a particular decision is taken. Provided that this additional cost is a cash flow, an incremental cost is a relevant cost.

Differential cost

A differential cost is the amount by which future costs will be different, depending on which course of action is taken. A differential cost is therefore an amount by which future costs will be higher or lower, if a particular course of action is chosen. Provided that this additional cost is a cash flow, a differential cost is a relevant cost.

Example

A company needs to hire a large laser printer for the next six months. It has to decide whether to continue using a particular type of printer, which it currently rents for $600 each month, or whether to switch to using a larger printer that will cost $1,000 each month. If it hires the larger laser printer, it will be able to terminate the rental agreement for the current printer immediately.

The decision is whether to continue to use the current printer, or to switch to the larger printer. One way of analysing the comparative costs is to say that the larger printer will be more expensive to rent, by $400 each month for six months. The differential cost of hiring the larger printer for six months is therefore $2,400 (6 months × $400).

Avoidable and unavoidable costs

An avoidable cost is a cost that could be saved (avoided), depending whether or not a particular decision is taken. An unavoidable cost is a cost that will be incurred anyway.

Avoidable costs are relevant costs. Unavoidable costs are not relevant to a decision, because the decision will not affect the cost in any way.

Example

A company has one year remaining on a short-term lease agreement on a warehouse. The rental cost is $50,000 per year. The warehouse facilities are no longer required, because operations have been moved to another warehouse that has spare capacity.

If a decision is taken to close down the warehouse, the company would be committed to paying the rental cost up to the end of the term of the lease. However, it would save local taxes of $8,000 for the year, and it would no longer need to hire the services of a security company to look after the empty building, which currently costs $20,000 each year.

The decision about whether to close down the unwanted warehouse should be based on relevant costs only. Local taxes and the costs of the security services ($28,000 in total for the next year) could be avoided and so these are relevant costs. The rental cost of the warehouse cannot be avoided, and so should be ignored in the economic assessment of the decision whether to close the warehouse or keep it open for another year.

Sunk costs

Sunk costs are costs that have already been incurred (historical costs) or costs that have already been committed by an earlier decision. Sunk costs must be ignored for the purpose of evaluating a decision, and cannot be relevant costs.

For example, suppose that a company must decide whether to launch a new product on to the market. It has already spent $500,000 on developing the new product, and a further $40,000 on market research.

A financial evaluation for a decision whether or not to launch the new product should ignore the development costs and the market research costs, because the $540,000 has already been spent. The costs are sunk costs.

1.5 Opportunity costs

Relevant costs can also be measured as an opportunity cost. An opportunity cost is a benefit that will be lost by taking one course of action instead of the next-most profitable course of action.

Example

A company is offered the opportunity to do a job for a customer that will earn net cash inflow of $4,000. However in order to do this job, it would be necessary to use equipment that is operating at full capacity on other work. If the equipment is used for this job, the company will have to give up other work that would earn net cash inflow of $1,800.

An opportunity cost of doing the work for the customer is $1,800, because this is the benefit that would be lost by doing the job instead of using the equipment for the other work.

	$
Net cash flow from job for the customer	4,000
Opportunity cost of using the equipment	(1,800)
Net benefit from the job for the customer	2,200

Identifying relevant costs

- Relevant costs of materials
- Relevant costs of labour
- Relevant costs and overheads
- Relevant costs of non-current assets
- Using relevant costs

2 Identifying relevant costs

For your examination, you need to understand the concept of relevant costs, and be able to identify a relevant cost in a given situation.

In many cases, the relevant cost of materials or labour is the additional variable costs that will be incurred as a consequence of a decision. CVP analysis therefore provides the relevant costs in many situations. However, there are some situations where the variable costs are not the relevant costs of a decision, or are not the only relevant costs.

There are certain rules or guidelines that might help you to identify the relevant costs for the purpose of decision-making.

2.1 Relevant costs of materials

The relevant costs of a decision to do some work or make a product will usually include costs of materials. Relevant costs of materials are the additional cash flows that will be incurred (or benefits that will be lost) by using materials for the purpose that is under consideration.

The relevant cost of materials for a decision is the effect on cash flows that will occur as a consequence of using the materials. The relevant cost of materials depends first of all on whether the materials:

- have not yet been purchased and will have to be purchased if a particular decision is taken, or
- have already been purchased and are currently held as inventory.

If **none of the required materials are currently held as inventory**, the relevant cost of the materials is simply their purchase cost. If the decision is to go ahead with the proposal, materials will have to be purchased and the relevant cost is the cash that will have to be paid to acquire and use the materials.

If **the required materials are currently held as inventory**, identifying the relevant costs is a bit more complex.

- The materials have been purchased already; therefore their historical purchase cost is irrelevant. Costs that have already been incurred are sunk costs and cannot be relevant.

- The relevant costs of materials held as inventory depend on what the consequences of using these materials will be for future cash flows.

Relevant costs of materials are identified by applying the following rules:

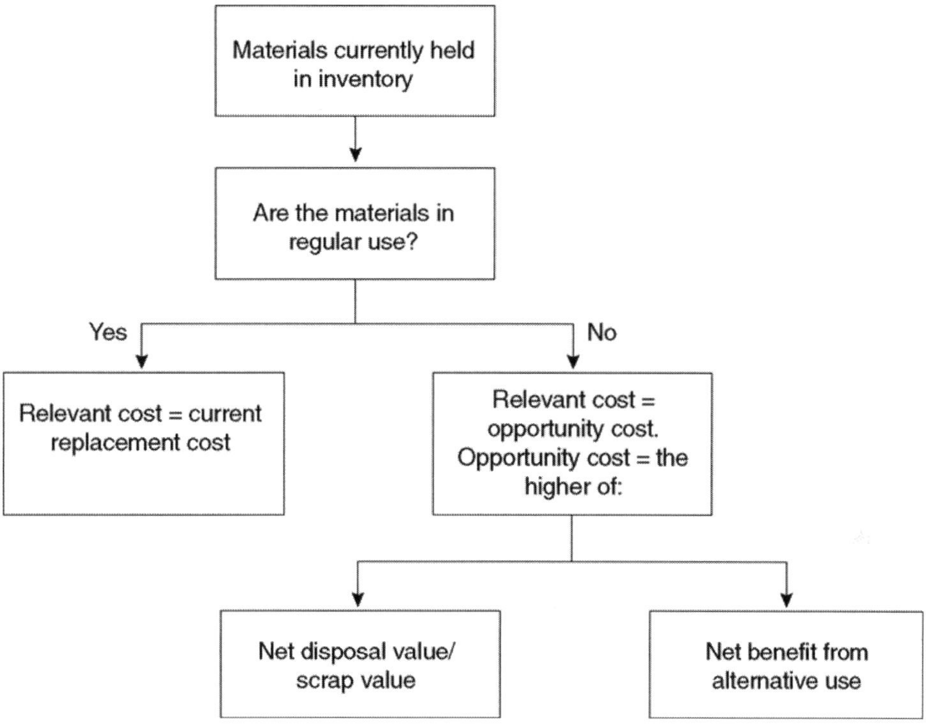

Materials already purchased (held in inventory)

It is essential to remember that the historical cost of materials held in inventory cannot be the relevant cost of the materials, because their historical cost is a sunk cost. The rule for identifying relevant costs for materials, as set out in the above chart, can be explained as follows.

If materials are held in inventory and will be required if a particular decision is taken:

- If the materials are in regular use, more materials will have to be purchased to replace them.
- If the materials are not in regular use, the consequences for future cash flows will depend on what the materials would otherwise be used for.

Example

A company is considering whether to do a special job for a customer. The job will need 200 units of direct materials. These are already held in inventory, but they are used regularly for other work that the company does. These 200 units were purchased for $3 per unit, but their purchase cost has recently been increased to $3.20 by the supplier.

If the decision is taken to do the job for the supplier, the 200 units already held will be used. However, because the materials are used regularly for other work, additional replacement materials will have to be purchased. These will cost $3.20 per unit, which is the relevant cost. The relevant cost of using the 200 units of materials is therefore $640 (200 units × $3.20).

A different situation applies when materials are already held in inventory, but they are not in regular use. Their historical purchase cost is not relevant, because this is a sunk cost. The relevant cost of the materials depends on how the materials would be used or disposed of if they are not used for the purpose under consideration. There are only two possible uses of such materials.

- They can be disposed of, and they might have a sales value from disposal.
- They might have an alternative use, from which there would be some net cash benefit.

The relevant cost of the materials is the higher of the net sales proceeds from disposal and the net cash inflow from putting them to an alternative use. The higher of these two amounts is the opportunity cost of the materials.

Example

A company has been asked to quote a price for a one-off contract.

The contract would require 5,000 kilograms of material X. Material X is used regularly by the company. The company has 4,000 kilograms of material X currently in inventory, which cost $2 per kilogram. The price for material X has since risen to $2.10 per kilogram.

What are the relevant costs of the material X for the contract?

Answer

Material X

This is in regular use. Any units of the material that are held in inventory will have to be replaced for other work if they are used for the contract. The relevant cost is their replacement cost.

Relevant cost = replacement cost = 5,000 kilograms × $2.10 = $10,500.

Example

A company has been asked to quote a price for a one-off contract.

The contract would require 2,000 kilograms of material Y. There are 1,500 kilograms of material Y in inventory, but because of a decision taken several weeks ago, material Y is no longer in regular use by the company. The 1,500 kilograms originally cost $7,200, and have a scrap value of $1,800. New purchases of material Y would cost $5 per kilogram.

What are the relevant costs of the materials for the contract?

Answer

Material Y

This is not in regular use. There are 1,500 kilograms in inventory, and unless they are used for the contract they will be sold as scrap. The contract would need 2,000 kilos, so an additional 500 kilograms would have to be purchased. The relevant cost of material Y for the contract would be as follows:

	$
Material held in inventory (scrap value)	1,800
New purchases (500 × $5)	2,500
Total relevant cost of Material Y	4,300

The scrap value of the 1,500 kilos already purchased is their scrap value. This is the benefit that would be lost if the materials are used for the contract instead of using them for the next-most beneficial use (which is to sell them as scrap).

Example

In order to carry out some work, a company would need to use 500 kilos of Material M. It already has sufficient quantities of the material in inventory, but due to the recent closure of a business operation, the materials are no longer in regular use.

The material M has a scrap value of $3 per kilo after selling costs. However, they could also be used as an alternative material in another operation, where it could be used instead of the same quantity of material P. Material P is in regular use and costs $4 per kilo to buy.

What are the relevant costs of the material M?

Answer

Material M

This is not in regular use. There are 500 kilograms in inventory, and if they are not used for the work, they will either by sold as scrap (for $3 per kilo) or used in a different operation, which would save purchases of 500 kilos of material P at $4 per kilo.

The relevant cost is the higher of these two values – 500 kilos × $4 = $2,000 – because this is how the materials should be used if they are not used for the work under consideration.

2.2 Relevant costs of labour

The relevant costs of a decision to do some work or make a product will usually include costs of labour.

The relevant cost of labour for any decision is the additional cash expenditure (or saving) that will arise as a direct consequence of the decision.

- **If the cost of labour is a variable cost**, and labour is not in restricted supply, the relevant cost of the labour is its variable cost. For example, suppose that part-time employees are paid $10 per hour, they are paid only for the hours that they work and part-time labour is not in short supply. If management is considering a decision that would require an additional 100 hours of part-time labour, the relevant cost of the labour would be $10 per hour or $1,000 in total. This represent additional cash spending that would be incurred.
- **If labour is a fixed cost and there is spare labour time available**, the relevant cost of using labour is $0. The spare time would otherwise be paid for as idle time, and there is no additional cash cost of using the labour to do extra work. For example, suppose that a new contract would require 30 direct labour hours, direct labour is paid $15 per hour, and the direct work force is paid a fixed weekly wage for a 40-hour week. If there is currently spare capacity, so that the labour cost would be idle time if it is not used for the new contract, the relevant cost of using 30 hours on the new contract would be $0. The 30 labour hours must be paid for whether or not the contract work is undertaken.
- **If labour is in limited supply**, the relevant cost of labour should include the opportunity cost of using the labour time for the purpose under consideration instead of using it in its next-most profitable way.

Labour in limited supply

When labour is in restricted supply, there are alternative ways of using the labour time in order to earn cash for the entity. If labour is used for a particular purpose, it cannot be used for something else.

The relevant cost of labour is therefore:

- the cost of the labour, plus
- the contribution that would otherwise be earned from putting the labour to its alternative use.

The **contribution forgone** is a relevant cost, not the profit forgone. Fixed costs will not be affected by a switch of labour from one job to another. The relevant cash flows are the net cash revenue that would be lost. This is the contribution forgone. **Labour costs can be treated as a variable cost whenever it is in short supply**, for the purpose of calculating the relevant cost of labour

Example

A company has been asked by a customer to carry out a special job. The work would require 20 hours of skilled labour time. There is a limited availability of skilled labour, and if the special job is carried out for the customer, skilled employees would have to be moved from doing other work that earns a contribution of $40 per labour hour. Skilled labour is paid $30 per hour.

What is the relevant cost of the labour?

a

Answer

Skilled labour is in restricted supply and using labour for the job will mean that other work that earns $30 per hour will be lost.

	$
Cost of labour hours (20 hours × $30)	600
Contribution forgone – an opportunity cost: (20 hours × $40)	800
Total relevant cost of skilled labour	1,400

e

Example

A company has been asked to do a special job for a customer. This would require 8 hours of Grade A labour and 6 hours of Grade B labour. Grade A labour is paid $20 per hour and Grade B labour is paid $15 per hour.

The Grade A labour would have to be taken off other work that earns a contribution of $40 per hour. There is sufficient Grade B labour available: if the Grade B employees do not work on this job, they will be paid but will have no other revenue-earning work to do.

Required
What are the relevant costs of the labour for the job?

a

Answer

Grade A labour is in restricted supply. Grade B labour time is available and would otherwise be paid for as idle time. The relevant labour costs are therefore as follows.

	$
Grade A labour: basic pay (8 hours × $20)	160
Grade A labour: opportunity cost (8 hours × $40)	320
Grade B labour: no incremental cost	0
Relevant cost of labour	480

e

Example

A company is considering a contract that will require labour time in three departments.

Department 1. The contract would require 200 hours of work in department 1, where the work force is paid $10 per hour. There is currently spare labour capacity in department 1 and there are no plans to reduce the size of the workforce in this department.

Department 2. The contract would require 100 hours of work in department 2 where the workforce is paid $12 per hour. This department is currently working at full capacity. The company could ask the work force to do overtime work, paid for at the normal rate per hour plus 50% overtime premium. Alternatively, the work force could be diverted from other work that earns a contribution of $4 per hour.

Department 3. The contract would require 300 hours of work in department 3 where the workforce is paid $20 per hour. Labour in this department is in short supply and all the available time is currently spent making product Z, which earns a contribution of $10 per hour.

Required

What is the relevant cost for the contract of labour in the three departments?

a

Answer

Department 1. There is spare capacity in department 1 and no additional cash expenditure would be incurred on labour if the contract is undertaken.

Relevant cost = $0.

Department 2. There is restricted labour capacity. If the contract is undertaken, there would be a choice between:

- overtime work at a cost of $18 per hour ($12 plus overtime premium of 50%) – this would be an additional cash expense, or
- diverting the labour from other work, and losing contribution of $4 per hour – cost per hour = $12 basic pay + contribution forgone $4 = $16 per hour.

It would be better to divert the work force from other work, and the relevant cost of labour is therefore 100 hours × $16 per hour = $1,600.

Department 3. There is restricted labour capacity. If the contract is undertaken, labour would have to be diverted from making product Z which earns a contribution of $10 per labour hour. This is an opportunity cost of labour if the contract work is undertaken. The relevant cost of the labour in department 3 is:

	$
Labour cost (300 hours × $20)	6,000
Contribution forgone (300 hours × $10)	3,000
Total relevant cost , Department 3	9,000

Summary of relevant costs of labour:

	$
Department 1	0
Department 2	1,600
Department 3	9,000
	10,600

2.3 Relevant costs and overheads

Relevant costs of expenditures that might be classed as overhead costs should be identified by applying the normal rules of relevant costing. Relevant costs are future cash flows that will arise as a direct consequence of making a particular decision.

Fixed overhead absorption rates are therefore irrelevant, because fixed overhead absorption is not overhead expenditure and does not represent cash spending

However, it might be assumed that the overhead absorption rate for **variable** overheads is a measure of actual cash spending on variable overheads. It is therefore often appropriate to treat a variable overhead hourly rate as a relevant cost, because it is an estimate of cash spending per hour for each additional hour worked.

The only overhead fixed costs that are relevant costs for a decision are extra cash spending that will be incurred, or cash spending that will be saved, as a direct consequence of making the decision.

Example

A company has three car showrooms, A, B and C. The budgeted sales and profit or loss for each showroom next year are as follows.

	A	B	C	Total
	$000	$000	$000	$000
Sales	2,000	1,600	2,400	6,000
Contribution	300	150	150	600
Less: Fixed costs	(180)	(120)	(200)	(500)
Profit/(Loss)	120	30	(50)	100

60% of the total fixed costs are general company overheads. These are apportioned to the three stores on the basis of sales revenue. The other fixed costs are specific to each store and are avoidable if the store is closed down.

Required

What would be the annual profit if showroom C is closed down?

Answer

The general overhead costs apportioned to Showroom C would not be saved if the showroom is closed down.

Total general overhead costs = 60% × $500,000 = $300,000.

These are apportioned on the basis of sales revenue; therefore the apportionment to showroom C is:

$300,000 × (2,400/6,000) = $120,000.

The fixed costs saved or avoided if showroom C is closed = $(200,000 – 120,000) = $80,000.

If showroom C is closed:	$
Loss of contribution	150,000
Saving in fixed costs	80,000
Reduction in profit	70,000

The profit would therefore fall from $100,000 to $30,000.

2.4 Relevant costs of non-current assets (NCAs)

Non-current assets are 'capital assets' such as buildings, plant and equipment etc that an entity acquires for long-term use.

The costs of non-current assets or the revenue from non-current assets are sometimes a factor in a management decision.

- A decision might be concerned with whether or not to buy a new non-current asset. When a new non-current asset is purchased, its relevant cost is its purchase cost, and there might also be a residual value at the end of its life when the asset is eventually sold. Decisions about buying non-current assets (capital expenditure decisions) are outside the syllabus for the examination.
- A decision might be concerned with whether to dispose of a non-current asset now. Alternatively, a decision might involve using a non-current asset in a different way and for a different purpose.

You might be required to identify the relevant costs or benefits of a non-current asset that is already owned by a business entity. The relevant costs of these non-current assets are identified in a similar way to the relevant costs of materials.

- If, as a consequence of taking a decision, the **non-current asset would have to be replaced**, a relevant cost is its replacement cost.
- If, as a consequence of taking a decision to use the asset for a different purpose, the **non-current asset would not be replaced**, the relevant cost (opportunity cost) of the non-current asset is the higher of its:
  - net disposal value (or scrap value), and
  - the net benefit that would be obtained from using the asset in the next-best way.

The relevant cost of non-current assets can also be described as their 'deprival value'. It is calculated in a similar way to the relevant cost of materials that have already been purchased.

The following diagram shows the rules that should be applied in order to identify the relevant costs of non-current assets such as machinery. (Compare this diagram with the previous diagram showing the relevant cost of materials. They are the same!)

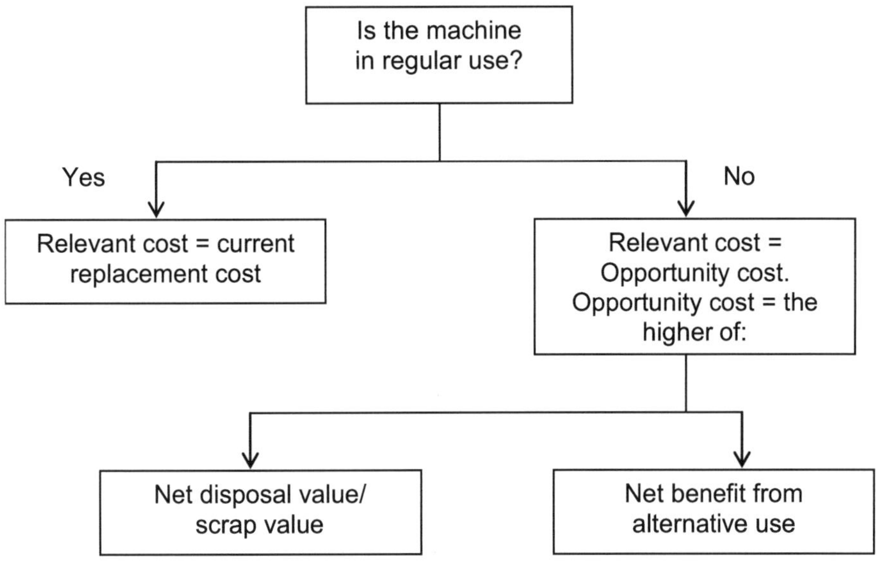

Note on terminology for non-current assets

If you have already studied financial accounting (financial reporting) you will be familiar with non-current assets, depreciation of non-current assets and net book value. If you are not familiar with financial accounting yet, the following brief explanation might be useful.

- A non-current asset is held for a number of years. The cost of a non-current asset is 'written off' as an expense in the income statement over its expected useful life.
- There is a annual notional charge in the income statement for the use of an asset. This is a depreciation charge. For example, if a non-current asset has a life of four years and costs $40,000, there might be an annual depreciation charge for the asset of $10,000 each year for four years.
- The net book value of a non-current asset is its original cost (assuming that it is not-re-valued at any time) less the accumulated depreciation to date. The asset above that cost $40,000 would therefore have a net book value of $30,000 after one year, $20,000 after two years, $10,000 after three years and $0 at the end of the fourth year.

The points to note about depreciation and net book value, for the purpose of relevant costing, are that:

- Depreciation charges are a notional annual charge: they do not represent cash flows
- Net book value is a notional value of an asset: it has no economic or 'cash flow' significance.
- Depreciation and net book value should always be ignored when identifying the relevant costs of non-current assets.

Example

A machine was purchased eight years ago for $20,000 and is depreciated at the rate of $2,000 per year. The net book value of the machine is $4,000 and its net disposal value is $3,000. A similar machine would cost $45,000 today.

The machine is not due to be replace for another two years, but as it has developed a fault which cannot be repaired, the company must replace the machine immediately.

Required

What is the relevant cost of the machine?

Answer

The machine is obviously in regular use. The relevant cost of the machine is therefore its replacement cost, $45,000.

Note the following points.

- The purchase price of $20,000 is not a relevant cost. It is a sunk cost that was incurred in the past.
- Net book values are not relevant costs. They do not represent cash flows or disposal values. In this example the NBV of $4,000 is not a relevant cost.
- The net disposal value of $3,000 is only relevant if the machine will not be replaced and has no alternative use.

Example

A company has an item of equipment that originally cost $50,000. It would now cost $60,000 to replace. Its current carrying amount (net book value) is $20,000 and it is being depreciated by $10,000 each year.

The company does not use the equipment any more, and does not foresee any further use for it. Another company, not a competitor, has offered to buy the equipment for $12,000.

What is the relevant cost of the equipment?

Answer

The asset has no other use and would not be replaced if it is disposed of. The options are to sell the equipment and earn $12,000 or not to sell it and earn nothing. The relevant cost is $0.

Example

A company has an item of equipment that originally cost $30,000. Its net book value is now $12,000. It could be used now on a three-month contract. If it is not used for the contract it would be sold off, and the net disposal proceeds would be $4,000. After use on the contract, the equipment would no longer have any sale value, and it would have to be dismantled and disposed of at a cost of $2,000.

What is the relevant cost of the equipment?

Answer

The asset has no other use and will not be replaced. If the contract is undertaken, the company will lose the opportunity to sell the equipment for $4,000. In addition, it would have to pay disposal costs of $2,000 at the end of the three months. The total relevant cost is therefore $4,000 + $2,000 = $6,000.

(The net book value is totally irrelevant.)

2.5 Using relevant costs

Relevant costs are used in accounting for decision-making. The costs and revenues that are taken into consideration when evaluating the effect of a decision must be the costs and revenues that are relevant to that decision. Non-relevant costs and revenues must be ignored when evaluating a decision.

The examination syllabus does not cover the use of relevant costs for specific decision-making problems, but you will come across these in your future studies of accounting.

Practice multiple choice questions

1 A company is considering whether to undertake a job for a customer. The job would require 1,800 kilos of a material that is used regularly in production. The company already holds 1,200 kilos of the material in inventory, which cost $7,200 last month. The supplier has recently announced a price increase of 5% for the material.

What is the total relevant cost of the material for the contract?

A $3,780

B $7,560

C $10,980

D $11,340 *(2 marks)*

2 A company is considering a contract that would require 120 hours of skilled labour. The skilled labour is paid $24 per hour and all skilled employees are fully employed manufacturing a product to which the following data relates:

	$	$
Selling price		75
Less: Variable costs		
Skilled labour	36	
Other variable costs	15	
		51
Contribution per unit		24

No other supply of skilled labour is available.

What is the total relevant cost of the labour for the contract?

A $1,920

B $2,880

C $4,800

D $6,000 ***(2 marks)***

3 A company would need 800kg of material D for a contract it is considering. It already has 600 kg of the material held in inventory. These materials were purchased last month, but since then the supplier has increased the purchase price by 6% to $53. The company uses material D regularly in normal production.

What is the total relevant cost for the contract of raw material D?

A $40,492

B $40,600

C $42,400

D $44,944 ***(2 marks)***

4 A company owns a machine that has a current net book value of $2,700. It has not been used for several months, but it could now be used on a job for a customer which would last for up to six months. If the machine is not used for this job, it will be sold immediately to earn net income of $2,900. After using the machine for the contract, it would have no further use or value, and it would have to be disposed of at a cost of $500.

What is the total relevant cost of the machine for the contract?

A $2,400

B $2,700

C $2,900

D $3,400 ***(2 marks)***

CHAPTER 15

Limiting factors and linear programming

Contents

Limiting factor decisions: single limiting factor

- Definition of a limiting factor
- Deciding whether there is a limiting factor
- Maximising profit when there is a single limiting factor
- Budgeting with one limiting factor

1 Limiting factor decisions: single limiting factor

1.1 Definition of a limiting factor

It is normally assumed in budgeting that a company can produce as many units of its products (or services) that are necessary to meet the available sales demand. Sales demand is therefore normally the factor that sets a limit on the volume of sales in each period.

Sometimes, however, there could be a shortage of a key production resource, such as an item of direct materials, or skilled labour, or machine capacity. In these circumstances, the limiting factor setting a limit to the volume of sales and profit in a particular period is the availability of the scarce resource.

It is assumed in this chapter that an entity makes and sells more than one different product. When there is a limiting factor, the problem is therefore to decide how many of each different product to make and sell in order to maximise profits.

1.2 Deciding whether there is a limiting factor

A limiting factor needs to be identified when the budget is prepared. The existence of a limiting factor can be established by comparing:

- the amount of each resource required to produce the quantities of products in the budget, and
- the total amount of the resource that will be available.

Example

A company makes three products, A, B and C, using the same direct labour work force and the same machines to make all the products. Budgeted data for the company is as follows.

	Product X	Product Y	Product Z
Budgeted production (units)	30,000	24,000	18,000
Time required per unit	minutes	minutes	minutes
Direct labour time (minutes)	15	20	40
Machine time (minutes	10	15	30

The company expects to have 26,000 direct labour hours and 21,000 machine hours available in the period.

Required
Is either direct labour time or machine time a limiting factor?

Answer

We need to compare the time required for production and the time available

	Labour time	Machine time
Time required	hours	hours
Product X	7,500	5,000
Product Y	8,000	6,000
Product Z	12,000	9,000
Total time required	27,500	20,000
Time available	26,000	21,000
Surplus/(shortfall)	(1,500)	1,000

Direct labour time is a limiting factor but machine time is not a limiting factor.

1.3 Maximising profit when there is a single limiting factor

Limiting factor analysis uses the same principles as CVP analysis and relevant costing, although it is normally sufficient to use the concepts of simple CVP analysis.

When there is just one limiting factor (other than sales demand), total profit will be maximised in a period by maximising the total contribution earned with the available scarce resources.

- The objective should be to maximise total contribution.
- This will be achieved by maximising the contribution in total from the scarce resource.
- Products should therefore be ranked in order or priority for manufacture and sale.
- The priority ranking should be according to the **contribution earned by each product (or service) for each unit of the scarce resource that the product uses**.
- The products or services should be produced and sold in this order of priority, up to the expected sales demand for each product.
- The planned output and sales should be decided by working down through the priority list until all the units of the limiting factor have been used.

In other words, in order to maximise profit, the aim should be to maximise the contribution for each unit of limiting factor used.

Example

A company makes four products, A, B, C and D, using the same direct labour work force on all the products. Budgeted data for the company is as follows.

Product	A	B	C	D
Annual sales demand (units)	4,000	5,000	8,000	4,000
	$	$	$	$
Direct materials cost	3.0	6.0	5.0	6.0
Direct labour cost	6.0	12.0	3.0	9.0
Variable overhead	2.0	4.0	1.0	3.0
Fixed overhead	3.0	6.0	2.0	4.0
Full cost	14.0	28.0	11.0	22.0
Sales price	15.5	29.0	11.5	27.0
Profit per unit	1.5	1.0	0.5	5.0

Direct labour is paid $12 per hour. However, only 6,000 direct labour hours are available during the year.

Required

Identify the quantities of production and sales of each product that would maximise annual profit.

Answer

The products should be ranked in order of priority according to the contribution that they make per direct labour hour.

	A	B	C	D
	$	$	$	$
Sales price per unit	15.5	29.0	11.5	27.0
Variable cost per unit	11.0	22.0	9.0	18.0
Contribution per unit	4.5	7.0	2.5	9.0
Direct labour hours perunit	0.5	1.0	0.25	0.75
Contribution per direct labour hour	9.0	7.0	10.0	12.0
Priority for making and selling	3rd	4th	2nd	1st

The products should be made and sold in the order D, C, A and then B, up to the volume of sales demand for each product and until all the available direct labour hours (limiting factor resources) are used up.

Profit-maximising budget

Product	Sales units	Direct labour hours	Contribution per unit	Total contribution
			$	$
D (1st)	4,000	3,000	9.0	36,000
C (2nd)	8,000	2,000	2.5	20,000
A (3rd)	2,000 (balance)	1,000	4.5	9,000
		6,000		65,000

1.4 Budgeting with one limiting factor

You might not be told by an examination question that a limiting factor exists, although you might be told that there is a restricted supply of certain resources. You might be expected to identify the limiting factor by calculating the budgeted availability of each resource and the amount of the resource that is needed to meet the available sales demand.

Example

A company manufactures and sells two products, Product X and Product Y. The two products are manufactured on the same machines. There are two types of machine, and the time required to make each unit of product is as follows:

	Product X	Product Y
Machine type 1	10 minutes per unit	6 minutes per unit
Machine type 2	5 minutes per unit	12 minutes per unit

Sales demand each year is for 12,000 units of Product X and 15,000 units of Product Y.

The contribution per unit is $7 for Product X and $5 for Product Y.

There is a limit to machine capacity, however, and in each year there are only 3,000 hours of Machine 1 time available and 4,200 hours of Machine 2 time available.

Required

Recommend the quantities of Product X and Y that the company should make and sell in order to maximise its annual profit.

Answer

The first step is to identify whether or not there is any limiting factor other than sales demand. To do this we calculate the required machine time to manufacture units of Product X and Y to meet the maximum sales demand. We then compare this requirement for machine time with the actual time available.

	Machine type 1	Machine type 2
	hours	hours
Time required		
To make 12,000 units of Product X	2,000	1,000
To make 15,000 units of Product Y	1,500	3,000
Hours needed to meet sales demand	3,500	4,000
Hours available	3,000	4,200
Shortfall	(500)	-

Machine type 1 is a limiting factor, but Machine type 2 is not. To maximise contribution and profit, we should therefore give priority to the product that gives the higher contribution per Machine type 1 hour.

	Product X	Product Y
Contribution per unit	$7	$5
Machine type 1 time per unit	10 minutes	6 minutes
Contribution per hour (Machine type 1)	$42	$50
Priority for making and selling	2nd	1st

Profit-maximising budget

Product	Sales units	Machine type 1 hours	Contribution per unit	Total contribution
			$	$
Y (1st)	15,000	1,500	5.0	75,000
X (2nd) - balance	9,000	1,500	7.0	63,000
		3,000		138,000

Exercise 1

A company makes four products, W, X, Y and Z, using the same single item of direct material in the manufacture of all the products. Budgeted data for the company is as follows.

Product	W	X	Y	Z
Annual sales demand (units)	4,000	4,000	6,000	3,000
	$	$	$	$
Direct materials cost	5.0	4.0	8.00	6.00
Direct labour cost	4.0	6.0	3.00	5.00
Variable overhead	1.0	1.5	0.75	1.25
Fixed overhead	8.0	12.0	6.00	10.00
Full cost	18.0	23.5	17.75	22.25
Sales price	50.0	31.5	59.75	54.25
Profit per unit	32.0	8.0	42.00	32.00

Due to restricted supply, only $78,000 of direct materials will be available during the year.

Required

Identify the quantities of production and sales of each product that would maximise annual profit.

Limiting factor decisions: linear programming

- Two or more limiting factors
- Formulating a linear programming problem
- The objective function
- Formulating the constraints

2 Limiting factor decisions: linear programming

2.1 Two or more limiting factors

When there is more than one limiting factor (other than sales demand for the products), the contribution-maximising plan cannot be identified simply by ranking products in order of contribution per unit of limiting factor.

For example, suppose that a company makes two products, X and Y, and there are two limiting factors, labour time and machine time. The contribution per unit of limiting factor might be as follows:

	Product X	Product Y	
Contribution per labour hour	$12	$9	Rank Product X first
Contribution per machine hour	$7	$10	Rank Product Y first

In this situation, the products cannot be ranked in order of contribution per unit of limiting factor because the ranking is different for each limiting factor. The problem is therefore to decide how to maximise total contribution given two (or more) limiting factors.

The problem can be formulated as a linear programming problem.

2.2 Formulating a linear programming problem

A linear programming problem is formulated by:

- identifying an objective function, and
- formulating two or more constraints, one for each limiting factor or other restriction (such as maximum sales demand).

2.3 The objective function

The objective of a linear programming problem is to maximise or minimise the value of something. For the purpose of your examination, it is likely to be the objective of maximising total contribution. (The objective might possibly be something else, such as the objective of minimising costs.)

An objective function expresses the objective, such as total contribution, as a formula.

Example

A company makes and sells two products, Product X and Product Y. The contribution per unit is $8 for Product X and $12 for Product Y. The company wishes to maximise profit.

If it is assumed that total fixed costs are the same at all levels of output and sales, the objective of the company is to maximise total contribution.

Total contribution can be expressed as a formula, as follows:

Let the number of units (made and sold) of Product X be x
Let the number of units (made and sold) of Product Y be y

The objective function is therefore to maximise:

(Total contribution): 8x + 12y.

2.4 Formulating the constraints

In a linear programming problem, there is a separate constraint for each item that might put a limitation on the objective function. Maximum sales demand for a product might be a constraint, as well as a restricted supply of a resource such as direct labour hours.

For each item that might be a limiting factor, a constraint must be included in the linear programming problem. There is one constraint for each limiting factor.

Each constraint, like the objective function, is expressed as a formula. Each constraint must also specify the amount of the limit or constraint.

A constraint is a formula that is not an equation with a equals sign ('=). It normally has an 'equal to or less than' sign (≤), although a constraint might possibly have an 'equal to or more than' sign (≥).

The basic technique for formulating the constraints for resources

To formulate the constraints for a problem, you must identify each item that might be a limiting factor, such as labour time for a specific grade or type of labour, machine time for a specific type of machine, the availability of a specific type of materials, or maximum sales demand for a product.

For each of these possible limiting factors, there must be a separate constraint in the problem.

The variables in the problem (x and y) are the same as for the objective function.

In a limiting factor problem, it is usual to find that material, labour time or machine time are constraints.

- **Materials**. If materials might be a limiting factor, a constraint is formulated as follows, when there are M units of materials available in total, and one unit of

Product X needs m_1 units of the material and one unit of Product Y needs m_2 units of the material. The constraint is:

$m_1x + m_2y \leq M$

For example, suppose that each unit of Product X needs 3kg of material and each unit of Product Y needs 4 kg of the same material, and the total material available is 6,000 kg, the constraint for materials is:

$3x + 4y \leq 6{,}000$.

- **Labour**. A grade or type of **labour** might be a limiting factor. If there are T hours of the labour time available in total, and one unit of Product X needs t_1 hours of the labour time and one unit of Product Y needs t_2 hours, the constraint is:

  $t_1x + t_2y \leq T$

  For example, suppose that each unit of Product X needs 30 minutes of skilled labour time and each unit of Product Y needs 15 minutes of skilled labour time, and total skilled labour is restricted to 200 hours per week, the constraint for skilled labour is:

  $0.50x + 0.25y \leq 200$.

  If you don't like fractions or decimal figures in a constraint, you can multiply this constraint by 4 to get rid of the decimals, and the constraint will be:

  $2x + y \leq 800$.

- **Machine time**. Machine time might be a limiting factor. If time on a particular type of machine or equipment might be a limiting factor, there are T hours of the machine time available in total, and one unit of Product X needs t_1 hours of the machine time and one unit of Product Y needs t_2 hours, the constraint is:

  $t_1x + t_2y \leq T$

  Formulating a constraint for machine time is therefore very similar to formulating constraints for materials or labour time.

Maximum sales demand constraint

If there is a **maximum limit**, the constraint must be expressed as 'must be equal to or less than'.

For example, if there is a maximum sales demand for Product X of 5,000 units, the constraint for sales demand for X would be expressed as:

$x \leq 5{,}000$

Minimum sales demand constraint

Similarly, if there is a **minimum limit**, the constraint must be expressed as 'must be equal to or more than'. For example, if there is a requirement to supply a customer with at least 2,000 units of Product X, this constraint would be expressed as:

$x \geq 2{,}000$

Non-negativity constraints

A requirement of linear programming problems is that there should be no negative values in the final solution. For example, it is not possible to make and sell *minus 4,000* units of Product Y.

Constraints in the linear programming problem should therefore be that each 'variable' must be equal to or greater than 0.

For example:

(Non-negativity constraint): $x, y \geq 0$.

Example

A company makes and sells two products, Product X and Product Y. The contribution per unit is $8 for Product X and $12 for Product Y. The company wishes to maximise profit.

The expected sales demand is for 6,000 units of Product X and 4,000 units of Product Y. However, there are limitations to the amount of labour time and machine time that is available in the period:

	Product X	**Product Y**
Direct labour hours per unit	3 hours	2 hours
Machine hours per unit	1 hour	2.5 hours

	Total hours
Direct labour hours available, in total	20,000
Machine hours available, in total	12,000

A linear programming problem can be formulated as follows:

Let the number of units (made and sold) of Product X be x
Let the number of units (made and sold) of Product Y be y

The objective function is to maximise total contribution: $8x + 12y$.

Subject to the following constraints:

Direct labour	$3x + 2y$	$\leq$	20,000
Machine time	$x + 2.5y$	$\leq$	12,000

Sales demand, X	x	≤	6,000
Sales demand, Y	y	≤	4,000
Non-negativity	x, y	≥	0

If you do not like figures with fractions in a constraint, the constraint for machine time could be expressed (by doubling it) as:

Machine time	2x + 5y	≤	24,000

Exercise 2

A company manufactures and sells two models of a product, the Standard model and the Economy model. The models are made from the same materials, but the Standard model includes more material than the Economy model. The Standard model makes a contribution of $6 per unit and the Economy model makes a contribution of $4 per unit.

Sales demand each year for the Standard model is 20,000 units and for the Economy model it is 16,000 units.

There are several resources in short supply. The annual availability of materials and labour are as follows:

Direct materials	$105,000
Skilled labour	16,500 hours
Unskilled labour	56,000 hours

The resources required per unit of product are as follows:

	Standard	**Economy**
	per unit	per unit
Direct materials per unit	$4.00	$2.50
Skilled labour hours per unit	0.5 hours	0.5 hours
Unskilled labour hours per unit	1.25 hours	2 hours

Required

Formulate a linear programming problem for the maximisation of annual contribution and profit.

Let the number of units (made and sold) of the Standard model be x
Let the number of units (made and sold) of the Economy model be y.

Linear programming: graphical solution

- Three-stage graphical method
- Drawing the constraints on a graph
- Maximising (or minimising) the objective function
- Calculating the value for the objective function: simultaneous equations
- An alternative approach to a solution: simultaneous equations
- Linear programming: problems with more than two variables

3 Linear programming: graphical solution

3.1 Three-stage graphical method

When there are just two variables in a linear programming problem (x and y), the problem can be solved by a graphical method. The solution identifies the values of x and y that maximise (or minimise) the value of the objective function. A graphical solution can therefore be used to solve a linear programming problem only when there are two products, although there might be more than two constraints.

There are three stages in solving a problem by the graphical method:

- **Step 1**: Draw the constraints on a graph, to establish the feasible combinations of values for the two variables x and y that are within all the constraints in the problem.
- **Step 2**: Identify the combination of values for x and y, within this feasible area, that maximises (or minimises) the objective function. This is the solution to the problem.
- **Step 3**: Calculate the value for the objective function that this solution provides.

3.2 Drawing the constraints on a graph

The constraints in a linear programming problem can be drawn as straight lines on a graph, provided that there are just two variables in the problem (x and y). One axis of the graph represents values for one of the variables, and the other axis represents values for the second variable.

The straight line for each constraint is the boundary edge of the constraint – its outer limit (or inner limit, in the case of minimum values).

For example, suppose we have a constraint:

$2x + 3y \leq 600$

The outer limit of this constraint is represented by a line:

$2x + 3y = 600$.

Combinations of values of x and y beyond this line on the graph (with higher values for x and y) will have a value in excess of 600. These exceed the limit of the constraint, and so cannot be feasible for a solution to the problem.

The constraint is drawn as a straight line. To draw a straight line on a graph, you need to plot just two points and join them up. The easiest points to plot are the combinations of x and y:

- where x = 0, and
- where y = 0.

For the equation 2x + 3y = 600:

- when x = 0, y = 200 (= 600/3). So plot the point x = 0, y = 200 on the graph
- when y = 0, x = 300 (= 600/2). So plot the point y = 0, x = 300 on the graph

Join these two points, and you have a line showing the values of x and y that are the maximum possible combined values that meet the requirements of the constraint.

Example

Suppose that we have the following linear programming problem:

The objective function is to maximise total contribution: 5x + 5y

subject to the following constraints:

Direct labour	2x + 3y	≤	6,000
Machine time	4x + y	≤	4,000
Sales demand, Y	y	≤	1,800
Non-negativity	x, y	≥	0

The non-negativity constraints are represented by the lines of the x axis and y axis.

The other three constraints are drawn as follows, to produce a combination of values for x and y that meet all three constraints. These combinations of values for x and y represent the 'feasible region' on the graph for a solution to the problem.

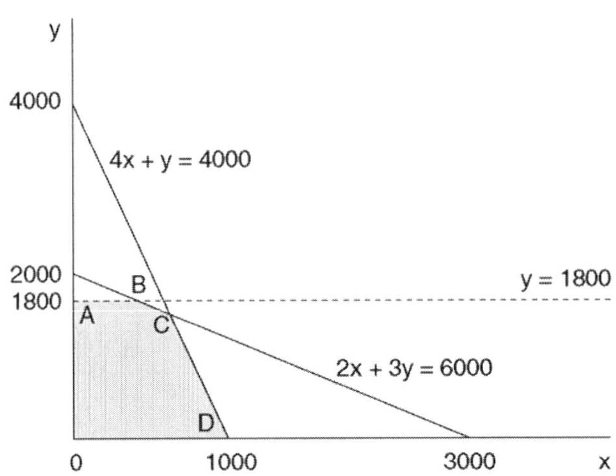

The feasible area for a solution to the problem is shown as the shaded area OABCD. To solve the linear programming problem, we now need to identify the feasible combination of values for x and y that maximises the objective function.

3.3 Maximising (or minimising) the objective function

As a starting point, you might recognise that the combination of values for x and y that maximises the objective function will be a pair of values that lies somewhere along the outer edge of the feasible area.

In the graph above, the solution to the problem will normally be the values of x and y at one of the following points on the graph:

- A
- B
- C, or
- D

In other words, we will normally expect the solution to be the combination of values for x and y that lies at one of the 'corners' of the outer edge of the feasible area.

(In some cases, the solution might be:

- any combination of values of x and y along the line AB, or
- any combination of values of x and y along the line BC, or
- any combination of values of x and y along the line CD.

However, this would be unusual.)

To identify the combination of values for x and y that are feasible (within all the constraints) and that also maximises the objective function, we need to look at the objective function itself.

Drawing an iso-contribution line

We do not know the maximum value (or minimum value) of the objective function. However, we can draw a line that shows all the combinations of x and y that provide the same total value for the objective function.

For example, suppose that the objective function is to maximise contribution 4x + 3y. We can draw a line on a graph that shows combinations of values for x and y that give the same total contribution, when x has a contribution of 4 and y has a contribution of 3. Any total contribution figure can be chosen, but a convenient multiple of 4 and 3 is simplest and easiest.

- For example, we could select a total contribution value of 4x + 3y = 12,000. This contribution line could be found by joining the points on the graph x = 0, y = 4,000 and y = 0, x = 3,000.
- Instead, we might select a total contribution value of 4x + 3y = 24,000. This contribution line could be found by joining the points on the graph x = 0, y = 8,000 and y = 0, x = 6,000.

If you draw both of these contribution lines on a graph, you will find that:

- the two lines are parallel to each other on the graph, and
- the line with the higher total contribution value for values of x and y (24,000) is further away from the origin of the graph (where x = 0 and y = 0, i.e. Point 0)).

A contribution line can be used to identify the solution to a linear programming problem.

- Draw a line showing combinations of values for x and y that give the same total value for the objective function. (This might be called an 'iso-contribution' line – meaning 'the same' contribution: every combination of values on the contribution line will give the same total contribution.)
- Look at the slope of the contribution line, and (using a ruler if necessary) identify which combination of values of x and y within the feasible area for the constraints is furthest away from the origin of the graph. This is the combination of values for x and y where an iso-contribution line can be drawn as far to the right as possible that just touches one corner of the feasible area.

This is the combination of values of x and y that provides the solution to the linear programming problem.

Example: using an iso-contribution line

Returning to the previous example, we can draw an iso-contribution line for, say, 5x + 5y = 10,000, by joining the points x = 0, y = 2,000 and y = 0, x = 2,000. (The value 10,000 is chosen here as a convenient multiple of the values 5 and 5.)

The iso-contribution line shows us the slope of all other iso-contribution lines. The optimal solution to the linear programming problem, when we want to maximise contribution, is a combination of x and y that:

- is as far away from the origin of the graph as possible, and
- provides a feasible solution to the problem.

This will give us a combination of x any y that provides a maximum value for contribution, which satisfies all the constraints in the problem.

In this example, the optimal solution lies at point A, point B, point C or point D.

If you look at the slope of the iso-contribution line is the graph below, you should see that the optimal solution is at point C.

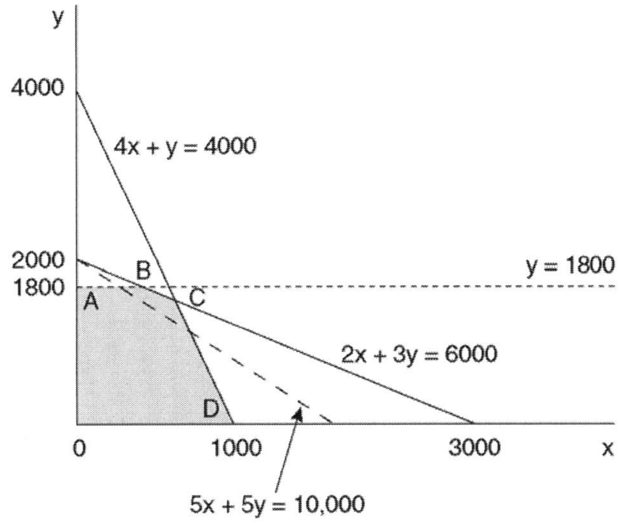

3.4 Calculating the value for the objective function: simultaneous equations

Having identified which combination of values for x and y provides the solution to the linear programming problem, the final step is to:

- establish the exact values for x and y at this point, and
- use these values to calculate the value of the objective function at this point.

You can do this by **solving two simultaneous equations** for the values of x and y.

At the point on the graph where total contribution is maximised, two constraint lines intersect. Both lines are equations at this profit-maximising point. When we have two equations that are both 'correct' for x and y, we can use them to calculate the values for x and y.

Example

In the previous example, the solution is the combination of values of x and y at point C on the graph. At point C, we have the simultaneous equations:

$2x + 3y = 6,000$
$4x + y \;= 4,000$

We can solve these simultaneous equations to obtain values for x and y:

(1)	$2x + 3y$	=	6,000
(2)	$4x + y$	=	4,000
Multiply (1) by 2:			
(3)	$4x + 6y$	=	12,000
Subtract (2) from (3):			
	$5y$	=	8,000
Therefore	y	=	1,600

Substitute in equation (2)	4x + 1,600	=	4,000
	4x	=	2,400
	x	=	600

The objective in this problem is to maximise 5x + 5y.

The total contribution where x = 600 and y = 1,600 is:

($5 × 600) + ($5 × 1,600) = $11,000.

This is the amount of the maximum achievable contribution.

3.5 An alternative approach to a solution: simultaneous equations

An alternative method of identifying the solution to a linear programming problem is to solve a number of simultaneous equations.

To obtain a solution, you should draw the feasible area on a graph, and identify the feasible combinations of values for x and y. You will know that the solution lies at one of the corners of this feasible area.

- At each corner point, you should identify the constraints that are equations.
- Solve these simultaneous equations to obtain the values for x and y at that point.
- Calculate the total contribution for those values of x and y.
- The optimal solution is at the corner of the feasible area where the combinations of x and y give the largest total contribution.

Example

In the previous example, the solution has to be at points A, B, C or D.

The optimal solution is obviously not at point A, because at point B, the value of y is the same as at A and the value of x is higher. So the answer is at point B, C or D.

Point B
At point B, we have the simultaneous equations:

(1)	2x + 3y	=	6,000
(2)	y	=	1,800
Substitute (2) in equation (1)			
	2x + (3 × 1,800)	=	6,000
(3)	2x + 5,400	=	6,000
	2x	=	600
	x	=	300

At point D, x = 300 and y = 1,800.
Total contribution = ($5 × 300) + ($5 × 1,800) = $10,500.

Point C
X = 600, y = 1,600

Total contribution = $11,000. (Calculated earlier, in the previous example)

Point D
At point D we have the equations:

(1)	4x + y	=	4,000
(2)	y	=	0
Substitute (2) in equation (1)	4x	=	4,000
	x	=	1,000

Total contribution = $5 × 1,000 = $5,000.

The total contribution at each point should be compared. This shows that total contribution is maximised at Point C.

3.6 Linear programming: problems with more than two variables

A linear programming problem can have more than two variables. Problems with more than two variables are formulated in exactly the same way as problems with two variables. The only difference is that the objective function and the constraints include more than two variables.

A linear programming problem with more than two variables cannot be solved by a graphical method, however, and another solution method is used. A non-graphical method of solving linear programming problems is the simplex method, but you do not need to know this method for your examination.

Practice multiple choice questions

1 A company manufactures two products S and T using the same materials and labour. It holds no inventories. Information about the variable costs and maximum sales demand for each product are as follows:

	Product S	Product T
	$/unit	$/unit
Material ($5 per kg)	12	10
Labour ($20 per hour)	45	30
	units	units
Maximum sales per month	4,000	6,000

Each month a maximum of 21,500 kilograms of material and 18,200 hours of labour are available.

Which one of the following statements is correct?

A Material is a limiting factor but labour is not a limiting factor

B Labour is a limiting factor but material is not a limiting factor

C Both material and labour are limiting factors

D Neither material nor labour is a limiting factor *(2 marks)*

2 A company manufactures and sells two products, Product X and Product Y, which can be sold for $120 per unit and $54 per unit respectively. Variable costs of the two products are:

	Product X	Product Y
	$/unit	$/unit
Material ($10 per kg)	30	10
Labour ($12 per hour)	48	6
Other variable costs	12	14
Total	90	30

Next month only 4,700 kg of materials and 3,300 labour hours will be available. The company holds no inventory. It is committed to selling at least 700 units of Product Y each month.

In a linear programming problem to identify the profit-maximising production quantities, which one of the following is a constraint?

A $x + 3y \leq 4{,}400$

B $0.5x + 4y \leq 3{,}300$

C $30x + 24y \geq 700$

D $8x + y \leq 6{,}600$

(2 marks)

The following information relates to questions 3, 4 and 5

A company manufactures and sells two products (X and Y) and it aims to maximise profits. It holds no inventory. Product X makes a contribution of $3 per unit and Product Y makes a contribution of $4 per unit.

Next period the company has three constraints on production and sales (all of them 'less than' constraints) and these are shown as the lines marked (1) (2) and (3). The line shown in dashes is an iso-contribution line.

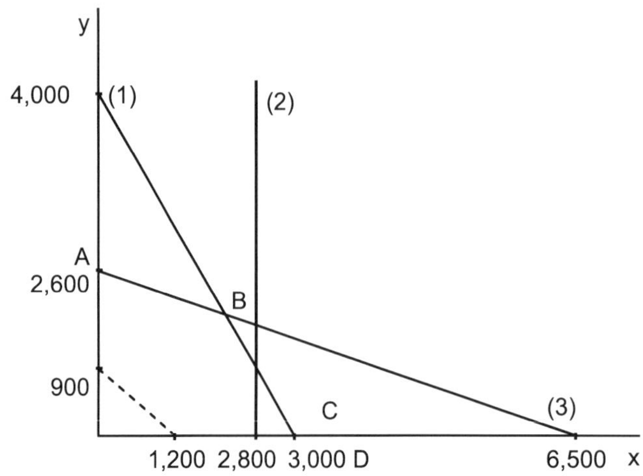

3 Which of the following points on the graph shows the optimal production and sales for next period?

A Point A

B Point B

C Point C

D Point D

(2 marks)

4 Which one of the following constraint formulations is represented by the line labelled as (1) on the graph?

A $3x + 4y \leq 12,000$

B $4x + 3y \leq 12,000$

C $2x + 5y \leq 13,000$

D $5x + 2y \leq 13,000$

(2 marks)

5 What is the maximum total contribution obtainable in the period?

A $12,267

B $12,500

C $14,120

D $16,080

(2 marks)

6 A company manufactures three products, X Y and Z, for which maximum sales demand in the period is 24,000units, 30,000 units and 16,000 units respectively. The selling prices per unit are $30 for X, $40 for Y and $50 for Z. All products are made with the same labour, and only 27,000 labour hours are available each month. The following costs per unit apply to each product.

	Product X	**Product Y**	**Product Z**
	$	$	$
Labour ($18 per hour)	9.0	12	16
Other variable costs	14.0	16	20
	23.0	28	36
Fixed costs	3.5	8	7
	26.5	36	43

The company holds no inventory and wishes to maximise the profit in each month.

Which of the following production quantities are achievable that will maximise the monthly profit?

A Make 24,000 units of X 1,500 units of Y and 16,000 units of Z

B Make 24,000 units of X and 22,500 units of Y

C Make 14,000 units of X and 30,000 units of Y

D Make 30,000 units of Y and 8,000 units of Z *(2 marks)*

APPENDIX

Spreadsheets

Contents

What is a spreadsheet?

- Introduction
- What is a spreadsheet?
- Spreadsheet language

1 What is a spreadsheet?

1.1 Introduction

This appendix is designed to introduce spreadsheets to those of you who are not familiar with the basic features and uses of spreadsheet packages. The most commonly-used spreadsheet package is Microsoft Excel and so this appendix has been written in order to guide you through this particular package.

All spreadsheet packages have the same basic features so don't worry if any spreadsheets that you see are slightly different to the ones shown here. All spreadsheet packages have the same basic features.

1.2 What is a spreadsheet?

A spreadsheet is a computer package that is used to present data in a table format. The data in the table can be text, numbers or symbols.

A spreadsheet can also be used to make calculations on some of the data in the table, and present the answers.

An example of a blank spreadsheet is shown on the next page.

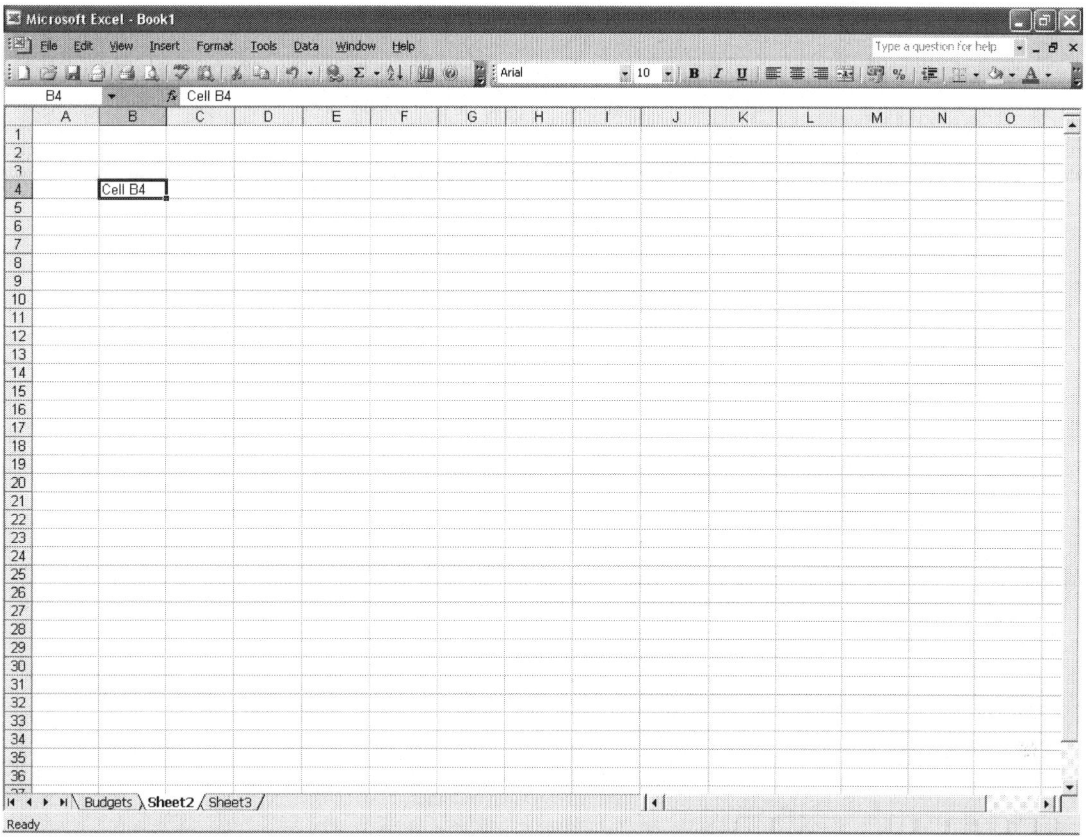

Spreadsheets are made up of a large number of 'cells'. Each cell has a unique reference. The cell highlighted above is cell B4 which means that it is found at the intersection of column B and row 4.

You should be able to find any cell easily. If you have never seen a spreadsheet before, make sure that you can find, say, cells K12 and D23.

Each spreadsheet 'workbook' is a computer file. Like every other computer file, it has to be given a name by its creator when the file is saved for the first time. A blank spreadsheet is called 'Book 1'.

1.3 Spreadsheet language

The following terms relate to spreadsheet packages. Make sure that you learn them if you don't know them already.

- **Cells** - each cell has a cell address that is unique to that cell. For example, B4 is shown in the spreadsheet above.
- **Rows** – there are more than 65,000 rows in an Excel spreadsheet. They run from top to bottom, with row 1 at the very top of the spreadsheet.
- **Columns** – whereas rows are referenced by numbers, columns are referenced by letters. They run from left to right across the top of the spreadsheet.
- **Worksheet** – the spreadsheet shown above is a worksheet (entitled 'Budgets'). There are two other sheets also shown which can be renamed as required.
- **Workbook** – the three worksheets (Budgets, Sheet 1 and Sheet 2) shown above make up the workbook entitled 'Book 1'.

- **Cell pointer** - Cell B4 shown in the spreadsheet above is 'highlighted' by the cell pointer. The cell pointer shows the cell that you are working in and is also indicated on the formula bar between the top of the spreadsheet and the toolbar.

Creating a spreadsheet

- How are spreadsheets created?
- Formulae
- Copying data
- Saving a file
- Formatting a spreadsheet

2 Creating a spreadsheet

2.1 How are spreadsheets created?

When you open Microsoft Excel, a blank spreadsheet like the one shown earlier appears on the screen. A spreadsheet is created by entering data in its cells, with keyboard and mouse.

The cell pointer indicates which cell is being worked on. Make sure that the cell pointer is highlighting the cell that you wish to enter data in. You can move the cell pointer from cell to cell using a mouse. You can also use the arrow keys on the keyboard. Once you have highlighted the relevant cell, you simply enter data using the keyboard and press the <Enter> key.

Data may be entered in the form of:

- Text
- Numbers
- Formulae

Entering text

If you type a letter as the first character in a cell, the program will treat all the data in the cell as text, and not as a formula. This is fine if the entry is text; however, if you are entering a formula in a cell, the formula has to begin with a character that is not a letter. With Excel, it is often '='.

If you enter a long piece of text that 'runs into' the next cell, you will only see part of the data as it will be 'cut off' when it reaches the next cell. This can be rectified by formatting the cells, for example by making the cell wider.

Entering numbers

Numbers are entered into a spreadsheet by typing them straight into a cell. As with text, columns can be made wider if numbers entered need more space to be shown fully.

Numbers can be formatted to make them look how you want them to look on screen and in printouts of the spreadsheet. This might involve having commas in large numbers (1,000 and higher) or if you wish them to be stated to a given number of decimal places (so that 1.226, for example, would be shown as 1.23 if you want every figure to be shown to 2 decimal places).

2.2 Formulae

The most commonly-used formulae in a spreadsheet are formulae for addition, multiplication, subtraction and division.

- Basic formulae always begin with an '=' in Excel.
- The 'operators' (plus, minus, multiply and divide) are shown as follows:
  - + indicates add
  - - indicates subtract
  - * indicates multiply
  - / indicates 'divide by'
- A basic formula also indicates the cells in which the numbers to be added, subtracted, multiplied or divided can be found.

Here are a few examples:

- If you want to enter in cell B6 the sum of the numbers in cells B4 and B5, the formula to enter in cell B6 is: = B4 + B5.
- If you want to subtract the value in cell D24 from the value in cell D23 and enter the answer in cell E25, the formula in cell E25 should be: = D23 – D24.
- If in cell H30 you want to enter the value of the number in cell C6 multiplied by the number in cell D6 multiplied by the number in cell G6, the formula to enter in cell H30 is: = C6*D6*G6.

Entering formulae in cells

Excel makes it even easier to enter formulae in cells using your mouse, without having to key cell numbers into a formula with your keyboard.

- In order to add two cells together, select the cell you want to display the total in and type an '=' sign, then click on the first cell, followed by a '+' sign and then click on the second cell. For example, if you want to enter in cell B6 the sum of the numbers in cells B4 and B5, click on cell B6, then key = into cell B6. Next click on cell B4. Then go back to cell B6 and key in +. Finally go to cell B5 and click on it. The formula will appear in full in cell B6.
- In order to multiply two cells together, select the cell you want to display the total in and type an '=' sign, then click on the first cell, followed by a * sign (to carry out the multiplication) and then click on the second cell.
- There is a formula bar towards the top of the screen. This shows the formula that is contained in a cell. When you click on a cell, the formula in the cell appears in the formula bar. You can use the formula bar to edit or amend any formula in ay cell. Check the formula bar in the following spreadsheet. The formula shows

how the total (30) is calculated by adding together cells C7, C8, C9, C10 and C11 using the formula shown in the formula bar. You can amend the formula in the cell, if you wish to do so, by making the amendments to the formula in the formula bar.

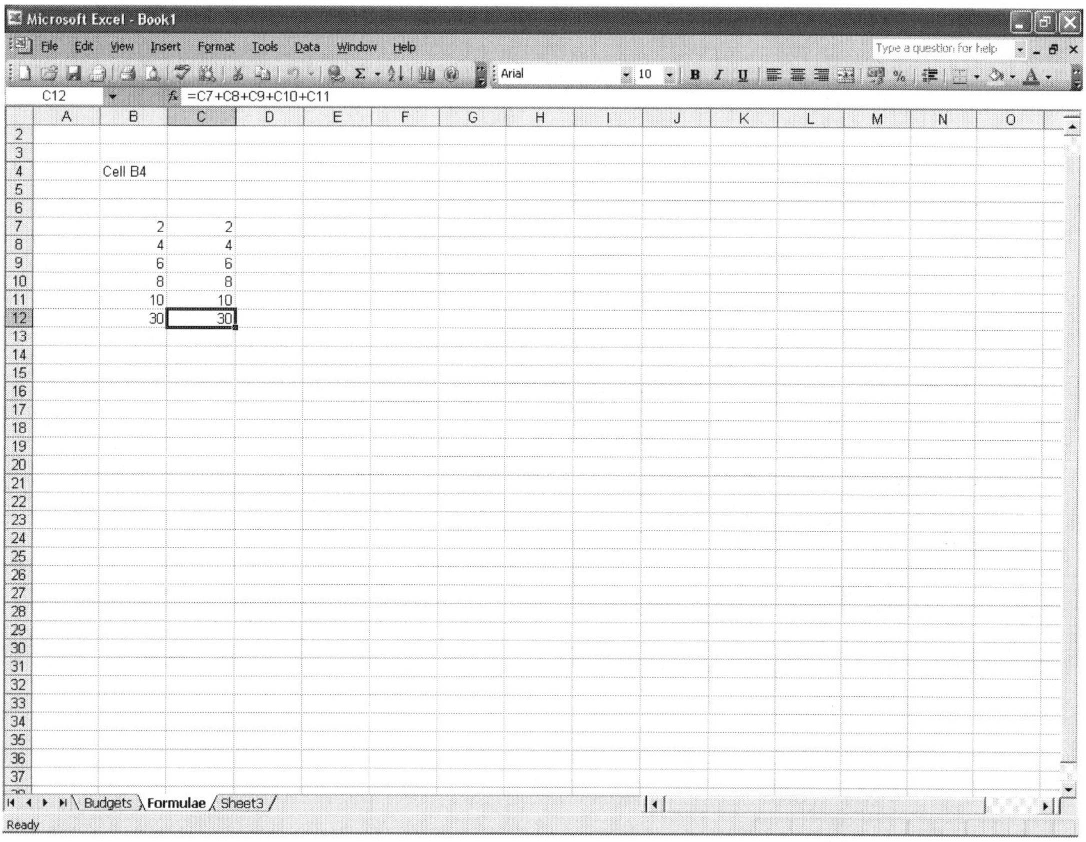

- In order to subtract one cell from another, select the cell you want to display the total in and type an '=' sign, then click on the first cell, followed by a '-' sign (to carry out the subtraction) and then click on the second cell.
- In order to divide one cell by another, select the cell you want to display the total in and type an '=' sign, then click on the first cell, followed by a '/' sign (to carry out the division) and then click on the second cell.

Most spreadsheet packages also have a number of statistical functions. For example, SUM (sum of the values in a list) and AVG (average of the values in a list). The Greek symbol, sigma (□) is a quick way of summing a list of values.

Examples of typical formulae include the following.

- =(B4+B5)-B6 Adds B4 to B5 and subtracts B6
- =(B4*B5)/B6 Multiplies B4 with B5 and divides this total by B6

2.3 Copying data

Apart from entering data and formulae, you can also copy data and formulae from another document or spreadsheet. There are three main ways of copying data once you have defined the cells that you want to copy:

- Select edit from the menu and then choose 'Copy'. Then paste the cells to the area that you wish to copy to.
- Use the 'Copy' button on the toolbar to copy data and then the 'Paste' button to paste the data.
- Right click on the mouse and select 'Copy'. Then paste the cells to the area that you wish to copy to by right clicking on the mouse and selecting 'Paste'.

Alternatively, if you wish to move cells or data from one are to another, you can 'cut and paste' the data as follows:

- Select edit from the menu and then choose 'Copy'. Then paste the cells to the area that you wish to copy to.
- Use the 'Copy' button on the toolbar to copy data and then the 'Paste' button to paste the data.
- Right click on the mouse and select 'Cut'. Then paste the cells to the area that you wish to transfer the data to by right clicking on the mouse and selecting 'Paste'.

Copying formulae

You can also copy formulae from one cell to another. When formulae are copied the cell references change automatically. When cell references change automatically, this is known as relative copying.

If you do not wish cell references to change automatically, you can insert a '$' sign before the column reference if you do not wish the column reference to change. Similarly, if you do not wish the row reference to change, then you insert a '$' before the row reference. If you want the formula to be copied exactly, then you need to insert a '$' sign before both the row and the column references. This is known as absolute copying.

2.4 Saving a file

Once you have created your spreadsheet, you will need to save it properly and give it a 'proper' name. You can save a spreadsheet file by carrying out the following instructions.

- Select the 'save as' option from the menu.
- Select the drive where you wish the file to be saved.
- Type in the file name.
- Click on 'Save'.

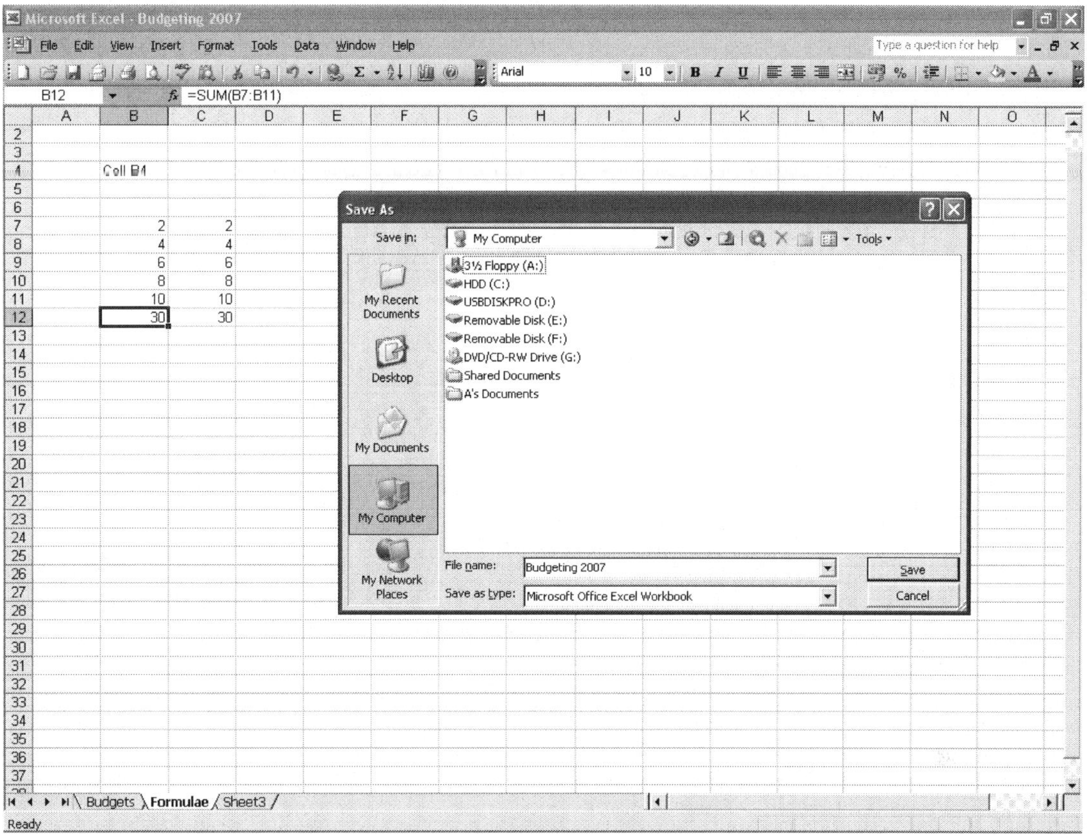

- You only need to save a file using the 'Save as' option the first time that you save a file. Every time you save a file after this, you can simply choose 'Save' from the menu bar or click on the 'save' button on the toolbar.

2.5 Formatting a spreadsheet

Once you have completed your spreadsheet you might wish to 'tidy it up' and make it look more 'professional' and presentable. The easiest way to format a spreadsheet is to select 'format' from the menu bar, followed by 'cells'. This will give you an enormous amount of options for formatting your spreadsheet:

- Number
- Alignment
- Font
- Border
- Patterns

Numbers

It is very important that numbers relating to monetary data are as clear as possible. For example, you might wish to state the numbers in your spreadsheet to a certain number of decimal places, and if they are relating to money, then you may wish to assign $ signs to your figures.

Text

You can make the text on your spreadsheet look good by selecting different fonts, emboldening, colours, italics and underlining and applying these characteristics to your text.

For example, if you want to put the column totals in bold in order to make them stand out and be easy to read, you can highlight these totals and embolden them by selecting the 'B' on the menu bar or selecting the 'format' option from the menu bar, followed by cells and font and bold. You can also apply italics and underlining to your text by following similar procedures but making the final selection as 'I' or italics and 'U' or Underline (single, double, single accounting or double accounting).

The best way of discovering how to format your spreadsheets is by playing around with the formatting options yourself.

A

Answers to exercises and practice multiple choice questions

Chapter 1: The nature and purpose of cost and management accounting

1 **True**

2 **D**

Management accountants provide information for decision-making but do not make the decisions themselves. A cost accounting system gathers data, not information. Management accounting systems provide some but not all the information needed for strategic and tactical planning. Information should be timely and relevant: it should also be reliable but need not be 100% accurate.

3 **A**

The factory manager does not appear to have responsibility for revenues (or profits) since all output is transferred to a processing centre. The manager is also not responsible for capital investment. The factory is therefore likely to be a cost centre.

4 **C**

Weekly cost reports are likely to be too frequent to be useful – especially since many costs such as salaries and rent are incurred on a monthly basis. Monthly cost reporting is the most probable frequency.

5 **B**

6 **B**

Budgets are a form of tactical plan, even when they do not extend over a one-year financial period.

Chapter 2: Cost classification

1 **True**

Inspectors and testers are indirect labour. They work in the production department and so are production overhead costs.

2 **C**

Workers in a stores department are indirect labour. The other employees in the question are all engaged in the direct production of the items produced or the direct provision of the services sold by the entity.

3 **A**

A writer's fee is a direct expense of publishing. The cost of a copy editor is a direct labour cost if the editor is employed by the publisher or a direct expense if an external editor is used. The cost of copies sent for review is a marketing overhead cost. The cost of buying printed copies of the book fro a printer is a direct material cost.

Chapter 3: Cost behaviour and cost estimation

Exercise

	Units		$
High: Total cost of	16,100 units	=	107,450
Low: Total cost of	12,600 units	=	91,700
Difference: Variable cost of	3,500 units	=	15,750

Therefore variable cost per unit = $15,750/3,500 units = $4.50 per unit.

(Tutorial note: take the highest volume of activity (= 16,100 units), not the volume of activity with the highest cost, which in this exercise was 16,000 units.)

Substitute in high or low equation	**Cost**
	$
Total cost of 12,600 units	91,700
Variable cost of 12,600 units (× $4.50)	56,700
Therefore fixed costs per month	35,000

Cost estimate for August	**Cost**
	$
Fixed costs	35,000
Variable cost (15,000 units × $4.50)	67,500
Estimated total costs	102,500

1 **C**

Adjust cost of 'low' activity level: adjusted cost = $960,000 + $36,000 = $996,000

Variable cost per unit = $(1,104,000 – 996,000)/(72,000 – 60,000) units = $9 per unit.

Fixed costs = $1,104,000 – (72,000 × $9) = $456,000.

Total cost of 70,000 units = (70,000 × $9) + $456,000 = $1,086,000.

2 **D**

Use 16,000 and 20,000 activity levels.

Variable cost (above 15,000 units) = $(154,000 – 139,600)/(20,000 – 16,000) units = $3.60.

Variable cost per unit below 15,000 units = $3.60 × 100/90 = $4.

Fixed costs = $130,000 – (12,000 × $4) = $82,000.

Total costs of 14,000 units = (14,000 × $4) + $82,000 = $138,000.

Chapter 4: Business mathematics and computer spreadsheets

Exercise 1

Profit/(loss)	Probability	
x	p	px
$		$
800,000	0.7	560,000
(150,000)	0.3	(45,000)
Expected value of profit		515,000

Exercise 2

Sales price	Probability		Unit cost	Probability	
x	p	px	x	p	px
$		$	$		$
4	0.3	1.20	3.60	0.75	2.70
5	0.6	3.00	4.20	0.25	1.05
6	0.1	0.60			
Expected value of price		4.80		EV of unit cost	3.75

The EV of profit per unit = $4.80 - $3.75 = $1.05.
For 10,000 units, the EV of profit = 10,000 × $1.05 = $10,500.

If the company uses expected values to make decisions, it should make and sell the batch of glasses.

However, there is a 0.30 probability that the sales price will be just $4 and a 0.25 probability that the unit cost will be $4.20. This means that there is a 0.075 probability (7.5%) that there will be a loss of $0.20 per glass, or $2,000 in total.

1 **C**

Profit/(loss)	Probability	
x	p	px
$		$
64,000	0.50	32,000
10,000	0.25	2,500
(20,000)	0.25	(5,000)
EV =		29,500

2 **A**

3 **A**

$$b = \frac{5(138{,}546) - (258)(2{,}670)}{5(13{,}732) - (258)^2}$$

$$= 3{,}870/2{,}096 = 1.846$$

$$a = \frac{2{,}670}{5} - \frac{1.846(258)}{5}$$

$$= 439$$

4 **B**

The correlation coefficient must have a value in the range – 1 to + 1.

5 **C**

Spreadsheets can be used to prepare any table of figures, and this includes calculating a line of best fit from data entered into the spreadsheet model. Spreadsheets are not unsuitable for the recording and storage of large quantities of data.

Chapter 5: Accounting for materials and labour

Exercise 1

Remember that holding costs and usage quantities should refer to the same length of time. In this example, holding costs are 8% of \$60 = \$4.80 per unit per year. Usage is 5,000 units in three months, which is 20,000 units per year.

$$EOQ = \sqrt{\frac{2C_oD}{C_H}}$$

Where:

$C_o = 250$

$D = 20{,}000$

$C_H = 4.80$

$$= \sqrt{\left(\frac{2 \times 20{,}000 \times 250}{4.80}\right)} = 1{,}443 \text{ units}$$

Exercise 2

Average number of employees = (600 + 630)/2 = 615.

Labour turnover rate = (35/615) × 100% = 5.7%.

1 **D**

EOQ = $\sqrt{(2 \times 240 \times 8{,}000)/0.54}$ = 2,667 units

2 **A**

An increase in the holding cost of inventory means that the EOQ will become smaller (since the holding cost is 'below the line' in the EOQ formula). A smaller EOQ means more orders on average each year; therefore annual ordering costs will increase.

3 **C**

EOQ = √ (2 × 500 × 10,000)/2.50 = 2,000 units.
Costs will be minimised by purchasing either 2,000 units (the EOQ) or the minimum quantity required to obtain the large order discount (5,000 units).

	Order size 2,000	Order size 5,000
	$	$
Purchase costs (10,000 units)	250,000	230,000
Holding costs (at $2.50)	2,500	6,250
Ordering costs ($500 per order)	2,500	1,000
Total costs	255,000	237,250

4 **C**

$$\sqrt{\frac{2 \times 800 \times (200 \times 50)}{2\left(1 - \dfrac{200}{1{,}000}\right)}}$$

= 3,162 units, or 3,200 units to the nearest 100 units.

5 **B**

Reorder level = Demand per day × Maximum supply lead time = 150 units × 10 days = 1,500 units.

6 **B**

Actual output = 2,100 units.
Capacity = 15 employees × 36 hours per week = 540 hours.
These two measurements need to be put on to the same basis, hours or units.
Actual output of 2,100 units is the equivalent of 525 hours of work at the standard rate of efficiency.
Production volume ratio = (525/540) × 100% = 97.2%.

Check: Capacity utilisation ratio = 500/540 = 92.6%.
Productivity or efficiency ratio = 2,100/(500 × 4) = 105%
Production volume ratio = 92.6% × 10597.2%.% = 97.2%.

7 **A**

Employees at the beginning of the year = 5,700 – 360 + 600 = 5,940
Average number of employees = (5,700 + 5,940)/2 = 5,820
Labour turnover = (600/5,820) × 100% = 10.3%

Chapter 6: Accounting for overheads

Exercise 1

Reciprocal method of cost apportionment of service department costs

	Total	P1	P2	S1	S2
	$	$	$	$	$
Allocated/apportioned overhead costs	92,000	32,520	22,000	15,000	22,480
Apportion costs of service departments:					
S1 (20:60:20)		3,000	9,000	(15,000)	3,000
				0	25,480
S2 (70:20:10)		17,836	5,096	2,548	(25,480)
Now repeat:					
S1 (20:60:20)		510	1,529	(2,548)	509
S2 (70:20:10)		356	102	51	(509)
Repeat again					
S1 (20:60:20)		10	31	(51)	10
S2 (70:20:10)		7	2	1	(10)
Repeat again					
S1 (20:60:20)		0	1	(1)	0
	92,000	54,239	37,761	0	0

Exercise 2

(a)

	Machine hours
Product A: (3,000 units × 0.2 hours)	600
Product B: (4,000 units × 0.1 hours)	400
Product C: (1,000 units × 0.2 hours)	200
Total machine hours	1,200
Production overhead expenditure	$24,000
Absorption rate per machine hour	$20
Overheads absorbed by each product:	$
Product A: (600 hours × $20)	12,000
Product B: (400 hours × $20)	8,000
Product C: (200 hours × $20)	4,000
Total	24,000

	Product A	Product B	Product C
	$	$	$
Prime cost per unit	3.00	4.00	5.00
Absorbed overhead at $20/machine hour	4.00	2.00	4.00
Full production cost/unit	7.00	6.00	9.00

(b)

	Labour cost
Product A	$3,500
Product B	$8,000
Product C	$4,500
Total direct labour cost	$16,000
Production overhead expenditure	$24,000
Absorption rate as % of labour cost	150%
Overheads absorbed by each product:	$
Product A: ($3,500 × 150%)	5,250
Product B: ($8,000 × 150%)	12,000
Product C: ($4,500 × 150%)	6,750
Total	24,000

Exercise 3

(a)

Absorption rate = Budgeted overheads/Budgeted direct labour hours
= $240,000/30,000 hours = $8 per direct labour hour.

The overheads charged to the cost of production in Year 7 were 33,000 hours × $8 = $264,000.

(b)

	$
Overheads absorbed (see above)	264,000
Actual overhead expenditure	258,000
Over-absorbed overhead	6,000

Exercise 4

(a)

Absorption rate = Budgeted overheads/Budgeted direct labour hours
= $720,000/120,000 hours = $6 per direct labour hour.

The overheads charged to the cost of production in the year were 106,000 hours × $6 = $636,000.

	$
Overheads absorbed (see above)	636,000
Actual overhead expenditure	704,000
Under-absorbed overhead	68,000

Reasons for the under-absorbed overhead

Expenditure variance

	$	
Budgeted (expected) overhead expenditure	720,000	
Actual overhead expenditure	704,000	
Expenditure variance	16,000	Favourable

Volume variance

	Hours	
Budgeted direct labour hours	120,000	
Actual direct labour hours	106,000	
Volume variance in hours	14,000	Adverse
Absorption rate per hour	$6	
Volume variance in $	$84,000	Adverse

The volume variance and the expenditure variance together add up to the under-absorbed overhead of $68,000.

(b)

		Job 123		Job 124
		$		$
Prime costs		270,000		360,000
Production overhead	(50,000 × $6)	300,000	(56,000 × $6)	336,000
Full production cost		570,000		696,000

Exercise 5

The fixed overhead absorption rate = $800,000/100,000 direct labour hours = $8 per direct labour hour.

Absorbed overheads	$
Fixed overheads (97,000 hours × $8)	776,000
Variable overheads (97,000 hours × $4)	388,000
Total absorbed overheads	1,164,000
Actual overhead expenditure	1,120,000
Over-absorbed overheads	44,000

Explaining the over-absorbed overhead

Expected overhead expenditure	$	
Fixed overheads (= Budgeted fixed overhead)	800,000	
Variable overheads (97,000 × $4)	388,000	
Total expected overhead expenditure	1,188,000	
Actual overhead expenditure	1,120,000	
Expenditure variance	68,000	Favourable

	hours	
Budgeted volume (direct labour hours)	100,000	
Actual volume (direct labour hours)	97,000	
Volume variance (direct labour hours)	3,000	Adverse
Fixed overhead absorption rate/direct labour hour	$8	
Volume variance in $ (fixed overhead only)	$24,000	Adverse

Summary	$	
Expenditure variance	68,000	Favourable
Volume variance	24,000	Adverse
Total over-absorbed overhead	44,000	Favourable

1 **C**

	Basis of apportionment	P1	P2	S1	S2
		$	$	$	$
Initial costs		300,000	450,000	320,000	350,000
Apportion S2	(30:40:30)	105,000	140,000	105,000	(350,000)
				425,000	
Apportion S1	(30:70)	127,500	297,500	(425,000)	
		532,500	887,500		

2 **A**

	CC1	CC2
	hours	hours
Product Y	80,000	100,000
Product Z	40,000	80,000
Total hours	120,000	180,000
Cost	$660,000	$540,000
Absorption rate per hour	$5.50	$3

Cost per unit of Product Z = (2 hours × $5.50) + (4 hours × $3) = $23.

3 A

	C1	C2
	hours	hours
Product P	30,000	75,000
Product Q	60,000	45,000
Total hours	90,000	120,000
Cost	$324,000	$583,200
Absorption rate per hour	$3.60	$4.86

Cost per unit of Product Q	$
C1: 4 hours × $3.60	14.40
Product Q: 3 hours × $4.86	14.58
Total hours	28.98

4 D

If actual labour hours are less than budget, overhead will be under-absorbed. If actual overhead spending is more than budget, overhead will be under-absorbed.

5 D

Overhead absorption rate = $144,000/36,000 hours = $4 per direct labour hour

	$
Overhead absorbed (37,500 × $4)	150,000
Actual overhead expenditure	157,500
Under-absorbed overhead	7,500

6 A

Overhead absorption rate = $300,000/24,000 hours = $12.50 per direct labour hour.

	$
Overhead absorbed (26,000 × $12.50)	325,000
Actual overhead expenditure	318,500
Over-absorbed overhead	6,500

Chapter 7: Accounting for costs: ledger entries

Exercise 1

Materials

	$		$
Opening balance	1,000		
Financial ledger control	20,000		

Wages and salaries

	$		$
Financial ledger control	25,000		

Production overheads

	$		$
Financial ledger control	4,000		

Other overheads

	$		$
Financial ledger control	7,000		

Sales

	$		$
		Financial ledger control	90,000

Financial ledger control account

	$		$
Sales	90,000	Opening balance	5,000
		Materials	20,000
		Wages and salaries	25,000
		Production overheads	4,000
		Other overheads	7,000

Exercise 2

Materials

	$		$
Opening balance	7,000	Work-in-progress	33,000
Financial ledger control (purchases)	50,000	Production overheads	17,000
		Other overheads	2,000
		Closing balance c/f	5,000
	57,000		57,000
Opening balance b/f	5,000		

Wages and salaries

	$		$
Financial ledger control	45,000	Work-in-progress	28,000
		Production overheads	7,000
		Other overheads	10,000
	45,000		45,000

Production overheads

	$		$
Materials	17,000	Work-in-progress (absorbed)	50,000
Wages and salaries	7,000		
Financial ledger control (expenses)	24,000		
Over-absorbed overhead	2,000		
	50,000		50,000

Work-in-progress

	$		$
Opening balance	3,000	Finished goods (balancing figure)	106,000
Materials	33,000		
Wages and salaries	28,000		
Production overhead	50,000	Closing balance c/f	8,000
	114,000		114,000
Opening balance b/f	8,000		

Finished goods

	$		$
Opening balance	4,000	Cost of sales	109,000
Work-in-progress	106,000	Closing balance c/f	1,000
	110,000		110,000
Opening balance b/f	1,000		

Other overheads

	$		$
Materials	2,000	Cost of sales	27,000
Wages and salaries	10,000		
Financial ledger control (expenses)	15,000		
	27,000		27,000

Sales

	$		$
Income statement	160,000	Financial ledger control	160,000

Cost of sales

	$		$
Finished goods	109,000	Income statement	136,000
Other overheads	27,000		
	136,000		136,000

Under- or over-absorbed overhead account

	$		$
Income statement	2,000	Production overhead	2,000

Costing income statement

	$		$
Cost of sales	136,000	Sales	160,000
Profit (financial ledger control account)	26,000	Over-absorbed overhead	2,000
	162,000		162,000

Financial ledger control account

	$		$
Sales	160,000	Opening balance	14,000
		Materials	50,000
		Wages and salaries	45,000
		Production overheads	24,000
		Other overheads	15,000
Closing balance c/f	14,000	Income statement (profit)	26,000
	174,000		174,000
		Opening balance b/f	14,000

Statement of closing balances

	Debit	Credit
	$	$
Materials	5,000	
Work-in-progress	8,000	
Finished goods	1,000	
Financial ledger control		14,000
	14,000	14,000

Chapter 8: Marginal costing and absorption costing

Exercise 1

Contribution per unit:

Product X: \$8 – \$3 = \$5
Product Y: \$6 – \$2 = \$4

	\$
Contribution from Product X: (40,000 × \$5)	200,000
Contribution from Product Y: (30,000 × \$4)	120,000
Total contribution per month	320,000
Fixed costs	(250,000)
Profit per month	70,000

Exercise 2

Income statement, marginal costing	\$	\$
Sales (40,000 × \$11)		440,000
Variable cost of sales (40,000 × \$5)		200,000
Contribution		240,000
Fixed costs:		
Production fixed costs	120,000	
Other fixed costs	80,000	
Total fixed costs		200,000
Profit		40,000

	units
Sales volume	40,000
Production volume	37,000
Reduction in inventory	(3,000)

Fixed production overhead cost per unit = \$111,000/37,000 units = \$3 per unit

Since sales are more than production volume, there will be a fall in inventory and the marginal costing profit will be higher than the absorption costing profit.

	\$
Marginal costing profit	40,000
Difference in profit (3,000 units × \$3)	9,000
Absorption costing profit (lower)	31,000

1 **A**

	$000	$000
Sales		250
Direct materials	24	
Direct labour	36	
Direct expenses	5	
Variable production overheads	6	
Variable selling overheads	8	
Total variable costs		79
Contribution		171

2 **B**

There is a reduction in inventory by 1,000 units, since production volume (24,000 units) is less than sales volume (25,000 units).

If absorption costing is used, the fixed production overhead cost per unit is $4 (= $96,000/24,000 units).

The difference between the absorption costing profit and marginal costing profit is therefore $4,000 (= 1,000 units × $4).

Absorption costing profit is lower, because there has been a reduction in inventory.

Absorption costing profit would therefore be $65,000 – $4,000 = $61,000.

3 **B**

There is an increase in inventory by 2,000 units, since production volume (32,000 units) is more than sales volume (30,000 units).

If absorption costing is used, the fixed production overhead cost per unit is $5 (= $160,000/32,000 units).

The difference between the absorption costing profit and marginal costing profit is therefore $10,000 (= 2,000 units × $5).

Absorption costing profit is higher, because there has been an increase in inventory.

Marginal costing profit would therefore be $101,000 – $10,000 = $91,000.

4 **D**

Fixed production cost per unit = $5 (= $125,000/25,000 units).

Difference between marginal and absorption costing profits = $15,000.

Therefore difference between sales volume and production volume = $15,000/$5 = 3,000 units.

Absorption costing profit is lower, which means that sales volume is higher t than production volume.

Expected sales volume = 25,000 units + 3,000 units = 28,000 units.

Chapter 9: Job costing, batch costing and service costing

1 **B**

Job cost

	$
Direct materials	125
Direct labour (4 hours at $20)	80
Direct expenses	25
Prime cost	230
Production overhead (4 hours at $35)	140
Production cost of the job	370
Non-production overheads (60% of prime cost)	138
Total job cost	508

2 **D**

Job costing is appropriate where each cost unit (job) differs in some respects from other cost units. Installing elevators differs between each job (with the location of the building, the layout and height of the building, number of elevators to install, type of elevator and so on).

3 **A**

Number of tonne/kilometres = 80,000 kilometres carrying an average of 3 tonnes = 240,000.

Cost per tonne-kilometre = $720,000/240,000 = $3.

Chapter 10: Process costing

Exercise 1

Normal loss = 5% × 6,000 units = 300 units
Expected output = 95% × 6,000 units = 5,700 units

	$
Direct materials	21,600
Direct labour	8,000
Production overheads	16,000
	45,600
Scrap value of normal loss (300 × $3.80)	1,140
	44,460
Expected output	5,700 units
Cost per unit	$7.80

Process account

	units	$		units	$
Direct materials	6,000	21,600	Finished goods (at $7.80)	5,500	42,900
Direct labour		8,000	Normal loss (300 at $3.80)	300	1,140
Production overheads		16,000	Abnormal loss (at $7.80)	200	1,560
	6,000	45,600		6,000	45,600

Abnormal loss account

	units	$		units	$
Process account	200	1,560	Scrap (200 at $3.80)	200	760

Exercise 2

Normal loss = 4% × 10,000 units = 400 units
Expected output = 96% × 10,000 units = 9,600 units

	$
Direct materials	35,200
Conversion costs	29,600
	64,800

Expected output	9,600 units
Cost per unit	$6.75

Process account

	units	$		units	$
Direct materials	10,000	35,200	Finished goods (at $6.75)	9,750	65,813
Conversion costs		29,600	Normal loss	400	0
Abnormal gain (at $6.75)	150	1,013			
	10,150	65,813		10,150	65,813

Exercise 3

Statement of equivalent units

Equivalent units	Total	Direct materials		Conversion costs
	Total units	Equivalent units		Equivalent units
Completed units	11,000	11,000		11,000
Closing inventory	5,000	5,000	(5,000 × 40%)	2,000
Total equivalent units	16,000	16,000		13,000

Statement of cost per equivalent unit

Costs	Direct materials	Conversion costs
	$	$
Opening inventory	14,800	6,100
Costs incurred in the period	70,000	34,200
Total costs	84,800	40,300
Equivalent units	16,000	13,000
Cost per equivalent unit	$5.30	$3.10

Statement of evaluation

Statement of evaluation		Direct materials		Conversion costs	Total cost
		$		$	$
Completed units	(11,000 × $5.3)	58,300	(11,000 × $3.1)	34,100	92,400
Closing inventory	(5,000 × $5.3)	26,500	(2,000 × $3.1)	6,200	32,700

The **process account** is prepared as follows:

Process account

	units	$		units	$
Opening inventory	2,000	20,900	Finished goods	11,000	92,400
Direct materials	14,000	70,000			
Conversion costs		34,200	Closing inventory c/f	5,000	32,700
	16,000	125,100		16,000	125,100

Exercise 4

Statement of equivalent units (work done in the current period)

Equivalent units	Total units	Direct materials	Equivalent units	Conversion costs	Equivalent units
To complete opening inventory, finished first	2,000	(0%)	0	(20% × 2,000)	400
Units started and completed in the current period	9,000		9,000		9,000
Finished output	11,000		9,000		9,400
Closing inventory	5,000		5,000	(40% × 5,000)	2,000
Total equivalent units	16,000		14,000		11,400

Statement of cost per equivalent unit (work in the current period)

Cost per equivalent unit	Direct materials	Conversion costs
Total cost in current period	$70,000	$34,200
Total equivalent units in the current period	14,000	11,400
Cost per equivalent unit	$5.00	$3.00

Statement of evaluation

		Direct materials		Conversion costs	Total cost
		$		$	$
Finished units					
Opening WIP					
Cost b/f		14,800		6,100	20,900
Cost to complete		0	(400 × $3)	1,200	1,200
		14,800		7,300	22,100
Units started and finished	(9,000 × $5)	45,000	(9,000 × $3)	27,000	72,000
Finished units		59,800		34,300	94,100
Closing inventory	(5,000 × $5)	25,000	(2,000 × $3)	6,000	31,000
		84,800		40,300	125,100

The process account is prepared as follows:

Process 2 account

	units	$		units	$
Opening inventory	2,000	20,900	Finished goods	11,000	94,100
Direct materials	14,000	70,000			
Conversion costs		34,200	Closing inventory c/f	5,000	31,000
	16,000	125,100		16,000	125,100
Opening inventory b/f	5,000	31,000			

1 **B**

Actual loss = 1,000 units (= 12,000 – 11,000). Normal loss = 600 units (= 5% of 12,000). Therefore abnormal loss = 400 units.

Total costs = $60,000 + $15,240 = $75,240.

Expected output = 12,000 units less 6% = 11,400 units.

Cost per unit of expected output = $75,240/11,400 = $6.60

Therefore cost of abnormal loss = 400 × $6.60 = $2,640.

2 **C**

Actual loss = 400 units (= 3,600 – 3,200). Normal loss = 600 units (= 1/6 of 3,600). Therefore abnormal gain = 200 units.

Total costs = $15,000 + $5,160 = $20,160.

Expected output = 3,600 units × 5/6 = 3,000 units.

Cost per unit of expected output = $20,160/3,000 = $6.72

Therefore cost of abnormal loss = 200 × $6.72 = $1,344.

3 **B**

Statement of equivalent units

	Direct materials equivalent units		Closing WIP equivalent units
Finished output	1,600		1,600
Closing WIP	400	(400 × 25%)	100
	2,000		1,700

Statement of cost per equivalent unit

		Direct materials		Conversion costs
Cost	(7,935 + 25,605)	$33,540	(1,020 + 5,440)	$6,460
Equivalent units		2,000		1,700
Cost per equivalent unit		$16.77		$3.80

Valuation of closing WIP = (400 × $16.77) + (100 × $3.80) = $7,088

4 **C**

	Direct materials equivalent units		Closing WIP equivalent units
Opening WIP finished	0	(400 × 25%)	100
Other finished output	1,500		1,500
Total finished output	1,500		1,600
Closing WIP	500	(500 × 40%)	200
	2,000		1,800

Statement of cost per equivalent unit in the current period

	Direct materials	Conversion costs
Cost	$12,200	$3,060
Equivalent units	2,000	1,800
Cost per equivalent unit	$6.10	$1.70

Valuation of finished output

	$
Opening WIP: cost brought forward	2,920
Costs in current period	
Direct materials (1,500 × $6.10)	9,150
Conversion costs (1,600 × $1.70)	2,720
Total cost of finished output	14,790

5 **A**

Actual loss = 1,000 units. Normal loss = 400 units. Therefore abnormal loss is 600 units.

Statement of equivalent units

	Direct materials equivalent units		Abnormal loss equivalent units
Finished output	7,000		7,000
Abnormal loss	600	(600 × 60%)	360
	7,600		7,360

Statement of cost per equivalent unit

	Direct materials	Conversion costs
Cost	$30,400	$11,040
Equivalent units	7,600	7,360
Cost per equivalent unit	$4	$1.50

Valuation of abnormal loss = (600 × $4) + (360 × $1.50) = $2,940

6 C

Cost of output net of by-product revenue = $(42,000 + 15,000 – 1,500) = $55,500

Units of joint product = 2,000 + 3,000 = 5,000

Cost per unit of joint product output = $55,500/5,000 = $11.10

Cost of output units of JP2 = 2,000 × $11.10 = $22,200

Chapter 11 Budgeting

Exercise 1

Materials usage budget

	Raw material X	Raw material Y	Total
	kilos	kilos	Kilos
To make 5,000 A	25,000	35,000	60,000
To make 10,000 B	40,000	30,000	70,000
Total quantities	65,000	65,000	130,000
Price per kilo	$10	$20	
Total cost	$650,000	$1,300,000	$1,950,000

Materials purchases budget

	Raw material X	Raw material Y	Total
	kilos	kilos	
Materials usage budget	65,000	65,0000	
Closing inventory	8,000	4,000	
	73,000	69,000	
Opening inventory	(10,000)	(8,000)	
Budgeted materials purchases	63,000	61,000	
Price per kilo	$10	$20	
Materials purchases budget in $	$630,000	$1,220,000	$1,850,000

1 A

2 B

Budgeted production = 20,000 + 4,000 – 5,000 units of product X = 19,000 units

Budgeted usage of material B = 19,000 units × 3 kilos per unit = 57,000 kilos

Budgeted purchase quantity of material B = 18,000 + 57,000 – 9,000 = 66,000 kilos

3 B

A flexed budget is for a fixed quantity of sales and output. It is not necessarily correct to state that no changes are permitted to a fixed budget.

4 D

Budgeted purchases of material T = 40,000 kilos

Budgeted usage of material T = 40,000 + 4,000 = 44,000 kilos

Budgeted production of Product Z = 22,000 units (= 44,000 kilos/2 kilos per unit)

Budgeted sales of Z = 19,000 units.

Therefore an increase of 3,000 units in Product Z inventory is planned.

5 **C**

	Product A	Product B
	units	units
Sales budget	12,000	15,000
Closing inventory	1,000	5,000
Opening inventory	(2,000)	(3,000)
Production budget	11,000	17,000
	hours	hours
Hours per unit	2	1.5
Total direct labour hours	22,000	25,500

Direct labour budget = 22,000 + 25,500 = 47,500 hours at $18 per hour = $855,000

Chapter 12 Standard costing and variance analysis

Exercise 1

Budgeted direct labour hours	hours
Product X: (2,000 units × 1.5 hours)	3,000
Product Y (1,000 units × 2 hours)	2,000
	5,000
Budgeted fixed production overheads	$60,000
Fixed overhead absorption rate/hour	$12

	Product X		Product Y	
		$		$
Direct materials				
Material A	(2 units × $4)	8	(1.5 units × $4)	6
Material B	(1 unit × $3)	3	(3 units × $3)	9
Direct labour	(1.5 hours × $10)	15	(2 hours × $10)	20
Variable production overhead	(1.5 hours × $2)	3	(2 hours × $2)	4
Standard variable prod'n cost		29		39
Fixed production overhead	(1.5 hours × $12)	18	(2 hours × $12)	24
Standard full production cost		47		63

Exercise 2

Note: In standard costing, output is valued at the standard cost per unit produced. Output in this example is therefore costed as 4,000 units at $3 each, not as 5,500 hours at $2 each.

	$	
4,000 units of output should cost (× $3)	12,000	
They did cost	11,700	
Variable overhead total cost variance	300	(F)

The variance is favourable, because actual costs were lower than the standard cost.

Exercise 3

Direct materials total cost variance:	$	
6,000 units of output should cost (× $6)	36,000	
They did cost	35,900	
Total direct materials cost variance	100	(F)

Materials price variance		
	$	
12,800 kilos of materials should cost (× $3)	38,400	
They did cost	35,900	
Materials price variance	2,500	(F)

Materials usage variance		
	kilos	
6,000 units of Product P44 should use (× 2 kilos)	12,000	
They did use	12,800	
Materials usage variance in kilos	800	(A)
Standard price per kilo of material L	$3	
Materials usage variance in $	$2,400	(A)

The materials price variance and the materials usage variance add up to the materials total cost variance.

Exercise 4

Standard fixed production overhead cost per unit = $72,000/6,000 units = $12 per unit.

Fixed production overhead expenditure variance		
	$	
Budgeted fixed overhead expenditure	72,000	
Actual fixed overhead expenditure	71,200	
Fixed overhead expenditure variance	800	(F)

Fixed production overhead volume variance		
	units	
Budgeted production volume	6,000	
Actual production volume	5,600	
Volume variance in units	400	(A)
Standard fixed overhead rate per unit	$12	
Fixed production overhead volume variance in $	$4,800	(A)

Exercise 5

Standard fixed production overhead cost per unit = $96,000/16,000 units = $6 per unit.

Standard fixed production overhead rate per hour = $6 per unit/0.25 hours per unit = $24 per hour.

Budgeted hours of work = $96,000/$24 per hour = 4,000 hours.

(Alternatively: Budgeted hours of work = 16,000 units × 0.25 hours per unit = 4,000 hours.)

Fixed production overhead expenditure variance		
	$	
Budgeted fixed overhead expenditure	96,000	
Actual fixed overhead expenditure	98,500	
Fixed overhead expenditure variance	2,500	(A)

Fixed production overhead volume variance		
	units	
Budgeted production volume	16,000	
Actual production volume	15,700	
Volume variance in units	300	(A)
Standard fixed overhead rate per unit	$6	
Fixed production overhead volume variance in $	$1,800	(A)

Fixed overhead efficiency variance		
	hours	
15,700 units should take (× 0.25 hours)	3,925	
They did take	4,200	
Efficiency variance in hours	275	(A)
Standard fixed overhead rate per hour	$24	
Fixed overhead efficiency variance in $	$6,600	(A)

Fixed overhead capacity variance		
	hours	
Budgeted hours of work	4,000	
Actual hours of work	4,200	
Capacity variance in hours	200	(F)
Standard fixed overhead rate per hour	$24	
Fixed overhead capacity variance in $	$4,800	(F)

Exercise 6

Sales price variance	$	
39,200 units should sell for (× $20)	784,000	
They did sell for	802,300	
Sales price variance	18,300	(F)

Sales volume profit variance		
	units	
Actual sales volume (units)	39,200	
Budgeted sales volume (units)	42,000	
Sales volume variance in units	2,800	(A)
Standard profit per unit ($20 – $16 = $4)	$4	
Sales volume profit variance	$11,200	(A)

Exercise 7

Direct labour rate variance	$	
1,240 hours should cost (× $16)	19,840	
They did cost	?	
Direct labour rate variance	1,700	(F)

The rate variance was favourable, which means that actual costs were less than standard.
Actual cost of labour = $19,840 - $1,700 = $18,140.

Exercise 8

Labour efficiency variance

	hours
3,200 units of Product H should take	?
They did take	5,150
Labour efficiency variance in hours	?
Standard rate per hour	$18
Labour efficiency variance in $	$8,100 (F)

Labour efficiency variance in hours = $8,100 (F)/$18 per hour = 450 hours (F).
The variance is favourable. This means that actual hours were less than standard hours (and so standard hours are more than actual hours).
Standard hours to make 3,200 units = 5,150 + 450 = 5,600 hours.
Standard time per unit = 5,600 hours/3,200 units = 1.75 hours per unit.

Standard direct labour cost of Product H =
1.75 hours at $18 per hour = $31.50.

1 D

	$
18,000 hours should cost (× $18.50)	333,000
They did cost	328,500
Direct labour rate variance	4,500 (F)

The variance is favourable because actual costs were lower than standard cost.

2 C

	hours
8,800 units of Product P234 should take (× 2 hours)	17,600
They did take	18,000
Efficiency variance in hours	400 (A)
Standard direct labour rate per hour	$18.50
Direct labour efficiency variance in $	$7,400 (A)

The efficiency variance is adverse because the output took longer to make than it should have done.

3 B

	$
6,450 units should sell for (× $15)	96,750
They did sell for	92,880
Sales price variance	3,870 (A)

	units	
Actual sales volume (units)	6,450	
Budgeted sales volume (units)	6,000	
Sales volume variance in units	450	(F)
Standard contribution per unit (80% × $15)	$12	
Sales volume variance (contribution variance)	5,400	(F)

4 **A**

Budgeted expenditure = 100%

Actual expenditure = 97% of budget

Expenditure variance = $4,800 which is 3% of budget

Budgeted expenditure = $2,000/0.03 = $160,000

Actual expenditure = 97% of budget = $155,200

5 **C**

	units	
Actual sales volume (units)	1,600	
Budgeted sales volume (units)	1,500	
Sales volume variance in units	100	(F)
Standard profit per unit ($48 – $34)	$14	
Sales volume profit variance	1,400	(F)

6 **B**

The senior buying manager is the person most responsible for the prices paid for raw materials. Variances should be reported to the manager who is in the best position to explain or control their causes.

7 **A**

	$	
10,500 kilos should cost (× $8)	84,000	
They did cost	82,500	
Material price variance	1,500	(F)

The variance is favourable because actual purchase costs were lower than expected.

8 **B**

	hours	
Actual hours worked	?	
Budgeted hours worked (35,000 units × 3)	105,000	
Capacity variance in hours	?	
Standard fixed overhead rate per hour	$12	
Fixed overhead capacity variance	7,200	(F)

The capacity variance is $7,200 (F), and at $12 per hour, this means that the capacity variance was 600 hours (F). When the capacity variance is favourable, actual hours worked were more than budgeted hours. Budgeted hours were 105,000. Therefore actual hours were 105,000 + 600 = 105,600 hours.

Chapter 13: Cost-volume-profit (CVP) analysis

Exercise 1

Method 1

Contribution per unit = $12 – $7.50 = $4.50

Total contribution to break even = fixed costs = $1,350,000.

Break-even point = $1,350,000/$4.50 per unit = 300,000 units.

At the break-even point, sales will be 300,000 × $12 = $3,600,000.

Method 2

Contribution per unit = $4.50.

Contribution/sales ratio = $4.50/$12 = 0.375.

Break-even point in sales ($) = $1,350,000/0.375 = $3,600,000.

At a selling price of $12 per unit, break-even point is 300,000 units (= $3,600,000/$12).

Exercise 2

Break-even point = Fixed costs/C/S ratio = $2,100,000/60% = $3,500,000.

Margin of safety = $4,000,000 – $3,500,000 = $500,000 (in sales revenue).

As a percentage of the budgeted sales, the margin of safety = 500,000/4,000,000 = 0.125 or 12.5%.

Exercise 3

	$
Fixed costs	3,200,000
Target profit	400,000
Target contribution	3,600,000

C/S ratio = 75%.

Therefore sales needed to achieve the target profit = $3,600,000/0.75 = $4,800,000.

1 C

Variable cost per unit = $(4 + 3 + 1 + 2) = $10.

Contribution per unit = $32 – $10 = $22

Contribution/Sales ratio = 22/32 = 0.6875 or 68.75%

2 C

Sales revenue required to break even = $360,000/0.40 = $900,000.

	$
Variable cost (= 60% of sales price)	12
Contribution (= 40% of sales price	8
Sales price per unit	20

Sales units required to break even = $900,000/$20 = 45,000 units.

3 C

Sales revenue required to break even = $234,000/0.60 = $390,000.

	$
Variable cost (= 40% of sales price)	48
Contribution (= 60% of sales price	72
Sales price per unit	120

Sales units required to break even = $390,000/$120 = 3,250 units.

Margin of safety = 5,100 units – 3,250 units = 1,850 units

4 B

Sales revenue required to break even = $810,000/0.60 = $1,350,000.

	$
Variable cost (= 40% of sales price)	36
Contribution (= 60% of sales price	54
Sales price per unit	90

Sales units required to break even = $1,350,000/$90 = 15,000 units.

5 D

Target contribution = $1,440,000 + $300,000 = $1,740,000

C/S ratio = 40%

Sales required to achieve target profit = $1,740,000/0.40 = $4,350,000

Chapter 14: Relevant costs

1 D

Cost of materials purchased last month = $7,200/1,200 kg = $6 per kg.

Materials held in inventory but in regular use: relevant cost = replacement cost

Materials not yet purchased: relevant cost = purchase cost.

Total relevant cost = 1,800 kg × $6 × 1.05 price increase = $11,340

2 C

Each unit of normal output earns a contribution of $24

Labour time per unit = $36 labour cost/$24 per direct labour hour = 1.5 hours

Therefore contribution per normal unit = $24/1.5 hours = $16 per labour hour.

	$
Variable cost of 120 hours of labour (× $24)	2,880
Opportunity cost: contribution forgone = 120 hours × $16	1,920
Total relevant cost of labour	4,800

3 **C**

Materials held in inventory but in regular use: relevant cost = replacement cost

Materials not yet purchased: relevant cost = purchase cost.

Total relevant cost = 800 kg × $53 = $42,400

(Note: The $53 price already includes the recent price increase.)

4 **D**

	$
Opportunity cost: sale value forgone	2,900
Disposal cost after completion of contract	500
Total relevant cost of machine	3,400

If the machine is used for the contract, the company will lose the sale (opportunity cost $2,900) and in addition it will have to pay an extra $500 when the contract is complete in order to dispose of the machine which will now be worthless.

Chapter 15: Limiting factors and linear programming

Exercise 1

	W	X	Y	Z
	$	$	$	$
Sales price/unit	50.0	31.5	59.75	54.25
Variable cost/unit	10.0	11.5	11.75	12.25
Contribution per unit	40.0	20.0	48.00	42.00
Direct materials per unit ($)	5	4	8	6
Contribution/$1 direct material	$8.0	$5.0	$6.0	$7.0
Priority for making and selling	1st	4th	3rd	2nd

Profit-maximising budget

Product	Sales units	Direct materials	Contribution per unit	Total contribution
		$	$	$
W (1st)	4,000	20,000	40	160,000
Z (2nd)	3,000	18,000	42	126,000
Y (3rd) - balance	5,000	40,000	48	240,000
		78,000		526,000

Exercise 2

The objective function is to maximise total contribution: 6x + 4y.

Subject to the following constraints:

Direct materials	4x + 2.5y	≤	105,000
Skilled labour	0.5 x + 0.5y	≤	16,500
Unskilled labour	1.25x + 2y	≤	56,000
Sales demand, Standard	x	≤	20,000
Sales demand, Economy	y	≤	16,000
Non-negativity	x, y	≥	0

If you do not like figures with fractions in a constraint, the constraints could be expressed as follows:

Direct materials	8x + 5y	≤	210,000
Skilled labour	x + y	≤	33,000
Unskilled labour	5x + 8y	≤	224,000

1 **A**

	Total units	**Material**		**Labour**	
		Per unit	**Total**	**Per unit**	**Total**
Required		kg	kg	hours	hours
Product S	4,000	2.4	9,600	2.25	9,000
Product T	6,000	2.0	12,000	1.50	9,000
			21,600		18,000
Available			21,500		18,200
Surplus/(shortfall)			(100)		200

Materials are a limiting factor but labour time is not a limiting factor.

2 **D**

The labour constraint is 4x + 0.5y ≤ 3,300, but this can be multiplied by two to remove the decimal figures: 8x + y ≤ 6,600.

3 **B**

An iso-contribution line furthest from the origin of the graph but within the feasible area for a solution is at point B.

4 **B**

On line (1), when x = 0, y = 4,000. When y = 0, x = 3,000.
The appropriate equation for the constraint line is therefore 4x + 3y = 12,000.

5 **B**

The optimal solution is at point B, where the following simultaneous equations apply:

Line(1)	4x + 3y	=	12,000
Line (3)	2x + 5y	=	13,000
Multiply Line (3) by 2:			
(4)	4x + 10y	=	26,000
Subtract (1) from (4):			
	7y	=	14,000
Therefore	y	=	2,000
Substitute in Line (1)	4x + 6,000	=	12,000
	4x	=	6,000
	x	=	1,500

Therefore total contribution = (1,500 × \$3) + (2,000 × \$4) = \$12,500.

6 **D**

	X	**Y**	**Z**
Labour hours per unit	0.5	0.667	0.875
Contribution per unit	\$7	\$12	\$14
Contribution per hour	\$14	\$18	\$16
Priority for manufacture	3	1	2

Product	**Units**	**Hours**	**Contribution**
			\$
Y	30,000	20,000	360,000
Z (balance)	8,000	7,000	112,000
		27,000	472,000

Q&A

Practice questions

Contents

1 Income statement

From the following information, prepare a budgeted income statement for the year to 31 December Year 6.

	$
Purchases of direct materials	243,000
Production overheads	270,000
Administration overheads	150,000
Marketing overheads	220,000
Sales	1,200,000
Direct labour cost	187,500
Inventories at 1 January Year 6:	
Direct materials	21,000
Work in progress	5,000
Finished goods	34,000
Inventories at 31 December Year 6:	
Direct materials	19,000
Work in progress	7,500
Finished goods	50,000

2 Cost behaviour

From the information in this cost behaviour graph, describe the behaviour of this item of cost, and calculate the total cost at 10,000 units of output.

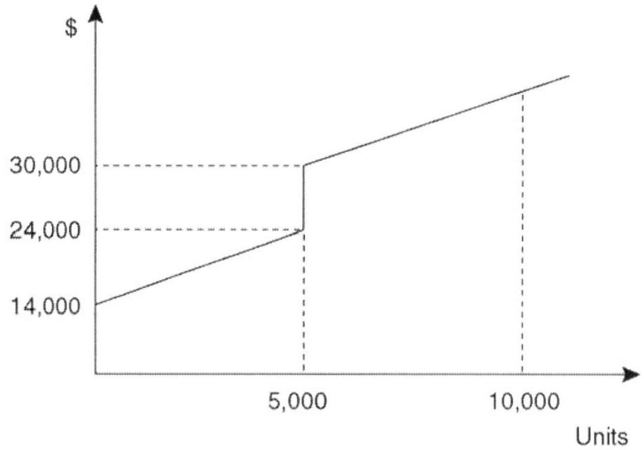

3 High/low analysis

A manufacturing company has budgeted to operate for 110,500 hours in the year, which is 85% capacity. Expected total costs for the year are $615,200.

The management accountant has also estimated that at 100% capacity, total annual costs would be $662,000.

Required

Using high/low analysis, estimate the variable cost per hour worked and the total annual fixed costs.

4 Maintenance and repair costs

Entity Z is trying to obtain a cost estimate for the costs of repairs. The following monthly repair costs have been recorded for the past six months.

Month	Number of machines repaired	Cost of repairs
		$
1	38	31,000
2	41	32,700
3	25	26,500
4	21	23,600
5	36	29,900
6	32	28,900

Required

Use high/low analysis to estimate the fixed costs of repairs each month and the variable cost per machine repaired.

Estimate the expected costs of repairs in a month when 30 machines are repaired.

5 Regression

Total production costs each week in a production department have been measured for the past five weeks, as follows.

Week	Units produced	Total cost
		$000
1	5	20
2	9	27
3	4	17
4	5	19
5	6	23

Required

(a) Use linear regression analysis to obtain an estimate of fixed costs per week and the variable cost of production per unit.

(b) Use your results to estimate total costs in a week when 8 units are produced.

(c) Calculate the correlation coefficient and comment on the value of r that you have obtained.

(d) Estimate a value for fixed costs and variable costs from the same data, using the high/low analysis, and use the values that you obtain to estimate total costs in a week when 8 units are produced.

6 Stock items 6786 and 6787

(a) A company uses 15,000 units of stock item 6786 each year. The item has a purchase cost of $4 per unit. The cost of placing an order for re-supply is $220. The annual holding cost of one unit of the item is 10% of its purchase cost.
Required

(i) What is the economic order quantity for item 6786, to the nearest unit?

(ii) What would be the effect of an increase in the annual holding cost per unit on (1) the EOQ and (2) total annual ordering costs?

(b) Data relating to stores item 6787 are as follows.

Daily use:	300 units
Lead time for re-supply:	5 – 20 days
Reorder quantity:	10,000 units

Required

What should be the reorder level for this stock item, to avoid the possibility of inventory-outs?

7 Inventory control

Entity G uses 105 units of an item of inventory every week. These cost $150 per unit. They are stored in special storage units and the variable costs of holding the item is $4 per unit each year plus 2% of the inventory's cost.

Required

(a) If placing an order for this item of material costs $390 for each order, what is the optimum order quantity to minimise annual costs? Assume that there are 52 weeks in each year.

(b) Suppose that the supplier offers a discount of 1% on the purchase price for order sizes of 2,000 units or more. What will be the order size to minimise total annual costs?

8 Economic batch quantity

A machine has the capacity to operate for 40 weeks each year during a 50-week year. It is used to manufacture several items, including component 3456. Component 3456 is produced in batches.

The machine is able to produce 8,000 units of item 3456 per hour. The cost of set-up for each batch is $6,000. Demand for the component occurs at an even rate throughout the year, and totals 2.5 million units per year. The cost of holding one unit of component 3456 in inventory is $1.50 per unit per year.

Required

(a) Calculate the economic batch production quantity for component 3456 to the nearest 10,000 units.

(b) Calculate the total costs per year of setting up the batches and inventory holding costs for this component, assuming the item is produced in batches of the size calculated in your answer to part (a).

9 Piece work

A production company pays the workers in a production department on a piece work basis. The workers produce a standard item, and the standard time allowed for the purpose of calculating pay is five minutes per unit. The company also guarantees these workers 75% of a time-based rate of pay, based on a rate of $24 per hour for a 7.5 hour day, and a five-day week. Piece work is paid at the rate of $20 per standard hour.

Required

What will be the weekly pay for a worker who produces:

(a) 444 units per week

(b) 400 units per week?

10 Labour cost

Two grades of direct labour workers are employed to produce units of Product 1234. There are 40 Grade 1 employees and 20 Grade 2 employees. All employees work a basic week of 40 hours. Grade 1 employees are paid $10 per hour and Grade 2 employees are paid $15 per hour. If employees work any overtime, they are paid at time-and-one-third (a premium of one third over the basic rate). There are also five 'support workers', such as maintenance engineers, who are paid $12 per hour for a basic 40-hour week.

During Week 23, the Grade 1 employees and support workers each worked 40 hours, and the Grade 2 employees worked 46 hours. Due to difficulties with some equipment, 250 hours of Grade 1 labour and 100 hours of Grade 2 labour were recorded as idle time in the week.

During Week 23, 4,000 units of Product 1234 were manufactured.

Required

(a) Calculate the direct labour costs and the indirect labour costs in Week 23.

(b) Calculate the direct labour cost per unit of Product 1234 in Week 23.

11 Overhead cost per unit

A company makes two products, Product X and Product Y. Each product is processed through two cost centres, CC1 and CC2. The following budgeted data is available.

	CC1	CC2
Allocated and apportioned overheads	$126,000	$180,000
(All overheads are fixed costs.)		
Direct labour hours per unit		
Product X	1.5	2.0
Product Y	1.2	2.6

The budgeted production is 12,000 units of Product X and 10,000 units of Product Y. Fixed overheads are absorbed into costs on a direct labour hour basis.

Required

Calculate the budgeted total fixed overhead cost per unit for Product X and for Product Y.

12 Apportionment

A production centre has three production departments, A, B and C.

Budgeted production overhead costs for the next period are as follows:

	$
Factory rent	60,000
Equipment depreciation	80,000
Insurance	20,000
Heating and lighting	18,000
Indirect materials:	
Department A	7,000
Department B	6,600
Department C	9,400
Indirect labour:	
Department A	40,000
Department B	27,000
Department C	20,000

Insurance costs relate mainly to health and safety insurance, and will be apportioned on the basis of the number of employees in each department. Heating and lighting costs will be apportioned on the basis of volume.

Other relevant information is as follows:

	Total	**Department A**	**Department B**	**Department C**
Direct labour hours	18,000	8,000	6,000	4,000
Number of employees	50	20	16	14
Floor area (square metres)	1,200	300	400	500
Cost of equipment ($000s)	1,000	200	600	200
Volume (cubic metres)	18,000	8,000	6,000	4,000

Required

(a) Calculate the overhead costs for each production department.

(b) Calculate an overhead absorption rate for the period for each department, assuming that a separate direct labour hour absorption rate is used for each department.

(c) Calculate an overhead absorption rate for the period, assuming that a single factory-wide direct labour hour absorption rate is used.

13 Service departments

In a factory with four production departments and two service departments, the operating costs for the month of October were as shown below.

	$
Production Department 1	700,000
Production Department 2	300,000
Production Department 3	400,000
Service departments	
Canteen	78,000
Boiler house	100,000
	1,578,000

The costs of running the canteen are apportioned to each department on the basis of the estimated use of the canteen by employees in each department.

The costs of the boiler house are apportioned on the basis of the estimated consumption of power by each department.

The service departments' costs are therefore apportioned as follows:

	Canteen	**Boiler house**
	%	%
Production Department 1	40	30
Production Department 2	20	30
Production Department 3	30	20
Service departments		
Canteen	-	20
Boiler house	10	-

Required

Prepare a statement showing the allocation of costs to the production departments using:

(a) the repeated distribution method

(b) the algebraic method or simultaneous equations method.

14 Volume and expenditure variances

A production manager is studying the cost report for the six-month period that has just ended. The production department incurred overhead costs of $680,000 and had under-absorbed overheads of $46,400. The actual direct labour hours worked in the department were 48,000 hours, which was 2,000 hours less than budgeted.

Required

(a) Calculate the budgeted absorption rate per direct labour hour.

(b) Calculate the budgeted overhead expenditure.

(c) Calculate the overhead expenditure and overhead volume variances in the period.

15 Plack Company

Plack Company is a manufacturing company that makes and sells a single product. The following information relates to the company's manufacturing operations in the next financial year.

Opening and closing stock:	Nil
Production:	18,000 units
Sales:	15,000 units
Fixed production overheads:	$117,000
Fixed sales overheads:	$72,000

Using absorption costing, the company has calculated that the budgeted profit for the year will be $43,000.

Required

What would be the budgeted profit if marginal costing is used, instead of absorption costing?

16 Differences

Entity T manufactures a single product, and uses absorption costing. The following data relates to the performance of the entity during October.

Profit	$37,000
Over-absorbed overhead	$24,000
Sales (48,000 units)	$720,000
Non-production overheads (all fixed costs)	$275,000
Opening inventory	$144,000
Closing inventory	$162,000

Units of inventory are valued at $9 each, consisting of a variable cost (all direct costs) of $3 and a fixed overhead cost of $6. All overhead costs are fixed costs.

Required

Calculate:

(a) the actual production overhead cost for October

(b) the profit that would have been reported in October if Entity T had used marginal costing.

17 Marginal and absorption

Entity RH makes and sells one product. Currently, it uses absorption costing to measure profits and inventory values. The budgeted production cost per unit is as follows:

		$
Direct labour	3 hours at $6 per hour	18
Direct materials	4 kilograms at $7 per kilo	28
Production overhead	(Fixed cost)	20
		66

Normal output volume is 16,000 units per year and this volume is used to establish the fixed overhead absorption rate for each year.

Costs relating to sales, distribution and administration are:

- Variable 20% of sales value
- Fixed $180,000 per year.

There were no units of finished goods inventory at 1 October Year 5.
The fixed overhead expenditure is spread evenly throughout the year.
The selling price per unit is $140.

For the two six-monthly periods detailed below, the number of units to be produced and sold are budgeted as follows:

	Six months ending 31 March Year 6	**Six months ending 30 September Year 6**
Production	8,500 units	7,000 units
Sales	7,000 units	8,000 units

The entity is considering whether to abandon absorption costing and use marginal costing instead for profit reporting and inventory valuation.

Required

(a) Calculate the budgeted fixed production overhead costs each year.

(b) Prepare statements for management showing sales, costs and profits for each of the six-monthly periods, using:

(i) marginal costing

(ii) absorption costing

(c) Prepare an explanatory statement reconciling for each six-monthly period the profit using marginal costing with the profit using absorption costing.

18 Job 6789

A company operates a job costing system. Job number 6789 will require $345 of direct materials and $210 of direct labour, which is paid $14 per hour. Production overheads are absorbed at the rate of $30 per direct labour hour and non-production overheads are absorbed at the rate of 40% of prime cost.

Required

What is the total expected cost of the job?

19 Process costing: the basic rules

The following examples take you through the basic rules for process costing.

Required

For each of the following examples, calculate:

(a) the cost of completed output from the process, and

(b) if there is any, the cost of any abnormal loss or the value of any abnormal gain

Example 1

1,500 litres of a liquid were input to a process at a cost of $7,200. Normal loss is 20% of the input quantity. Actual loss was equal to the normal loss.

Example 2

1,500 litres of liquid were input to a process at a cost of $7,200. A normal loss of 20% of the input is expected. The actual output for the period was only 1,100 litres.

Example 3

1,500 litres of liquid were input to a process at a cost of $7,200. A normal loss of 20% of the input is expected. Loss is sold as scrap, for a net sales price of $0.40 per litre. The actual output from the process was 1,200 litres.

Example 4

1,500 litres of liquid were input to a process at a cost of $7,200. The output from the process was 1,100 litres. Normal loss is 20% of the input quantity. Any lost units have a scrap value of $0.40 per litre.

Example 5

1,500 litres of liquid were input to a process at a cost of $7,200. Normal loss is 20% of the input quantity but the actual output for the period was 1,250 litres. Loss has no scrap value.

Example 6

1,500 litres of liquid were input to a process at a cost of $7,200. The output from the process was 1,250 units. Normal loss is 20% of the input quantity. Any lost units have a scrap value of $0.40 per litre.

20 Process 1 and Process 2

A manufacturing company operates two processes. Output from Process 1 is transferred as input to Process 2. Output from Process 2 is the finished product.

Data for the two processes in January are as follows:

Process 1

Opening work in process	Nil
Units introduced into the process	14,000
Units completed and transferred to the next process (Process 2)	10,000
Closing work-in-progress	4,000
Material cost added during the period	$70,000
Conversion cost added during the period	$48,000

Materials are input into Process 1 at the start of the process and conversion costs are incurred at a constant rate throughout processing. The closing work-in-progress in Process 1 at the end of January is estimated to be 50% complete for the conversion work.

Process 2

Opening work-in-process	Nil
Units transferred into the process from Process 1	10,000
Closing work-in-progress	1,000
Units completed and transferred to finished goods inventory	9,000
Costs for the period:	
Cost of production transferred from Process 1	$90,000
Conversion cost added during the period	$57,000
Added materials during Process 2	$36,000

The materials from Process 1 are introduced at the start of processing in Process 2, but the added materials are introduced at the end of the process. Conversion costs are incurred at a constant rate throughout processing. The closing work-in-progress in Process 2 at the end of January is estimated to be 50% complete.

Required

Calculate:

(a) the cost of completed output from Process 1 and Process 2

(b) the cost of the closing work-in-process in each process at the end of January.

(c) Prepare the Process 1 account and the Process 2 account for January.

21 Equivalent units

XYZ operates several process production systems.

(a) For Process 5, the FIFO method of valuing opening work-in-progress is used, and the following details relate to September Year 5.

Opening work-in-process was 600 units, each 80% processed as to materials and 60% processed as to conversion costs.

Finished output was 14,500 units. There were no abnormal losses or gains.

Closing work-in-process was 800 units, each 70% processed as to materials and 40% processed as to conversion costs.

Costs of processing during the current period were:

Materials: $36,450

Conversion costs: $17,352.

Required

Calculate the cost per equivalent unit of output produced during September (= one unit started and completed during the month).

(b) The following details relate to Process 16 in September Year 5:

Opening work-in-progress	2,000 litres, fully complete as to materials and 40% complete as to conversion. The cost of materials in the opening WIP was $9,860 and conversion costs in the opening WIP were $4,700.
Material input	24,000 litres, cost $130,540
Conversion costs in the month	$82,960
Output to process 2	23,000 litres
Closing work-in-progress	3,000 litres, fully complete as to materials and 45% complete as to conversion.

The weighted average cost system is used for inventory valuation in Process 16.

Required

Calculate the cost per unit of output from this process during September.

22 Joint process

In a joint process, two joint products are made, Product A and Product B. There are no inventory of work-in-process. Information relating to last month's production is set out in the table below.

Joint product	Opening inventory	Closing inventory	Sales
	units	units	units
A	800	1,200	8,000
B	700	300	10,000

The costs of the joint process in the month were $144,000. These are apportioned between the joint products on the basis of units produced.

Required

Calculate the joint processing costs for the month that are charged to each product.

23 Sales budget

A company makes and sells two products, Product A and Product B. The sales price and expected sales volume for each product next year are as follows:

	Product A	Product B
Sales price per unit	$2.50	$4.00
Budgeted sales volume	50,000	80,000

Required

Prepare the sales budget for the company for next year.

24 Production budget

A company produces Product L. Budgeted sales for Product L are 20,000 units for next year. Opening inventory is 2,500 units and planned closing inventory is 2,000 units.

Required

Prepare the production budget for Production L for next year.

25 Labour budget

A company makes Product DOY which requires two grades of labour, Grade I and Grade II.

Product DOY requires 4 hours of Grade I labour and (at $12 per hour) and 7 hours of Grade II labour (at $15 per hour).

Budgeted production of Product DOY is 25,000 units for the forthcoming year.

Required

Prepare the labour budget for Product DOY for the forthcoming year.

26 Materials budget

A company manufactures a single product. A single direct material, material X, is used in its manufacture. A budget is being prepared for next year. Opening inventory is expected to be 2,000 units of finished goods and 30,000 units of direct material X. Each unit of the product requires 5 kilos of material X.

Budgeted sales next year are 25,000 units of the product. It is also planned to increase finished goods inventory to 4,000 units before the end of the year and to reduce inventories of direct material X by 50%.

Required

Prepare a materials usage budget and a material purchase budget for material X

27 Simple variances

(a) Z plc uses a standard costing system and has the following labour cost standard in relation to one of its products:

4 hours of skilled labour at $6.00 per hour: $24.00

During October, 3,350 units of this products were made, which was 150 units less than budgeted. The labour cost incurred was $79,893 and the number of direct labour hours worked was 13,450.

Required

Calculate the direct labour rate and efficiency variances for the month.

(b) Entity J uses a standard costing system and has the following data relating to one of its products:

	$ per unit	$ per unit
Selling price		9.00
Variable cost	4.00	
Fixed cost	3.00	
		7.00
Profit		2.00

The budgeted sales for October Year 5 were 800 units, but the actual sales were 850 units. The revenue earned from these sales was $7,480.

Required

Calculate the sales price and sales volume variances for October using:

(i) standard absorption costing

(ii) standard marginal costing.

The standard fixed production cost of a product is $20, which is 4 hours at a rate of $5 per direct labour hour.

(c) The budget was to produce 15,000 units. The standard fixed production cost of a product is $20, which is 4 hours at a rate of $5 per direct labour hour. Actual production was 14,600 units and actual fixed production overhead expenditure was $325,000. The production output was manufactured in 58,000 hours of work.

Required

Calculate:

(i) the fixed production overhead total cost variance

(ii) the fixed production overhead expenditure variance and volume variance

(iii) the fixed production overhead efficiency variance and capacity variance

28 Overhead variances

A company operates a standard overhead absorption costing system. The standard fixed overhead rate per hour is $25. The following data relate to last month:

Actual hours worked	8,250
Budgeted hours	9,000
Standard hours of actual production	7,800
Actual fixed overhead expenditure	$211,000

Required

Calculate for the month:

(a) the fixed overhead capacity variance

(b) the fixed overhead efficiency variance

(c) the fixed overhead expenditure variance.

29 Standard cost sheet

The following data relates to actual output, actual costs and variances for the four-weekly accounting period number 4 of a company which makes only one product.

The value of work-in-progress at the end of period 4 was the same as the value of work-in-progress at the beginning of the month.

Actual production of Product XY	18,000 units
Actual costs incurred:	$000
Direct materials purchased and used (150,000 kg)	210
Direct labour costs (32,000 hours)	136
Variable production overhead	38

Variances:	$000	
Direct materials price	15	Favourable
Direct materials usage	9	Adverse
Direct labour rate	8	Adverse
Direct labour efficiency	16	Favourable
Variable production overhead expenditure	6	Adverse
Variable production overhead efficiency	4	Favourable

Variable production overhead varies with labour hours worked.
A standard marginal costing system is operated.

Required

Present a standard product cost sheet for one unit of Product XY, showing how the standard marginal production cost of the product is made up.

30 Margin of safety

A company makes a single product that it sells at $80 per unit. The total fixed costs are $360,000 for the period and the contribution/sales ratio is 60%. Budgeted production and sales for the period is 8,000 units.

Required

Calculate the margin of safety for the period, as a percentage of the budgeted sales.

31 Current year and next year

A company makes and sells a single product. The following data relates to the current year's budget.

Sales and production (units):	8,000
Variable cost per unit:	$20
Fixed cost per unit:	$25
Contribution/sales ratio:	60%

The selling price next year will be 6% higher than the price in the current year budget and the variable cost per unit will be 5% higher than in the current year budget. Budgeted fixed costs next year will be 10% higher than budgeted fixed costs in the current year.

Required

(a) For the current year, calculate:

(i) the budgeted contribution per unit

(ii) the budgeted total profit

(b) For next year, calculate the number of units that will have to be sold in order to achieve a total profit that is equal to the budgeted profit in the current year.

32 CVP

(a) Entity D makes a single product which it sells for $10 per unit. Fixed costs are $48,000 each month and the product has a contribution/sales ratio of 40%.

Required

If budgeted sales for the month are $140,000, what is the margin of safety in units?

(b) Entity E has monthly sales of $128,000, but at this level of sales, its monthly profit is only $2,000 and its margin of safety is 6.25%.

Required

Calculate:

(i) the monthly fixed costs

(ii) the level of monthly sales needed to increase the monthly profit to $5,000.

33 Break-even

You are a management accountant for a business that develops specialist computers. You are consulted to investigate the viability of marketing a new type of hand-held computer.

With the help of the manager of research and development, the production manager, the buyer and the sales manager, you have made the following estimates of annual sales and profitability:

Sales	Profit/(loss)
units	$
12,000	(30,000)
15,000	150,000
18,000	330,000

The selling price will be $150.

Required

(a) Prepare a traditional break-even chart using the information given above.

(b) Calculate the margin of safety if annual sales are expected to be 15,000 units.

34 Machine

A company bought a machine six years ago for $125,000. Its written down value is now $25,000. The machine is no longer used for normal production work, and it could be sold now for $17,500. A project is being considered that would make use of this machine for six months. After this time the machine would be sold for $10,000.

Required

Calculate the relevant cost of the machine to the project.

35 Relevant cost of labour

A contract is under consideration which would require 1,400 hours of direct labour. There is spare capacity of 500 hours of direct labour, due to the cancellation of another order by a customer. The other time would have to be found by asking employees to work in the evenings and at weekends, which would be paid at 50% above the normal hourly rare of $15.

Alternatively, the additional hours could be found by switching labour from other work which earns a contribution of $5 per hour.

Required

Calculate the relevant cost of direct labour if the contract is accepted and undertaken.

36 Domco

Domco makes and sells a single product, Product P. It is currently producing 112,000 units per month, and is operating at 80% of full capacity. Total monthly costs at the current level of capacity are $611,000. At 100% capacity, total monthly costs would be $695,000. Fixed costs would be the same per month at all levels of capacity between 85% and 100%.

At the normal selling price for Product P, the contribution/sales ratio is 60%.

A new customer has offered to buy 25,000 units of Product P each month, at 20% below the normal selling price. Domco estimates that for every five units that it sells to this customer, it will lose one unit of its current monthly sales to other customers.

Required

(a) Calculate the variable cost per unit of Product P and total fixed costs per month.

(b) Calculate the current normal sales price per unit, and the contribution per unit at this price.

(c) Calculate the effect on total profit each month of accepting the new customer's offer, and selling 25,000 units per month to this customer. Recommend whether the customer's offer should be accepted.

37 Limiting factors

Entity X manufactures four liquids: A, B, C and D. The selling price and unit cost details for these products are as follows:

	Liquid A	Liquid B	Liquid C	Liquid D
	$ per litre	$ per litre	$ per litre	$ per litre
Selling price	100	110	120	120
Costs:				
Direct materials	24	30	16	21
Direct labour ($6/hour)	18	15	24	27
Direct expenses	0	0	3	0
Variable overhead	12	10	16	18
Fixed overhead (note 1)	24	20	32	36
Total cost per litre	78	75	91	102
Profit per litre	22	35	29	18

Note 1

Fixed overhead is absorbed on the basis of labour hours, based on a budget of 1,600 hours per quarter (three months).

During the next three months the number of direct labour hours is expected to be limited to 1,345 hours. The same labour is used for all products.

The marketing director has identified the maximum demand for each of the four products during the next three months as follows:

Liquid A	200 litres
Liquid B	150 litres
Liquid C	100 litres
Liquid D	120 litres

No inventory is held at the beginning of the period that could be used to satisfy demand in the period.

Required

(a) Determine the number of litres of liquids A, B, C and D to be produced and sold in the next three months in order to maximise profits.

(b) Calculate the profit that this would yield.

38 Proglin

Proglin is a manufacturing company. It makes and sells two versions of a product, Mark 1 and Mark 2. The two products are made from the same direct materials and by the same direct labour employees.

The following budgeted data has been prepared for next year.

	Mark 1	Mark 2
Direct materials per unit	$2	$4
Direct labour hours per unit	3 hours	2 hours
Maximum sales demand	5,000 units	unlimited
Contribution per unit	$10 per unit	$15 per unit

Direct materials and direct labour will be in restricted supply next year, as follows:

	Maximum available
Direct materials	$24,000
Direct labour hours	18,000 hours

There is no inventory of finished goods at the beginning of the year.

Required

Use the graphical method of linear programming to identify the quantities of Mark 1 and Mark 2 that should be made and sold during the year in order to maximise profit and contribution.

Calculate the amount of contribution that will be earned.

Q&A

Answers to practice questions

Contents

1 Income statement

Income statement for the year to 31 December Year 6

	$	$
Sales		1,200,000
Opening inventory, direct materials	21,000	
Purchases	243,000	
	264,000	
Closing inventory, direct materials	(19,000)	
Direct materials used in production	245,000	
Direct labour	187,500	
Production overheads	270,000	
Production costs in the period	702,500	
Opening inventory, work-in-progress	5,000	
Closing inventory, work-in-progress	(7,500)	
Cost of finished production	700,000	
Opening inventory, finished goods	34,000	
Closing inventory, finished goods	(50,000)	
Production cost of sales	684,000	
Administration overheads	150,000	
Sales and distribution overheads	220,000	
Cost of sales		1,054,000
Profit		146,000

2 Cost behaviour

The cost item is a mixed cost. Up to 5,000 units of output, total fixed costs are $14,000 and the variable cost per unit is $(24,000 – 14,000)/5,000 units = $2 per unit.

At the 5,000 units of output, there is a step increase in fixed costs of $6,000 (from $24,000 total costs to $30,000 total costs). Total fixed costs therefore rise from $14,000 to $20,000. The variable cost per unit remains unchanged.

At the 10,000 units level, total costs are therefore:

	$
Variable costs (10,000 × $2)	20,000
Fixed costs	20,000
Total costs	40,000

3 High/low analysis

110,500 hours = 85% capacity.
Therefore 100% capacity = 110,500 hours/85% = 130,000 hours.

	hours		$
High: Total cost of	130,000	=	662,000
Low: Total cost of	110,500	=	615,200
Difference: Variable cost of	19,500	=	46,800

Therefore the variable cost per hour = $46,800/19,500 hours = $2.40.

Substitute in high equation	**Cost**
	$
Total cost of 130,000 hours	662,000
Variable cost of 130,000 hours (× $2.40)	312,000
Therefore fixed costs	350,000

4 Maintenance and repair costs

	Units		**$**
High: Total cost of	41	=	32,700
Low: Total cost of	21	=	23,600
Difference: Variable cost of	20	=	9,100

Therefore variable cost per unit repaired = $9,100/20 hours = $455.

Substitute in low equation	**Cost**
	$
Total cost of 21 units	23,600
Variable cost of 21 units (≥ $455)	9,555
Therefore fixed costs per month	14,045

Cost estimate for 30 units	**Cost**
	$
Fixed costs	14,045
Variable cost of 30 units (x $455)	13,650
Estimated total costs	27,695

If this estimate is used to prepare a budget for a period, it might be rounded to a convenient number, say $27,700.

5 Regression

Workings

Output	**Total cost**			
units	**$000**			
x	y	Σx²	Σxy	Σy²
5	20	25	100	400
9	27	81	243	729
4	17	16	68	289
5	19	25	95	361
6	23	36	138	529
29	106	183	644	2,308
= Σx	= Σy	= Σx²	= Σxy	= Σy²

There are five pairs of data, so n = 5.

$$b = \frac{n\Sigma xy - \Sigma x \Sigma y}{n\Sigma x^2 - (\Sigma x)^2}$$

$$b = \frac{5(644) - (29)(106)}{5(183) - (29)^2} = \frac{3{,}220 - 3{,}074}{915 - 841} = \frac{146}{74}$$

b (in $000) = 1.97

$$a = \frac{\Sigma y}{n} - \frac{b\,\Sigma x}{n}$$

$$a = \frac{106}{5} - \frac{1.97\,(29)}{5} = 21.2 - 11.4$$

a (in $000) = 9.8

Answer

(a) The estimate of monthly fixed costs and the variable cost per unit is therefore:

y = 9,800 + 1,970x.

(b) When output is expected to be 8 units, the expected total costs will be:

	$
Fixed	9,800
Variable (8 x $1,970)	15,760
Total costs	25,560

(c) The value of the correlation coefficient, r, in this example is:

$$r = \frac{146}{\sqrt{(74)[5(2{,}308) - (106)^2]}}$$

$$= \frac{146}{\sqrt{(74)(11{,}540 - 11{,}236)}}$$

$$= \frac{146}{\sqrt{(74)(304)}}$$

$$= \frac{146}{150} = +0.97$$

The correlation coefficient is + 0.97. This is high, indicating a high degree of positive correlation and suggesting that the estimates of costs based on the formula should be reliable.

(d) **Using the high/low analysis:**

	units		$000
High: Total cost of	9	=	27
Low: Total cost of	4	=	17
Difference: Variable cost of	5	=	10

Therefore variable cost per unit produced = $10,000/5 units = $2,000.

Substitute in low equation	**Cost**
	$
Total cost of 4 units	17,000
Variable cost of 4 units (× $2,000)	8,000
Therefore fixed costs per week	9,000

Cost estimate for 8 units	**Cost**
	$
Fixed costs	9,000
Variable cost of 8 units (× $2,000)	16,000
Estimated total costs	25,000

6 Stock items 6786 and 6787

(a) (i) $\text{EOQ} = \sqrt{\dfrac{2 \times 220 \times 15{,}000}{0.40}} = 4{,}062 \text{ units}$

(ii) If the annual holding cost per unit increases to more than $0.40 per unit, the EOQ will become smaller.

If the EOQ is smaller, there will be more orders each year; therefore total annual ordering costs will increase.

(b) Reorder level to avoid inventory-outs
= Daily demand × Maximum lead time
= 300 units × 20 days
= 6,000 units.

7 Inventory control

(a) The annual holding cost per unit of inventory = $4 + (2% × $150) = $7.
Annual demand = 52 weeks × 105 units = 5,460 units.

$$\text{EOQ} = \sqrt{\frac{2 \times 390 \times 5{,}460}{7}} = 780 \text{ units.}$$

(b) A discount on the price is available for order sizes of 2,000 units or more, which is above the EOQ.

The order size that minimises cost is therefore either the EOQ or the minimum order size to obtain the discount, which is 2,000 units.

Annual costs	Order size 780 units	Order size 2,000 units
	$	$
Purchases		
(5,460 × \$150): ((5,460 × \$150 × 99%)	819,000	810,810
Holding costs	2,730	7,000
(\$7 × 780/2): (\$7 × 2,000/2)		
Ordering costs	2,730	1,065
(\$390 × 5,460/780): (\$390 × 5,460/2,000)		
Total costs	824,460	818,875

Conclusion

The order size that will minimise total annual costs is 2,000 units.

8 Economic batch quantity

(a) Production capacity of the machine = 8,000 per hour × 40 hours per week × 50 weeks per year = 16 million units. Economic batch quantity =

$$\sqrt{\frac{2 \text{ x } 6{,}000 \text{ x } 2.5 \text{ million}}{1.50\left(1-\dfrac{2.5 \text{ million}}{16 \text{ million}}\right)}}$$

= 153,960 units.

To the nearest 10,000 units, this is 150,000 units.

(b) Average inventory = Q (1 – D/R)/2
= 150,000 [1 – (2.5 million/16 million)]/2
= 126,562.5/2 units = 63,281.25 units

		$
Annual holding costs	63,281.25 units × \$1.50	94,922
Annual set-up costs	(2.5 million/390,000) × \$6,000	38,462
		133, 384

(With the economic batch quantity formula, the total annual holding costs and total annual set-up costs are not equal.)

9 Piece work

The minimum guaranteed wage = 75% of (7.5 hours × 5 days × \$24 per hour) = 75% of \$900 = \$675 per week.
For piece work calculations, 1 unit = 5/60 standard hours.

(1) Piecework value of 444 units per week = 444 × 5/60 × \$20 per hour = \$740

(2) Piecework value of 400 units per week = 400 × 5/60 × \$20 per hour = \$666.67

(a) If output is 444 units in the week, pay will be \$740.

(b) If output is 400 units per week, pay will be \$675 (the guaranteed minimum).

10 Labour cost

(a)

		Total worked	Idle time	Worked on production		Overtime
		hours	hours	hours		hours
Grade 1	(40 × 40)	1,600	250	1,350		
Grade 2	(20 × 46)	920	100	820	(20 × 6)	120

	Direct labour		Indirect labour (overhead)	
		$		$
Grade 1 basic wages	(1,350 × $10)	13,500	(250 × $10)	2,500
Grade 2 basic wages	(820 × $15)	12,300	(100 × $15)	1,500
Overtime premium			(120 x $15 × 1/3)	600
Support staff			(5 x 40 × $12)	2,400
Total		25,800		7,000

(b)

Units produced	4,000	
Direct labour cost/unit = $25,800/4,000 =	$6.45	per unit

11 Overhead cost per unit

		CC1		CC2
		Total hours		Total hours
Product X	12,000 × 1.5	18,000	12,000 × 2.0	24,000
Product Y	10,000 × 1.2	12,000	10,000 × 2.6	26,000
		30,000		50,000
Total overheads		$126,000		$180,000
Absorption rate per hour		$4.20		$3.60

Fixed overhead cost/unit		**Product X**		**Product Y**
		$		$
CC1	1.5 × $4.20	6.30	1.2 × $4.20	5.04
CC2	2.0 × $3.60	7.20	2.6 × $3.60	9.36
Total		13.50		14.40

12 Apportionment

Tutorial note: The answers to all three parts of the question are shown here, but are not labelled.

	Basis of apportionment	Total	A	B	C
		$	$	$	$
Indirect materials	Allocation	23,000	7,000	6,600	9,400
Indirect labour	Allocation	87,000	40,000	27,000	20,000
Rent	Floor area	60,000	15,000	20,000	25,000
Depreciation	Equipment cost	80,000	16,000	48,000	16,000
Insurance	Employee numbers	20,000	8,000	6,400	5,600
Heating, lighting	Volume	18,000	8,000	6,000	4,000
Total		288,000	94,000	114,000	80,000
Direct labour hours			8,000	6,000	4,000
Absorption rate	(per direct labour hour)		$11.75	$19	$20

If a single factory-wide absorption rate is used instead of separate absorption rates for each department, the absorption rate would be $16 per direct labour hour (= $288,000/18,000 hours).

13 Service departments

(a) **Repeated distribution method**

C = Canteen

BH = Boiler house

	Dept 1	Dept 2	Dept 3	C	BH
	$	$	$	$	
Initial overheads	700,000	300,000	400,000	78,000	100,00
Apportion:					
BH (30:30:20:20)	30,000	30,000	20,000	20,000	(100,000
				98,000	
C (40:20:30:10)	39,200	19,600	29,400	(98,000)	9,80
BH (30:30:20:20)	2,940	2,940	1,960	1,960	(9,800
C (40:20:30:10)	784	392	588	(1,960)	19
BH (30:30:20:20)	59	59	39	39	(196
C (40:20:30:10)	15	8	12	(39)	
BH (30:30:20:20)	1	1	1	1	(4
C (40:20:30:10)	1	0	0	(1)	
Total overhead	773,000	353,000	452,000		

(b) **Simultaneous equations method**

Let X = the total overheads apportioned from the Canteen

Let Y = the total overheads apportioned from the Boiler House

This gives us the simultaneous equations:

$$X = 78{,}000 + 0.2\,Y \quad \ldots (1)$$
$$Y = 100{,}000 + 0.1\,X \quad \ldots (2)$$

Re-arrange:

$$78{,}000 = X - 0.2\,Y \quad \ldots (1)$$
$$100{,}000 = -0.1\,X + Y \quad \ldots (2)$$

Multiply (2) by 10

$$1{,}000{,}000 = -X + 10Y \quad \ldots (3)$$

Add (1) and (3)

$1{,}078{,}000 = 9.8Y$

$Y = 110{,}000$

Therefore, from (1) and substituting $Y = 110{,}000$:

$X = 78{,}000 + 0.2\,(110{,}000) = 100{,}000$.

	Dept 1	Dept 2	Dept 3
	$	$	$
Initial overheads	700,000	300,000	400,000
Apportion:			
BH (30%, 30% and 20% of 110,000)	33,000	33,000	22,000
C (40%, 20% and 30% of 100,000)	40,000	20,000	30,000
Total overhead apportionment	773,000	353,000	452,000

14 Volume and expenditure variances

(a)

	$
Actual overhead expenditure	680,000
Under-absorbed overhead	(46,400)
Absorbed overhead	633,600
Hours worked	48,000
Therefore budgeted absorption rate per hour ($633,600/48,000)	$13.20

(b)

	hours
Actual hours worked	48,000
This was less than budget by	2,000
Budgeted hours	50,000
Absorption rate per hour	$13.20
Budgeted overhead expenditure (50,000 hours × $13.20)	$660,000

(c)

Volume variance in hours	2,000 hours	Adverse
Absorption rate per hour	$13.20	
Volume variance in $	$26,400	Adverse

	$	
Actual overhead expenditure	680,000	
Budgeted overhead expenditure	660,000	
Expenditure variance	20,000	Adverse

15 Plack Company

Production overhead per unit, with absorption costing:

= $117,000/18,000 units
= $6.50 per unit.

The budgeted increase in inventory = 3,000 units (18,000 – 15,000).
Production overheads in the increase in inventory = 3,000 × $6.50 = $19,500.
With marginal costing, profit will be lower than with absorption costing, because there is an increase in inventory levels.

Marginal costing profit = $43,000 - $19,500 = $23,500.

16 Differences

(a)

	units
Opening inventory (\$144,000/\$9)	16,000
Closing inventory (\$162,000/\$9)	18,000
Increase in inventory in October	2,000
Sales	48,000
Production in October	50,000

	\$
Absorbed production overhead (50,000 × \$6)	300,000
Over-absorbed overheads	24,000
Actual production overhead expenditure	276,000

(b) Inventory increased during October; therefore the reported profit will be higher with absorption costing than with marginal costing.

	\$
Absorption cost profit	37,000
Increase inventory × fixed production overhead per unit (2,000 × \$6)	12,000
Marginal costing profit	25,000

Proof:

	\$	\$
Sales		720,000
Variable cost of sales (48,000 × \$3)		144,000
Contribution		576,000
Fixed production overheads (see above)	276,000	
Other fixed overheads	275,000	
Total fixed overheads		551,000
Marginal costing profit		25,000

17 Marginal and absorption

(a) Budgeted production overhead expenditure =
Normal production volume × Absorption rate per unit
= 16,000 units × \$20 = \$320,000.
Since expenditure occurs evenly throughout the year, the budgeted production overhead expenditure is \$160,000 in each six-month period.

(b)

Workings	**\$ per unit**
Direct material	18
Direct labour	28
	46
Sales, distribution, administration (20% × \$140)	28
Marginal cost of sale	74

(i) **Marginal costing**

	Six months to 31 March		Six months to 30 September	
Units sold		7,000		8,000
	$	$	$	$
Sales at $140		980,000		1,120,000
Marginal cost of sales (at $74)		518,000		592,000
Contribution		462,000		528,000
Fixed costs				
Production ($320,000/2)	160,000		160,000	
Other ($180,000/2)	90,000		90,000	
Total fixed costs		250,000		250,000
Profit		212,000		278,000

(ii) **Absorption costing**

The fixed overhead absorption rate is based on the normal volume of production. Since budgeted output in each six-month period is different from the normal volume, there will be some under- or over-absorption of production overhead in each six-month period.

	Six months to 31 March		Six months to 30 September	
Units sold		7,000		8,000
	$	$	$	$
Sales at $140		980,000		1,120,000
Production cost of sales (at $66)		462,000		528,000
		518,000		592,000
Production overhead absorbed (8,500 × $20: 7,000 × $20)	170,000		140,000	
Actual production overhead	160,000		160,000	
Over-/(under-) absorbed overheads		10,000		(20,000)
		528,000		572,000
Sales, distribution, admin costs				
Variable (7,000 × $28: 8,000 × $28)	196,000		224,000	
Other	90,000		90,000	
		286,000		314,000
Profit		242,000		258,000

(c) **Reconciliation of profit figures**

Six months to 31 March Year 6		
Increase in inventory	(8,500 – 7,000 units)	1,500 units
Production overhead absorbed in these units (absorption costing)		$20 per unit
Therefore absorption costing profit higher by		$30,000

Six months to 31 March Year 6		
Reduction in inventory	(7,000 – 8,000 units)	1,000 units
Production overhead absorbed in these units (absorption costing)		$20 per unit
Therefore absorption costing profit lower by		$20,000

The difference in reported profits is due entirely to differences in the valuation of inventory (and so differences in the increase or reduction in inventory during each period).

18 Job 6789

	$
Direct materials	345
Direct labour (15 hours)	210
Prime cost	555
Production overheads (15 hours × $30)	450
Full production cost	1,005
Non-production overheads (40% × $555)	222
Full cost of sale for the job	1,227

19 Process costing: the basic rules

Example 1

	litres
Input	1,500
Normal loss (20%)	300
Expected output	1,200

Cost per unit of expected output = $7,200/1,200 litres = $6 per litre.

Actual output = 1,200 litres.

Cost of actual output = 1,200 litres × $6 = $7,200.

There is no abnormal loss or abnormal gain.

Example 2

	litres
Input	1,500
Normal loss (20%)	300
Expected output	1,200
Actual output	1,100
Abnormal loss	100

Cost per unit = same as in Example 1, $6 per litre.
Cost of actual output = 1,100 litres × $6 = $6,600.
Cost of abnormal loss = 100 litres × $6 = $600.

Example 3

	$
Input cost	7,200
Scrap value of normal loss (300 × $0.40)	120
Net cost of the process	7,080

Cost per unit of expected output = $7,080/1,200 litres = $5.90 per litre.
Actual output = 1,200 litres.

Cost of actual output= 1,200 litres × $5.90 = $7,080.

There is no abnormal loss or abnormal gain.

Example 4

Cost per unit = same as in Example 3, $5.90 per litre.
Cost of actual output = 1,100 litres × $5.90 = $6,490.
Cost of abnormal loss = 100 litres × $5.90 = $590.

This cost of abnormal loss is the amount recorded in the process account.

The net cost of abnormal loss is reduced (in the abnormal loss account) by the scrap value of the lost units.

	$
Cost of abnormal loss in the process account	590
Scrap value of abnormal loss (100 × $0.40)	(40)
Net cost of abnormal loss (= expense in the income statement)	550

Example 5

	litres
Input	1,500
Normal loss (20%)	300
Expected output	1,200
Actual output	1,250
Abnormal gain	50

Cost per unit = same as in Example 1, $6 per litre.
Cost of actual output = 1,250 litres × $6 = $7,500.
Value of abnormal gain = 50 litres × $6 = $300 (= debit entry in the process account)

Example 6

	litres
Input	1,500
Normal loss (20%)	300
Expected output	1,200
Actual output	1,250
Abnormal gain	50

Cost per unit = same as in Example 3, $5.90 per litre.
Cost of actual output = 1,250 litres × $5.90 = $7,375.
Value of abnormal gain = 50 litres × $5.90 = $295.

This value of abnormal gain is the amount recorded in the process account (as a debit entry).

The value cost of abnormal gain is reduced (in the abnormal gain account) by the scrap value of the units that have not been lost.

	$
Value of abnormal gain in the process account	295
Scrap value forgone: (50 × $0.40)	(20)
Net value of abnormal gain (= income in the income statement)	275

20 Process 1 and Process 2

There is no opening inventory in either process; therefore there is no difference between the weighted average cost and FIFO valuation methods.

Process 1

Equivalent units	Total	Direct materials		Conversion costs
	Total units	Equivalent units		Equivalent units
Completed units	10,000	10,000		10,000
Closing inventory	4,000	4,000	(4,000 × 50%)	2,000
Total equivalent units	14,000	14,000		12,000
Cost		$70,000		$48,000
Cost per equivalent unit		$5		$4

Statement of evaluation		Direct materials		Conversion costs	Total cost
		$		$	$
Completed units	(10,000 × $5)	50,000	(10,000 × $4)	40,000	90,000
Closing inventory	(4,000 × $5)	20,000	(2,000 × $4)	8,000	28,000
		70,000		48,000	118,000

The process account is prepared as follows:

Process 1 account

	units	$		units	$
Direct materials	14,000	70,000	Process 2 account	10,000	90,000
Conversion costs		48,000	Closing inventory c/f	4,000	28,000
	14,000	118,000		14,000	118,000

Process 2

Equivalent units	Total	Materials from Process 1	Conversion costs	Added materials
	Total units	Equivalent units	Equivalent units	Equivalent units
Completed units	9,000	9,000	9,000	9,000
Closing inventory	1,000	1,000	500	0
Total equivalent units	10,000	10,000	9,500	9,000
Cost		$90,000	$57,000	$36,000
		$9	$6	$4

Note: The added materials are added at the end of the process, which means that there are no added materials in the (unfinished) closing inventory.

Statement of evaluation	Materials from Process 1	Conversion costs	Added materials	Total cost
	$	$	$	$
Completed units	81,000	54,000	36,000	171,000
Closing inventory	9,000	3,000	0	12,000
	90,000	57,000	36,000	183,000

The process account is prepared as follows:

Process 2 account

	units	$		units	$
Materials from Process 1	10,000	90,000	Finished goods	9,000	171,000
Conversion costs		57,000			
Added materials		36,000	Closing inventory c/f	1,000	12,000
	10,000	183,000		10,000	183,000

21 Equivalent units

(a) FIFO method

Equivalent units	Total	Direct materials		Conversion costs	
	Units	Equivalent units		Equivalent units	
Completion of opening WIP	600	(20%)	120	(40%)	240
Other completed units	13,900		13,900		13,900
	14,500		14,020		14,140
Closing inventory	800	(70%)	560	(40%)	320
Total equivalent units	15,300		14,580		14,460
Costs in the current period			$36,450		$17,352
Cost per equivalent unit			$2.5		$1.2

Cost per equivalent unit of fully completed units in the current period = $2.50 + $1.20 = $3.70.

(b) Weighted average cost

Equivalent units	Total	Direct materials		Conversion costs	
	Total units	Equivalent units		Equivalent units	
Completed units	23,000		23,000		23,000
Closing inventory	3,000	(100%)	3,000	(45%)	1,350
Total equivalent units	26,000		26,000		24,350
Costs:			$		$
Opening WIP			9,860		4,700
Current period costs			130,540		82,960
Total costs			140,400		87,660
Cost per equivalent unit			$5.40		$3.60

Cost per equivalent unit of fully completed units in the current period = $5.40 + $3.60 = $9.00.

22 Joint process

	Production
	units
Joint product A: (1,200 + 8,000 – 800)	8,400
Joint product B: (300 + 10,000 – 700)	9,600
Total production	18,000

Joint processing costs	$144,000
Joint processing costs per unit	$8

Apportionment of joint costs

	$
To Joint product A: (8,400 × $8)	67,200
To Joint product B: (9,600 × $8)	76,800
	144,000

23 Sales budget

Product	Sales quantity	Sales price	Sales revenue
A	50,000	$2.50	$125,000
B	80,000	$4.00	$320,000
Total			$445,000

24 Production budget

	Units
Sales budget in units	20,000
Plus budgeted closing inventory	2,000
Less closing inventory	(2,500)
	19,500

25 Labour budget

	Grade I	Grade II	Total
	hours	hours	
To make 25,000 units DOY	100,000	175,000	275,000
Labour cost per hour	$12	$15	
Total labour cost	$1,200,000	$2,625,000	$3,825,000

26 Materials budget

Production budget	Units
Closing inventory	4,000
Sales	25,000
	29,000
Opening inventory	(2,000)
Budgeted production	27,000

Materials usage budget, material X
= 27,000 units of product × 5 kilos per unit = 135,000 kilos.

Materials purchases budget	Kilos of material X
Closing inventory	15,000
Usage in production	135,000
	150,000
Opening inventory	(30,000)
Budgeted production	120,000

27 Simple variances

(a)

Direct labour rate variance		
	$	
13,450 hours should cost (× $6)	80,700	
They did cost	79,893	
Labour rate variance	807	(F)

Direct labour efficiency variance		
	hours	
3,350 units should take (× 4 hours)	13,400	
They did take	13,450	
Efficiency variance in hours	50	(A)
Standard rate per hour	$6	
Direct labour efficiency variance in $	$300	(A)

(b)

Sales price variance	$	
850 units should sell for (× $9)	7,650	
They did sell for	7,480	
Sales price variance	170	(A)

Sales volume variance, absorption costing		
	units	
Actual sales volume (units)	850	
Budgeted sales volume (units)	800	
Sales volume variance in units	50	(F)
Standard profit per unit	$2	
Sales volume variance (profit variance)	$100	(F)

Sales volume contribution variance, marginal costing		
Sales volume variance in units	50 (F)	
Standard contribution per unit ($9 - $4)	$5	
Sales volume variance (contribution variance)	$250	(F)

(c) (i)

Fixed production overhead total cost variance

	$	
Standard fixed overhead cost of 14,600 units (× $20)	292,000	
Actual fixed overhead expenditure	325,000	
Fixed overhead total cost variance (under absorption)	33,000	(A)

(ii)

Fixed production overhead expenditure variance

	$	
Budgeted fixed overhead expenditure (15,000 × $20)	300,000	
Actual fixed overhead expenditure	325,000	
Fixed overhead expenditure variance	25,000	(A)

Fixed production overhead volume variance

	units	
Budgeted production volume	15,000	
Actual production volume	14,600	
Volume variance in units	400	(A)
Standard fixed overhead rate per unit	$20	
Fixed production overhead volume variance in $	$8,000	(A)

(iii)

Fixed production overhead efficiency variance

	hours	
14,600 units should take (× 4 hours)	58,400	
They did take	58,000	
Efficiency variance in hours	400	(F)
Standard fixed overhead rate per hour	$5	
Fixed production overhead efficiency variance in $	$2,000	(F)

Fixed production overhead capacity variance	**hours**	
Budgeted hours of work (15,000 × 4 hours)	60,000	
Actual hours of work	58,000	
Capacity variance in hours	2,000	(A)
Standard fixed overhead rate per hour	$5	
Fixed production overhead capacity variance in $	$10,000	(A)

28 Overhead variances

Fixed production overhead capacity variance

	hours	
Budgeted production hours of work	9,000	
Actual production hours of work	8,250	
Capacity variance inhours	750	(A)

Standard fixed overhead rate per hour	$25	
Fixed production overhead capacity variance in $	$18,750	(A)

Fixed production overhead efficiency variance

	hours	
Standard hours produced	7,800	
Actual hours worked	8,250	
Efficiency variance in hours	450	(A)
Standard fixed overhead rate per hour	$25	
Fixed production overhead efficiency variance in $	$11,250	(A)

Fixed production overhead expenditure variance

	$	
Budgeted fixed overhead expenditure (9,000 hours × $25)	225,000	
Actual fixed overhead expenditure	211,000	
Fixed overhead expenditure variance	14,000	(F)

29 Standard cost sheet

Tutorial note: This problem tests your understanding of the formulae for calculating variances. Here, you are given the actual costs and the variances, and have to work back to calculate the standard cost. The answer can be found by filling in the balancing figures for each variance calculation.

Materials price variance

	$	
150,000 kilos of materials did cost	210,000	
Material price variance	15,000	(F)
150,000 kilos of materials should cost	225,000	

(The variance is favourable, so the materials did cost less to buy than they should have cost.)

Therefore the standard price for materials is $225,000/150,000 kilograms = $1.50 per kilo.

Materials usage variance

Materials usage variance in $ = $9,000 (A)
Standard price for materials = $1.50
Materials usage variance in kilograms = 9,000/1.50 = 6,000 kilos (A)

	kilos	
18,000 units of the product did use	150,000	
Material usage variance in kilos	6,000	(A)
18,000 units of the product should use	144,000	

Therefore the standard material usage per unit of product = 144,000 kilos/18,000 units = 8 kilos per unit.

Direct labour rate variance		
	$	
32,000 hours of labour did cost	136,000	
Direct labour rate variance	8,000	(A)
32,000 hours of labour should cost	128,000	

Therefore the standard direct labour rate per hour = $128,000/32,000 hours = $4 per hour.

Direct labour efficiency variance

Labour efficiency variance in $ = $16,000 (F)
Standard rate per hour = $4
Labour efficiency variance in hours = 16,000/4 = 4,000 hours (F)

	hours	
18,000 units of the product did take	32,000	
Labour efficiency variance in hours	4,000	(F)
18,000 units of the product should take	36,000	

Therefore the standard time per unit of product = 36,000 hours/18,000 units = 2 hours per unit.

This number of hours per unit also applies to variable production overheads.

Variable overhead expenditure variance		
	$	
32,000 hours did cost	38,000	
Variable overhead expenditure variance	6,000	(A)
32,000 hours should cost	32,000	

Therefore the variable production overhead rate per hour = $32,000/32,000 hours = $1 per hour.

Standard marginal production cost – Product XY		$
Direct materials	(8 kilos at $1.50 per kilo)	12.0
Direct labour	(2 hours at $4 per hour)	8.0
Variable production overhead	(2 hours at $1 per hour)	2.0
Standard marginal production cost		22.0

30 Margin of safety

Contribution per unit = 60% × $80 = $48
Fixed costs = $360,000
Break-even point = $360,000/$48 per unit = 7,500 units
Budgeted sales = 8,000 units
Margin of safety = (8,000 – 7,500) units = 500 units
As a percentage of budgeted sales, the margin of safety is (500/8,000) × 100% = 6.25%.

31 Current year and next year

(a) Contribution/sales ratio = 60%
Therefore variable costs/sales ratio = 40%.
Variable cost per unit = $20
Therefore sales price per unit = $20/0.40 = $50.
Contribution per unit = $50 – $20 = $30.

	$
Budgeted contribution (8,000 × $30)	240,000
Budgeted fixed costs (8,000 × $25)	200,000
Budgeted profit, current year	40,000

(b) Sales price next year = $50 × 1.06 = $53 per unit
Variable cost per unit next year = $20 × 1.05 = $21
Therefore contribution per unit next year = $53 – $21 = $32

	$
Target profit next year	40,000
Fixed costs next year (200,000 × 1.10)	220,000
Target contribution for same profit as in the current year	260,000

Therefore target sales next year = $260,000/$32 per unit = 8,125 units.

32 CVP

(a) Break-even point = $48,000/0.40 = $120,000 (sales revenue).
Margin of safety (in sales revenue) = $140,000 – $120,000 = $20,000.
Selling price per unit = $10.
Margin of safety (in units) = $20,000/$10 = 2,000 units.

(b) (i) The margin of safety is 6.25%. Therefore the break-even volume of sales = 93.75% of budgeted sales = 0.9375 × $128,000 = $120,000

	Budget	**Break-even**
	$	$
Sales	128,000	120,000
Profit	2,000	0
Total costs	126,000	120,000

This gives us the information to calculate fixed and variable costs, using high/low analysis.

	$ Revenue		**$ Cost**
High: Total cost at	128,000	=	126,000
Low: Total cost at	120,000	=	120,000
Difference: Variable cost of	8,000	=	6,000

Therefore variable costs = $6,000/$8,000 = 0.75 or 75% of sales revenue.

Substitute in high or low equation	**Cost**
	$
Total cost at $128,000 revenue	126,000
Variable cost at $128,000 revenue (× 0.75)	96,000
Therefore fixed costs	30,000

(ii) At sales of $128,000, profit is $2,000.
The contribution/sales ratio = 100% – 75% = 25% or 0.25.
To increase profit by $3,000 to $5,000 each month, the increase in sales must be:
(Increase in profit and contribution) ÷ C/S ratio

= $3,000/0.25
= $12,000.
Sales must increase from $128,000 (by $12,000) to $140,000 each month.

Alternative approach to the answer

	$
Target profit	5,000
Fixed costs	30,000
Target contribution	35,000
C/S ratio	0.25
Therefore sales required ($35,000/0.25)	$140,000

33 Break-even

Workings

	Sales	**Sales (at $150)**	**Profit**
	units	$	$
	18,000	2,700,000	(30,000)
	12,000	1,800,000	330,000
Difference	6,000	900,000	360,000

An increase in sales from 12,000 units to 18,000 units results in an increase of $900,000 in revenue and $360,000 in contribution and profit.

From this, we can calculate that the contribution is $60 per unit ($360,000/6,000) and the C/S ratio is 0.40 ($360,000/$900,000). Variable costs are therefore 0.6 or 60% of sales.

To draw a break-even chart, we need to know the fixed costs.

Substitute in high or low equation	
When sales are 18,000 units:	$
Sales (at $150 each)	2,700,000
Variable cost (sales × 60%)	1,620,000
Contribution (sales × 40%)	1,080,000
Profit	330,000
Therefore fixed costs	750,000

When sales are 18,000 units:	**$**
Fixed costs	750,000
Variable cost (see above)	1,620,000
Total costs	2,370,000

There is now enough information to draw a break-even chart.

(a)

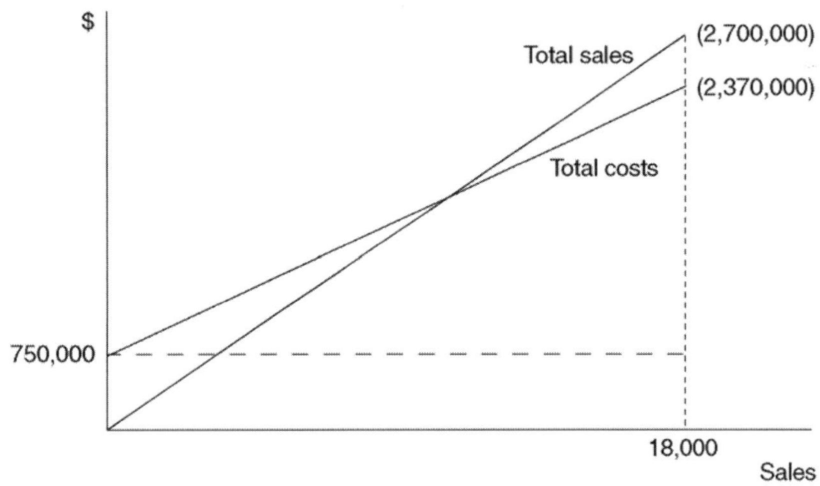

(b) Break-even point = Fixed costs ÷ C/S ratio
= $750,000/0.40 = $1,875,000
Break-even point in units = $1,875,000/$150 per unit = 12,500 units.

If budgeted sales are 15,000 units, the margin of safety is 2,500 units (15,000 – 12,500).
This is 1/6 or 16.7% of the budgeted sales volume.

34 Machine

Relevant cost = Difference between sale value now and sale value if it is used. This is the relevant cost of using the machine for the project.

Relevant cost = $17,500 - $10,000 = $7,500.

35 Relevant cost of labour

A total of 900 hours would have to be found by either working overtime at a cost of $15 × 150% = $22.50 per hour, or diverting labour from other work that earns a contribution of $5 per hour after labour costs of $15 per hour. The opportunity cost of diverting labour from other work is therefore $20 per hour. This is less than the cost of working overtime. If the contract is undertaken, labour will therefore be diverted from the other work.

It is assumed that the 500 hours of free labour time (idle time) available would be paid for anyway, even if the contract is not undertaken. The relevant cost of these hours is therefore $0.

Relevant cost of labour	$
500 hours	0
900 hours (× $20)	18,000
Total relevant cost of labour	18,000

36 Domco

(a) 100% capacity each month = 112,000 units/0.80 = 140,000 units.

Using high/low analysis:

	units		$
High: Total cost of	140,000	=	695,000
Low: Total cost of	112,000	=	611,000
Difference: Variable cost of	28,000	=	84,000

Therefore variable cost per unit = $84,000/28,000 units = $3.

Substitute in high equation	**Cost**
	$
Total cost of 140,000 units	695,000
Variable cost of 140,000 units (× $3)	420,000
Therefore fixed costs per month	275,000

(b) Contribution/sales ratio = 60%
Therefore variable cost/sales ratio = 40%
The normal sales price per unit = $3/0.40 = $7.50

The contribution per unit at the normal selling price is $7.50 – $3 = $4.50 per unit.

(c) If the customer's offer is accepted, the sales price for the 25,000 units will be $7.50 – 20% = $6 per unit.

The contribution per unit for these units will be $6 – $3 = $3.

The reduction in monthly sales at the normal price will be 1/5 × 25,000 = 5,000 units.

	$
Increase in contribution from 25,000 units sold (25,000 × $3)	75,000
Loss of contribution from fall in other sales (5,000 × $4.50)	22,500
Net increase in profit each month	52,500

By accepting the new customer's offer, the profit would increase by $52,500 each month. The offer should therefore be accepted.

37 Limiting factors

	A	B	C	D
	$	$	$	$
Sales price	100	110	120	120
Variable cost per litre	54	55	59	66
Contribution per litre	46	55	61	54
Direct labour hours/unit	3	2.5	4	4.5
Contribution /direct labour hour	$15.33	$22	$15.25	$12
Priority for manufacture/sale	2nd	1st	3rd	4th

The fixed overhead absorption rate is $8 per hour. This can be calculated from the overhead cost and direct labour hours for any of the four products.

The budgeted labour hours for calculating this absorption rate was 1,600 hours, therefore budgeted fixed costs are 1,600 hours × $8 = $12,800.

The output and sales that will maximise contribution and profit is as follows.

Product	Litres	Hours	Contribution/litre	Contribution/profit
			$	$
B	150.0	375	55	8,250.0
A	200.0	600	46	9,200.0
C (balance)	92.5	370	61	5,642.5
		1,345		23,092.5
Fixed costs (see above)				12,800.0
Profit				10,292.5

38 Proglin

Let the number of units of Mark 1 be x
Let the number of units of Mark 2 be y.

The objective function is to maximise total contribution: 10x + 15y.
Subject to the following constraints:

Direct materials	$2x + 4y$	$\leq$	24,000
Direct labour	$3x + 2y$	$\leq$	18,000
Sales demand, Mark 1	x	$\leq$	5,000
Non-negativity	x, y	$\geq$	0

These constraints are shown in the graph below. The graph also shows an iso-contribution line 10x + 15y = 60,000.

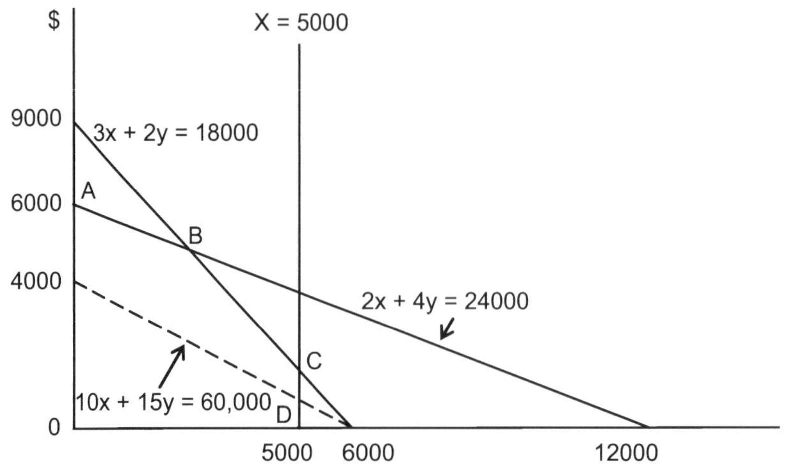

The feasible solutions are shown by the area 0ABCD in the graph.

Using the slope of the iso-contribution line, it can be seen that contribution is maximised at point B on the graph.

At point B, we have the following simultaneous equations:

(1)	2x + 4y	=	24,000
(2)	3x + 2y	=	18,000
Multiply (2) by 2			
(3)	6x + 4y	=	36,000
Subtract (1) from (3)			
	4x	=	12,000
Therefore	x	=	3,000
Substitute in equation (1)			
	2 (3,000) + 4y	=	24,000
	4y	=	18,000
	y	=	4,500

The objective in this problem is to maximise 10x + 15y.

The total contribution where x = 3,000 and y = 4,500 is as follows

	$
3,000 units of Mark 1 (× $10)	30,000
4,500 units of Mark 2 (× $15)	67,500
Total contribution	97,500

i

Index

A

B

C

D

E

F

